T0103059

"The ***Fix-It and Forget-It*** series is the country's bestselling crockpot cookbook series.

"The six books in the series compile edited versions of recipes contributed by everyday cooks and have sold more than nine million copies."

— *Publishers Weekly*

"The author who came in second to Rachael Ray in total foodie sales was Phyllis Good, who does not have a TV show."

— *Summary of Bestsellers*
Publishers Weekly

"One reason why the books are so popular is that they aren't intended for folks who dabble in cooking as a hobby or a whim.

"'The audience that I have in mind is those who have to cook every day of the week,' says Good."

— *Los Angeles Times*

"Good's books have sold more in the United States than the *combined* works of popular Food Network hosts Ina Garten, Giada De Laurentiis, and Jamie Oliver." — *The New York Times*
Front-page feature

"One of the losses in our lives is that it's so hard to sit down at the dinner table, night after night, and have parents and children eating together," says Phyllis Good.

"With the slow cooker, you can prepare food early and bring everyone together at the table," she says. "It helps immensely."

— *The Associated Press*

Fix-It and Forget-It®

Christmas Slow Cooker Feasts

650 Easy Holiday Recipes

Phyllis Good

Good Books®
New York, New York

FIX-IT AND FORGET-IT® CHRISTMAS SLOW COOKER FEASTS

Copyright © 2016 by Good Books, an imprint of Skyhorse Publishing, Inc.

All rights reserved. No part of this book may be reproduced in any manner without the express written consent of the publisher, except in the case of brief excerpts in critical reviews or articles. All inquiries should be addressed to Good Books, 307 West 36th Street, 11th Floor, New York, NY 10018.

Good Books books may be purchased in bulk at special discounts for sales promotion, corporate gifts, fund-raising, or educational purposes. Special editions can also be created to specifications. For details, contact the Special Sales Department, Good Books, 307 West 36th Street, 11th Floor, New York, NY 10018 or info@skyhorsepublishing.com.

Good Books is an imprint of Skyhorse Publishing, Inc.®, a Delaware corporation.

Visit our website at www.goodbooks.com.

10 9 8 7 6 5 4 3

Comb bound ISBN: 978-1-68099-177-2
Paperback ISBN: 978-1-68099-176-5
ebook ISBN: 978-1-68099-180-2

Cover illustration and illustrations throughout the book by Cheryl Benner
Design by Cliff Snyder

Printed in China

The information in this book has been developed with care and accuracy and is presented in good faith. However, no warranty is given nor are results guaranteed. Neither the author nor the publisher has control over the materials or procedures used, and neither has any liability for any loss or damage related to the use of information contained in the book. Should any corrections be needed, they will be posted at www.GoodBooks.com.

Table of Contents

Welcome to *Fix-It and Forget-It Christmas Slow Cooker Feasts* 3

Tips for Using Your Slow Cooker 5

Appetizers, Snacks, and Spreads 9

Breakfast and Brunch Dishes 21

Soups, Stews, and Chilis 27

Main Dishes

- **Beef Main Dishes** 75
- **Pork and Ham Main Dishes** 127
- **Chicken Main Dishes** 157
- **Turkey Main Dishes** 183
- **Meat and Bean Main Dishes** 191
- **Other Main Dish Favorites** 199

Vegetables 205

Beverages 233

Desserts and Sweets 241

Go-Alongs 261

Equivalent Measurements 280

Assumptions about Ingredients 281

Three Hints 281

Substitute Ingredients 282

Kitchens Tools and Equipment You Really Ought to Have 283

Index 284

About the Author 299

Welcome to *Fix-It and Forget-It Christmas Slow Cooker Feasts*

It seemed like a good idea...

If you've invited your family or your special friends or neighbors to your home for a holiday meal, you might be caught somewhere between anticipation and dread right now.

Who doesn't like to have loved ones around the table, murmuring with delight about the food they've been eating? But which of us hasn't had panic nearly paralyze us on the way to that lovely moment?

Running out...

Or maybe your energy and your cooking ideas left you before your holiday guests did? How do you prepare without running out of time—or graciousness?

Never fear. You absolutely can make holiday meals with ease and with pleasure!

Phyllis Good

Beat the panic

Most of us prepare dozens of meals during the 60 days between early November and early January. Well, here are 600 *manageable* slow-cooker recipes (plus 50 Go-Alongs)—all from cooks who want to feast with their loved ones without being exhausted and frazzled.

A bonus

Don't miss the "Ideas for Meaningful Holidays" and "Happy Hosting Tips," spread among the recipes. One more reason that this cookbook can quickly become your kitchen companion.

Thank you, all you wonderful cooks and hosts who so generously shared your holiday recipes and tips for happiness at this special time of year. And thank you, too, testers, for your care and comments. Each of you has demonstrated the wonder of hospitality.

Make this cookbook your own

Most of the recipes in this collection are flexible and forgiving. You'll notice that most of them offer a range of cooking times; many of the recipes suggest optional ingredients.

Make this book your own. Write in it. Note the cooking time that worked for you. Star the recipe you liked. If you added or subtracted ingredients, write them in the neighboring column. Flip to the Index and put a big dot next to a recipe you especially liked. Then you can spot it at a glance when you're looking for cooking inspiration.

One more thing

These recipes work at any time of the year! Don't restrict them to your holiday table.

Phyllis Good

Christmas Smells

Mary Kathryn Yoder
Harrisonville, MO

Prep. Time: 10 minutes

Ideal slow cooker size: 2-quart

4 cups water
rind of 1 lemon
rind of 1 orange
1-oz. box whole cloves
1-oz. box cinnamon sticks
2 bay leaves

1. Pour water into 2-qt. slow cooker so it's half to ⅔ full.
2. Add all other ingredients. Stir well.
3. Cover. Turn cooker to High until mixture boils.
4. Remove lid. Reduce heat to Low. Let mixture simmer and fill your home with good smells. Add water as needed.

Note:
Do not leave your house with Christmas Smells cooking. This needs continual checking so it doesn't boil dry.

Tips for Using Your Slow Cooker

A Friendly Holiday Appliance

1. What to buy

• A good standard size for a household of four is a 4-quart slow cooker.

But holiday-time may be the perfect opportunity to add to your slow-cooker collection. Because these babies are so absolutely useful and relieve so much hosting tension, I recommend:

- *one large cooker (6- or 7-quart)*
  Then you're set for preparing sizable roasts, turkey breasts, chicken legs and thighs, or a big pot of soup.
- *one or two medium cookers (4- or 5-quart)*
  Do your vegetables in these. Or if you're cooking for a smaller group, you can do your main dish in one or both of them. Don't forget that you can prepare brunch dishes or desserts in these, too.
- *one or two small cookers (1½- 3-quart)*
  These are ideal for dips, breakfast fruit, dessert toppings, and more.

• Cookers which allow you to program "On," the length of the cooking time, and "Off," are convenient. If your model doesn't include that feature, you might want to get a digital appliance timer, which gives you that option. Make sure the timer is adequate for the electrical flow that your cooker demands.

• A baking insert, a cooking rack, a temperature probe, and an insulated carrying tote are all useful additions offered with some models. Or you can buy some of them separately by going to the manufacturers' websites.

2. Learn to know your slow cooker

• Some newer slow cookers cook at a very high temperature. You can check the temperature of your slow cooker this way:

1. Place 2 quarts of water in your slow cooker.
2. Cover. Heat on Low 8 hours.
3. Lift the lid. Immediately check the water temp with an accurate thermometer.
4. The temperature of the water should be 185°F. If the temperature is higher, foods may overcook and you should reduce the overall cooking time. If the temperature is lower, your foods will probably not reach a safe temperature quickly enough, and the cooker should be discarded.

3. Maximizing what a slow cooker does best

• Slow cookers tend to work best when they're ⅔ full. You many need to increase the cooking time if you've exceeded that amount, or reduce it if you've put in less than that.

• Cut the hard veggies going into your cooker into chunks of about equal size. In other words, make your potato and carrot pieces about the same size. Then they'll be done cooking at nearly the same time. Softer veggies, like bell peppers and zucchini, cook faster, so they don't need to be cut as small. But again, keep them similar in size to each other so they finish together.

• Because raw vegetables are notoriously tough customers in a slow cooker, layer them over the bottom and around the sides of the cooker, as much as possible. That puts them in more direct contact with the heat.

• There are consequences to lifting the lid on your slow cooker while it's cooking. To compensate for the lost heat, you should plan to add 15-20 minutes of cooking time for each time the lid was lifted off.

On the other hand, moisture gathers in a slow cooker as it works. To allow that to cook off, or to thicken the cooking juices, take the lid off during the last half hour of cooking time.

• Use only the amount of liquid called for in a recipe. In contrast to an oven or a stovetop, a slow cooker tends to draw juices out of food and then harbor it.

Of course, if you sense that the food in your cooker is drying out, or browning excessively before it finishes cooking, you may want to add ½ cup of *warm* liquid to the cooker.

- Important variables to remember that don't show up in recipes:
  - *The fuller your slow cooker, the longer it will take its contents to cook.*
  - *The more densely packed the cooker's contents are, the longer they will take to cook.*
  - *The larger the chunks of meat or vegetables, the more time they will need to cook.*

4. Debunking the myths

- You certainly can cook holiday-worthy dishes in a slow cooker! These appliances can put out a meal at any level—elegant or comfortable.

One hard-won piece of advice. You'll notice that many of the recipes in this cookbook give a range of cooking times (for example, Chicken ala Orange on page 168 tells you to cook the dish 6-7 hours). Every slow cooker is different, so learn to know your cooker before you ask it to make your holiday turkey.

Do a test-run of a sample recipe, note the length of time it took to cook the dish to perfection, and then write that next to the recipe in this book. Make that experiment your baseline for judging the appropriate length of cooking time in your cooker for similar recipes. Now you can relax as you wait for your guests to arrive.

Two more reasons to put your cooker(s) to work during the holidays:

1. If your oven is full, use your slow cooker to relieve the space crunch.
2. When you want to avoid lots of last-minute work and enjoy your guests instead, make whatever you can in your slow cooker.

- Slow cookers are also *a handy year-round appliance.* They don't heat up a kitchen in warm weather. They allow you to escape to the pool or lake or lawn or gardens – so why not let them work for you when it's hot outdoors. A slow cooker fixes your dinner while you're at your child's soccer game, too.

- You can overdo food in a slow cooker. If you're tempted to stretch a recipe's 6-hour stated cooking time to 8 or 10 hours, you may be disappointed in your dinner. Yes, these cookers work their magic using slow, moist heat. Yes, many dishes cook a long time. But these outfits have their limits.

For example, chicken can overcook in a slow cooker. Especially boneless, skinless breasts. But legs and thighs aren't immune either. Once they go past the falling-off-the-bone stage, they are prone to move on to deeply dry.

Cooked pasta and sour cream do best if added late in the cooking process, ideally 10 minutes before the end of the cooking time if the cooker is on high; 30 minutes before the end of the cooking time if it's on low.

5. Safety

- A working slow cooker gets hot on the outside – and I mean the outer electrical unit as well as the inner vessel. Make sure that curious and unsuspecting children or adults don't grab hold of either part. Use oven mitts when lifting any part of a hot cooker.
- To prevent a slow cooker from bubbling over, either when its sitting still on a counter, or when its traveling to a carry-in dinner, fill the cooker only ⅔ full.

If you're going to exceed that limit, pull out your second slow cooker (what – you have only one?!) and divide the contents between them.

6. Adapting stove-top or oven recipes for a slow cooker

- Many stove-top and oven recipes can be adapted for a slow cooker.

If you want to experiment, use these conversion factors:

- *Low (in a slow cooker) = 200°F approximately (in an oven).*
- *High (in a slow cooker) = 300°F approximately (in an oven).*
- *In a slow cooker, 2 hours on Low = 1 hour, approximately, on High.*

Appetizers, Snacks, and Spreads

Creamy Artichoke Dip

Jessica Stoner
West Liberty, OH

Makes 7-8 cups

Prep. Time: 15-20 minutes
Cooking Time: 1-1½ hours
Ideal slow cooker size: 3-qt.

2 14-oz. cans water-packed artichoke hearts, coarsely chopped (drain one can; stir juice from other can into Dip)
2 cups (8 oz.) shredded, part-skim mozzarella cheese
8-oz. pkg. cream cheese, softened
1 cup grated Parmesan cheese
½ cup mayonnaise
½ cup shredded Swiss cheese
2 Tbsp. lemon juice
2 Tbsp. plain yogurt
1 Tbsp. seasoned salt
1 Tbsp. chopped, seeded jalapeño pepper
1 tsp. garlic powder
Dippers: tortilla chips

1. In slow cooker, combine artichoke hearts, cheeses, mayonnaise, lemon juice, yogurt, salt, jalapeño pepper, and garlic powder.
2. Cover. Cook on Low 1 hour, or until cheeses are melted and Dip is heated through.
3. Serve with tortilla chips.

Variation:
Add 2 10-oz. pkgs. frozen chopped spinach, thawed and squeezed dry, to Step 1.

Steven Lantz
Denver, CO

Red Pepper-Cheese Dip

Ann Bender
Ft. Defiance, VA

Makes 4-5 cups

Prep. Time: 10 minutes
Cooking Time: 2 hours
Ideal slow cooker size: 3-qt.

2 Tbsp. olive oil
4-6 large red peppers, cut into 1" squares
crackers and/or pita bread
½ lb. feta cheese, crumbled

1. Pour oil into slow cooker. Stir in peppers.
2. Cover. Cook on Low 2 hours.
3. Serve on crackers or pita bread, topped with feta cheese.

Ratatouille

Barb Yoder
Angola, IN

Makes about 3½ cups

Prep. Time: 20-30 minutes
Cooking Time: 7-8 hours
Ideal slow cooker size: 4-qt.

1½ cups chopped onion
6-oz. can tomato paste
1 Tbsp. olive oil
2 minced cloves garlic (1 tsp.)
1½ tsp. crushed dried basil
½ tsp. dried thyme
15-oz. can chopped tomatoes, with juice drained but reserved
1 large zucchini, halved lengthwise and sliced thin
salt and pepper to taste
slices of French bread *or* **baguette**

1. Mix all ingredients except bread in slow cooker.
2. Cover. Cook on Low 7-8 hours.
3. If mixture is stiffer than you wish, stir in some of reserved tomato juice.
4. Serve hot or cold on top of French bread or baguette slices.

Hot Cheddar Mushroom Spread

Amber Swarey
Honea Path, SC

Makes 3¼-½ cups

Prep. Time: 10 minutes
Cooking Time: 1-1½ hours
Ideal slow cooker size: 2-qt.

1 cup mayonnaise
1 cup (4 oz.) shredded cheddar cheese
⅓ cup grated Parmesan cheese
2 4½-oz. cans sliced mushrooms, drained
half an envelope Ranch salad dressing mix
minced fresh parsley
assorted crackers

1. Combine mayonnaise, cheeses, mushrooms, and dressing mix in slow cooker.
2. Cover. Cook on Low 1 hour, or until cheeses are melted and Dip is heated through.
3. Sprinkle with parsley and serve with crackers.

Nacho Dip

Rose Hankins
Stevensville, MD

Makes 3-4 cups

Prep. Time: 5 minutes
Cooking Time: 3-4 hours
Ideal slow cooker size: 4-qt.

4 cups (16 oz.) shredded cheddar cheese
14-oz. can diced tomatoes, drained, with juice reserved
7-oz. can chopped green chilies, drained
1 cup chopped onions
1 Tbsp. cumin
1 tsp. chili powder
1 tsp. hot pepper sauce
tortilla chips

1. Mix all ingredients except chips in slow cooker.
2. Cover. Cook on Low 3-4 hours.
3. Stir before serving. If Dip is stiffer than you like, stir in some of reserved tomato juice
4. Serve with tortilla chips for dipping.

I like to keep a basket full of small gifts by the door to give to guests as they leave. These are simple gifts like home-made dip mixes in jars or freshly baked cookies, wrapped in colorful papers or gift bags. Sending friends home with a little something extra is a fun way to end a get-together.
Mary Rogers, Waseca, MN

Hot Chili Dip

Lavina Hochstedler
Grand Blanc, MI
Anna Stoltzfus
Honey Brook, PA
Kathi Rogge
Alexandria, IN

Makes 5-6 cups

Prep. Time: 5-10 minutes
Cooking Time: 1-2 hours
Ideal slow cooker size: 3-qt.

24-oz. jar hot salsa
15-oz. can chili with beans
2 2¼-oz. cans sliced ripe olives, drained
12 ozs. mild cheese, cubed
tortilla chips

1. Combine all ingredients except tortilla chips in slow cooker.
2. Cover. Cook on Low 1-2 hours, or until cheese is melted, stirring halfway through.
3. Serve with tortilla chips.

Hot Hamburger Dip

Kristi See
Weskan, KS

Makes 7-8 cups

Prep. Time: 20 minutes
Cooking Time: 1-2 hours
Ideal slow cooker size: 2-qt.

1 lb. ground beef
1 small onion, chopped
1 lb. Velveeta cheese, cubed
8-oz. can tomatoes and green chilies, undrained
2 tsp. Worcestershire sauce
½ tsp. chili powder
1 tsp. garlic powder
½ tsp. pepper
10¾-oz. can tomato soup
10¾-oz. can cream of mushroom soup
corn chips
little barbecued smokies

1. Brown ground beef and onions in skillet. Drain off drippings. Place beef and onions in slow cooker.
2. Add remaining ingredients, except corn chips and smokies, and stir well.
3. Cover. Simmer until cheese is melted.
4. Serve with corn chips and little barbecued smokies.

Cheesy Hot Bean Dip

John D. Allen, Rye, CO

Makes 4-5 cups

Prep. Time: 10 minutes • Cooking Time: 2 hours
Ideal slow cooker size: 2-qt.

16-oz. can refried beans
1 cup salsa
2 cups (8 oz.) shredded Jack and cheddar cheeses, mixed
1 cup sour cream
3-oz. pkg. cream cheese, cubed
1 Tbsp. chili powder
¼ tsp. ground cumin
tortilla chips

1. Combine all ingredients except chips in slow cooker.
2. Cover. Cook on High 2 hours. Stir 2-3 times during cooking time.
3. Serve warm from cooker with chips.

Note:
This bean dip is a favorite of ours. Once you start on it, it's hard to leave it alone.
We have been known to dip into it even when it's cold.

Creamy Taco Dip

Nanci Keatley
Salem, OR

Makes 7-8 cups

Prep. Time: 15 minutes
Cooking Time: 1-2 hours
Ideal slow cooker size: 4-qt.

8-oz. pkg. cream cheese, softened
1 cup sour cream
¾ cup mayonnaise
1 lb. ground beef
1 envelope taco seasoning
12-oz. jar salsa
2 cups (8 oz.) shredded cheddar cheese
garnishes: 4 cups lettuce, shredded; 2 medium tomatoes, chopped; 1 small onion, chopped
tortilla chips

1. In good-sized mixing bowl, mix together cream cheese, sour cream, and mayonnaise. Spread in bottom of lightly greased slow cooker.
2. Brown ground beef in skillet, breaking up clumps of meat with a wooden spoon as it browns. Drain off drippings.
3. Mix taco seasoning and salsa into browned meat. Spoon mixture over cream cheese mixture in slow cooker.
4. Sprinkle shredded cheddar over top.
5. Cover. Cook on Low 1-2 hours, or until cheese is melted.
6. Serve with lettuce, tomatoes, onions, and tortilla chips.

TNT Dip

Sheila Plock
Boalsburg, PA

Makes 8 cups

Prep. Time: 15 minutes
Cooking Time: 1-1¼ hours
Ideal slow cooker size: 3-qt.

1½ lbs. ground beef
10¾-oz. can cream of mushroom soup
half a stick (4 Tbsp.) butter, melted
1 lb. Velveeta, cubed
1 cup salsa
2 Tbsp. chili powder
tortilla chips and/or corn chips
party rye bread

1. Brown ground beef in skillet. Drain off drippings. Place browned beef in slow cooker.
2. Add all remaining ingredients, except chips and bread, to slow cooker. Mix well.
3. Cover. Cook on High 1-1¼ hours, or until cheese is melted. If you're at home, stir occasionally during cooking.
4. Serve with tortilla chips, corn chips, and/or party rye bread.

Variation:

To change the balance of flavors, use only 1 lb. browned ground beef and add 1½ cups salsa.

Note:

My son has hosted a Super Bowl party for his college friends at our house the past two years. He served this Dip the first year, and the second year it was requested.

His friends claim it's the best Dip they've ever eaten. With a bunch of college kids it disappears quickly.

Hot Beef Dip

Paula Showalter
Weyers Cave, VA

Makes about 3 cups

Prep. Time: 15 minutes
Cooking Time: 2-3 hours
Ideal slow cooker size: 2-qt.

2 8-oz. pkgs. cream cheese, softened
2 cups (8 oz.) mild cheddar cheese, grated
1 green bell pepper, chopped fine
1 small onion, chopped fine
¼ lb. chipped dried beef, shredded
assortment of crackers

1. Combine cheeses in slow cooker.
2. Fold in pepper, onions, and beef.
3. Cover. Cook on Low 2-3 hours.
4. Serve hot with crackers.

Variation:

For more kick, add a few finely diced chili peppers to Step 2.

Taco Appetizer

Annie C. Boshart
Lebanon, PA

Makes 8 cups

Prep. Time: 15-30 minutes
Cooking Time: 30-60 minutes
Ideal slow cooker size: 3-qt.

½ lb. lean ground beef
½ lb. hot Italian sausage
1 large onion, finely chopped
salt to taste
2 tsp. hot pepper sauce, *or* **more or less to taste**
2 16-oz. cans refried beans
4-oz. can chopped green chilies, drained
2-3 cups (8-12 oz.) grated Monterey Jack cheese
¾ cup hot, *or* **mild, taco sauce**
tortilla chips *or* **corn chips**
garnishes: chopped tomatoes, chopped green onions, chopped ripe olives, smashed ripe avocado, sour cream

1. In skillet, sauté meats with onion until browned. Drain off drippings. Season meat with salt and hot pepper sauce to taste.
2. Meanwhile, spread refried beans in lightly greased slow cooker.
3. Spoon browned meat over refried beans.
4. Top with chopped chilies.
5. Sprinkle with grated cheese.
6. Pour taco sauce on top of cheese. (Do not stir.)
7. Heat in slow cooker for 30-60 minutes on Medium High, or until Dip is heated through.
8. Serve with chips and garnishes.

Cheesy Sausage Dip

Marissa Pinon
Rio Rancho, NM
Cynthia Morris
Grottoes, VA

Makes 4-5 cups

Prep. Time: 15-25 minutes
Cooking Time: 30-60 minutes
Ideal slow cooker size: 3- to 4-qt.

1 lb. loose sausage
14½-oz. can Rotel tomatoes—hot, medium, *or* **mild**
2 lbs. Velveeta, *or* **3 8-oz. blocks cream cheese, cut into 1" squares**
chips and/or tortilla scoops

1. Brown sausage in skillet, breaking up clumps of meat as it browns. Drain off drippings.
2. Transfer sausage to slow cooker. Stir in tomatoes and cheese cubes.
3. Cover. Cook on Low until melted, stirring occasionally.
4. Once cheese melts, turn slow cooker to "Keep Warm" or Low setting. Serve with chips or tortilla scoops.

Bacon Cheese Dip

Genelle Taylor
Perrysburg, OH

Makes 6 cups

Prep. Time: 10-20 minutes
Cooking Time: 2 hours or less
Ideal slow cooker size: 3-qt.

2 8-oz. pkgs. cream cheese, cubed
4 cups shredded sharp cheddar cheese
1 cup half-and-half
2 tsp. Worcestershire sauce
1 tsp. dried minced onion
1 tsp. prepared mustard
16 bacon strips, cooked and crumbled
tortilla chips and/or French bread slices

1. Combine first six ingredients in slow cooker.
2. Cover. Cook on Low 2 hours, or until cheeses are melted. Stir occasionally if you're home and able to do so.
3. Just before serving, stir in bacon.
4. Serve warm with tortilla chips and/or French bread.

Cheesy Spinach and Bacon Dip

Amy Bauer
New Ulm, MN

Makes 3½ cups

Prep. Time: 15 minutes
Cooking Time: 1 hour
Ideal slow cooker size: 3-qt.

10-oz. pkg. frozen chopped spinach, thawed and squeezed dry
1 lb. Velveeta, *or* **your choice of soft cheese, cut into ½" cubes**
3-oz. pkg. cream cheese, softened
14½-oz. can Rotel diced tomatoes and green chilies, undrained
8 slices bacon, cooked crisp and crumbled
crackers and/or chips

1. Combine all ingredients except bacon, crackers and chips in slow cooker.
2. Cover. Heat on Low 1 hour, or until cheeses have melted and Dip is heated through. Stir occasionally if you're around to do so.
3. Just before serving, stir in crumbled bacon.
4. Serve warm with crackers and/or chips.

Variation:
This is also tasty with half a package of spinach.

Creamy Pizza Dip

Rosalie Buckwalter
Narvon, PA

Makes 4½ cups

Prep. Time: 15-20 minutes
Cooking Time: 2-4 hours
Ideal slow cooker size: 3-qt.

8-oz. pkg. cream cheese, cubed and softened
¾ cup salad dressing, *or* **mayonnaise (regular** *or* **light)**
1 cup shredded mozzarella cheese
8 oz. sliced pepperoni, chopped
2 ripe plum tomatoes, chopped
10 large, black olives, chopped
4 crusty Italian rolls, toasted if you wish, and then cut into ½" cubes and/or crackers

1. Mix all ingredients, except rolls and crackers for dipping, in slow cooker.
2. Cover. Cook on High 2-4 hours, or until cheese is melted and Dip is heated through.
3. Turn on Low to keep warm while serving.
4. Remove cover. Allow to cool slightly before serving with rolls and/or crackers for dipping.

Cheese Pizza Fondue

Annie C. Boshart
Lebanon, PA

Makes 6-7 cups

Prep. Time: 30 minutes
Cooking Time: 1¼ hours
Ideal slow cooker size: 2-qt.

1 lb. ground beef
½ cup chopped onions
3 8-oz. cans pizza sauce with cheese
1 Tbsp. cornstarch
¾ tsp. oregano
¼ tsp. garlic powder
1 cup shredded mozzarella cheese
2 cups shredded cheddar cheese
cubed French bread, tortilla chips, crackers

1. Brown ground beef and onion in skillet. Stir frequently with wooden spoon, breaking up clumps of meat. When brown, drain off drippings. Spoon meat and onion into slow cooker.
2. Add pizza sauce, cornstarch, oregano, and garlic powder to slow cooker. Stir into meat mixture.
3. Cover. Cook on Low 1 hour, or until mixtures bubbles and thickens. Stir occasionally if you're able to.
4. Add cheese gradually, stirring well until it melts.
5. Serve hot with bread cubes, chips, and/or crackers for dipping.

Tester's Idea:

I served this to my family as a main dish for supper. I made angel-hair pasta and we put the fondue over it as a sauce. We loved it! I also offered breadsticks for dipping into the sauce.

Meatless Pizza Fondue

Virginia Graybill
Hershey, PA

Makes 4 cups

Prep. Time: 5 minutes
Cooking Time: 3 hours
Ideal slow cooker size: 3-qt.

29-oz. jar meatless spaghetti sauce
2 cups (8 oz.) shredded mozzarella cheese
¼ cup shredded Parmesan cheese
2 tsp. dried oregano
1 tsp. dried minced onion
¼ tsp. garlic powder
1 lb. unsliced loaf Italian bread, cut into cubes

1. Combine spaghetti sauce, cheeses, oregano, onion, and garlic powder in slow cooker.
2. Cover. Cook on Low 3 hours, or until cheese is melted and sauce is hot.
3. Serve with bread cubes.

Note:

Each Christmas season, we have an evening set aside for a fondue meal. This recipe is always a hit.

Note from Tester:

I had some leftover sauce that I served as a topping for steamed cauliflower. My family loved it!

Slow Cooker Reuben Dip

Allison Ingels
Maynard, IA

Makes 5 cups

Prep. Time: 10 minutes
Cooking Time: 3-4 hours
Ideal slow cooker size: 3-qt.

8 oz. sour cream
2 8-oz. pkgs. cream cheese, softened
8-oz. can sauerkraut, drained
3 2½-oz. pkgs. dried corned beef, finely chopped
6-oz. pkg. shredded Swiss cheese
rye crackers and/or rye party bread

1. Combine all ingredients except crackers and/or bread in slow cooker.
2. Cover. Heat on Low 3-4 hours, or until cheeses are melted.
3. Serve from cooker with rye crackers or rye party bread.

I like to set up an appetizer table so that I don't feel as pressured if I'm running a little late with my meal. I try to make appetizers that can be prepared ahead and quickly set out. Kristine Martin, Newmanstown, PA

Cranberry Meatballs

Char Hagner
Montague, MI

Makes about 50-60 meatballs

Prep. Time: 30-45 minutes
Cooking Time: 2 hours
Ideal slow cooker size: 3- to 4-qt.

Meatballs:

2 lbs. ground beef
⅓ cup parsley flakes
2 Tbsp. soy sauce
½ tsp. garlic powder
2 Tbsp. minced onion
1 cup cornflake crumbs
2 eggs
½ cup ketchup

Sauce:

1 can jellied cranberry sauce
12-oz. bottle chili sauce
2 Tbsp. brown sugar
1 Tbsp. lemon juice

1. In a large mixing bowl, combine Meatball ingredients until well mixed.
2. Form into 50-60 Meatballs and put in lightly greased 9x13 baking pan.
3. Bake at 350 degrees for about 30 minutes, or until Meatballs are cooked through. (Cut one open to test.)
4. While meatballs are baking, combine Sauce ingredients in saucepan. Heat over low heat until jellied sauce and brown sugar melt. Stir frequently.
5. Place baked Meatballs in slow cooker. Pour Sauce over Meatballs, making sure that all are covered in Sauce if you've layered them into the cooker.
6. Cover. Cook on Low 2 hours, or until Sauce is bubbly.
7. Turn slow cooker to Warm and serve with toothpicks.

Variations:

1. Use 1 lb. ground beef and 1 lb. ground pork instead of 2 lbs. ground beef.
2. Use 10¾-oz. can condensed tomato soup, mixed with 1 tsp. prepared mustard, instead of chili sauce.

Jane Geigley
Honey Brook, PA

3. Here's an alternative meatball recipe:

2 egg whites
2 lbs. ground turkey
2 green onions with tops, sliced
4 tsp. grated orange peel
2 tsp. reduced-sodium soy sauce
½ tsp. black pepper
⅛ tsp. cayenne pepper, *optional*

Follow Steps 1-3 above, and then continue with rest of recipe.

Mary Ann Bowman
East Earl, PA

Buffalo Chicken Dip

Gail Skiff
Clifton Park, NY

Makes 3-4 cups

Prep. Time: 30-40 minutes
Cooking Time: 1 hour
Ideal slow cooker size: 2- to 3-qt.

8-oz. pkg. cream cheese, softened
½-¾ cup bleu cheese dressing
½ cup bleu cheese crumbles
½ cup buffalo wing sauce (I use Anchor Bar Buffalo Wing Sauce)
1 lb. boneless skinless chicken breasts, cooked and shredded
celery sticks and/or your favorite chips

1. Mix cream cheese, dressing, blue cheese crumbles, and sauce in slow cooker.
2. Stir in chicken.
3. Cover. Heat on Low 1 hour, or until cheeses melt and Dip is heated through. Stir several times during the hour if you're home and able to do so.
4. Serve warm with celery sticks and/or your favorite chips.

Keep it simple. Too many different items, especially finger foods, are a lot of work. A few (3-4) very nice items will be remembered and enjoyed.

Carol Findling, Carol Stream, IL

Sweet Chili Chicken Bites

Nanci Keatley
Salem, OR

Makes 4 cups

Prep. Time: 10 minutes
Cooking Time: 4-6 hours
Ideal slow cooker size: 4-qt.

4 lbs. boneless skinless chicken breasts
1 bottle Asian sweet chili sauce (we use May Ploy brand)

1. Cut chicken into bite-size pieces. Place in slow cooker.
2. Pour bottle of sauce over chicken. Stir together well.
3. Cover. Cook on Low 4-6 hours, or until chicken is fully cooked.
4. Serve with toothpicks.

Tester's Idea

This is also good as a main dish served over cooked rice.

Sweet and Sour Chicken Wings

Irma H. Schoen, Windsor, CT

Makes 6-8 servings

Prep. Time: 15 minutes • Cooking Time: 7 hours
Ideal slow cooker size: 3- to 4-qt.

1½ cups sugar
1 cup cider vinegar
½ cup ketchup
1 chicken bouillon cube
2 Tbsp. soy sauce
¼ tsp. salt, *optional*
¼ tsp. pepper, *optional*
16 chicken wings
¼ cup cornstarch
½ cup cold water

1. On stove in medium-sized saucepan, mix together sugar, vinegar, ketchup, bouillon cube, soy sauce, and salt and pepper if you wish.
2. Bring to a boil over medium heat. Stir to dissolve sugar and bouillon cube.
3. Put wings in slow cooker. Pour sauce over wings.
4. Cover. Simmer on Low 6½ hours, or until wings are tender but not dry.
5. A few minutes before end of cooking time, combine water and cornstarch in a small bowl. When smooth, stir gently into wings and sauce.
6. Cover. Simmer on High until liquid thickens, about 30 minutes.
7. To serve, keep cooker turned to Low. Stir occasionally.

Hot Crab Dip

Cassandra Ly
Carlisle, PA
Miriam Nolt
New Holland, PA

Makes 6-7 cups

Prep. Time: 10-15 minutes
Cooking Time: 3-4 hours
Ideal slow cooker size: 3-qt.

½ cup milk
⅓ cup salsa
3 8-oz. pkgs. cream cheese, cubed
2 8-oz. pkgs. imitation crabmeat, flaked
1 cup thinly sliced green onions
4-oz. can chopped green chilies, drained
assorted crackers and/or bread cubes

1. Grease interior of slow cooker.
2. Combine milk and salsa in slow cooker.
3. Stir in cream cheese, crabmeat, onions, and chilies.
4. Cover. Cook on Low 3-4 hours, stirring every 30 minutes if you're home and able to do so.
5. Serve with crackers and/or bread.

Cheese and Crab Dip

Donna Lantgen, Rapid City, SD

Makes 5 cups

Prep. Time: 10 minutes • Cooking Time: 2 hours
Ideal slow cooker size: 2-qt.

3 8-oz. pkgs. cream cheese, softened
2 6-oz. cans crabmeat, drained
1 can broken shrimp, drained
6 Tbsp. finely chopped onions
1 tsp. horseradish
½ cup toasted almonds, broken
assorted crackers and/or bread cubes

1. Combine all ingredients, except crackers and/or bread cubes, in slow cooker.
2. Cover. Cook on Low 2 hours.
3. Serve with crackers or bread cubes.

Variation:

Add 2 tsp. Worcestershire sauce to Step 1 for added zest.

Dorothy VanDeest • Memphis, TN

Liver Paté

Barbara Walker
Sturgis, SD

Makes 1½ cups paté

Prep. Time: 10-15 minutes
Cooking Time: 4-5 hours
Cooling Time: 1-2 hours
Ideal slow cooker size: 1½-qt.

1 lb. chicken livers
½ cup dry wine
1 tsp. instant chicken bouillon granules
1 tsp. minced fresh, *or* **dry, parsley**
1 Tbsp. instant minced onion
¼ tsp. ground ginger
½ tsp. seasoning salt
1 Tbsp. soy sauce
¼ tsp. dry mustard
half a stick (4 Tbsp.) butter, softened
1 Tbsp. brandy
crackers and/or toast cubes

1. In slow cooker, combine all ingredients except butter, brandy, crackers, and/or toast cubes.
2. Cover. Cook on Low 4-5 hours. Let stand in liquid until cool.
3. Drain. Place in blender or food grinder.
4. Add butter and brandy. Process until smooth.
5. Serve with crackers and/or toast cubes.

Snack Mix

Yvonne Boettger
Harrisonburg, VA

Makes 14 cups

Prep. Time: 10 minutes
Cooking Time: 2 hours
Ideal slow cooker size: 5-qt.

8 cups Chex cereal, of any combination
6 cups from the following: pretzels, snack crackers, goldfish, Cheerios, nuts, bagel chips, toasted corn
¾ stick (6 Tbsp.) butter, melted
2 Tbsp. Worcestershire sauce
1 tsp. seasoning salt
½ tsp. garlic powder
½ tsp. onion salt
½ tsp. onion powder

1. Combine 14 cups of dry ingredients in slow cooker.
2. In a mixing bowl, combine butter and seasonings.
3. Pour over dry ingredients in slow cooker. Toss until well mixed.
4. Cover. Cook on Low 2 hours, stirring every 30 minutes.

Variation:

To liven up the Snack Mix a bit more, increase Worcestershire sauce to 4 Tbsp. and add a dash of Tabasco sauce.

Dorothy van Deest
Memphis, TN

Spicy Party Mix

Sharon Miller
Holmesville, OH

Makes 13 cups

Prep. Time: 15 minutes
Cooking Time: 3-4 hours
Ideal slow cooker size: 4- to 5-qt.

¾ stick (6 Tbsp.) butter, melted
1-oz. packet taco seasoning mix
¾ tsp. ground cinnamon
⅛-¼ tsp. cayenne, depending on your taste preferences
2 cups pecan halves
2 cups roasted cashews, unsalted
2 cups walnut halves
2 cups whole almonds, unblanched
3 cups goldfish, *or* **bite-size cheese, crackers**
2 cups pretzel nuggets *or* **sticks**

1. Mix butter and seasonings in slow cooker.
2. Add all remaining ingredients and toss together gently.
3. Cook uncovered on Low 3-4 hours, stirring every 30 minutes until nuts are toasted. Turn off heat.
4. Serve from slow cooker with large spoon, or pour into big serving bowl.

Tip:
You can make this a day before your party. Just be sure to store it in an airtight container.

Christmas Sugared Walnuts

Lavina Hochstedler
Grand Blanc, MI

Makes 3-4 cups

Prep. Time: 10 minutes
Cooking Time: 2-3 hours
Ideal slow cooker size: 2- to 3-qt.

1 lb. walnut pieces
1 stick (8 Tbsp.) unsalted butter, melted
½ cup confectioners sugar
1½ tsp. ground cinnamon
¼ tsp. ground ginger
¼ tsp. ground allspice
⅛ tsp. ground cloves

1. In slow cooker, stir walnuts and butter together until combined.
2. Add confectioners sugar, stirring to coat nuts evenly.
3. Cover. Cook on High 15 minutes. Then reduce heat to Low.
4. Cook uncovered, stirring occasionally until nuts are coated with a crisp glaze, about 2 hours.
5. Transfer nuts to a serving bowl.
6. In a small bowl, combine spices. Sift over nuts, stirring to coat evenly.
7. Cool nuts completely before serving.

Caramel Peanut Butter Dip

Genelle Taylor
Perrysburg, OH

Makes about 1½ cups

Prep. Time: 20 minutes
Ideal slow cooker size: 1-qt.

30 caramels, unwrapped
1-2 Tbsp. water
¼ cup, plus 2 Tbsp., creamy peanut butter
¼ cup finely crushed peanuts, *optional*
sliced apples, unpeeled

1. In a microwave-safe bowl, microwave caramels and water for 1 minute on High. Stir. Microwave 1 minute more, or until smooth.
2. Add peanut butter and mix well. Microwave 30 seconds on High, or until smooth.
3. Stir in peanuts if you wish.
4. Transfer to a 1-qt. slow-cooker. Turn to Warm while serving.
5. Serve with sliced apples.

Note:
Red and green apples look very festive for the holiday season.

Have a popcorn and cranberry stringing party.
Lena Sheaffer, Port Matilda, PA

Chunky Sweet Spiced Apple Butter

Jennifer Freed
Harrisonburg, VA

Makes 4 cups

Prep. Time: 20 minutes
Cooking Time: 8 hours
Ideal slow cooker size: 2- to 3-qt.

4 cups (about 1¼ lbs.) peeled, chopped Granny Smith apples
¾ cup packed dark brown sugar
2 Tbsp. balsamic vinegar
half a stick (4 Tbsp.) butter, *divided*
1 Tbsp. ground cinnamon
½ tsp. salt
¼ tsp. ground cloves
1½ tsp. vanilla

1. Combine apples, sugar, vinegar, 2 Tbsp. butter, cinnamon, salt, and cloves in slow cooker.
2. Cover. Cook on Low 8 hours.
3. Stir in remaining 2 Tbsp. butter and vanilla.
4. Cool completely before serving, storing, or giving away.

Pumpkin Butter

Emily Fox
Bethel, PA

Makes approximately 6½ cups

Prep. Time: 5-10 minutes
Cooking Time: 11-12 hours
Ideal slow cooker size: 3-qt.

6 cups pumpkin purée
2¾ cups light brown sugar
2½ tsp. pumpkin pie spice

1. Mix pumpkin purée, brown sugar, and pumpkin pie spice together in slow cooker.
2. Cook *uncovered* on Low for 11-12 hours, depending on how thick you'd like the butter to be. Cool.
3. Serve on bread or rolls for seasonal eating.

Note:
Refrigerate or freeze until ready to use.

Tip from Tester:
You could replace 3 cups pumpkin purée with 3 cups applesauce for a different twist on pumpkin butter.

Pear Butter

Betty Moore
Plano, IL

Makes 2-3 pints

Prep. Time: 15 minutes
Cooking Time: 11-13 hours
Ideal slow cooker size: 4-qt.

10 large pears (about 4 lbs.)
1 cup orange juice
2½ cups sugar
1 tsp. ground cinnamon
1 tsp. ground cloves
½ tsp. ground allspice

1. Peel and quarter pears. Place in slow cooker.
2. Cover. Cook on Low 10-12 hours. Drain. Discard liquid.
3. Mash or purée pears. Add remaining ingredients. Mix well and return to slow cooker.
4. Cover. Cook on High 1 hour.
5. Place in hot sterile jars and process, following the instructions of your canning equipment. Allow to cool undisturbed for 24 hours.

Use Christmas cookie-baking time as an opportunity to teach your children about how to measure ingredients, break eggs, and pour milk. Share your special cooking secrets. For example, I keep two knives or narrow spatulas in hot water while frosting cookies. When one gets sticky, I'm prepared with a fresh hot knife. Orpha Herr, Andover, NY

Breakfast and Brunch Dishes

Western Omelet Casserole

Mary Louise Martin, Boyd, WI
Jan Mast, Lancaster, PA

Makes 10 servings

Prep. Time: 15 minutes
Cooking Time: 4-6 hours
Ideal slow cooker size: 5-qt.

32-oz. bag frozen hash brown potatoes, *divided*
1 lb. cooked ham, cubed, *divided*
1 medium onion, diced, *divided*
1½ cups shredded cheddar cheese, *divided*
18 eggs
1½ cups milk
1 tsp. salt
1 tsp. pepper

1. Layer one-third each of frozen potatoes, ham, onion, and cheese in bottom of slow cooker. Repeat 2 times.
2. Beat together eggs, milk, salt, and pepper in a large mixing bowl. Pour over mixture in slow cooker.
3. Cover. Cook on Low 4-6 hours.

Note:
This is a great breakfast, served along with orange juice and fresh fruit.

Eggs 'n' Spinach

Shirley Unternahrer
Wayland, IA

Makes 8 servings

Prep. Time: 20 minutes
Cooking Time: 1½-8 hours
Ideal slow cooker size: 6-qt.

1 lb. sausage with bacon (Farmland offers this)
1½ 10-oz. pkgs. frozen spinach, thawed and squeezed dry
⅓ cup, plus 2 Tbsp., grated Parmesan cheese, *divided*
8 eggs
⅛ tsp. black pepper, ground *or* **cracked**

1. Sauté sausage with bacon in skillet until browned. Drain off half the drippings.
2. Coat interior of slow cooker with cooking spray. Place sausage and reserved drippings in slow cooker.
3. Stir spinach into slow cooker.
4. Stir in ⅓ cup Parmesan cheese.
5. Break eggs directly onto mixture in slow cooker. Be careful not to break yolks. Do not stir.
6. Cover. Cook on High 1½ hours, or on Low up to 8 hours (you can turn it on right before you go to bed).
7. Sprinkle with pepper and 2 Tbsp. Parmesan cheese before serving.

Breakfast Skillet

Sue Hamilton
Minooka, IL

Makes 4-5 servings

Prep. Time: 15 minutes
Cooking Time: 2½-6 hours
Ideal slow cooker size: 3½-qt.

3 cups milk
5½-oz. box au gratin potatoes
1 tsp. hot sauce
5 eggs, lightly beaten
1 Tbsp. prepared mustard
4-oz. can sliced mushrooms, drained
8 slices bacon, fried and crumbled
1 cup cheddar cheese, shredded

1. Combine milk, au gratin-sauce packet, hot sauce, eggs, and mustard in slow cooker until well blended.
2. Stir in dried potatoes, drained mushrooms, and bacon.
3. Cover. Cook on High 2½-3 hours, or on Low 5-6 hours.
4. Sprinkle cheese over top. Cover and let stand a few minutes until cheese melts.

Apple Oatmeal

Sheila Plock
Boalsburg, PA

Makes 6-8 servings

Prep. Time: 15 minutes
Cooking Time: 6 hours
Ideal slow cooker size: 5-qt.

3-4 apples, peeled and sliced
½ cup brown sugar
1 tsp. nutmeg
1 tsp. cinnamon
¼ stick (2 Tbsp.) butter
½ cup walnuts
3 cups uncooked rolled oats
6 cups milk

1. Layer apples in bottom of slow cooker.
2. Sprinkle with brown sugar, nutmeg, and cinnamon.
3. Dot with butter.
4. Scatter walnuts evenly over top.
5. Layer oatmeal over fruit and nuts.
6. Pour milk over oatmeal. Stir together until well blended.
7. Cover. Cook on Low 6 hours.

Note:
Wake up to the smell of freshly baked apple pie!

Slow-Cooker Oatmeal

Betty B. Dennison
Grove City, PA

Makes 2 servings

Prep. Time: 5 minutes
Cooking Time: 6-8 hours
Ideal slow cooker size: 1½-qt.

1 cup uncooked rolled oats
2 cups water
salt
⅓-½ cup raisins
¼ tsp. ground nutmeg
¼ tsp. ground cinnamon

1. Combine all ingredients in slow cooker.
2. Cover. Cook on Low 6-8 hours.
3. Eat warm with milk and brown sugar.

Oatmeal Morning

Barbara Forrester Landis
Lititz, PA

Makes 6 servings

Prep. Time: 5 minutes
Cooking Time: 2½-6 hours
Ideal slow cooker size: 3-qt.

1 cup uncooked steel cut oats
1 cup dried cranberries
1 cup walnuts
½ tsp. salt
1 Tbsp. cinnamon
4 cups liquid – milk, water, *or* combination of the two

1. Combine all dry ingredients in slow cooker. Stir well.
2. Pour in liquid ingredient(s). Mix together well.
3. Cover. Cook on High 2½ hours or on Low 5-6 hours.

Variation:
If you wish, substitute fresh or dried blueberries, or raisins, for the dried cranberries.

Fruit and Grains Breakfast Cereal

Jean Butzer
Batavia, NY
Katrina Eberly
Wernersville, PA

Makes 10 servings

Prep. Time: 10 minutes
Cooking Time: 6-7 hours
Ideal slow cooker size: 5-qt.

5 cups water
2 cups uncooked whole-grain cereal of your choice
1 medium apple, peeled and chopped
1 cup unsweetened apple juice
¼ cup dried apricots, chopped
¼ cup dried cranberries
¼ cup raisins
¼ cup chopped dates
2-4 Tbsp. maple syrup, according to your preference for sweetness
1 tsp. cinnamon
½ tsp. salt

1. Combine all ingredients in slow cooker.
2. Cover. Cook on Low 6-7 hours, or until fruits and grain are as soft as you like them.

Note:
This hearty breakfast dish reminds me of the old-fashioned oatmeal that was a winter staple in our country kitchen many years ago. My dad would put it on to cook before he went to the barn to milk cows. It would be cooked to perfection by the time he was done with chores and ready for breakfast.

Jean Butzer
Batavia, NY

Our local historical museum hosts an annual "Wonderland of Trees," inviting organizations to decorate a tree for display. Our quilt guild decorates one with homemade fabric ornaments and fabric garlands. A kitchen shop uses kitchen notions—whisks, measuring spoons, etc. The garden club does one in a gardening theme. There are usually 20-30 trees on display from November through December for the public to enjoy.
Jean Butzer, Batavia, NY

Hot Wheatberry Cereal

Rosemarie Fitzgerald
Gibsonia, PA

Makes 4 servings

Prep. Time: 5 minutes
Soaking Time: 8 hours
Cooking Time: 10 hours
Ideal slow cooker size: 3-qt.

1 cup dry wheatberries
5 cups water
butter
milk
honey

1. Rinse and sort berries. Cover with water and soak 8 hours in slow cooker.
2. Cover. Cook on Low overnight (or up to 10 hours).
3. Drain, if needed. Serve hot with honey, milk, and butter.

Variation:

Eat your hot wheatberries with raisins and maple syrup as a variation.

Note:

Wheatberries can also be used in pilafs or grain salads. Cook as indicated, drain, and cool.

Mexican-Style Grits

Mary Sommerfeld
Lancaster, PA

Makes 10-12 servings

Prep. Time: 10 minutes
Cooking Time: 2-6 hours
Ideal slow cooker size: 3-qt.

1½ cups instant grits
1 lb. Velveeta cheese, cubed
½ tsp. garlic powder
2 4-oz. cans diced chilies, drained
1 stick (8 Tbsp.) butter, cut in chunks

1. Prepare grits according to package directions.
2. Stir in cheese, garlic powder, and chilies, until cheese is melted.
3. Stir in butter. Pour into greased slow cooker.
4. Cover. Cook on High 2-3 hours, or on Low 4-6 hours.

Cornmeal Mush

Betty Hostetler
Allensville, PA

Makes 15-18 servings

Prep. Time: 5-10 minutes
Cooking Time: 4-7 hours
Ideal slow cooker size: 4-qt.

2 cups cornmeal
2 tsp. salt
2 cups cold water
6 cups hot water
2 sticks (½ lb.) butter, *optional*

1. Combine cornmeal, salt, and cold water in greased slow cooker.
2. Stir in hot water, stirring until well blended.
3. Cover. Cook on High 1 hour. Stir well. Cook on Low 3-4 hours. (Or cook on Low 5-6 hours, stirring once every hour during the first 2 hours.)
4. Serve hot with butter alongside for those who want to add a chunk to their individual servings. Or serve warm with milk and syrup.

Variations:

1. Pour cooked cornmeal mush into loaf pans. Chill until set (several hours or overnight). Cut into ½"-thick slices.
2. Dredge each slice in flour. Melt butter in large skillet. Fry slices in butter, being careful not to crowd the skillet or mush will steam and not brown. When the first side is well browned, flip each slice to brown the other side.

3. Serve slices for breakfast with maple syrup, bacon, sausage, or ham and eggs.
4. Mush is much like polenta. It is also delicious topped with chili for a lunch or supper.

Note:

When we lived on the farm, Mother would prepare boiled mush for the evening meal.

The rest she poured into pans and fried for supper the next evening. I adapted this recipe for the slow cooker several years ago when Mother was living with us and I needed to go to work.

Breakfast Apple Cobbler

Anona M. Teel
Bangor, PA

Makes 6-8 servings

Prep. Time: 15 minutes
Cooking Time: 2-9 hours
Ideal slow cooker size: 3½- to 4-qt.

8 medium apples, cored, peeled, sliced
¼ cup sugar
dash of cinnamon
juice of 1 lemon
half a stick (4 Tbsp.) butter, melted
2 cups granola

1. Combine all ingredients in slow cooker.
2. Cover. Cook on Low 7-9 hours (while you sleep), or on High 2-3 hours (after you're up in the morning).

Hot Applesauce Breakfast

Colleen Konetzni
Rio Rancho, NM

Makes 8 servings

Prep. Time: 15 minutes
Cooking Time: 8-10 hours
Ideal slow cooker size: 3½-qt.

10 apples, peeled and sliced
½-1 cup sugar, according to the sweetness of the apples and your taste preference
1 Tbsp. ground cinnamon
¼ tsp. ground nutmeg

1. Combine all ingredients in slow cooker.
2. Cover. Cook on Low 8-10 hours (while you're asleep?).

Serving suggestion: This is yummy over ***oatmeal*** *or mixed with* ***vanilla yogurt****. Or serve it over* ***pancakes*** *or* ***waffles****.*

Variation:

Add chopped nuts for an extra treat, either before cooking or before serving.

Breakfast Prunes

Jo Haberkamp
Fairbank, IA

Makes 6 servings

Prep. Time: 10 minutes
Cooking Time: 8-10 hours
Ideal slow cooker size: 2-qt.

2 cups orange juice
¼ cup orange marmalade
1 tsp. ground cinnamon
¼ tsp. ground cloves
¼ tsp. ground nutmeg
1 cup water
12-oz. pkg. pitted dried prunes (1¾ cups)
2 thin lemon slices

1. Combine orange juice, marmalade, cinnamon, cloves, nutmeg, and water in slow cooker.
2. Stir in prunes and lemon slices.
3. Cover. Cook on Low 8-10 hours, or overnight.
4. Serve warm as a breakfast food, or warm or chilled as a side dish with a meal later in the day.

Variation:

If you prefer more citrus flavor, eliminate the ground cloves and reduce the cinnamon to ½ tsp. and the nutmeg to ⅛ tsp.

Boston Brown Bread

Jean Butzer
Batavia, NY

Makes 3 loaves

Prep. Time: 15-20 minutes
Cooking Time: 4 hours
Ideal slow cooker size: large enough to hold 3 cans upright

3 16-oz. vegetable cans, cleaned and emptied
½ cup rye flour
½ cup yellow cornmeal
½ cup whole wheat flour
3 Tbsp. sugar
1 tsp. baking soda
¾ tsp. salt
½ cup chopped walnuts
½ cup raisins
1 cup buttermilk*
⅓ cup molasses

1. Spray insides of vegetable cans, and one side of 3 6"-square pieces of foil, with nonstick cooking spray. Set aside.
2. Combine rye flour, cornmeal, whole wheat flour, sugar, baking soda, and salt in a large bowl.
3. Stir in walnuts and raisins.
4. Whisk together buttermilk and molasses in a separate bowl. Add to dry ingredients. Stir until well mixed. Spoon into prepared cans.
5. Place one piece of foil, greased side down, on top of each can. Secure foil with rubberbands or cotton string. Place upright in slow cooker.
6. Pour boiling water into slow cooker to come halfway up sides of cans. (Make sure foil tops do not touch boiling water).
7. Cover cooker. Cook on Low 4 hours, or until skewer inserted in center of bread comes out clean.
8. To remove bread, lay cans on their sides. Roll and tap gently on all sides until bread releases. Cool completely on wire racks.
9. Serve with butter or cream cheese.

* To substitute for buttermilk, pour 1 Tbsp. lemon juice into a 1-cup measure. Add enough milk to fill the cup. Let stand 5 minutes before mixing with molasses.

Dulce de Leche (Sweet Milk)

Dorothy Horst
Tiskilwa, IL

Makes 2½ cups

Prep. Time: 5 minutes
Cooking Time: 2 hours
Ideal slow cooker size: large enough to hold 2 cans upright

2 14-oz. cans sweetened condensed milk

1. Place unopened cans of milk in slow cooker. Fill cooker with warm water so that it comes above the cans by 1½-2 inches.
2. Cover cooker. Cook on High 2 hours.
3. Cool unopened cans.
4. When opened, the contents should be thick and spreadable. Use as a filling between 2 cookies or crackers.

Note:

When on a tour in Argentina, we were served this at breakfast time as a spread on toast or thick slices of bread. We were also presented with a container of prepared Dulce de Leche as a parting gift to take home. This dish sometimes appears on Mexican menus.

Soups, Stews, and Chilis

Hearty Bean and Vegetable Soup

Jewel Showalter
Landisville, PA

Makes 6-8 servings

Prep. Time: 20-25 minutes
Cooking Time: 6-8 hours
Ideal slow cooker size: 5-qt.

2 medium onions, sliced
2 garlic cloves, minced
2 Tbsp. olive oil
8 cups chicken, *or* **vegetable, broth**
1 small head cabbage, chopped
2 large red potatoes, chopped
2 cups chopped celery
2 cups chopped carrots
4 cups corn
2 tsp. dried basil
1 tsp. dried marjoram
¼ tsp. dried oregano
1 tsp. salt
½ tsp. pepper
2 15-oz. cans navy beans, drained

1. Sauté onions and garlic in oil in skillet. Transfer to large slow cooker.
2. Add remaining ingredients. Mix together well.
3. Cover. Cook on Low 6-8 hours.

Variation:
Add 2-3 cups cooked and cut-up chicken 30 minutes before serving if you wish.

Note:
I discovered this recipe after my husband's heart attack. It's a great nutritious soup using only a little fat.

Invite friends over. Have everyone bring a slow-cooker soup. Set all of the slow cookers around the counter with labels on each one. It's a great way to sample lots of different kinds of soups. (You can assign a different recipe to each person if you're concerned about having duplicates.)
Nancy Wagner Graves, Manhattan, KS

Minestrone

Bernita Boyts
Shawnee Mission, KS

Makes 8-10 servings

Prep. Time: 15 minutes
Cooking Time: 4-9 hours
Ideal slow cooker size: 3½- to 4-qt.

1 large onion, chopped
4 carrots, sliced
3 ribs celery, sliced
2 garlic cloves, minced
1 Tbsp. olive oil
6-oz. can tomato paste
14½-oz. can chicken, beef, *or* **vegetable, broth**
24-oz. can pinto beans, undrained
10-oz. pkg. frozen green beans
2-3 cups chopped cabbage
1 medium zucchini, sliced
8 cups water
2 Tbsp. parsley
2 Tbsp. Italian spice
1 tsp. salt, *or* **more**
½ tsp. pepper
¾ cup dry acini di pepe (small round pasta)
grated Parmesan, *or* **Asiago, cheese**

1. Sauté onion, carrots, celery, and garlic in oil in skillet until tender.
2. Combine all ingredients, except pasta and cheese, in slow cooker.
3. Cover. Cook 4-5 hours on High or 8-9 hours on Low.
4. Add pasta 1 hour before cooking is complete.
5. Top individual servings with cheese.

Zesty Minestrone

Lavina Hochstedler
Grand Blanc, MI

Makes 8 servings

Prep. Time: 15 minutes
Cooking Time: 3-6 hours
Ideal slow cooker size: 3- to 4-qt.

¼ cup zesty Italian dressing
1 onion, chopped
1 rib celery, chopped
1 carrot, peeled and chopped
14½-oz. can diced tomatoes, with juice
10-oz. can kidney beans, rinsed and drained
2 14-oz. cans vegetable broth
2 cups water
1 tsp. Italian seasonings
1½ cups small shell macaroni, uncooked
½ cup grated Parmesan cheese

1. Heat dressing in large skillet on medium-high heat. Add onions, celery, and carrots.
2. Cook 2 minutes, or until crisp-tender, stirring occasionally. Spoon into slow cooker.
3. Stir in tomatoes, beans, broth, water, and seasonings.
4. Cover. Cook on Low 6 hours or on High 3 hours.
5. Stir in macaroni 30 minutes before end of cooking time.
6. Sprinkle individual servings with cheese.

Variation:
White beans or garbanzo beans work just as well as kidney beans. Substitute if you wish.

Slow-Cooker Bean Soup

Betty B. Dennison
Grove City, PA

Makes 6 servings

Prep. Time: 30 minutes
Cooking Time: 8-9 hours
Ideal slow cooker size: 6-qt., or 2 4- to 5-qt.

3 15-oz. cans pinto beans, undrained
3 15-oz. cans great northern beans, undrained
4 cups chicken, *or* **vegetable, broth**
3 potatoes, peeled and chopped
4 carrots, sliced
2 celery ribs, sliced
1 large onion, chopped
1 green bell pepper, chopped
1 sweet red pepper, chopped, *optional*
2 garlic cloves, minced
1 tsp. salt, *or* **to taste**
¼ tsp. pepper, *or* **to taste**
1 bay leaf, *optional*
½ tsp. liquid barbecue smoke, *optional*

1. Empty beans into 6-qt. slow cooker, or divide ingredients between 2 4- or 5-qt. cookers.

2. Cover. Cook on Low while preparing vegetables.
3. Add remaining ingredients and mix well.
4. Cover. Cook on Low 8-9 hours, or until vegetables are as tender as you like.

Serving suggestion: Serve with ***tossed salad, Italian bread,*** *or* ***cornbread.***

Note:
This is a stress-free recipe when you're expecting guests, but you're not sure of their arrival time. Slow-Cooker Bean Soup can burble on Low heat for longer than its appointed cooking time without being damaged.

Great Northern Bean Soup

Alice Miller
Stuarts Draft, VA

Makes 6-8 servings

Prep. Time: 15-20 minutes
Cooking Time: 3 hours
Ideal slow cooker size: 3-qt.

2 1-lb. cans great northern beans, rinsed and drained
1-lb. can stewed, *or* **diced, tomatoes, including juice**
1-2 Tbsp. brown sugar
½ cup green bell peppers, chopped
½ cup red bell peppers, chopped

1. Put beans, tomatoes, and brown sugar into slow cooker. Stir until well mixed.
2. Cover. Cook on High 2½ hours.
3. Stir chopped red and green peppers into Soup.
4. Cover. Cook on High 30 more minutes.

Southwestern Bean Soup with Cornmeal Dumplings

Melba Eshleman
Manheim, PA

Makes 4 servings

Prep. Time: 20 minutes
Cooking Time: 4½-12½ hours
Ideal slow cooker size: 5-qt.

15½-oz. can red kidney beans, rinsed and drained
15½-oz. can black beans, pinto beans, *or* **great northern beans, rinsed and drained**
3 cups water
14½-oz. can Mexican-style stewed tomatoes
10-oz. pkg. frozen whole-kernel corn, thawed
1 cup sliced carrots
1 cup chopped onions
4-oz. can chopped green chilies, drained
2 Tbsp. instant beef, chicken, *or* **vegetable, bouillon granules**
1-2 tsp. chili powder
2 cloves garlic, minced

Dumplings:
⅓ cup flour
¼ cup yellow cornmeal
1 tsp. baking powder
dash of salt
dash of pepper
1 egg white, beaten
2 Tbsp. milk
1 Tbsp. oil

1. Combine all Soup ingredients in slow cooker.
2. Cover. Cook on Low 10-12 hours or on High 4-5 hours.
3. Make Dumplings by mixing together flour, cornmeal, baking powder, salt, and pepper in a large bowl.
4. Combine egg white, milk, and oil in a separate bowl. Add to flour mixture. Stir with fork until just combined.
5. At end of Soup's cooking time, turn slow cooker to High. Drop Dumpling mixture by rounded teaspoonfuls to make 8 mounds atop the soup.
6. Cover. Cook for 30 minutes. Do not lift lid during that time!

Back-on-Track Soup

Barbara Forrester Landis
Lititz, PA

Makes 8 servings

Prep. Time: 20 minutes
Cooking Time: 3-5 hours
Standing Time: 15 minutes
Ideal slow cooker size: 5-qt.

1 Tbsp. olive oil
2-4 cloves garlic, minced, depending on how much you like garlic
2 bay leaves
2 15-oz. cans pinto, *or* **kidney, beans, rinsed and drained**
2 lbs. potatoes cut into ½" pieces
8 cups vegetable broth
1 box frozen chopped spinach, thawed and squeezed dry
salt and pepper to taste

1. Combine everything except spinach, salt, and pepper in slow cooker.
2. Cover. Cook on High 3 hours or on Low 5 hours.
3. Fifteen minutes before serving, stir in spinach.
4. Cover cooker and allow to stand 15 minutes. Taste, then add salt and pepper to enhance flavoring.
5. If you wish, use a potato masher to partially mash and thicken the Soup.

Note:
This is a great Soup for getting back to healthy eating after holiday feasting. No punishment here!

Many-Bean Soup

Trudy Kutter
Corfu, NY

Makes 12 servings

Prep. Time: 15 minutes
Cooking Time: 8¼-10¼
Ideal slow cooker size: 6-qt

20-oz. pkg. dried 15-bean soup mix, *or* **2¼ cups dried beans of your choice**
5 14½-oz. cans chicken, *or* **vegetable, broth**
2 cups chopped carrots
1½ cups chopped celery
1 cup chopped onions
2 Tbsp. tomato paste
1 tsp. Italian seasoning
½ tsp. pepper
14½-oz. can diced tomatoes

1. Combine all ingredients except tomatoes in slow cooker.
2. Cover. Cook on Low 8-10 hours, or until beans are tender.
3. Stir in tomatoes.
4. Cover. Cook on High 10-20 minutes, or until soup is heated through.

Serving suggestion: Serve with ***bread*** *and* ***salad****.*

Blessing Soup

Alix Nancy Botsford
Seminole, OK

Makes 8-10 servings

Prep. Time: 20 minutes
Soaking Time: 8 hours, or overnight
Cooking Time: 4-12 hours
Ideal slow cooker size: 4- to 5-qt.

2 cups mixed dried beans—10-18 different kinds, if you can find them!
2-2½ qts. water
1 cup diced ham
1 large onion, chopped
1 garlic clove, minced
juice of 1 lemon
14½-oz. can Italian tomatoes, chopped
½ cup chopped sweet red peppers
½ cup chopped celery
2 carrots, thinly sliced
1 tsp. salt
1 tsp. pepper

1. Wash beans. Discard any stones. Place in slow cooker. Cover with water and soak 8 hours or overnight.
2. Drain water off beans.
3. Add 2-2½ qts. water to drained beans. Cook on High 2 hours.
4. Combine all remaining ingredients with beans in slow cooker.
5. Add more water if necessary so that everything is just covered with water.
6. Cover. Cook on High 4-6 hours or on Low 8-12 hours, or until beans and

other vegetables are tender but not mushy.

Note:
During one January that was especially dismal, I invited many friends, most of whom didn't know each other, to my home. I put on a video about rose gardens around the world. Then I made this soup and a fresh bread crouton that could be eaten on top of the soup and tossed a large salad.

Garbanzo Souper

Willard E. Roth
Elkhart, IN

Makes 6 servings

Prep. Time: 20 minutes
Soaking Time: 8 hours, or overnight
Cooking Time: 6 hours
Ideal slow cooker size: 4-qt.

1 lb. dry garbanzo beans
4 oz. raw baby carrots, cut in halves
1 large onion, diced
3 ribs celery, cut in 1" pieces
1 large green bell pepper, diced
½ tsp. dried basil
½ tsp. dried oregano
½ tsp. dried rosemary
½ tsp. dried thyme
2 28-oz. cans vegetable broth
1 broth can of water
8-oz. can tomato sauce
8 oz. prepared hummus
½ tsp. sea salt

1. Place beans in slow cooker. Cover with water. Soak 8 hours, or overnight.
2. Drain off water. Return soaked beans to slow cooker.
3. Add carrots, onion, celery, and green pepper.
4. Sprinkle with basil, oregano, rosemary, and thyme.
5. Add broth and water.
6. Cover. Cook on High 6 hours, or until beans and vegetables are tender but not over-cooked.
7. Half an hour before serving, stir in tomato sauce, hummus, and salt. Continue cooking until hot.

*Serving suggestion: Serve with **Irish soda bread** and **lemon curd**.*

Note:
A fine meal for vegetarians on St. Patrick's Day!

Russian Red Lentil Soup

Naomi E. Fast
Hesston, KS

Makes 8 servings

Prep. Time: 15 minutes
Cooking Time: 3¾-4¾ hours
Ideal slow cooker size: 3½- to 4-qt.

1 Tbsp. oil
1 large onion, chopped
3 cloves garlic, minced
½ cup diced, dried apricots
1½ cups dried red lentils
½ tsp. cumin
½ tsp. dried thyme
3 cups water
2 14½-oz. cans chicken, *or* **vegetable, broth**
14½-oz. can diced tomatoes
1 Tbsp. honey
¾ tsp. salt
½ tsp. coarsely ground black pepper
2 Tbsp. chopped fresh mint
1½ cups plain yogurt

1. Combine all ingredients except mint and yogurt in slow cooker.
2. Cover. Heat on High until soup starts to simmer.
3. Turn to Low and cook 3-4 hours, or until lentils and vegetables are tender.
4. Add mint and dollop of yogurt to each individual bowl of soup.

Lentil Soup

Tina Snyder
Manheim, PA

Makes 10 servings

Prep. Time: 15 minutes
Cooking Time: 8 hours
Ideal slow cooker size: 3½-qt.

4 cups hot water
14½-oz. can tomatoes
¼ cup tomato juice
3 medium potatoes, peeled and diced
3 carrots, thinly sliced
1 onion, chopped
1 rib celery, sliced
1 cup dry lentils
2 garlic cloves, minced
2 bay leaves
4 tsp. curry powder
1½ tsp. salt
sour cream

1. Combine all ingredients except sour cream in slow cooker.
2. Cover. Cook on Low 8 hours.
3. Serve with sour cream on top of individual servings and crusty bread as a go-along.

Black Bean and Tomato Soup

Sue Tjon
Austin, TX

Makes 6 servings

Prep. Time: 10-15 minutes
Soaking Time: 8 hours, or overnight
Cooking Time: 8 hours
Ideal slow cooker size: 4-qt.

1-lb. bag dry black beans
2 10-oz. cans Rotel tomatoes
1 medium onion, chopped
1 medium green bell pepper, chopped
1 Tbsp. minced garlic
14½-oz. can chicken, *or* **vegetable, broth**
water
Cajun seasoning to taste

1. Place beans in slow cooker. Cover with water and soak for 8 hours or overnight.
2. Drain well. Add tomatoes, onions, pepper, garlic, and broth to beans in slow cooker.
3. Add water just to cover all ingredients.
4. Stir in Cajun seasoning to taste.
5. Cover. Cook on High 8 hours.
6. Mash some of the beans before serving for a thicker consistency.

Serving suggestion: Serve over ***rice*** *or in* ***black bean tacos.***

Tip:
Leftovers freeze well.

Black Bean and Ham Soup

Janie Steele
Moore, OK

Makes 5-6 qts., or about 18 servings

Prep. Time: 20 minutes
Soaking Time: 8 hours, or overnight
Cooking Time: 7½-10 hours
Ideal slow cooker size: 6-qt. or 2 4- to 5-qt.

4 cups dry black beans
5 qts. water
ham bone, ham pieces, *or* **ham hocks**
3 bunches green onions, sliced thin
4 bay leaves
1 Tbsp. salt
¼-½ tsp. pepper
3 cloves minced garlic
4 celery ribs, chopped
3 large onions, chopped
10½-oz. can consommé
1 stick (8 Tbsp.) butter
2½ Tbsp. flour
1 cup Madeira wine, *optional*
chopped parsley

1. In 6-qt. slow cooker, soak beans in 5 qts. water for 8 hours or overnight.
2. Rinse. Drain. Pour beans back into slow cooker, or divide between 2 4- or 5-qt. cookers.
3. Add ham, green onions, bay leaves, salt, pepper, garlic, celery, and onions. Pour in consommé. Add water to cover vegetables and meat. Stir well.

4. Cover. Cook on High 1½-2 hours. Reduce heat to Low and cook 6-8 hours.
5. Remove ham bones and bay leaves. Cut ham off bones and set meat aside
6. Force vegetable mixture through sieve, if you wish.
7. Taste and adjust seasonings, adding more salt and pepper if needed. Return cooked ingredients and cut-up ham to cooker.
8. In saucepan, melt butter. Stir in flour until smooth. Stir into soup to thicken and enrich.
9. Prior to serving, add wine to heated soup mixture if you wish. Garnish with chopped parsley.

Party Bean Soup

Jo Haberkamp
Fairbank, IA

Makes 9 servings

Prep. Time: 10 minutes
Cooking Time: 20-22 hours
Ideal slow cooker size: 5-qt.

1 cup dry navy beans
1 qt. water
1 lb. smoked, *or* **plain, ham hocks**
1 cup chopped onions
½ cup chopped celery
1 garlic clove, minced
8-oz. can tomatoes, cut up
2 14½-oz. cans chicken broth
⅛ tsp. salt
⅛ tsp. pepper
1 cup (4 oz.) shredded cheddar cheese
1 Tbsp. dried parsley flakes

1. Place beans and water in slow cooker.
2. Cover. Cook on Low 12 hours.
3. Add ham hocks, onions, celery, garlic, tomatoes, chicken broth, salt, and pepper.
4. Cover. Cook on Low 8-10 more hours.
5. Add cheese and parsley just before serving. Stir until cheese is melted.

Red and Green Bean Soup

Carol Duree
Salina, KS

Makes 6-8 servings

Prep. Time: 15 minutes
Cooking Time: 6¼-8¼ hours
Ideal slow cooker size: 4-qt.

1 lb. dry navy beans
6 cups boiling water
1 cup sliced carrots
½ cup chopped onion
1½-2 lbs. ham hocks
salt and pepper to taste
1-2 cups chopped kale, spinach, *or* **chard**
½ cup roasted red peppers, chopped
Parmesan cheese, grated

1. Rinse beans; then place in slow cooker.
2. Add all other ingredients except kale, red peppers, and cheese.
3. Cover. Cook on Low 6-8 hours, or until beans are tender but not mushy.
4. Ten minutes before serving, add kale and peppers. Cover and continue to cook 10 more minutes.
5. Sprinkle Parmesan cheese on top of individual servings.

Navy Bean Soup

Lucille Amos
Greensboro, NC

Makes 8 servings

Prep. Time: 5-10 minutes
Soaking Time: 8 hours, or overnight
Cooking Time: 5-12 hours
Ideal slow cooker size: 2- to 3-qt.

2 cups dry navy beans
1 cup chopped onions
1 bay leaf
1 tsp. salt
1 tsp. pepper
½ lb. ham, chopped

1. Place dry beans in slow cooker. Cover with water. Allow to soak 8 hours, or overnight.
2. Drain off water. Add all remaining ingredients to beans in slow cooker.
3. Add water to cover.
4. Cover. Cook on Low 10-12 hours or on High 5-6 hours.
5. Remove bay leaf and serve.

Navy Bean and Bacon Chowder

Ruth A. Feister
Narvon, PA

Makes 6 servings

Prep. Time: 15 minutes
Soaking Time: 8 hours, or overnight
Cooking Time: 7¼-9¼ hours
Ideal slow cooker size: 5-qt.

1½ cups dry navy beans
2 cups cold water
8 slices bacon, cooked and crumbled
2 medium carrots, sliced
1 rib celery, sliced
1 medium onion, chopped
1 tsp. dried Italian seasoning
⅛ tsp. pepper
46-oz. can chicken broth
1 cup milk

1. Place beans in cooker. Add 2 cups cold water. Soak 8 hours, or overnight.
2. Drain off any water. Add all remaining ingredients, except milk, to beans in slow cooker.
3. Cover. Cook on Low 7-9 hours, or until beans are crisp-tender.
4. Place 2 cups cooked bean mixture into blender. (Cover lid of blender with heavy towel and hold it on tightly. Hot ingredients can blow the lid off as you run the blender.) Process until smooth.
5. Return blended beans to slow cooker.
6. Add milk. Cover and heat on High 10 minutes.

*Serving suggestion: Serve with crusty **French bread** and additional **herbs** and **seasonings** for diners to add as they wish.*

Bauer 24-Day Countdown to Christmas: Our family hangs a string of our own stockings in our living room each December. There are three of us, so we each choose eight socks and hang them using clothes pins. Each morning we take turns checking a sock for a surprise. We may find a small gift or something as simple as a note that says "Will cook supper for Mom tonight." We have fun thinking of unique ideas for each other, and before you know it, Christmas is here.
Amy Bauer, New Ulm, MN

Cassoulet Chowder

Miriam Friesen
Staunton, VA

Makes 8-10 servings

Prep. Time: 1¾ hours
Refrigeration Time: 4-8 hours
Cooking Time: 4-10 hours
Ideal slow cooker size: 5-qt.

1¼ cups dry pinto beans
4 cups water
12-oz. pkg. brown-and-serve sausage links, cooked and drained
2 cups cubed cooked chicken
2 cups cubed cooked ham
1½ cups sliced carrots
8-oz. can tomato sauce
¾ cup dry red wine
½ cup chopped onions
½ tsp. garlic powder
1 bay leaf

1. Combine beans and water in large saucepan. Bring to boil. Reduce heat and simmer 1½ hours.
2. Allow cooked beans to cool. Refrigerate beans and liquid 4-8 hours.
3. Combine all ingredients in slow cooker.
4. Cover. Cook on Low 8-10 hours or on High 4 hours.
5. If Chowder seems too thin, remove lid during last 30 minutes of cooking time to allow some liquid to cook off.
6. Remove bay leaf before serving.

Polish Sausage Bean Soup

Janie Steele
Moore, OK

Makes 10 servings

Prep. Time: 15 minutes
Soaking Time: 8 hours, or overnight
Cooking Time: 9-9½ hours
Ideal slow cooker size: 6-qt.

1-lb. pkg. dry great northern beans
28-oz. can whole tomatoes
2 8-oz. cans tomato sauce
2 large onions, chopped
3 cloves garlic, minced
1 tsp. salt
¼-½ tsp. pepper, according to your taste preference
3 celery ribs, sliced
bell pepper, sliced
large ham bone, *or* **ham hock**
1-2 lbs. smoked sausage links, sliced

1. Place beans in 6-qt. slow cooker. Cover with water and soak 8 hours, or overnight.
2. Rinse and drain. Return beans to cooker and cover with water again.
3. Combine all other ingredients, except sausage, with beans in slow cooker.
4. Cover. Cook on High 1-1½ hours. Reduce to Low and cook 7 hours.
5. Remove ham bone or hock and debone. Stir ham pieces back into soup.
6. Add sausage links.
7. Cover. Cook on Low 1 more hour.

Grandma's Barley Soup

Andrea O'Neil
Fairfield, CT

Makes 10-12 servings

Prep. Time: 10 minutes
Cooking Time: 6-8 hours
Ideal slow cooker size: 4- to 5-qt.

2 smoked ham hocks
4 carrots, sliced
4 potatoes, cubed
1 cup dry lima beans
1 cup tomato paste
1½-2 cups cooked barley
salt, if needed

1. Combine all ingredients in slow cooker, except salt.
2. Cover with water.
3. Cover. Simmer on Low 6-8 hours, or until both ham and beans are tender.
4. Debone ham hocks and return cut-up meat to soup.
5. Taste before serving. Add salt if needed.

Tip:
If you want to reduce the amount of meat you eat, this dish is flavorful using only 1 ham hock.

Split Pea Soup

Janette Anderson
Sedalia, MO

Makes 6-8 servings

Prep. Time: 20 minutes
Cooking Time: 8-11 hours
Ideal slow cooker size: 5- to 6-qt.

1 *or* 2 ham hocks
1 lb. (2 cups) dry split peas
2 carrots, sliced
1 onion, diced
2 ribs celery, diced
¼ tsp. pepper
1 tsp. salt
3 potatoes, diced
1 qt. water
1 qt. chicken broth

1. Place ham hock(s) in slow cooker.
2. Add remaining ingredients and stir well.
3. Cover. Cook on Low 8-10 hours, or until ham and split peas are tender.
4. Remove ham bone. Allow to cool until it's possible to handle it.
5. Debone and cut up meat. Stir meat back into soup.
6. For creamier soup, cook an hour or so longer. Stir occasionally to prevent sticking.

Variations:

1. Add 14½-oz. can diced tomatoes with juice in Step 2.

Holly Schwartz
Lac Du Flambeau, WI

2. Instead of ham hocks, use 1 lb. smoked kielbasa, sliced. Stir into Soup in Step 2.

Nathan LeBeau
Rapid City, SD

White Marrow Bean Soup

Becky Frey
Lebanon, PA

Makes 8 servings

Prep. Time: 30 minutes
Cooking Time: 4-5 hours
Ideal slow cooker size: 5-qt.

2 qts. cooked marrow beans, *or* your choice of cooked white beans, undrained
1 cup onions, chopped
1 cup cooked ham, chopped
1 cup celery, chopped
3 cups potatoes, peeled and diced
2 qts. ham broth
parsley to taste
salt to taste
pepper to taste

1. Put beans, onions, ham, celery, potatoes, broth, and seasonings in slow cooker.
2. Cover. Cook on High 4-5 hours, or until potatoes are soft.

Tip:

You can use dried beans in the recipe if you have time to soak and cook them before following the instructions above.

Note from Tester:

I would add a finely chopped jalapeño pepper to the Soup 1 hour before the end of cooking time. And I would add ¼ cup chopped red bell pepper and ¼ cup chopped green bell pepper to the Soup, just before serving it.

Before your main meal, serve a bowl of your favorite homemade soup. Don't forget your soup tureen. Your guests will feel special. Why have a soup tureen and not use it?
Leona M. Slabaugh, Apple Creek, OH

Rice & Bean Soup

Sharon Easter
Yuba City, CA

Makes 6 servings

Prep. Time: 10 minutes
Cooking Time: 3½-4 hours
Ideal slow cooker size: 5-qt.

½ lb. loose Italian sausage, hot *or* sweet
2 32-oz. boxes chicken, *or* vegetable, broth
28-oz. can diced tomatoes
½ tsp. salt
¼ tsp. pepper
½ tsp. dried oregano
1 cup long-grain rice, uncooked
15-oz. can white beans, rinsed and drained
1 cup diced celery
4 carrots, sliced

1. Brown sausage in skillet. Drain off drippings.
2. Put all ingredients in slow cooker. Stir until well blended.
3. Cover. Cook on Low 2 hours. Stir Soup.
4. Cover and cook an additional 1½-2 hours on Low, or until vegetables and rice are tender, but not mushy.

Mexican Rice and Bean Soup

Esther J. Mast
East Petersburg, PA

Makes 6 servings

Prep. Time: 15-20 minutes
Cooking Time: 6 hours
Ideal slow cooker size: 4- to 5-qt.

½ cup chopped onions
⅓ cup chopped green bell peppers
1 garlic clove, minced
1 Tbsp. oil
4-oz. pkg. thinly sliced, *or* chipped, dried beef
18-oz. can tomato juice
15½-oz. can red kidney beans, undrained
1½ cups water
½ cup long-grain rice, uncooked
1 tsp. paprika
½-1 tsp. chili powder
½ tsp. salt
dash of pepper

1. Cook onions, green peppers, and garlic in oil in skillet until vegetables are tender but not brown. Transfer to slow cooker.
2. Tear beef into small pieces and add to slow cooker.
3. Add remaining ingredients. Mix well.
4. Cover. Cook on Low 6 hours. Stir before serving.

*Serving suggestion: Serve with **relish tray** and **cornbread, home-canned fruit,** and **cookies**.*

Note:
This is a recipe I fixed often when our sons were growing up. We have all enjoyed it in any season of the year.

Green Beans and Ham Soup

Loretta Krahn
Mountain Lake, MN

Makes 6 servings

Prep. Time: 15 minutes
Cooking Time: 4¼-6¼ hours
Ideal slow cooker size: 5- to 6-qt.

1 meaty ham bone, *or* 2 cups cubed ham
1½ qts. water
1 large onion, chopped
2-3 cups cut-up green beans
3 large carrots, sliced
2 large potatoes, peeled and cubed
1 Tbsp. parsley
1 Tbsp. summer savory
½ tsp. salt
¼ tsp. pepper
1 cup cream, *or* milk

1. Combine all ingredients except cream in slow cooker.
2. Cover. Cook on High 4-6 hours.
3. Remove ham bone. Cut off meat and return to slow cooker.
4. Turn to Low. Stir in cream or milk. Heat through and serve.

Green Beans and Sausage Soup

Bernita Boyts
Shawnee Mission, KS

Makes 5-6 servings

Prep. Time: 20-25 minutes
Cooking Time: 7-10 hours
Ideal slow cooker size: 4- to 5-qt.

⅓ lb. link sausage, sliced, *or* bulk sausage
1 medium onion, chopped
2 carrots, sliced
2 ribs celery, sliced
1 Tbsp. olive oil
5 medium potatoes, cubed
10-oz. pkg. frozen green beans
2 14½-oz. cans chicken broth
2 broth cans water
2 Tbsp. chopped fresh parsley, *or* 2 tsp. dried parsley
1-2 Tbsp. chopped fresh oregano, *or* 1-2 tsp. dried oregano
1 tsp. Italian spice
salt to taste
pepper to taste

1. Brown sausage in skillet. Stir frequently for even browning.
2. Remove meat from skillet and place in slow cooker. Reserve drippings.
3. Sauté onion, carrots, and celery in skillet drippings until tender.
4. Place sautéed vegetables in slow cooker, along with all remaining ingredients. Mix together well.
5. Cover. Cook on High 1-2 hours and then on Low 6-8 hours.

Variation:
If you like it hot, add ground red pepper or hot sauce just before serving, or offer to individual eaters to add to their own bowls.

Broccoli and Cauliflower Soup

Wafi Brandt
Manheim, PA

Makes 4-6 servings

Prep. Time: 15 minutes
Cooking Time: 4¼ hours
Ideal slow cooker size: 3-qt.

16-oz. bag frozen broccoli and cauliflower
¼ stick (2 Tbsp.) butter
½ Tbsp. dried onion
2 cups water
2 chicken bouillon cubes
4 Tbsp. flour
2 cups milk, *divided*
½ tsp. Worcestershire sauce
½ tsp. salt
1 cup grated cheddar cheese
chopped chives
parsley

1. Put broccoli and cauliflower, butter, onion, water, and bouillon cubes in slow cooker.
2. Cover. Cook on High 4 hours.
3. When broccoli and cauliflower are soft, mix flour and 1 cup milk together in a jar with a tight-fitting lid. Cover jar and shake vigorously until flour dissolves and mixture is smooth.
4. Pour milk mixture into vegetables and stir. The soup will soon thicken.
5. Then stir in Worcestershire sauce, salt, and cheese.
6. When cheese is melted, stir in last cup of milk. Allow to heat through before serving.
7. Sprinkle chives and parsley over top of each individual serving bowl.

Broccoli, Potato, and Cheese Soup

Ruth Shank
Gridley, IL

Makes 6 servings

Prep. Time: 20-25 minutes
Cooking Time: 4 hours
Ideal slow cooker size: 4-qt.

2 cups cubed, *or* diced, potatoes
3 Tbsp. chopped onion
10-oz. pkg. frozen broccoli cuts, thawed
¼ stick (2 Tbsp.) butter, melted
1 Tbsp. flour
2 cups cubed Velveeta cheese
½ tsp. salt
5½ cups milk

1. Cook potatoes and onion in boiling water in saucepan until potatoes are crisp-tender. Drain. Place in slow cooker.
2. Add remaining ingredients. Stir together.
3. Cover. Cook on Low 4 hours.

Cheesy Broccoli Soup

Dede Peterson, Rapid City, SD

Makes 4 servings

Prep. Time: 15 minutes
Cooking Time: 5-6 hours
Ideal slow cooker size: 3-qt.

1 lb. frozen chopped broccoli, thawed
1 lb. Velveeta cheese, cubed
10¾-oz. can cream of celery soup
14½-oz. can chicken, *or* **vegetable, broth**
dash of pepper
dash of salt

1. Combine ingredients in slow cooker.
2. Cover. Cook on Low 5-6 hours.

Carrot Ginger Soup

Jean Harris Robinson, Pemberton, NJ

Makes 8-10 servings

Prep. Time: 30 minutes • Cooking Time: 3½-4½ hours
Ideal slow cooker size: 5-qt.

2 Tbsp. olive oil
3 lbs. carrots, peeled and thinly sliced
2 Tbsp. chopped gingerroot
2 Tbsp. minced green onion
3 ribs celery, chopped
49½-oz. can chicken broth
1-3 tsp. kosher salt
1 tsp. ground pepper
2 Tbsp. honey
¼ stick (2 Tbsp.) butter
1 cup heavy cream

1. Pour olive oil into slow cooker. Swirl to cover bottom of cooker.
2. Add carrots, ginger, onion, and celery.
3. Pour in broth. Add salt, pepper, honey, and butter. Stir to mix all ingredients well.
4. Cover. Cook on High 3-4 hours, or until carrots are soft.
5. Pulse with an immersion blender to purée.
6. Stir in one cup heavy cream. Heat Soup 15-20 minutes until heated through, but don't let it boil. Serve immediately.

Note:
I was first introduced to this Soup at one of my quilt guild's regular meetings. Even the professed carrot-haters loved it.

Ham and Broccoli Chowder

Rachel Olinger
Parkesburg, PA

Makes 6 servings

Prep. Time: 10 minutes
Cooking Time: 7 hours
Ideal slow cooker size: 4-qt.

2 Tbsp. flour
12-oz. can evaporated milk
2 cups diced ham
1 pkg. frozen chopped broccoli
¼ cup minced onion
1 cup grated Swiss cheese
2 cups water
1 cup light cream

1. Mix flour and milk in slow cooker until smooth.
2. Add all additional ingredients except cream.
3. Cover. Cook on Low 7 hours.
4. Before serving, stir in cream and heat through.

Curried Carrot Soup

Ann Bender
Ft. Defiance, VA

Makes 6-8 servings

Prep. Time: 20 minutes
Cooking Time: 2 hours
Ideal slow cooker size: 3-qt.

1 garlic clove, minced
1 large onion, chopped
2 Tbsp. oil
1 Tbsp. butter
1 tsp. curry powder
1 Tbsp. flour
4 cups chicken, *or* **vegetable, broth**
6 large carrots, sliced
¼ tsp. salt
¼ tsp. ground red pepper, *optional*
1½ cups plain yogurt, *or* **light sour cream**

1. In skillet cook minced garlic and onion in oil and butter until vegetables are limp but not brown.
2. Add curry and flour. Cook 30 seconds. Pour into slow cooker.
3. Add chicken broth and carrots. Mix together well.
4. Cover. Cook on High for about 2 hours, or until carrots are soft.
5. Purée mixture in blender. Hold top on tightly with a thick towel. (The heat tends to push the lid of the blender off.)
6. Return to slow cooker and add seasoning. Keep warm until ready to serve.
7. Add a dollop of yogurt or sour cream to each serving.

Corn Chowder

Betty Moore
Plano, IL

Makes 4-6 servings

Prep. Time: 20-30 minutes
Cooking Time: 6 hours
Ideal slow cooker size: 4-qt.

2½ cups milk
14¾-oz. can cream-style corn
10¾-oz. can cream of mushroom soup
1¾ cups frozen corn
1 cup frozen shredded hash brown potatoes
1 cup cooked ham, diced
1 medium-large onion, diced
¼ stick (2 Tbsp.) butter
2 tsp. parsley flakes
salt and pepper to taste

1. Combine all ingredients in slow cooker.
2. Cover and cook on Low 6 hours.

Note from Tester:

I would garnish each individual bowl of soup with diced red and green bell peppers. Looks like the holidays!

Variations:

1. Replace ham with 8 slices bacon, cooked and crumbled. Add just before serving in order to keep the bacon crisp.
2. Stir ½ tsp. Worcestershire sauce in with Step 1.

Orpha Herr
Andover, NY

Green Chile Corn Chowder

Kelly Evenson
Pittsboro, NC

Makes 8 servings

Prep. Time: 15 minutes
Cooking Time: 7¼-8¼ hours
Ideal slow cooker size: 4-qt.

16-oz. can cream-style corn
3 potatoes, peeled or not, and diced
2 Tbsp. chopped fresh chives
4-oz. can diced green chilies, drained
2-oz. jar chopped pimentos, drained
½-¾ cup chopped cooked ham
2 10½-oz. cans chicken broth
salt to taste
pepper to taste
Tabasco sauce to taste
1 cup milk
shredded Monterey Jack cheese

1. Combine all ingredients except milk and cheese in slow cooker.
2. Cover. Cook on Low 7-8 hours or until potatoes are tender.
3. Stir in milk. Heat until hot.
4. Top individual servings with cheese.

Chicken Corn Soup

Moreen Weaver
Bath, NY

Makes 8-10 servings

Prep. Time: 1 hour
Cooking Time: 4-5 hours
Ideal slow cooker size: 5- to 6-qt.

4-5 lbs. chicken leg quarters
3 qts. water
1 tsp. salt
1½ cups chopped celery
1 medium onion, chopped
4 cups fresh, *or* **frozen, corn**
3 chicken bouillon cubes
pepper to taste
12-oz. bag fine noodles, uncooked

1. If you wish, remove skin from chicken. Put chicken in large stockpot. Add salt and water. Cover and cook until tender.
2. Remove chicken. Allow to stand until cool enough to debone. Meanwhile, strain broth and pour into slow cooker.
3. Remove chicken from bones and cut in small pieces. Place in slow cooker.

4. Stir celery, onion, corn, bouillon, and pepper into slow cooker.
5. Cover. Cook on Low 4-5 hours.
6. Fifteen minutes before end of cooking time, stir in noodles.

Note:
My mother-in-law makes this recipe every Christmas. It just wouldn't be Christmas without it!

Red French Onion Soup

Marilyn Mowry
Irving, TX

Makes 6-8 servings

Prep. Time: 10-15 minutes
Cooking Time: 4-5 hours
Ideal slow cooker size: 3- *to 4-qt.*

5 large red onions
¼ stick (2 Tbsp.) butter
1 cup dry red wine
4 cups beef broth
½ tsp. dried thyme
2 Tbsp. fresh chopped parsley
French baguette
½ cup grated Swiss cheese

1. Cut onions into thin slices. Add with butter to cooker.
2. Turn to High. As butter melts, stir into onions.
3. Add wine, broth, thyme, and parsley. Stir well.
4. Cover. Cook 4-5 hours on Low, or until onions are tender.
5. Prepare bread toppers 30 minutes before Soup is finished cooking. Slice French bread into 1"-thick slices. Lay slices on a baking sheet. Bake 10 minutes at 350 degrees, or until bread is dry and crisp.
6. Sprinkle cheese over each slice of warm bread.
7. To serve, float a cheesy bread topper on top of each bowl of soup.

Variations:
1. Add 1½ tsp. Worcestershire sauce to Step 3.
2. Place cheese on top of bread slices before baking. Then broil them to make the cheese brown and bubble. Watch carefully so the cheese doesn't burn.
3. Instead of Swiss cheese, use ⅓ cup grated mozzarella mixed with ¼ cup grated Parmesan cheese.

Lucille Amos
Greensboro, NC

Betty Drescher
Quakertown, PA

Note:
This is a handy recipe at holiday-time when you need to do last-minute shopping.

Onion Soup

Lucille Amos
Greensboro, NC

Makes 10 servings

Prep. Time: 30 minutes
Cooking Time: 4-5 hours
Ideal slow cooker size: 4- to 5-qt.

6 large onions
1 stick (8 Tbsp.) butter
6 10½-oz. cans beef broth
1½ tsp. Worcestershire sauce
pepper to taste
10 ½"-thick slices French bread
shredded mozzarella cheese and Parmesan cheese, shredded

1. In large skillet or saucepan, sauté onions in butter until tender. Do not brown. Transfer to slow cooker.
2. Add broth, Worcestershire sauce, and pepper.
3. Cover. Cook on Low 4-5 hours or until onions are very tender.
4. Top each serving with French bread and cheese.

Creamy Potato Soup

Janeen Troyer
Fairview, MI

Makes 6-8 servings

Prep. Time: 30 minutes
Cooking Time: 3¼-3½ hours
Ideal slow cooker size: 4-qt.

3 cups chopped potatoes, peeled or unpeeled
1 cup water
½ cup chopped celery
½ cup chopped carrots
¼ cup chopped onions
2 cubes chicken, *or* **vegetable, bouillon**
1 tsp. parsley
½ tsp. salt
¼ tsp. pepper
1½ cups milk
2 Tbsp. flour
½ lb. cheese, your choice, shredded

1. Combine potatoes, water, celery, carrots, onion, bouillon, parsley, salt, and pepper in slow cooker.
2. Cover. Cook on High 3 hours, or until vegetables are tender.
3. In a jar with a tight-fitting lid, add milk to flour. Cover tightly and shake until flour dissolves in milk. When smooth, add mixture to vegetables in cooker. Stir well.
4. Cover. Cook on High another 15-30 minutes, or until soup is thickened and smooth. Stir occasionally to prevent lumps from forming.
5. Add cheese. Stir until melted.

Note from Tester:
For the Christmas holidays, garnish individual soup bowls with fresh parsley and chopped red bell peppers.

Ham and Potato Chowder

Penny Blosser
Beavercreek, OH

Makes 5 servings

Prep. Time: 10 minutes
Cooking Time: 8 hours
Ideal slow cooker size: 4-qt.

5-oz. pkg. scalloped potatoes
sauce mix from potato pkg.
1 cup cooked ham, cut into narrow strips
4 cups chicken broth
1 cup chopped celery
⅓ cup chopped onions
salt to taste
pepper to taste
2 cups half-and-half
⅓ cup flour

1. Combine potatoes, sauce mix, ham, broth, celery, onions, salt, and pepper in slow cooker.
2. Cover. Cook on Low 7 hours.
3. Combine half-and-half and flour in small bowl. Gradually stir into slow cooker, blending well.
4. Cover. Cook on Low up to 1 hour, stirring occasionally until thickened.

Creamy Tomato Soup

Susie Shenk Wenger
Lancaster, PA

Makes 4 servings

Prep. Time: 10-15 minutes
Cooking Time: 3-4 hours
Ideal slow cooker size: 3-qt.

29-oz. can tomato sauce, *or* **crushed tomatoes,** *or* **1 qt. home-canned tomatoes, chopped**
1 small onion, chopped
1-2 carrots, sliced thin
2 tsp. brown sugar
1 tsp. Italian seasoning
¼ tsp. salt
¼ tsp. pepper
1 tsp. freshly chopped parsley
½ tsp. Worcestershire sauce
1 cup heaving whipping cream
croutons, preferably homemade
freshly grated Parmesan cheese

1. Combine tomato sauce, onions, carrots, brown sugar, Italian seasoning, salt, pepper, parsley, and Worcestershire sauce in slow cooker.
2. Cover. Cook on Low 3-4 hours, or until vegetables are soft.
3. Cool Soup a bit. Purée with immersion blender.
4. Add cream and blend lightly again.
5. Serve hot with croutons and Parmesan as garnish.

Tip:
This recipe can be easily doubled.

Butternut Squash and Apple Soup

Tina Hartman
Lancaster, PA

Makes 25-28 1-cup servings

Prep. Time: 30-60 minutes
Cooking Time: 1-2 hours
Ideal slow cooker size: 8-qt.

¼ stick (2 Tbsp.) unsalted butter
2 Tbsp. olive oil
4 cups chopped yellow onions
2 Tbsp. mild curry powder
5 lbs. butternut squash (2 large ones)
1½ lbs. sweet apples
2 tsp. salt
½ tsp. ground pepper
2 cups water
2 cups apple cider, *or* **juice**

1. Warm butter, olive oil, onions, and curry powder in large stockpot over low heat on stove until onions are tender (15 to 20 minutes).
2. Peel squash and remove seeds. Cut squash into chunks.
3. Peel, core, and cut apples into about 8 wedges each.
4. Add squash, apples, salt, pepper, and water to pot. Cook until soft enough to purée.
5. Purée or process with a food processor.
6. Pour entire mixture into slow cooker. Add apple cider or juice.
7. Cover. Cook on Low 1-2 hours. Serve hot from the cooker.

Note:
This recipe is actually from my friends Brittany Leffler and Brian McKee. (They should get credit for it!) They host a cookie-exchange party every Christmas, and they serve this and chili. The rest of us bring the cookies. It is wonderful.

We have an old holiday storybook which my mother used to read to us children. It's pretty battered, but it's a family treasure. One year my sister crafted and painted a special box for it, and now whoever hosts Christmas (we take turns) gets to keep the book until the following Christmas, when it's always the first gift opened.

Carol L. Miller, Lockport, NY

Naturally Colorful Vegetable Soup

Darla Sathre
Baxter, MN

Makes 6 servings

Prep. Time: 20-30 minutes
Cooking Time: 9-11 hours
Ideal slow cooker size: 4-qt.

15-oz. can whole-kernel corn, undrained
2 cups frozen peas
16-oz. can kidney beans, undrained
14½-oz. can diced tomatoes with juice
15-oz. can tomato sauce
½ lb. baby carrots, halved lengthwise
1 onion, chopped
6 cloves garlic, thinly sliced
2 tsp. Italian seasoning
1 tsp. dried marjoram
1 tsp. dried basil

1. Put all ingredients into slow cooker. Stir well.
2. Cover. Cook on High 1-2 hours. Then cook on Low 8-9 hours, or until carrots and onions are as tender as you like them.

Cream of Pumpkin Soup

Nanci Keatley
Salem, OR

Makes 4-6 servings

Prep. Time: 10-15 minutes
Cooking Time: 2-3 hours
Ideal slow cooker size: 4-qt.

1 Tbsp. butter, melted
1 large onion, diced fine
32-oz. box vegetable stock
16-oz. can solid-pack pumpkin
1 tsp. salt
¼ tsp. cinnamon
¼ tsp. freshly ground nutmeg
⅛ tsp. ground ginger
⅛ tsp. ground cloves
⅛ tsp. ground cardamom
¼ tsp. freshly ground pepper
1½ cups half-and-half
1 cup heavy cream
chopped chives

1. Mix butter and onion in slow cooker.
2. Add stock, pumpkin, salt, and other seasonings. Mix well.
3. Cover. Cook on Low 2-3 hours.

Peanut Butter Pumpkin Soup

Carol L. Miller, Lockport, NY

Makes 8-10 servings

Prep. Time: 15 minutes* • Cooking Time: 6 hours
Ideal slow cooker size: 4-qt.

¼ stick (2 Tbsp.) butter
4 cups canned pumpkin
2 cups cooked puréed sweet potatoes, *or* **butternut squash**
1 cup smooth peanut butter
6 cups chicken broth
1 tsp. black pepper
¼ tsp. salt
croutons for garnish, *optional*
crumbled cooked bacon for garnish, *optional*

1. Place butter, pumpkin, sweet potatoes or squash, peanut butter, broth, pepper, and salt in slow cooker.
2. Cover. Cook on Low 6 hours, stirring well after first 2 hours.
3. Serve with croutons or crumbled bacon as garnishes if you wish.

*If you have to make your own puréed sweet potatoes or squash, add another hour to the Prep Time. Use 2 large sweet potatoes, or a medium-sized butternut squash, in order to get the 2 cups mashed.

4. Add half-and-half and cream.
5. Cover. Cook on Low 1 hour, or until heated through.
6. Garnish individual serving bowls with chives.

Savory Cheese Soup

Diane Eby
Holtwood, PA
Dorothy Lingerfelt
Stonyford, CA

Makes 4-5 servings

Prep. Time: 20 minutes
Cooking Time: 8-9 hours
Ideal slow cooker size: 5-qt.

3 14½-oz. cans chicken broth
1 small onion, chopped
1 large carrot, chopped
1 celery rib, chopped
¼ cup chopped sweet red bell pepper
¼ stick (2 Tbsp.) butter
1 tsp. salt
½ tsp. pepper
⅓ cup flour
⅓ cup cold water
8-oz. pkg. cream cheese, softened and cubed
2 cups shredded cheddar cheese
croutons, popcorn, crumpled bacon, sliced green onions, *optional*

1. In a slow cooker, combine chicken broth, onion, carrot, celery, sweet pepper, butter, salt, and pepper.
2. Cover and cook on Low 7-8 hours.
3. In a jar with a tight-fitting lid, combine flour and water. Put on lid and shake vigorously until mixture is smooth and without lumps. Stir into soup.
4. Cover. Cook on High 30 minutes, or until soup has thickened. Stir every 10 minutes or so to prevent lumps from forming.
5. Stir in cream cheese and cheddar cheese until blended.
6. Cover. Cook on Low until cheeses melt and Soup is heated through.
7. Serve with the toppings that you wish.

Easy Cheese Soup

Nancy Wagner Graves
Manhattan, KS

Makes 4 servings

Prep. Time: 5-10 minutes
Cooking Time: 4-6 hours
Ideal slow cooker size: 3½-qt.

2 10¾-oz. cans cream of mushroom, *or* **cream of chicken, soup**
1 cup beer, *or* **milk**
1 lb. cheddar cheese, grated
1 tsp. Worcestershire sauce
¼ tsp. paprika
croutons

1. Combine all ingredients except croutons in slow cooker.
2. Cover. Cook on Low 4-6 hours.
3. Stir thoroughly 1 hour before serving to make sure cheese is well distributed and melted.
4. Serve topped with croutons or in bread bowls.

I have made fabric bags for my friends. They each know which one is theirs (the bags are all different). I get them back every year at the end of the holiday season, ready to use again the next year. It sure saves on wrapping paper.
Sharon Easter, Yuba City, CA

Aunt Thelma's Homemade Soup

Janice Muller
Derwood, MD

Makes 10-12 servings

Prep. Time: 10 minutes
Cooking Time: 4½-6½ hours
Ideal slow cooker size: 6-qt.

7 cups water
4 chicken, *or* **vegetable, bouillon cubes**
1 cup thinly sliced carrots
1 lb. frozen peas
1 lb. frozen corn
1 lb. frozen lima beans
1 bay leaf
¼ tsp. dill seed
28-oz. can whole tomatoes
1 cup diced raw potatoes
1 cup chopped onions
2-3 tsp. salt
½ tsp. dried basil
¼ tsp. pepper
2 Tbsp. cornstarch
¼ cup cold water

1. Combine all ingredients except cornstarch and ¼ cup water in slow cooker.
2. Cover. Simmer on High 4-6 hours, or until vegetables are tender.
3. Thirty minutes before end of cooking time, mix cornstarch and cold water together in a small bowl until smooth.
4. Remove 1 cup broth from cooker and mix with cornstarch-water. When smooth, stir into soup.
5. Cover and continue cooking another half hour, or until soup thickens slightly.

Serving suggestion: A loaf of fresh ***Italian bread*** *goes well with a hot bowl of this soup.*

Note:
My aunt always makes this in the winter and freezes an extra batch for unexpected guests. I converted the recipe to slow-cooker use a few years ago, but I think of her whenever I make it.

Diet Soup Unlimited

Eileen Lehman
Kidron, OH

Makes 6 servings

Prep. Time: 15 minutes
Cooking Time: 4-8 hours
Ideal slow cooker size: 3½- to 4-qt.

4 cups water
2 cups tomato juice
2 beef, *or* **vegetable, bouillon cubes**
1 Tbsp. soy sauce, *optional*
2 tsp. sugar, *optional*
1 cup sliced cabbage
2 carrots, sliced
1 celery rib, sliced
1 onion, sliced
2 cups frozen green beans
1 tsp. salt
pepper to taste

1. Combine all ingredients in slow cooker.
2. Cover. Cook on Low 4-8 hours, or just until vegetables are as tender as you like them.

Variation:
Add fresh mushrooms, if you like, after the first 2 hours of cooking.

Note:
After the holidays this tasty, low-calorie soup is a welcome meal. It improves in flavor the longer it cooks.

The Soup

Joanne Kennedy
Plattsburgh, NY

Makes 8 servings

Prep. Time: 20 minutes
Cooking Time: 9 hours
Ideal slow cooker size: 5- to 6-qt.

2 14½-oz. cans vegetable broth
2 vegetable boullion cubes
4 cups water
1 qt. canned tomatoes
3-4 garlic cloves, minced
1 large onion, chopped
1 cup chopped celery
2 cups chopped carrots
1 small zucchini, cubed
1 small yellow squash, cubed
2 tsp. fresh basil
1 tsp. fresh parsley
pepper to taste
3 dashes Tabasco sauce

Norma's Vegetarian Chili

Kathy Hertzler, Lancaster, PA

Makes 8-10 servings

Prep. Time: 20 minutes • Cooking Time: 8½ hours
Ideal slow cooker size: 5-qt.

2 Tbsp. oil
2 cups minced celery
1½ cups chopped green bell pepper
1 cup minced onions
4 garlic cloves, minced
5½ cups stewed tomatoes
2 1-lb. cans kidney beans, undrained
1½-2 cups raisins
¼ cup wine vinegar
1 Tbsp. chopped parsley
2 tsp. salt
1½ tsp. dried oregano
1½ tsp. cumin
¼ tsp. pepper
¼ tsp. Tabasco sauce
1 bay leaf
¾ cup cashews
1 cup grated cheese, *optional*

1. Combine all ingredients except cashews and cheese in slow cooker.
2. Cover. Simmer on Low 8 hours. Add cashews and simmer 30 minutes more.
3. Garnish individual servings with grated cheese.

Wintertime Vegetable Chili

Maricarol Magill
Freehold, NJ

Makes 6 servings

Prep. Time: 20 minutes
Cooking Time: 6-8 hours
Ideal slow cooker size: 6-qt.

1 medium butternut squash, peeled and cubed
2 medium carrots, peeled and diced
1 medium onion, diced
3 tsp.—3 Tbsp. chili powder, depending upon how hot you like your chili
2 14-oz. cans diced tomatoes
4¼-oz. can chopped mild green chilies, drained
1 tsp. salt, *optional*
1 cup vegetable broth
2 16-oz. cans black beans, drained and rinsed
sour cream, *optional*

1. In slow cooker, layer all ingredients, except sour cream, in order given.
2. Cover. Cook on Low 6-8 hours, or until vegetables are as tender as you want.
3. Stir before serving.
4. Top individual servings with dollops of sour cream.

Serving suggestion: Serve with crusty ***French bread.***

1. Combine all ingredients in slow cooker.
2. Cover. Cook on Low 9 hours, or until vegetables are as tender as you like them.

Variation:
Add cooked pasta after soup is done cooking.

When guests visit I provide a set of slippers for each one to keep their feet toasty and more comfortable. I invite them to keep them when they leave.

Donna Conto, Saylorsburg, PA

Your-Choice-of-Vegetables Soup

Dawn Day
Westminster, CA

Makes 6-8 servings

Prep. Time: 10 minutes
Cooking Time: 6 hours
Ideal slow cooker size: 4- to 5-qt.

4 cups vegetable, beef, *or* **chicken stock**
4 cups vegetables (use any or all of corn, peas, carrots, broccoli, green beans, cauliflower, mushrooms), either fresh *or* **frozen**
leftover cooked meat, cut in small pieces, *or* **1 lb. cubed beef, browned in oil in skillet**
15-oz. can chopped tomatoes
1 bay leaf
¼ cup uncooked long-grain rice *or* **small pearl barley,** *or* **½ cup cooked orzo** *or* **small shells**

1. Combine all ingredients in slow cooker except rice, barley, or pasta.
2. Cover. Cook on Low 6 hours.
3. One hour before end of cooking time, stir in rice or barley. Or 30 minutes before end of cooking time, stir in cooked pasta.

Note:
Serve with rolls and a salad for a great comfort meal.

Homemade Vegetable Soup

Audrey Romonosky
Austin, TX

Makes 6-8 servings

Prep. Time: 15 minutes
Cooking Time: 6-8 hours
Ideal slow cooker size: 4-qt.

1 lb. stewing meat, cut into pieces
1 bay leaf
1 small onion, diced
3 carrots, sliced
2 ribs celery, sliced
2-3 potatoes, diced
14½-oz. can stewed tomatoes, cut up
8-oz. can tomato sauce
¼ cup frozen corn
½ cup frozen green beans
¼ cup frozen peas
¼ cup chopped cabbage
salt to taste
pepper to taste

1. Combine all ingredients in slow cooker. Add water to cover ingredients.
2. Cover. Cook on Low 6-8 hours, or until meat and vegetables are as tender as you like them.

Stay-in-Bed Stew

Janie Steele
Moore, OK
Judy Newman
St. Mary's, Ontario, Canada

Makes 6 servings

Prep. Time: 20 minutes
Cooking Time: 5-6 hours
Ideal slow cooker size: 3-qt.

1 lb. chuck stewing meat
1 large onion, chunked
2 potatoes, peeled and diced large
4 carrots, peeled and sliced
10¾-oz. can tomato soup
½ soup can water
dash of pepper
½ tsp. salt
1 bay leaf
1 cup frozen peas

1. Put all ingredients except peas in slow cooker.
2. Cover. Cook on Low 5-6 hours, or until vegetables are as tender as you like them.
3. Add peas ½ hour before serving.
4. Remove bay leaf before serving.

Beef Dumpling Soup

Barbara Walker
Sturgis, SD

Makes 5-6 servings

Prep. Time: 10-15 minutes
Cooking Time: 4½-6½ hours
Ideal slow cooker size: 4-qt.

1 lb. beef stewing meat, cubed
1 envelope dry onion soup mix
6 cups hot water
2 carrots, peeled and shredded
1 celery rib, finely chopped
1 tomato, peeled and chopped
1 cup buttermilk biscuit mix
1 Tbsp. finely chopped parsley
6 Tbsp. milk

1. Place meat in slow cooker. Sprinkle with onion soup mix. Pour water over meat.
2. Add carrots, celery, and tomato.
3. Cover. Cook on Low 4-6 hours, or until meat is tender.
4. Combine biscuit mix and parsley in bowl. Stir in milk with fork until moistened. Drop dumplings by teaspoonfuls into cooker.
5. Cover. Cook on High 30 minutes.

Variation:
Increase flavor of broth by adding 2 cloves garlic, ½ tsp. dried basil, and ¼ tsp. dill weed in Step 2.

Easy Hamburger Vegetable Soup

Winifred Paul
Scottdale, PA

Makes 8-10 servings

Prep. Time: 20 minutes
Cooking Time: 8-10 hours
Ideal slow cooker size: 5-qt.

1 lb. ground beef
oil
1 cup chopped onions
15-oz. can kidney beans, *or* **butter beans, undrained**
1 cup sliced carrots
¼ cup long-grain rice, uncooked
1 qt. stewed tomatoes
3½ cups water
5 beef bouillon cubes
1 Tbsp. parsley flakes
1 tsp. salt
⅛ tsp. pepper
¼ tsp. dried basil
1 bay leaf

1. Brown ground beef in skillet in oil if needed. Stir frequently to break up clumps of meat. Cook until meat is no longer pink. Drain off drippings.
2. Place meat in cooker, along with all other ingredients.
3. Cover. Cook on Low 8-10 hours.

Tip:
Add more herbs and additional seasonings for zestier flavor in Step 2.

Ruth's Ground Beef Vegetable Soup

Ruth Ann Penner
Hillsboro, KS

Makes 6 servings

Prep. Time: 15 minutes
Cooking Time: 8-10 hours
Ideal slow cooker size: 5-qt.

1 lb. ground beef
1½ qts. water
¾ cup chopped celery
1 cup chopped carrots
1 large onion, chopped
2 cups cubed potatoes
1½ tsp. salt
½ cup long-grain rice, uncooked
¼ tsp. pepper
10¾-oz. can tomato soup

1. Crumble ground beef into slow cooker. Add water.
2. Add remaining ingredients except soup. Mix together well.
3. Cover. Cook on Low 8-10 hours.
4. Add soup 30 minutes before serving and stir through.

Beef Barley Soup

Michelle Showalter
Bridgewater, VA

Makes 10-12 servings

Prep. Time: 15 minutes
Cooking Time: 4-10 hours
Ideal slow cooker size: 6-qt.

1 lb. ground beef
1½ qts. water
1 qt. canned tomatoes, stewed, crushed, *or* **whole**
3 cups sliced carrots
1 cup diced celery
1 cup diced potatoes
1 cup diced onions
¾ cup quick-cooking barley
3 tsp. beef bouillon granules, *or* **3 beef bouillon cubes**
2-3 tsp. salt
¼ tsp. pepper

1. Brown ground beef in skillet in oil if needed. Stir frequently to break up clumps of meat. When meat is no longer pink, drain off drippings.
2. Place meat in cooker, along with all other ingredients. Mix together well.
3. Cover. Cook on Low 8-10 hours or on High 4-5 hours.

Serving suggestion: Serve with fresh ***bread*** *and* ***cheese cubes.***

Variation:

You may use pearl barley instead of quick-cooking barley. Cook it in a saucepan according to package directions, and add halfway through Soup's cooking time.

Easy Veggie-Beef Soup

Rebecca Plank Leichty
Harrisonburg, VA

Makes 6-8 servings

Prep. Time: 20 minutes
Cooking Time: 4-8 hours
Ideal slow cooker size: 5-qt.

1 lb. ground beef, *or* **2 cups stewing beef**
2 cups sliced carrots
1 lb. frozen green beans, thawed
14½-oz. can corn, drained, *or* **16-oz. bag frozen corn, thawed**
28-oz. can diced tomatoes
3 cups beef, *or* **veggie, broth**
3 tsp. instant beef bouillon
2 tsp. Worcestershire sauce
1 Tbsp. sugar
1 Tbsp. minced onion
10¾-oz. can cream of celery soup

1. If using ground beef, place in skillet with a bit of oil if needed. Brown, stirring frequently to break up clumps. When no longer pink, drain off drippings.
2. Place meat in slow cooker.
3. Add all remaining ingredients except celery soup. Mix well.
4. Stir in soup.
5. Cover. Cook on Low 7-8 hours or on High 4 hours.
6. If using stewing meat, shred and mix through soup just before serving.

Serving suggestion: Serve with freshly baked ***bread*** *and homemade* ***jam.***

Note:

Two modern-day conveniences—the slow cooker and bread machine—allow me to prepare tasty meals without too much last-minute dashing around. Utilizing both gives me time to plan table settings and decorations, too.

Make sure your invitations inform your guests about whether your party is informal or formal. It's really uncomfortable to be over-dressed at an informal party or vice versa.
Anita Troyer, Fairview, MI

Hamburger Soup

Naomi Ressler
Harrisonburg, VA
Kay Magruder
Seminole, OK

Makes 8 servings

Prep. Time: 20 minutes
Cooking Time: 3-10 hours
Ideal slow cooker size: 4-qt.

1½ lbs. ground beef
oil
1 medium onion, chopped
1 cup sliced carrots
1 cup sliced celery
1 cup sliced cabbage
6-oz. can tomato paste
2 tsp. Worcestershire sauce
2-3 cups beef broth, depending upon how thick or thin you like your soup

1. Brown ground beef in skillet in oil if needed. Stir frequently in order to break up clumps of meat. When beef is no longer pink, drain off drippings.
2. Combine beef, onions, carrots, celery, and cabbage in slow cooker.
3. Combine tomato paste, Worcestershire sauce, and broth in bowl. When blended, pour into slow cooker. Mix with other ingredients.
4. Cover. Cook on Low 8-10 hours or on High 3-4 hours.

Variation:
Stir in ¼ tsp. black, *or* cayenne, pepper and 2 bay leaves in Step 3 for added flavor.

Ground Beef Soup

Nadine L. Martinitz
Salina, KS

Makes 6-8 servings

Prep. Time: 15-20 minutes
Cooking Time: 7-9 hours
Ideal slow cooker size: 4- to 5-qt.

1 lb. ground beef
1 medium onion, chopped
1 Tbsp. oil
15½-oz. can great northern beans, undrained
15-oz. can tomato sauce
1½-2 tomato-sauce cans water
2 large potatoes, cubed
14½-oz. can tomatoes
1 tsp. salt

1. Brown ground beef and onions in oil in skillet. Stir frequently, breaking up clumps of meat. When meat is no longer pink, drain off drippings.
2. Place beef and onions in slow cooker. Stir in remaining ingredients.
3. Cook on High 1 hour, and then on Low 6-8 hours.

*Serving suggestion: Serve with **grilled cheese sandwiches**.*

Hamburger Vegetable Soup

Joyce Shackelford
Green Bay, WI

Makes 8-10 servings

Prep. Time: 20 minutes
Cooking Time: 8-9 hours
Ideal slow cooker size: 5-qt.

1 lb. ground chuck
1 onion, chopped
2 garlic cloves, minced
oil
4 cups V-8 juice
14½-oz. can stewed tomatoes
2 cups cole slaw mix
2 cups frozen green beans
2 cups frozen corn
2 Tbsp.Worcestershire sauce
1 tsp. dried basil
½ tsp. salt
¼ tsp. pepper

1. Brown beef, onion, and garlic in skillet in oil. Stir frequently to break up clumps of meat. When meat is no longer pink, drain off drippings.
2. Transfer beef and vegetables to slow cooker.
3. Add all remaining ingredients and combine.
4. Cover. Cook on Low 8-9 hours, or until vegetables are as tender as you like them.

Snowmobile Soup

Jane Geigley
Honey Brook, PA

Makes 4-6 servings

Prep. Time: 20 minutes
Cooking Time: 3-4 hours
Ideal slow cooker size: 4- to 6-qt.

1 lb. ground beef
1 small onion, chopped
5 large potatoes, julienned like French fries (you can leave the skins on)
10¾-oz. can cream of mushroom soup
1 soup can milk
2 lbs. shredded cheddar cheese
1 tsp. salt
¼ tsp. pepper

1. Brown beef in skillet. Stir frequently to break up clumps. When meat is no longer pink, drain off all but 2 Tbsp. drippings.
2. Place browned beef in slow cooker.
3. Sauté onion in drippings in skillet until softened.
4. Stir onions, potatoes, soup, milk, cheese, salt, and pepper into meat in slow cooker.
5. Cover. Cook on High 3-4 hours, or until potatoes are as soft as you like them.

Taco Soup with Corn

Suzanne Slagel
Midway, OH

Makes 6-8 servings

Prep. Time: 15 minutes
Cooking Time: 4-6 hours
Ideal slow cooker size: 5- to 6-qt.

1 lb. ground beef
1 large onion, chopped
oil
16-oz. can Mexican-style tomatoes
16-oz. can ranch-style beans
16-oz. can whole-kernel corn, undrained
16-oz. can kidney beans, undrained
16-oz. can black beans, undrained
16-oz. jar picante sauce
corn, *or* **tortilla, chips**
sour cream
shredded cheddar cheese

1. Brown meat and onions in skillet in oil if needed. Stir frequently to break up clumps of meat. When meat is no longer pink, drain off drippings.
2. Place meat and onions in slow cooker. Add other vegetables and picante sauce. Stir well.
3. Cover. Cook on Low 4-6 hours.

Serving suggestion: Serve with ***corn*** *or* ***tortilla chips, sour cream,*** *and* ***shredded cheese*** *as toppings.*

Taco Soup with Hominy

Sue Tjon
Austin, TX

Makes 8 servings

Prep. Time: 15 minutes
Cooking Time: 4 hours
Ideal slow cooker size: 6-qt.

1 lb. ground beef
oil
1 envelope dry ranch dressing mix
1 envelope dry taco seasoning mix
3 12-oz. cans Rotel tomatoes, undrained
2 24-oz. cans pinto beans, undrained
24-oz. can hominy, undrained
14½-oz. can stewed tomatoes, undrained
1 onion, chopped
2 cups water

1. Brown meat in skillet in oil if needed. Stir frequently to break up clumps of meat. When meat is no longer pink, drain off drippings.
2. Spoon meat into slow cooker. Add all remaining ingredients. Mix well.
3. Cover. Cook on Low 4 hours.

Serving suggestion: Line each individual soup bowl with ***tortilla chips****. Then ladle Taco Soup on top and sprinkle with* ***grated cheese****.*

Tip:
Increase or decrease the amount of water you add to make the dish either stew-like or soup-like.

Slow-Cooker Chili

Kay Magruder
Seminole, OK

Makes 8-10 servings

Prep. Time: 25 minutes
Cooking Time: 6-12 hours
Ideal slow cooker size: 6-qt.

3 lbs. stewing meat
2 cloves garlic, minced
¼ tsp. pepper
½ tsp. cumin
¼ tsp. dry mustard
7½-oz. can jalapeño relish
1 cup beef broth
1-1½ onions, chopped, according to your taste preference
½ tsp. salt
½ tsp. dried oregano
1 Tbsp. chili powder
7-oz. can green chilies, chopped
14½-oz. can stewed tomatoes, chopped
15-oz. can tomato sauce
2 15-oz. cans red kidney beans, rinsed and drained
2 15-oz. cans pinto beans, rinsed and drained

1. Combine all ingredients except kidney and pinto beans in slow cooker.
2. Cover. Cook on Low 10-12 hours or on High 6-7 hours. Add beans halfway through cooking time.

Serving suggestion: Serve with ***Mexican cornbread.***

Chili con Carne Supreme

Jane Geigley
Honey Brook, PA

Makes 8 servings

Prep. Time: 30-35 minutes
Cooking Time: 2 hours
Ideal slow cooker size: 4-qt.

2 lbs. ground beef
2 Tbsp. olive oil
2 garlic cloves, minced, *optional*
2 medium onions, chopped
1 green bell pepper, chopped
3 beef bouillon cubes
1 cup boiling water
1½ tsp. salt
2 Tbsp. chili powder
1 tsp. ground cumin
2 tsp. dried oregano
¼ tsp. ground cinnamon
⅛ tsp. cayenne pepper
2 16-oz. cans stewed, *or* **diced, tomatoes with liquid**
15½-oz. can kidney beans, undrained

1. Brown ground beef in large skillet in oil. Stir frequently to break up clumps. When no longer pink, reserve drippings. Spoon meat into slow cooker.
2. In skillet drippings, sauté garlic, onions, and green peppers over low heat until onions are tender. Spoon veggies into slow cooker.
3. Dissolve bouillon cubes in boiling water. Pour into slow cooker.
4. Add rest of ingredients to slow cooker. Stir together until well mixed.
5. Cover. Cook on Low 2 hours.

We always have chili on Christmas Eve. We all enjoy a no-stress meal. Nancy Wagner Graves, Manhattan, KS

Our Favorite Chili

Ruth Shank
Gridley, IL

Makes 10-12 servings

Prep. Time: 20 minutes
Cooking Time: 4-10 hours
Ideal slow cooker size: 5-qt.

1½ lbs. ground beef
¼ cup chopped onions
1 rib celery, chopped
oil
29-oz. can stewed tomatoes
2 15½-oz. cans red kidney beans, undrained
2 16-oz. cans chili beans, undrained
½ cup ketchup
1½ tsp. lemon juice
2 tsp. vinegar
1½ tsp. brown sugar
1½ tsp. salt
1 tsp. Worcestershire sauce
½ tsp. garlic powder
½ tsp. dry mustard powder
1 Tbsp. chili powder
2 6-oz. cans tomato paste

1. Brown ground beef, onions, and celery in skillet in oil if needed. Stir frequently to break up clumps of meat. When meat is no longer pink, drain off drippings.
2. Place meat and vegetables in slow cooker. Add all remaining ingredients. Mix well.
3. Cover. Cook on Low 8-10 hours or on High 4-5 hours.

Serving suggestion: Serve with fresh warm ***cornbread*** *and slices of* ***Colby*** *or* ***Monterey Jack cheese****.*

Slow-Cooked Chili

Jean A. Shaner
York, PA

Makes 10 servings

Prep. Time: 20 minutes
Cooking Time: 8-10 hours
Ideal slow cooker size: 5-qt.

2 lbs. ground beef
oil
2 16-oz. cans kidney beans, rinsed and drained
2 14½-oz. cans diced tomatoes
8-oz. can tomato sauce
2 onions, chopped
1 green bell pepper, chopped
2 garlic cloves, minced
2 Tbsp. chili powder
2 tsp. salt
1 tsp. pepper
shredded cheddar cheese

1. Brown ground beef in skillet in oil if needed. Stir frequently to break up clumps of meat. When no longer pink, drain off drippings.
2. Spoon meat into slow cooker. Add all other ingredients to cooker, except cheese. Stir together well.
3. Cover. Cook on Low 8-10 hours.
4. Ladle chili into individual bowls and top with cheese just before serving.

Chili Soup

Glenna Fay Bergey
Lebanon, OR

Makes 5 qts.

Prep. Time: 25 minutes
Cooking Time: 2-6 hours
Ideal slow cooker size: 2 4- to 5-qt.

3 lbs. ground beef
¾ cup chopped onions
2 Tbsp. celery flakes
2 tsp. salt
1 Tbsp. chili powder, *or* **more, according to your taste preferences**
oil
3 15-oz. cans kidney beans, drained
1 qt. tomato juice
2 10¾-oz. cans tomato soup
1 cup ketchup
¼ cup brown sugar

1. Brown meat, onions, and seasonings in large skillet in oil if needed. Stir frequently to break up clumps of meat. When meat is no longer pink, drain off drippings.
2. Transfer mixture to slow cooker. Stir in all remaining ingredients.
3. Divide between 2 4- or 5-qt. slow cookers. (This is a large recipe!)
4. Cover. Cook on High 2 hours or on Low 4-6 hours.

Serving suggestion: Serve with ***cornbread****.*

Country Auction Chili Soup

Clara Newswanger
Gordonville, PA

Makes 20 servings

Prep. Time: 25 minutes
Cooking Time: 4-8 hours
Ideal slow cooker size: 6-qt.

1½ lbs. ground beef
¼ cup chopped onions
oil
½ cup flour
1 Tbsp. chili powder
1 tsp. salt
6 cups water
2 cups ketchup
⅓ cup brown sugar
3 15½-oz. cans kidney beans, undrained

1. Brown ground beef and onions in skillet in oil if needed. Stir frequently to break up clumps of meat. When no longer pink, drain off drippings.
2. Spoon meat mixture into slow cooker. Stir flour into meat and onions. Add seasonings.
3. Slowly stir in water. Add ketchup, brown sugar, and beans.
4. Cover. Cook on High 4 hours or on Low 8 hours.

Hot and Good Chili

Rose Hankins
Stevensville, MD

Makes 12 servings

Prep. Time: 20 minutes
Cooking Time: 4-10 hours
Ideal slow cooker size: 5-qt.

1 lb. ground beef
oil
1 cup chopped onions
1 cup chopped celery
1 cup chopped green bell peppers
28-oz. can tomatoes, broken up
14-oz. can tomato sauce
2 14-oz. cans kidney beans, undrained
2 Tbsp. chili powder
1 Tbsp. garlic powder
1 Tbsp. hot sauce

1. Brown beef in skillet in oil if needed. Stir frequently, breaking up clumps of meat. When meat is no longer pink, transfer meat to slow cooker. Reserve drippings
2. Sauté onions, celery, and green peppers in drippings until just wilted. Drain and transfer to slow cooker.
3. Stir in remaining ingredients.
4. Cover. Cook on High 4-5 hours or on Low 8-10 hours.

Slowly Cooked Chili

Beatrice Martin
Goshen, IN

Makes 6-8 servings

Prep. Time: 20 minutes
Cooking Time: 5-12 hours
Ideal slow cooker size: 4-qt.

2 lbs. ground beef, *or* **turkey**
oil
15½-oz. can kidney beans, undrained
3 cups tomato juice
3 Tbsp. chili powder
1 tsp. minced garlic
1 envelope dry onion soup mix
½-1 tsp. salt, according to taste
¼ tsp. pepper

1. Brown ground beef or turkey in skillet in oil if needed. Stir frequently, breaking up clumps of meat. When meat is no longer pink, drain off drippings.
2. Place browned meat in cooker. Stir in all remaining ingredients with meat.
3. Cover. Cook on Low 10-12 hours or on High 5-6 hours.

Serving suggestion: Serve in soup bowls with ***crackers****, or over* ***rice****.*

Tip:
This chili freezes well.

Have everyone bring a dish of food, plus its printed recipe to share. *Nancy Wagner Graves, Manhattan, KS*

Three-Bean Chili

Chris Kaczynski
Schenectady, NY

Makes 8-10 servings

Prep. Time: 25 minutes
Cooking Time: 8-10 hours
Ideal slow cooker size: 6-qt. or 2 4- to 5-qt.

2 lbs. ground beef
2 medium onions, diced
oil
16-oz. jar medium salsa
2 envelopes dry chili seasoning
2 16-oz. cans red kidney beans, drained
2 16-oz. cans black beans, drained
2 16-oz. cans white kidney, *or* **garbanzo, beans drained**
28-oz. can crushed tomatoes
16-oz. can diced tomatoes
2 tsp. sugar

1. Brown beef and onions in skillet in oil if needed. Stir frequently, breaking up clumps of meat. When beef is no longer pink, drain off drippings.
2. Spoon beef into slow cooker. Add all remaining ingredients to beef.
3. Cover. Cook on Low 8-10 hours.

Serving suggestion: Serve with ***chopped raw onion*** *and/or* ***shredded cheddar cheese*** *as toppings.*

Tip:
This recipe can be cut in half without injuring its flavor if you don't have a single cooker, or multiple cookers, large enough to handle the full amount.

Hearty Chili

Joylynn Keener
Lancaster, PA

Makes 8 servings

Prep. Time: 20-25 minutes
Cooking Time: 8 hours
Ideal slow cooker size: 5-qt.

1 onion, chopped
2 ribs celery, chopped
1 lb. ground beef
oil
2 14-oz. cans kidney beans, undrained
14-oz. can pinto beans, undrained
14-oz. can diced tomatoes
2 14-oz. cans tomato sauce
1 green bell pepper, chopped
1 Tbsp. sugar
1 tsp. salt
1 tsp. dried thyme
1 tsp. dried oregano
1 Tbsp. chili powder, *or* **to taste**

1. Brown onion, celery, and beef in skillet in oil if needed. Stir frequently to break up clumps of meat. When meat is no longer pink, drain off drippings.
2. Spoon meat into slow cooker. Stir in all remaining ingredients, mixing well.
3. Cover. Cook on Low 8 hours.

So Easy Chili

Sue Graber
Eureka, IL

Makes 4 servings

Prep. Time: 15 minutes
Cooking Time: 4-6 hours
Ideal slow cooker size: 3½-qt.

1 lb. ground beef
1 onion, chopped
oil
15-oz. can chili, with *or* **without beans**
14½-oz. can diced tomatoes with green chilies, *or* **with basil, garlic, and oregano**
1 cup tomato juice
chopped onion
grated cheddar cheese

1. Brown ground beef and onion in skillet in oil, if needed. Stir frequently to break up clumps of meat. When meat is no longer pink, drain off drippings.
2. Spoon meat into slow cooker.
3. Stir in chili, diced tomatoes, and tomato juice.
4. Cover. Cook on Low 4-6 hours.

Serving suggestion: Serve with ***onions*** *and* ***cheese*** *as toppings for individual servings.*

Tips:
1. This chili is a good consistency for serving over rice.
2. For a thicker chili, add 4-6 oz. tomato paste 20 minutes before end of cooking time.

The Chili Connection

Anne Townsend
Albuquerque, NM

Makes 6 servings

Prep. Time: 15-20 minutes
Cooking Time: 3-5 hours
Ideal slow cooker size: 3½-qt.

1½ lbs. ground beef
1 cup chopped onions
oil
28-oz. can tomatoes, chopped
15-oz. can kidney beans, undrained
1 Tbsp. brown, *or* **granulated, sugar**
2-4 tsp. chili powder, according to your taste preference
1 tsp. salt

1. Brown ground beef and onions in skillet in oil if needed. Stir frequently to break up clumps of meat. When meat is no longer pink, drain off drippings.
2. Spoon meat and onions into slow cooker. Stir in all other ingredients.
3. Cover. Cook on Low 3-5 hours.

Variation:

In order to have a thicker chili, stir in a 6-oz. can tomato paste in Step 2.

Tips:

An assortment of toppings can take the place of a salad with this chili. I usually offer chopped onions, tomatoes, grated cheddar cheese, picante sauce, and, when avocados are in season, guacamole.

Cornbread or refrigerated twist rolls sprinkled with garlic salt are delicious. Either chocolate or apple cake with ice cream makes a happy ending.

This is a fun informal party dish which connects the guests as they get involved in selecting their favorite toppings.

As a frequently enjoyed dish, this recipe has stood the test of time. Our children thought it was delicious when they were young and now they enjoy preparing it for their own families.

Extra Easy Chili

Jennifer Gehman
Harrisburg, PA

Makes 4-6 servings

Prep. Time: 5-10 minutes
Cooking Time: 3-8 hours
Ideal slow cooker size: 4-qt.

1 lb. ground beef, *or* **turkey**
1 envelope dry chili seasoning mix
16-oz. can chili beans in sauce
2 28-oz. cans crushed, *or* **diced, tomatoes seasoned with garlic and onion**

1. Crumble meat into slow cooker.
2. Stir in remaining ingredients.
3. Cover. Cook on High 3-4 hours or on Low 6-8 hours. Stir halfway through cooking time.

Serving suggestion: Serve over ***white rice****, topped with* ***shredded cheddar cheese*** *and* ***chopped raw onions****.*

Note:

I decided to make this Chili recipe one year for Christmas. Our family was hosting other family members—and we had had guests for about a week prior to Christmas.

Needless to say, I was tired of cooking so this seemed easy enough. It was so nice to put the ingredients in the slow cooker and let it cook all day long. Not only did the Chili warm us up on a cold day, but it was a welcomed change from the traditional Christmas meal. It has been my tradition ever since!

Grandma's Chili

Beverly Flatt-Getz
Warriors Mark, PA

Makes 8 servings

Prep. Time: 20 minutes
Cooking Time: 4 hours
Ideal slow cooker size: 5-qt.

1 large onion, chopped
2 lbs. ground beef
oil
28-oz. can stewed tomatoes
16-oz. can dark kidney beans, undrained
15-oz. can chili with beans
10¾-oz. can tomato soup
1 tsp. K.C. Masterpiece BBQ sauce
¼ tsp. garlic salt
¼ tsp. garlic powder
¼ tsp. onion salt
¼ tsp. chili powder
pinch of sugar

1. Brown onion and beef in skillet in oil, if needed. Stir meat frequently to make sure it's browning evenly, but leave meat in larger chunks. When meat is no longer pink, drain off drippings.
2. Spoon meat and onion into slow cooker. Stir in remaining ingredients.
3. Cover. Cook on High 4 hours.

*Serving suggestion: Serve with **crackers**, **rolls**, **butter**, and **apple crisp** with **whipped topping**.*

Note:
When the grandchildren come to visit from five different states, they always ask for Grandma's Chili. I just made up the recipe. Now I'm afraid to change it!

Hearty Potato Chili

Janice Muller
Derwood, MD

Makes 8 servings

Prep. Time: 20-25 minutes
Cooking Time: 4 hours
Ideal slow cooker size: 5-qt.

1 lb. ground beef
oil
½ cup chopped onions
½ cup chopped green bell pepper
1 Tbsp. poppy seeds, *optional*
1 tsp. salt
½ tsp. chili powder
1 pkg. au gratin, *or* **scalloped, potato mix**
1 cup hot water
15-oz. can kidney beans, undrained
16-oz. can stewed tomatoes
4-oz. can mushroom pieces, undrained

1. Brown ground beef in skillet in oil, if needed. Stir frequently, breaking up clumps of meat. When meat is no longer pink, spoon into slow cooker. Reserve drippings.
2. Sauté onions and green peppers in drippings until softened.
3. Place sautéed vegetables, along with all other ingredients in slow cooker. Mix together well.
4. Cover. Cook on High 4 hours, or until liquid is absorbed and potatoes are tender.

Spicy Chili

Deborah Swartz
Grottoes, VA

Makes 4-6 servings

Prep. Time: 20 minutes
Cooking Time: 2-3 hours
Ideal slow cooker size: 3½-qt.

½ lb. sausage, either cut in thin slices or removed from casings
½ lb. ground beef
½ cup chopped onions
½ lb. fresh mushrooms, sliced
⅛ cup chopped celery
⅛ cup chopped green bell peppers
1 cup salsa
16-oz. can tomato juice
6-oz. can tomato paste
½ tsp. sugar
½ tsp. salt
½ tsp. dried oregano
½ tsp. Worcestershire sauce
¼ tsp. dried basil
¼ tsp. pepper

1. Brown sausage, ground beef, and onions in skillet. Stir frequently to break up clumps of meat.
2. During last 3 minutes of

browning, add mushrooms, celery, and green peppers. Continue cooking; then drain off drippings.

3. Spoon meat and sautéed vegetables into cooker. Stir in remaining ingredients.

3. Cover. Cook on High 2-3 hours.

Variations:

Add any or all of the following to Step 3:

1 tsp. chili powder
1 tsp. ground cumin
15-oz. can black beans, undrained
15-oz. can whole-kernel corn, undrained

M&T's Chili

Sherry Conyers
McPherson, KS

Makes 4 servings

Prep. Time: 20 minutes
Cooking Time: 5-6 hours
Ideal slow cooker size: 5-qt.

1 lb. ground beef
½ lb. sausage links, sliced
1 envelope Williams chili seasoning
2 10-oz. cans Mexican tomatoes
15-oz. can chili with no beans
2 10-oz. cans Rotel tomatoes
1-lb. can refried beans
¼ cup diced onions

1. Brown beef and sliced sausage in skillet. Stir frequently to break up clumps of beef. When meat is no longer pink, drain off drippings.

2. Spoon meats into cooker. Stir in all additional ingredients.

3. Cover. Cook on Low 5-6 hours.

Variation:

If you want a soupier and less spicy chili, add a 1-lb. can of stewed tomatoes or 2 cups tomato juice in Step 2.

Black Bean Chili con Carne

Janie Steele
Moore, OK

Makes 18 1-cup servings

Prep. Time: 25-30 minutes
Soaking Time: 8 hours, or overnight
Cooking Time: 8 hours
Ideal slow cooker size: 6-qt. or 2 4- to 5-qt. cookers

1 lb. dry black beans
3 lbs. ground beef
oil
2 large onions, chopped
1 green bell pepper, chopped
3 cloves garlic, minced
2 tsp. salt
1 tsp. pepper
6-oz. can tomato paste
3 cups tomato juice, *or* **more**
1 tsp. celery salt
1 Tbsp. Worcestershire sauce
1 tsp. dry mustard
cayenne pepper to taste
cumin to taste
3 Tbsp. chili powder

1. Place beans in slow cooker. Cover with water. Soak 8 hours or overnight.

2. Rinse beans and drain. Return soaked beans to slow cooker.

3. Brown ground beef in batches in large skillet in oil, if needed. Stir frequently to break up clumps of meat. When beef is no longer pink, drain off drippings.

4. Spoon meat into slow cooker with beans.

5. Mix in all remaining ingredients.

6. Cover. Cook on Low 8 hours.

Serving suggestion: Serve over ***salad greens*** *or wrapped in* ***tortillas****, topped with* ***lettuce*** *and* ***grated cheese****.*

Beef Tortellini Soup

Char Hagner
Montague, MI

Makes 6 servings

Prep. Time: 30 minutes
Cooking Time: 8 hours
Ideal slow cooker size: 4- to 5-qt.

1 lb. ground beef
oil
28-oz. can stewed, *or* **diced, tomatoes**
10½-oz. can condensed French onion soup
9-oz. pkg. frozen green beans
9-oz. pkg. cheese tortellini
1 tsp. dried basil
1 medium zucchini, chopped
½-¾ tsp. salt
¼ tsp. pepper
3½ cups water

1. Brown beef in a skillet in oil, if needed. Stir frequently to break up clumps. When meat is no longer pink, drain off drippings.
2. Place meat in slow cooker. Stir in all other ingredients.
3. Cover. Cook on Low 8 hours.

Sausage, Tomato, Spinach Soup

Wendy B. Martzall, New Holland, PA

Makes 6-8 servings

Prep. Time: 15-20 minutes • Cooking Time: 5 hours
Ideal slow cooker size: 3- to 4-qt.

½ lb. loose pork, *or* **turkey, sausage**
1 medium onion, chopped
1 small green bell pepper, chopped
28-oz. can diced tomatoes
2 14½-oz. cans beef broth
8-oz. can tomato sauce
½ cup picante sauce
1½ tsp. sugar
1 tsp. dried basil
½ tsp. dried oregano
10-oz. pkg. frozen spinach, thawed and squeezed dry
½-¾ cup shredded mozzarella cheese

1. Brown sausage with onions and peppers in skillet. (If you use turkey sausage, you'll probably need to add 1-2 Tbsp. oil to the pan.) Stir frequently, breaking up clumps of meat. When meat is no longer pink, drain off drippings.
2. Spoon meat and vegetables into slow cooker.
3. Add all remaining ingredients except spinach and cheese. Stir until well blended.
4. Cover. Cook on Low 4¾ hours.
5. Stir spinach into Soup. Cover and continue cooking on Low another 15 minutes.
6. Top each individual serving with a sprinkling of mozzarella cheese.

Sausage Tortellini Soup

Susie Shenk Wenger
Lancaster, PA

Makes 12-15 servings

Prep. Time: 20-25 minutes
Cooking Time: 4-5 hours
Ideal slow cooker size: 4-qt.

2 lbs. sweet Italian sausage, casings removed
2-3 cups carrots, diced
1 large onion, diced
3 small zucchini, cubed
1½ cups fresh, *or* **frozen, sweet corn**
1 large can diced petite tomatoes with garlic and olive oil
2 10¾-oz. cans tomato soup
2 soup cans water
1 large can tomato purée
1 family-sized bag of 3-cheese frozen tortellini, cooked according to package directions
shredded cheese of your choice

1. In large skillet, brown sausage, stirring frequently to break up meat. Drain off

all but 2 Tbsp. drippings. Put sausage in slow cooker.

2. Sauté carrots and onions in sausage drippings just until softened.

3. Add carrots, onions, zucchini, corn, tomatoes, tomato soup, water and tomato purée to slow cooker. Stir until well mixed.

4. Cover. Cook on High 1 hour. Stir.

5. Cover. Cook on Low 3 hours, or until vegetables are softened.

6. Just before serving, stir in cooked tortellini.

Serving suggestion: Serve steaming hot with ***shredded cheddar cheese*** *sprinkled over each individual bowl of soup.*

Note:

Because we have three ovens in our home, we host a day-after-Thanksgiving cookie-bake every year at our house. Extended family join in, and we have all the ovens going full-time. This soup is always the lunch for this event. It's the fuel to keep the bakers going through the day, and it doesn't require oven space.

Vegetable Pork Soup

Naomi Ressler
Harrisonburg, VA

Makes 6 servings

Prep. Time: 25-30 minutes
Cooking Time: 6-7 hours
Ideal slow cooker size: 4-qt.

1-lb. pork tenderloin, cut into bite-sized pieces
1 tsp. garlic powder
2 tsp. oil
28-oz. can diced tomatoes
4 medium carrots, cut into bite-sized pieces
2 medium potatoes, peeled *or* **unpeeled, cubed**
14½-oz. can chicken broth
¼ cup quick-cooking tapioca
2 bay leaves
1 Tbsp. Worcestershire sauce
1 Tbsp. honey
1 tsp. dried thyme
¼ tsp. salt
¼ tsp. pepper
⅛ tsp. nutmeg

1. Sprinkle pork with garlic powder. In large skillet, brown pork in oil.

2. Transfer meat to slow cooker.

3. Stir remaining ingredients into pork.

4. Cover. Cook on Low 6-7 hours, or just until pork and vegetables are tender.

5. Discard bay leaves before serving.

Pork Chile

Carol Duree
Salina, KS

Makes 4-5 servings

Prep. Time: 15 minutes
Cooking Time: 4-8 hours
Ideal slow cooker size: 4-qt.

1½-2 lbs. boneless pork ribs, *or* **other cut of pork**
2 14½-oz. cans fire-roasted diced tomatoes
1, *or* **2 4¼-oz. cans diced green chili peppers, drained**
½ cup chopped onion
1, *or* **2 cloves garlic, minced**
salt and pepper to taste
1 Tbsp. chili powder, *or* **to taste**

1. Layer ingredients into slow cooker in order given.

2. Cover. Cook on High 4 hours or on Low 6-8 hours, or until pork is tender but not dry.

3. Cut up or shred meat. Stir through chile and serve.

Notes:

1. You can serve this as soup, but we especially like it over rice.

2. You can add a 1-lb. can of your favorite chili beans 30 minutes before end of cooking time.

Black-Eyed Pea Chili

Lena Mae Janes
Lane, KS

Makes 10 servings

Prep. Time: 20-30 minutes
Cooking Time: 2 hours
Ideal slow cooker size: 5- to 6-qt.

1 lb. loose pork sausage
1 medium onion, chopped
½ cup celery chopped
4 15-oz. cans black-eyed peas, undrained
14-oz. can diced tomatoes, undrained
10-oz. can diced tomatoes with green chilies, undrained
2 Tbsp. chili powder

1. Cook sausage in skillet until no longer pink, stirring frequently. Drain sausage on paper towel.
2. Discard all but 2 Tbsp. pan drippings. To these drippings, add onion and celery. Cook until translucent, stirring frequently.
3. Place peas, tomatoes, tomatoes with green chilies, cooked onions and celery, sausage, and chili powder in slow cooker. Stir well.
4. Cover. Cook on High until all ingredients are hot, about an hour. Then turn cooker to Low and cook 1 more hour.

Serving suggestion: ***Cornbread sticks*** *are a great accompaniment to this Chili.*

Note:
Black-Eyed Pea Chili, slow-cooked, is a New Year's must for our household. Black-eyed peas bring good luck, you know!

Asian Pork Soup

Judi Manos
West Islip, NY

Makes 6 servings

Prep. Time: 20 minutes
Cooking Time: 4-10 hours
Ideal slow cooker size: 4-qt.

1 lb. ground pork, chicken, *or* **turkey**
1 garlic clove, minced
oil
2 medium carrots, cut into julienne strips
4 medium green onions, cut into 1" pieces
1 garlic clove, minced
¼ cup soy sauce
½ tsp. gingerroot, chopped
⅛ tsp. pepper
49½-oz. can chicken broth
1 cup sliced mushrooms
1 cup bean sprouts

1. Cook meat with garlic in skillet in oil, if needed. Stir frequently to break up clumps of meat. When meat is no longer pink, drain off drippings.
2. Spoon meat and garlic into slow cooker. Stir in all other ingredients except mushrooms and sprouts.
3. Cover. Cook on Low 7-9 hours or on High 3-4 hours.
4. Stir in mushrooms and bean sprouts.
5. Cover. Cook on Low 1 more hour.

Variation:
For added flavor to the meat, add ⅛ tsp. five-spice blend to Step 2.

Lentil Soup with Ham Bone

Rhoda Atzeff
Harrisburg, PA

Makes 6-8 servings

Prep. Time: 15 minutes
Cooking Time: 8-9 hours
Ideal slow cooker size: 4-qt.

1 lb. dry lentils, washed and drained
1 celery rib, chopped
1 large carrot, grated
½ cup chopped onions
1 bay leaf
¼ tsp. dried thyme
7-8 cups water
1 ham bone, ½ lb. thinly sliced kielbasa, *or* **½ lb. hot smoked sausage, sliced**
¼-½ tsp. crushed red hot pepper flakes
pepper to taste
salt to taste

1. Combine all ingredients except pepper and salt in slow cooker.
2. Cover. Cook on Low 8-9 hours, or until meat and lentils are tender.

3. Remove bay leaf and ham bone. Allow ham bone to cool. Then dice meat from bone and return to cooker.
4. Season to taste with pepper and salt.

Serving suggestion: Serve alone, or over ***rice*** *with* ***grated cheese*** *on top.*

Everyone's Hungry Soup

Janie Steele
Moore, OK

Makes 20-25 servings

Prep. Time: 45 minutes
Cooking Time: 8-10 hours
Ideal slow cooker size: 2 6- to 7-qt. cookers

6 thick slices bacon
3 lbs. boneless beef stewing meat, cubed
1 lb. boneless pork, cubed
3 14½-oz. cans stewed, *or* **diced, tomatoes**
10-oz. can Rotel tomatoes with chilies
3 celery ribs, chopped
3 large onions, chopped
garlic to taste
salt to taste
pepper to taste
½ cup Worcestershire sauce
2 Tbsp. chili powder
2 cups water
6-8 medium potatoes, peeled and cubed
1 lb. carrots, sliced
15-oz. can peas, undrained
14½-oz. can green beans, undrained
15¼-oz. can corn, undrained
1 lb. cut-up okra, *optional*

1. Fry bacon in skillet until crisp. Remove bacon, but reserve drippings. Crumble bacon and divide between 2 large (6-qt. or larger) slow cookers.
2. Brown stewing beef and pork in skillet in bacon drippings. Drain off drippings.
3. Divide beef and pork between two cookers.
4. In a large bowl, combine all remaining ingredients and mix well. Divide between slow cookers.
5. Stir each cooker's ingredients well. Cover. Cook on Low 8-10 hours.

Serving suggestion: Serve with loaves of ***homemade bread*** *or pans of* ***cornbread.***

Hamburger Sausage Soup

Esther Becker
Gordonville, PA

Makes 4-6 servings

Prep. Time: 20-25 minutes
Cooking Time: 8-10 hours
Ideal slow cooker size: 5-qt.

1 lb. ground beef
1 lb. Polish sausage, sliced
½ tsp. seasoning salt
¼ tsp. dried oregano
¼ tsp. dried basil
1 envelope dry onion soup mix
6 cups boiling water
16-oz. can diced tomatoes
1 Tbsp. soy sauce
½ cup sliced celery
¼ cup chopped celery leaves
1 cup pared, sliced carrots
1 cup uncooked macaroni

1. Brown ground beef and sausage in skillet. Stir frequently, breaking up clumps of beef. When meats are no longer pink, drain off drippings.
2. Place meats in slow cooker. Add seasoning salt, oregano, basil, and onion soup mix to cooker.
3. Stir in boiling water, tomatoes, and soy sauce.
4. Add celery, celery leaves, and carrots. Stir well.
5. Cover. Cook on Low 8-10 hours.
6. One hour before end of cooking time, stir in dry macaroni.

Serving suggestion: Serve with ***cornbread*** *or* ***corn muffins.***

Delicious Sausage Soup

Karen Waggoner
Joplin, MO

Makes 4 servings

Prep. Time: 15-20 minutes
Cooking Time: 4-5 hours
Ideal slow cooker size: 5-qt.

1 lb. spicy Italian sausage
5½ cups chicken broth
½ cup heavy cream
3 carrots, grated
4 potatoes, sliced, *or* **cubed**
4 cups kale, chopped
½ tsp. salt
½ tsp. crushed red pepper flakes

1. Slice sausage into thin pieces, or squeeze out of casings. Place in skillet. Cook, stirring frequently to brown all sides. When no more pink remains in meat, drain off drippings.
2. Place meat in slow cooker. Add broth, cream, and vegetables.
3. Sprinkle spices over top.
4. Cover. Cook on High 4-5 hours, stirring occasionally if you're home and able to do so.

Spicy Sausage Soup

Janie Steele
Moore, OK

Makes 8-10 servings

Prep. Time: 25 minutes
Cooking Time: 6-8 hours
Ideal slow cooker size: 5-qt.

1 lb. ground beef
1 lb. bulk spicy sausage, casings removed
half a large onion, chopped
2 cups chopped carrots
2 cups chopped celery
1 green, *or* **red, bell pepper, chopped,** *optional*
2 tsp. salt, *or* **to taste**
¼ tsp. pepper, *or* **to taste**
1 tsp. dried oregano, *or* **to taste**
2 *or* **3 garlic cloves, minced**
14½-oz. can stewed tomatoes with chilies
14½-oz. can green beans
¼ tsp. chili powder
1 cup instant rice, uncooked

1. Combine beef, sausage, and onions in a large bowl. Form into balls. Place in slow cooker.
2. Place all remaining ingredients, except rice, in another large bowl. Stir together well.
3. Stir vegetable mixture and meatballs together gently so as not to break up the meatballs.
4. Cover. Cook on Low 6-8 hours. Stir in rice 20 minutes before serving.

Serving suggestion: Serve with ***rolls*** *or* ***cornbread.***

Sauerkraut-Sausage Bean Soup

Bonnie Goering
Bridgewater, VA

Makes 8-10 servings

Prep. Time: 10 minutes
Cooking Time: 2-3 hours
Ideal slow cooker size: 4-qt.

3 15-oz. cans white beans, undrained
16-oz. can sauerkraut, drained and rinsed
1 lb. link sausage, sliced thin
¼ cup brown sugar
½ cup ketchup

1. Combine all ingredients in slow cooker.
2. Cover. Cook on High 2-3 hours.

Serving suggestion: Serve with ***cornbread, applesauce,*** *and/or* ***cole slaw.***

Tip:
Add some tomato juice or water if you prefer a thinner soup.

Jambalaya

Mary Ann Lefever
Lancaster, PA

Makes 10-12 servings

Prep. Time: 30 minutes
Cooking Time: 2-3 hours
Ideal slow cooker size: 4- to 5-qt.

1 lb. hot, *or* **mild, Italian sausage, removed from casings**
½ cup chopped celery
1 cup chopped onion
½ cup chopped green bell pepper
1 tsp. minced garlic
16-oz. can chopped, *or* **diced, tomatoes**
12-oz. can chicken broth
6-oz. can tomato juice
½ cup long-grain rice, uncooked
¼ tsp. black pepper
14 drops hot pepper sauce, *or* **to taste,** *optional*
1 chicken breast, cooked, cut into small pieces, *or* **2 cups leftover cooked turkey**
½ lb. uncooked medium shrimp, peeled

1. Brown sausage in skillet with celery and onions, breaking up sausage as it cooks. When the meat is no longer pink, drain off drippings.
2. Spoon meat, celery, and onion into slow cooker.
3. Add green pepper, garlic, tomatoes, broth, tomato juice, rice, pepper, and hot sauce if you wish to cooker. Stir together well.
4. Cover. Cook on Low 2-3 hours, or until rice has cooked tender.
5. Five minutes before end of cooking time, stir in cooked chicken and shrimp.
6. Cover and cook 5 more minutes.

Serving suggestion: Serve with plenty of cooked ***rice****.*

Note:

This has become our traditional Christmas dish ever since we stopped doing a big sit-down meal. With family coming at different times during the day, a slow-cooker Jambalaya is perfect.

White Chicken Chili

Jewel Showalter
Landisville, PA

Makes 6-8 servings

Prep. Time: 25 minutes
Cooking Time: 3½-5 hours
Ideal slow cooker size: 5-qt.

2 whole skinless chicken breasts
6 cups water
2 chopped onions
2 garlic cloves, minced
1 Tbsp. oil
2-4 4¼-oz. cans chopped green chilies, drained, depending on your taste preference
1-2 diced jalapeño peppers
2 tsp. ground cumin
1½ tsp. dried oregano
¼ tsp. cayenne pepper
½ tsp. salt
3-lb. can navy beans, undrained
1-2 cups shredded cheese
sour cream
salsa

1. Place chicken in slow cooker. Add 6 cups water.
2. Cover. Cook on Low 3-4 hours, or until chicken is tender but not dry.
3. Remove chicken from slow cooker. When cool enough to handle, cube and set aside.
4. Sauté onions and garlic in oil in skillet. Add chilies, jalapeño peppers, cumin, oregano, pepper, and salt. Sauté 2 minutes. Transfer to broth in slow cooker.
5. Add navy beans.
6. Cover. Cook on Low 30-60 minutes.
7. Right before serving add chicken and cheese.
8. Serve topped with sour cream and salsa.

Serving suggestion: ***Cornbread*** *and/or* ***corn chips*** *are good go-alongs with this Chili.*

Variation:

If you want to use dried beans, use 3 cups navy beans. Cover with water in saucepan, soaking overnight. In the morning, drain and cover with fresh water. Cook in saucepan over low heat, 7-8 hours, or until tender. Drain off excess moisture and stir into chicken and broth.

White Chili

Rebecca Plank Leichty
Harrisonburg, VA

Makes 6-8 servings

Prep. Time: 15 minutes
Cooking Time: 4-10 hours
Ideal slow cooker size: 5-qt.

15-oz. can chickpeas, *or* garbanzo beans, undrained
15-oz. can small northern beans, undrained
15-oz. can pinto beans, undrained
1 qt. frozen corn, *or* 2 1-lb. bags frozen corn
1½ cups shredded cooked chicken
2 Tbsp. minced onion
1 red bell pepper, diced
3 tsp. minced garlic
3 tsp. ground cumin
½ tsp. salt
½ tsp. dried oregano
2 15-oz. cans chicken broth

1. Combine all ingredients in slow cooker.
2. Cover. Cook on Low 8-10 hours or on High 4-5 hours.

Serving suggestion: Serve with warmed ***tortilla chips*** *topped with melted* ***cheddar cheese.***

Variation:
For more zip, add 2 tsp. chili powder, or one or more chopped jalapeño peppers, to Step 1.

Italian Chicken Chili

Betty K. Drescher, Quakertown, PA

Makes 8 servings

Prep. Time: 20-30 minutes • Cooking Time: 6¾ hours
Ideal slow cooker size: 5-qt.

½ lb. loose Italian sausage, hot, *or* sweet
1 tsp. olive oil
1 lb. boneless, skinless chicken breasts, uncooked and cut into 1" cubes
28-oz. can crushed tomatoes, undrained
28-oz. can diced tomatoes, undrained
15-oz. can white kidney, *or* cannellini, beans, rinsed and drained
2 celery ribs, chopped
1 cup onions, chopped
1 small red bell pepper, chopped
½ cup chicken broth
2 Tbsp. chili powder
2 tsp. dried oregano
2 tsp. minced garlic
2 tsp. dried thyme
1 medium zucchini, diced
1 cup sliced fresh mushrooms
¼ cup minced fresh parsley
shredded Italian cheese blend, *optional*

1. In large skillet, cook sausage in oil over medium heat. Stir frequently to break up clumps. Cook until no longer pink. Drain off drippings.
2. Transfer sausage to slow cooker. Stir in chicken, crushed and diced tomatoes, beans, celery, onion, red bell pepper, broth, chili powder, oregano, garlic, and thyme.
3. Cover. Cook on Low 6 hours.
4. Stir in zucchini and mushrooms.
5. Cover. Cook on High 45 minutes.
6. Sprinkle with parsley.
7. Serve individual bowls of soup with shredded Italian cheese blend, if you wish.

Chicken Sausage Fennel Soup

Jean Harris Robinson
Pemberton, NJ

Makes 12-14 cups

Prep. Time: 20 minutes
Cooking Time: 4-5 hours
Ideal slow cooker size: 4- to 5-qt.

1 stick (8 Tbsp.) butter
¾ cup flour
2 fennel bulbs cut into large strips (plus some fennel fronds, chopped)
3 celery ribs, chopped
1 medium onion, chopped
2 Tbsp. olive oil
8 cups chicken stock
½ lb. loose mild turkey sausage
3 cups cooked and diced chicken breast
salt and pepper to taste

1. Melt butter in a small skillet. Blend in flour. Cook over medium heat just until roux turns golden. Stir frequently so mixture doesn't stick. Set aside.
2. In a larger skillet, sauté fennel, celery, and onion in olive oil for 10 minutes. Spoon vegetables into slow cooker.
3. Stir chicken stock into slow cooker. Turn cooker on High.
4. Sauté sausage in skillet, breaking up into small pieces with a wooden spoon, just until cooked through. Drain off drippings. Add meat to cooker.
5. Stir in chopped chicken. Cover cooker.
6. When Soup begins to bubble, add roux, stirring constantly until it dissolves into the Soup.
7. Cover cooker. Turn back to Low and cook 4 hours.

Apple Chicken Stew

Lorraine Pflederer
Goshen, IN

Makes 4 servings

Prep. Time: 30-40 minutes
Cooking Time: 4-5 hours
Ideal slow cooker size: 5-qt.

4 medium potatoes, cubed
4 medium carrots, cut ¼"-thick slices
1 medium red onion, halved and sliced
1 celery rib, thinly sliced
1½ tsp. salt
¾ tsp. dried thyme
½ tsp. pepper
¼-½ tsp. caraway seeds
2 lbs. boneless, skinless chicken breasts, cubed
2 Tbsp. olive, *or* **vegetable, oil**
1 large tart apple, peeled and cubed
1¼ cups apple cider, *or* **juice**
1 Tbsp. cider vinegar
1 bay leaf
minced fresh parsley

1. Layer potatoes, carrots, onion, and celery into slow cooker.
2. In a small bowl, combine salt, thyme, pepper, and caraway seeds. Sprinkle half over vegetables.
3. In a skillet, sauté chicken in oil just until lightly browned. Drain off drippings.
4. Transfer chicken to slow cooker. Top with cubed apple.
5. In another small bowl, combine apple cider and vinegar. Pour over chicken and apple.
6. Sprinkle with remaining salt mixture. Lay bay leaf on top.
7. Cover. Cook on High 4-5 hours, or until vegetables are tender and chicken juices run clear.
8. Discard bay leaf. Stir before serving.
9. Sprinkle individual serving bowls with parsley.

If you've made a thick slow-cooker stew or chili, you can serve it in individual hard rolls. Cut the top off each roll. Hollow out the bottom, leaving a half inch of bread inside. Spoon about a cup of the stew or chili into each roll, just before serving. — *Jean M. Butzer, Batavia, NY*

Santa Fe Chicken Soup

Sherry Conyers
McPherson, KS

Makes 6-8 servings

Prep. Time: 30 minutes if using cooked chicken, or 4½-5½ hours if using uncooked chicken
Cooking Time: 3-4 hours
Ideal slow cooker size: 6-qt.

4 whole chicken breasts, cooked* and shredded
1 small onion, diced
15¼-oz. can whole-kernel corn, undrained
24-oz. can pinto beans, undrained
14½-oz. can diced tomatoes, undrained
10-oz. can Rotel tomatoes, undrained
1 lb. Velveeta cheese, cubed
¼ cup milk

1. Place chicken and onions in slow cooker.
2. Add corn, beans, tomatoes, cubed cheese, and milk. Stir together well.
3. Cover. Cook on Low 3-4 hours, or until cheese is melted. Try not to let soup boil.

*To prepare cooked chicken in a slow cooker for this recipe, see White Chicken Chili, on page 65 of this cookbook. Follow Steps 1-3 of the instructions, but increase water to 8 cups and cooking time to 4-5 hours on Low, or until chicken is tender but not dry.

Pixie's Chicken Stew

Janice Muller
Derwood, MD

Makes 8-10 servings

Prep. Time: 15 minutes
Cooking Time: 5-6 hours
Ideal slow cooker size: 5- to 6-qt.

2-3-lb. chicken
2 qts. water
1 pkg. dry chicken noodle soup
2 chicken bouillon cubes
15-oz. can whole-kernel corn, undrained
1 Tbsp. onion flakes
½ tsp. dried thyme, *or* **according to your taste preference**

1. Place chicken in slow cooker. Add water.
2. Cover. Cook on High 3-4 hours. Cool.
3. Strain broth into container and reserve.
4. When chicken is cool enough to handle, debone. Return cut-up meat and strained broth to slow cooker.
5. Stir in all remaining ingredients.
6. Cover. Cook on High 2 hours.

Tip:
I've found that if I make this a day ahead so that it can sit overnight in the refrigerator, it's easy to skim the fat off the top.

Note:
Pixie invited friends in for soup after long walks in the snow. She always served this with fresh bread in front of a roaring fire. Pixie finished these meals by offering us a plate of chocolate fudge. Life couldn't get any better.

Chicken Noodle Soup

Jennifer J. Gehman
Harrisburg, PA

Makes 6-8 servings

Prep. Time: 5-10 minutes
Cooking Time: 4-8 hours
Ideal slow cooker size: 5-qt.

2 cups uncooked cubed chicken, dark, *or* **white meat**
15¼-oz. can corn, *or* **2 cups frozen corn**
1 cup green beans, *or* **peas***
10 cups water
10-12 chicken bouillon cubes
3 Tbsp. bacon drippings
½ pkg. dry Kluski (or other very sturdy) noodles

1. Combine all ingredients except noodles in slow cooker.
2. Cover. Cook on High 4-6 hours or on Low 6-8 hours.

3. Two hours before end of cooking time, stir in noodles.

Serving suggestion: Serve with ***potato rolls*** *and* ***butter*** *or* ***grilled cheese sandwiches.***

*If using green beans, stir in during Step 1. If using peas, stir into slow cooker just 20 minutes before end of cooking time.

Matzo Ball Soup

Audrey Romonosky
Austin, TX

Makes 6 servings

Prep. Time: 30 minutes
Chilling Time: 20 minutes
Cooking Time: 2-6 hours
Ideal slow cooker size: 2-qt.

2 eggs
2 Tbsp. oil
2 Tbsp. water
½ cup matzo meal*
1 tsp. salt, *optional*
1½ qts. water
32-oz. can chicken broth

1. Lightly beat eggs, oil, and 2 Tbsp. water together in a good-sized bowl.
2. Add matzo meal and salt. Mix well.
3. Cover and refrigerate 20 minutes.
4. Bring 1½ qts. water to boil in saucepan.
5. Wet hands. Roll chilled matzoh mixture into 1" balls.
6. Drop into boiling water and cook 20 minutes. Using a slotted spoon, remove from water. Drain. (Cooked balls can be stored in refrigerator for up to 2 days.)
7. Pour chicken broth into slow cooker. Add matzoh balls.
8. Cover. Cook on High 2-3 hours or on Low 5-6 hours.

*Finely crushed matzo may be substituted.

Note:
I made this soup for an ethnic luncheon at work. Everyone enjoyed it. Matzo ball soup is traditionally served on the Jewish holiday of Passover. It is also tasty all year-round.

Pumpkin Black-Bean Turkey Chili

Rhoda Atzeff
Harrisburg, PA

Makes 10-12 servings

Prep. Time: 20 minutes
Cooking Time: 7-8 hours
Ideal slow cooker size: 5-qt.

1 cup chopped onions
1 cup chopped yellow bell pepper
3 garlic cloves, minced
2 Tbsp. oil
1½ tsp. dried oregano
1½-2 tsp. ground cumin
2 tsp. chili powder
2 15-oz. cans black beans, rinsed and drained
2½ cups chopped cooked turkey
16-oz. can pumpkin
14½-oz. can diced tomatoes
3 cups chicken broth

1. Sauté onions, yellow pepper, and garlic in oil in skillet for 8 minutes, or until soft.
2. Stir in oregano, cumin, and chili powder. Cook 1 minute. Transfer to slow cooker.
3. Stir in remaining ingredients.
4. Cover. Cook on Low 7-8 hours.

Host a soup bar with everyone bringing their favorite soup or stew.
Amber Swarey, Honea Path, SC

Turkey Green Chili Chowder

Colleen Konetzni
Rio Rancho, NM

Makes 12 servings

Prep. Time: 45 minutes
Cooking Time: 6 hours
Ideal slow cooker size: 6-qt.

1 cup chopped celery
1 cup chopped onion
¼ stick (2 Tbsp.) butter
3 cups chopped cooked turkey
4 cups turkey broth
4 potatoes, peeled, *or* **unpeeled, and cubed**
½ cup green chili, chopped
½ cup cubed cheese, your choice
2 cans creamed corn
2 cups milk

1. In a skillet, sauté celery and onion in butter until vegetables soften and begin to brown.
2. Place sautéed vegetables, turkey, broth, potatoes, chili, cheese, corn, and milk in slow cooker.
3. Cover. Cook on High 6 hours, or until potatoes are soft.
4. If you wish, mash the Chowder a few times with a potato masher to make it thicker.
5. Turn slow cooker to Low until time to serve.

Turkey Frame Soup

Joyce Zuercher
Hesston, KS

Makes 6-8 servings

Prep. Time: 40 minutes
Cooking Time: 3-4 hours
Ideal slow cooker size: 6-qt.

2-3 cups cooked and cut-up turkey*
3 qts. turkey broth
1 onion, diced
½-¾ tsp. salt, *or* **to taste**
16-oz. can chopped tomatoes
1 Tbsp. chicken bouillon granules
1 tsp. dried thyme
⅛ tsp. pepper
1½ tsp. dried oregano
4 cups chopped fresh vegetables –any combination of sliced celery, carrots, onions, rutabaga, broccoli, cauliflower, mushrooms, and more
1½ cups uncooked noodles

1. Place turkey, broth, onion, salt, tomatoes, bouillon granules, thyme, pepper, oregano, and vegetables into slow cooker. Stir.
2. Cover. Cook on Low 8 hours, or until vegetables are nearly done.
3. Fifteen to 30 minutes before serving time, stir in noodles. Cover. Cook on Low. If noodles are thin and small, they'll cook in 15 minutes or less. If heavier, they may need 30 minutes to become tender.
4. Stir well before serving.

*If you've got a big turkey frame, and you know it's got some good meaty morsels on it, here's what to do. Break it up enough to fit into your Dutch oven. Add 3 qts. water, 1 onion, quartered, and 2 tsp. salt. Cover, and simmer 1½ hours. Remove turkey bones from Dutch oven and allow to cool. Then debone and chop meat coarsely. Discard bones and skin. Strain broth. Begin with Step 1 above!

Picking a color theme and re-purposing everyday items makes holiday decorating easy. Fill glass flower vases with candy (red, green, white) and tie red ribbons around knobs and handles. Your kitchen will look festive without losing work space.
Susan Tjon, Austin, TX

Turkey Mushroom Soup

Lois Stoltzfus
Honey Brook, PA

Makes 6-8 servings

Prep. Time: 20-30 minutes
Cooking Time: 6-9 hours
Ideal slow cooker size: 4-qt.

2 cups cooked turkey
2 qts. turkey broth (add water if necessary to reach 2 quarts)
2 cups carrots, chopped
1 cup celery, chopped
2 cups potatoes, cubed
1 small onion, chopped
1 cup long-grain rice, uncooked
1 tsp. garlic salt
¼ tsp. pepper
1 tsp. dried parsley
10¾-oz. cream of mushroom soup

1. Place all ingredients except cream of mushroom soup in slow cooker.
2. Cover. Cook on Low 6-9 hours, or until potatoes and rice are as tender as you like them.
3. Add cream of mushroom soup during last hour of cooking time.

Note:
This recipe, with some changes, comes from an old cookbook first published in 1950. The quote at the end of the recipe said, "A grand end to a noble bird!"

Turkey Meatball Soup

Mary Ann Lefever
Lancaster, PA

Makes 8 servings

Prep. Time: 30 minutes
Cooking Time: 8 hours
Ideal slow cooker size: 5- to 6-qt.

4-5 large carrots, chopped
10 cups chicken broth
¾ lb. escarole, washed and cut into bite-size pieces
1 lb. ground turkey, uncooked
1 medium onion, chopped
2 large eggs, beaten
½ cup Italian bread crumbs
½ cup freshly grated Parmesan, plus more for serving
1 tsp. salt
¼ tsp. pepper

1. In slow cooker, combine carrots and chicken broth.
2. Stir in escarole.
3. Cover. Cook on Low 4 hours.
4. Combine turkey, onion, eggs, bread crumbs, ½ cup Parmesan cheese, salt, and pepper in good-sized bowl. Mix well and shape into 1" balls. Drop carefully into soup.
5. Cover cooker. Cook on Low 4 more hours, or just until meatballs and vegetables are cooked through.
6. Serve hot sprinkled with extra Parmesan cheese.

Variation:
If you wish, you can substitute 3 cups cut-up, cooked turkey for the ground turkey meatballs.

Turkey Chili

Reita F. Yoder
Carlsbad, NM

Makes 6-8 servings

Prep. Time: 10 minutes
Cooking Time: 6-8 hours
Ideal slow cooker size: 4- to 5-qt.

2 lbs. ground turkey
16-oz. can pinto, *or* kidney, beans
2 cups fresh, *or* canned, tomatoes, chopped
2 cups tomato sauce
1 garlic clove, minced
1 small onion, chopped
16-oz. can Rotel tomatoes
1-oz. pkg. Williams chili seasoning

1. Crumble ground turkey into slow cooker.
2. Add remaining ingredients. Mix well.
3. Cover. Cook on Low 6-8 hours.

Chilly Chili

Alix Nancy Botsford
Seminole, OK

Makes 6-8 servings

Prep. Time: 15 minutes
Soaking Time: 6-8 hours, or overnight
Cooking Time: 3-11 hours
Ideal slow cooker size: 3½-qt.

2 cups dry beans of your choice
1 tsp. salt
1 large onion, chopped
1 lb. ground turkey
2 tsp. minced garlic
2 Tbsp. olive oil
1 tsp. salt
2 celery ribs, chopped
1 green bell pepper, diced
10-oz. can tomatoes and green chilies

1. Wash beans and remove any stones. Place beans in slow cooker and cover with water. Soak 6-8 hours, or overnight.
2. Drain off water. Return beans to cooker and cover with fresh water.
3. Stir in 1 tsp. salt.
4. Cover. Cook on High 2-3 hours, or until a bean can be crushed with a fork.
5. Drain off liquid.
6. While beans are cooking, place onion, turkey, and garlic in oil in skillet over medium heat. Stir frequently, breaking up clumps of meat. When meat is no longer pink, drain off drippings.
7. Place meat and vegetables in slow cooker.
8. Add 1 tsp. salt, celery, and green pepper. Stir in tomatoes.
9. Cover. Cook on Low 1-8 hours, or until vegetables are as tender as you like them.

Serving suggestion: Serve with slices of ***cheese*** *and* ***crackers****.*

Note:

This is a good meal for guests—or when we're all working outdoors and need our meal to be ready when we come in, like during early spring when we're getting the garden ready.

When relatives from far come and stay, we make special sleep-over accommodations. We move the cars out of our 3 car garage and put some furniture in. We even make it warm and cozy with lights, an electric space heater, and an electric fireplace. *Annie C. Boshart, Lebanon, PA*

Smoked Salmon Corn Chowder

Sandra Haverstraw
Hummelstown, PA

Makes 8-10 servings

Prep. Time: 30 minutes
Cooking Time: 4½-5½ hours
Ideal slow cooker size: 5- to 6-qt.

1 large onion, chopped
½ cup chopped celery
⅓ cup chopped red bell pepper
¼ stick (2 Tbsp.) butter
3 cups peeled, cubed potatoes, cooked
2 cups chicken broth
15-oz. can creamed corn
16-oz. bag frozen corn
½ tsp. salt, *optional*
½ tsp. ground black pepper
2 tsp. dried dill weed
2 oz. smoked salmon, chopped
1 cup whole milk
1 cup shredded cheddar cheese
½ tsp. hot pepper sauce, *optional*
1 cup sour cream, *optional*

1. In medium skillet, sauté onion, celery, and red bell pepper in butter until soft.
2. Mix sautéed vegetables, cooked potatoes, chicken broth, creamed corn, frozen corn, salt if you wish, pepper, dill, and smoked salmon in slow cooker.
3. Cover. Cook on High 1 hour.

4. Reduce heat to Low and cook 3-4 hours.

5. One half hour prior to serving, add milk and cheese, and hot pepper sauce and sour cream if you wish, to Chowder in slow cooker.

6. Cover and continue cooking 25-30 minutes, or until cheese has melted and chowder is fully heated.

Note:

Our family always goes to Christmas Eve Services, and we enjoy corn chowder on our return home. During a trip to Alaska, I was served a delicious corn chowder with smoked salmon. Now I've added that to our favorite recipe.

The rest of the menu for our Christmas Eve Buffet: cold steamed shrimp with cocktail sauce, cocktail meatballs in a small slow cooker, fresh vegetables with Ranch dip, assorted cheeses and crackers. Plus hot mulled cider or wine in a large slow cooker. And, of course, coconut cake, fruit, and cookies.

Corn and Shrimp Chowder

Naomi E. Fast, Hesston, KS

Makes 6 servings

Prep. Time: 20 minutes • Cooking Time: 3-4 hours
Ideal slow cooker size: 3½-qt.

4 slices bacon, diced
1 cup chopped onions
2 cups diced, unpeeled red potatoes
2 10-oz. pkgs. frozen corn
1 tsp. Worcestershire sauce
½ tsp. paprika
½ tsp. salt
⅛ tsp. pepper
2 6-oz. cans shrimp
2 cups water
¼ stick (2 Tbsp.) butter
12-oz. can evaporated milk
chopped chives

1. Fry bacon in skillet until lightly crisp. Add onions to drippings and sauté until transparent. Using slotted spoon, transfer bacon and onions to slow cooker.

2. Add remaining ingredients to cooker, except milk and chives. Stir together well.

3. Cover. Cook on Low 3-4 hours.

4. Add milk and chives 30 minutes before end of cooking time.

Serving suggestion: Serve with ***broccoli salad****.*

Note:

I learned to make this recipe in a 7th-grade home economics class. It made an impression on my father who liked seafood very much. The recipe calls for canned shrimp, but I often increase the taste appeal with extra cooked shrimp.

Variation:

I frequently use frozen hash brown potatoes for speedy preparation. There is no difference in the taste.

Wonderful Clam Chowder

Carlene Horne
Bedford, NH

Makes 4-6 servings

Prep. Time: 10-15 minutes
Cooking Time: 4-5 hours
Ideal slow cooker size: 3½-qt.

2 12-oz. cans evaporated milk
1 evaporated milk can of water
1 small onion, chopped
2 small potatoes, diced
2 6-oz. cans whole clams, undrained
6-oz. can minced clams, undrained
2 Tbsp. cornstarch
¼ cup water

1. Combine all ingredients except clams, cornstarch, and ¼ cup water in slow cooker.
2. Cover. Cook on Low 3-4 hours, or until vegetables are tender, or nearly so.
3. One hour before end of cooking time, stir clams with their juice into slow cooker.
4. Immediately following that, mix cornstarch and ¼ cup water together in small bowl. When smooth, stir into soup. Stir until soup thickens.
5. Cover and continue cooking another 50 minutes or so.

Clam Chowder

Ruth Shank
Gridley, IL

Makes 8-12 servings

Prep. Time: 15 minutes
Cooking Time: 2-3 hours
Ideal slow cooker size: 4-qt.

2 10¾-oz. cans cream of potato soup
10¾-oz. can cream of celery soup
2 6½-oz. cans minced clams, drained
3 slices bacon, diced and fried
1 soup can of water
1 small onion, minced
1 Tbsp. fresh parsley
dash of dried marjoram
1 Tbsp. Worcestershire sauce
pepper to taste
2 soup cans of milk

1. Combine all ingredients, except 2 soup cans of milk, in slow cooker.
2. Cover. Cook on Low 2-3 hours.
3. Twenty minutes before end of cooking time, stir in milk. Continue cooking until heated through.

Oyster Stew

Nadine Martinitz
Salina, KS

Makes 6 servings

Prep. Time: 20 minutes
Ideal slow cooker size: 4-qt.

1 cup celery, chopped
3 Tbsp. butter
1 tsp. Worcestershire sauce
2 8-oz. cans whole stewing oysters with their juices
4 cups hot milk, *or* **2 cups milk and 2 cups light cream**
salt & pepper
sherry, *optional*
paprika

1. In a large skillet, simmer celery in butter until tender.
2. Add Worcestershire sauce and oysters with their juices. Heat just until oysters begin to curl.
3. Place oyster mixture in slow cooker. Add milk and salt and pepper to taste. Season with sherry if you wish.
4. Keep hot in slow cooker turned on Low until time to serve.
5. Serve steaming in bowls, garnished with a sprinkling of paprika.

One night during December the children like to sleep by the Christmas tree. — *Karen Sauder, Adamstown, PA*

Beef Main Dishes

Spicy Beef Roast

Karen Ceneviva
Seymour, CT

Makes 8-10 servings

Prep. Time: 15-20 minutes
Cooking Time: 4-10 hours
Ideal slow cooker size: 4- to 5-qt.

1-2 Tbsp. cracked black peppercorns
2 cloves garlic, minced
3 lbs. round tip roast, *or* **brisket, trimmed of fat**
3 Tbsp. balsamic vinegar
¼ cup reduced-sodium soy sauce
2 Tbsp. Worcestershire sauce
2 tsp. dry mustard

1. Rub cracked pepper and garlic onto roast. Put roast in slow cooker.
2. Make several shallow slits in top of meat.
3. In a small bowl, combine remaining ingredients. Spoon over meat.
4. Cover. Cook on Low 8-10 hours or on High 4-5 hours, just until meat is tender but not dry.

Note:
Once when I had made this roast for friends, my son said—in front of all the guests—"Mom, you always cook so well and you have a smile while you're doing it." That's the kind of comment you don't forget. And this roast is that good!

Wine Tender Roast

Rose Hankins
Stevensville, MD

Makes 8-10 servings

Prep. Time: 10 minutes
Cooking Time: 8-10 hours
Ideal slow cooker size: 4- to 5-qt.

2½-3-lb. chuck roast
1 cup thinly sliced onion
½ cup chopped apple, peeled, *or* **unpeeled**
3 cloves garlic, chopped
1 cup red wine
salt and pepper

1. Put roast in slow cooker. Layer onions, apples, and garlic on top of roast.
2. Carefully pour wine over roast without disturbing its toppings.
3. Sprinkle with salt and pepper.
4. Cover. Cook on Low 8-10 hours, or until meat is tender but not dry.

Plum Roast

Shirley Unternahrer
Wayland, IA

Makes 8 servings

Prep. Time: 10-15 minutes
Cooking Time: 6-8 hours
Ideal slow cooker size: 6-qt.

3½-4-lb. beef roast, any cut
12-oz. can cola
½-¾ tsp. salt
1 large onion, sliced
1 rib celery, sliced
1 whole clove garlic
2 cups fresh, *or* **canned, plums, cut up**

1. Layer first six ingredients into slow cooker in order.
2. Cover. Cook on High 6-8 hours, or just until roast is tender but not dry.
3. Add plums (including juice if they're canned) for last hour of cooking. Cover.

Machaca Beef

Jeanne Allen, Rye, CO

Makes 10-12 servings

Prep. Time: 5-7 minutes • Cooking Time: 10-12 hours
Ideal slow cooker size: 3½-qt.

1½-lb. beef roast
1 large onion, sliced
4-oz. can chopped green chilies, undrained
2 beef bouillon cubes
1½ tsp. dry mustard
½ tsp. garlic powder
1 tsp. seasoning salt
½ tsp. pepper
1 cup salsa

1. Combine all ingredients except salsa in slow cooker. Add just enough water to cover meat.
2. Cover cooker and cook on Low 10-12 hours, or until beef is tender but not dry. Drain and reserve liquid.
3. Shred beef using two forks to pull it apart.
4. Combine beef, salsa, and enough of reserved liquid to have the consistency you want.
5. Use as filling for burritos, chalupas, quesadillas, or tacos.

Note:
After living in New Mexico for the past 30 years, I get homesick for New Mexican cuisine now that I live in Colorado. I keep memories of New Mexico alive by cooking foods that remind me of home.

Cranberry Brisket

Roseann Wilson
Albuquerque, NM

Makes 5-6 servings

Prep. Time: 10-15 minutes
Cooking Time: 8-10 hours
Ideal slow cooker size: 5-qt.

2½-lb. beef brisket
½ tsp. salt
¼ tsp. pepper
16-oz. can whole berry cranberry sauce
8-oz. can tomato sauce
½ cup chopped onion
1 Tbsp. prepared mustard

1. Rub brisket with salt and pepper. Place in slow cooker.
2. Combine cranberry sauce, tomato sauce, onion, and mustard in a mixing bowl. Spoon over brisket, being careful not to disturb seasoning on meat.
3. Cover. Cook on Low 8-10 hours, or until meat is tender but not dry.
4. Remove brisket. Slice thinly across grain. Skim fat from juices. Serve juices with brisket.

Smoked Beef Brisket

Joy Martin
Myerstown, PA

Makes 4-5 servings

Prep. Time: 10-12 minutes
Cooking Time: 8-9 hours
Ideal slow cooker size: 3- to 4-qt.

2½ lbs. beef brisket
1 Tbsp. liquid smoke
1 tsp. salt
½ tsp. pepper
½ cup chopped onion
½ cup ketchup
2 tsp. prepared Dijon mustard
½ tsp. celery seed

1. Cut brisket in half. Rub both pieces with liquid smoke, salt, and pepper.
2. Place brisket halves in slow cooker. Top with onion.
3. In a small bowl, combine ketchup, mustard, and celery seed. Spread over meat.
4. Cover. Cook on Low 8-9 hours, or until meat is tender but not dry.
5. Remove brisket and keep warm.
6. Transfer cooking juices to a blender. Cover and process until smooth. (Cover lid of blender with thick towel and hold it on tightly while using.) Serve juices with brisket.

Salsa Chuck Roast

Hazel L. Propst
Oxford, PA

Makes 6 servings

Prep. Time: 15 minutes
Cooking Time: 7-8 hours
Ideal slow cooker size: 5-qt.

3-4-lb. chuck, *or* **round, roast**
1 Tbsp. oil
1 pkg. dry onion soup mix
2 cups water
1 cup salsa

1. Brown meat in skillet in oil on both sides. Place in slow cooker.
2. Add remaining ingredients to drippings in pan. Simmer 2-3 minutes. Pour over roast in slow cooker.
3. Cover. Cook on Low 7-8 hours.

Serving suggestion: This is a good topping for ***noodles*** *or* ***rice****, along with the roast's rich broth.*

Melt-in-Your-Mouth Mexican Meat Dish

Marlene Bogard, Newton, KS

Makes 6 servings

Prep. Time: 15 minutes
Cooking Time: 8-10 hours
Ideal slow cooker size: 4-qt.

4-lb. chuck roast
1 tsp. salt
1 tsp. pepper
2 Tbsp. oil
1 onion, chopped
1 tsp. chili powder
1 tsp. garlic powder
1¼ cups diced green chili peppers
½ cup chipotle salsa
¼ cup hot pepper sauce
water
flour, *optional*

1. Season roast with salt and pepper. Sear on all sides in oil in skillet. Place in slow cooker.
2. In a bowl, mix together remaining ingredients, except water, and spoon over meat.
3. Pour water down along side of the cooker (so as not to wash off the topping) until roast is ⅓ covered.
4. Cover cooker. Cook on High 6 hours. Reduce to Low and cook 2-4 more hours, or until meat falls apart but doesn't dry out.
5. Thicken hot sauce with several Tbsp. flour, if you like, in the slow cooker.

Serving suggestion: This highly seasoned meat is perfect for ***shredded beef Mexican tacos*** *and* ***burritos****.*

Apple and Onion Beef Pot Roast

Betty K. Drescher
Quakertown, PA

Makes 8-10 servings

Prep. Time: 20 minutes
Cooking Time: 5-6 hours
Ideal slow cooker size: 4-qt.

3-lb. boneless beef roast, cut in half
oil
1 cup water
1 tsp. seasoning salt
½ tsp. soy sauce
½ tsp. Worcestershire sauce
¼ tsp. garlic powder
1 large tart apple, quartered
1 large onion, sliced
2 Tbsp. cornstarch
2 Tbsp. water

1. Brown roast on all sides in oil in skillet. Transfer to slow cooker.
2. Add water to skillet. Stir with wooden spoon to loosen browned bits. Pour over roast.
3. Sprinkle with seasoning salt, soy sauce, Worcestershire sauce, and garlic powder.
4. Top with apple and onion.
5. Cover. Cook on Low 5-6 hours.
6. Remove roast and onion. Let stand 15 minutes.
7. To make gravy, pour juices from roast into saucepan and simmer until reduced to 2 cups.
8. Combine cornstarch and water until smooth in small bowl.
9. Stir into beef broth. Bring to boil. Cook and stir 2 minutes, or until thickened.
10. Slice pot roast and serve with gravy.

There's-No-Easier Roast Beef

Sue Pennington
Bridgewater, VA

Makes 6-8 servings

Prep. Time: 5 minutes
Cooking Time: 6-8 hours
Ideal slow cooker size: 4-qt.

12-oz. bottle barbecue sauce, *divided*
3-4-lb. beef roast

1. Pour half of barbecue sauce into bottom of slow cooker.
2. Add roast. Top with remaining barbecue sauce.
3. Cover. Cook on Low 6-8 hours.
4. Slice roast and serve with sauce.

Variation:

Use an 18-oz. bottle of barbecue sauce if you prefer a juicier outcome.

8-Hour Tangy Beef

Mary Martins
Fairbank, IA

Makes 6-8 servings

Prep. Time: 5 minutes
Cooking Time: 8-9 hours
Ideal slow cooker size: 4-qt.

3½-4-lb. beef roast
12-oz. can ginger ale
1½ cups ketchup

1. Put beef in slow cooker.
2. Blend ginger ale and ketchup together in a good-sized bowl. Pour over roast.
3. Cover. Cook on Low 8-9 hours.

Serving suggestion: Shred with 2 forks and serve on ***buns****. Or break up into chunks and serve over* ***rice****,* ***potatoes****, or* ***pasta****.*

Variations:

1. This recipe produces a lot of juice. You can add chopped onions, potatoes, and green beans in Step 2, if you want. Or stir in sliced mushrooms and/or peas 30 minutes before the end of the cooking time.
2. For a tangier finished dish, add chili powder or cumin, along with black pepper, in Step 2.

Beef Roast in Beer

Evelyn Page
Riverton, WY

Makes 5-6 servings

Prep. Time: 5 minutes
Marinating Time: 8 hours
Cooking Time: 6-8 hours
Ideal slow cooker size: 3-qt.

2-3-lb. beef roast
12-oz. can beer
1 onion, sliced

1. Place roast in slow cooker. Poke all over surface with fork.
2. Pour beer over roast. Cover. Refrigerate 8 hours.
3. Add sliced onion to top of roast.
4. Cover. Cook on Low 6-8 hours.

Variations:

1. Brown roast in oil in skillet on top and bottom before placing in cooker.
2. Mix together 1 cup cider vinegar and 2 Tbsp. Worcestershire sauce in slow cooker. Marinate roast in mixture in refrigerator for 2-4 hours. When ready to cook roast, either discard marinade, or add other ingredients to it.
3. To thicken broth, mix together ¼ cup flour and 1 cup water until smooth. Twenty minutes before end of cooking time, remove roast from cooker. Stir flour paste into beef broth in cooker until smooth. Return roast to cooker and continue cooking. When finished, cut roast into chunks and serve with gravy.

Italian Beef au Jus

Carol Sherwood
Batavia, NY

Makes 8 servings

Prep. Time: 5 minutes
Cooking Time: 8 hours
Ideal slow cooker size: 4- to 5-qt.

3-5-lb. boneless beef roast
4-5-oz. pkg. au jus mix
1 pkg. Italian salad dressing mix
14½-oz. can beef broth
half a soup can water

1. Place beef in slow cooker.
2. Combine remaining ingredients in bowl. Pour over roast.
3. Cover. Cook on Low 8 hours.

Serving suggestion: Slice meat and spoon onto hard ***rolls*** *with straining spoon to make sandwiches. Or shred with 2 forks and serve over* ***noodles*** *or* ***rice*** *in broth thickened with flour.*

Tip:

To thicken broth, mix 3 Tbsp. cornstarch into ¼ cup cold water in small bowl. Stir until smooth. Remove ½ cup beef broth from cooker and blend into cornstarch-water. Stir back into broth in cooker, stirring until smooth. Cook 10-15 minutes on High until broth reaches gravy consistency.

Saucy Italian Roast

Sharon Miller
Holmesville, OH

Makes 8-10 servings

Prep. Time: 5-10 minutes
Cooking Time: 8-9 hours
Ideal slow cooker size: 4-qt.

3-3½-lb. boneless rump roast
½ tsp. salt
½ tsp. garlic powder
¼ tsp. pepper
4½-oz. jar mushroom pieces, drained
1 medium onion, diced
14-oz. jar spaghetti sauce
¼-½ cup beef broth

1. Cut roast in half.
2. Combine salt, garlic powder, and pepper in a small bowl. Rub over both halves of roast. Place in slow cooker.
3. Top with mushrooms and onions.
4. Combine spaghetti sauce and broth in a good-sized bowl. Spoon over roast, being careful not to disturb toppings and seasonings covering it.
5. Cover. Cook on Low 8-9 hours.

Serving suggestion: Slice roast. Serve in sauce over ***pasta****.*

Simply Super Supper

Anne Townsend
Albuquerque, NM

Makes 4 servings

Prep. Time: 10 minutes
Cooking Time: 7-8 hours
Ideal slow cooker size: 3- to 4-qt.

2 ribs celery, sliced
3 carrots, cut in strips
2 potatoes, cubed
2 onions, coarsely chopped
2-lb. beef roast
1 pkg. dry onion soup mix
1 Tbsp. liquid smoke
1½ cups water

1. Place vegetables in slow cooker.
2. Place roast on top of vegetables.
3. Sprinkle with dry soup mix.
4. Combine liquid smoke and water in a small bowl. Pour over roast.
5. Cover. Cook on Low 7-8 hours, or until vegetables are tender.

Serving suggestion: Slice meat and serve with ***cole slaw*** *and* ***French bread****.* ***Lemon pie*** *makes a nice finish.*

Note:
This is a welcoming dinner to come home to because the house smells so yummy as you walk in. And the wonderful aroma lingers.

Sunday Roast Beef

Beverly Flatt-Getz
Warriors Mark, PA

Makes 8 servings

Prep. Time: 15 minutes
Cooking Time: 8½-10½ hours
Ideal slow cooker size: 4-qt.

4 potatoes, peeled and quartered
½ cup peeled small onions
1 cup carrot chunks
4-lb. beef chuck roast
1 Tbsp. olive oil
1 pkg. George Washington Seasoning
½ tsp. onion salt
½ tsp. minced garlic
½ tsp. garlic salt
1 cup water
few drops Worcestershire sauce
1 Tbsp. cornstarch
½ cup cold water

1. Place potatoes, onions, and carrots in bottom of slow cooker.
2. Sear beef on all sides in olive oil in skillet. Add to vegetables in slow cooker.
3. Sprinkle with seasonings.
4. Pour water around roast.
5. Cover. Cook on Low 8-10 hours.
6. Remove roast and vegetables from juice. Season juice with Worcestershire sauce.
7. Dissolve cornstarch in cold water in a small bowl. Stir into slow cooker. Cook on High until thick and bubbly. Serve with juice alongside.

Note:
When I was growing up we often had this for Sunday lunch after church. Mom put it in the oven very early. I adapted the recipe for making it in a slow cooker.

Bavarian Beef

Naomi E. Fast
Hesston, KS

Makes 6 servings

Prep. Time: 15 minutes
Cooking Time: 6½-7½ hours
Ideal slow cooker size: 4-qt.

3-3½-lb. boneless beef chuck roast
oil
3 cups sliced carrots
3 cups sliced onions
2 large kosher dill pickles, chopped
1 cup sliced celery
½ cup dry red wine, *or*

Every year I buy a new game for the whole extended family to play after dinner. Some we've especially enjoyed are Pictionary, Guesstures, Family Feud, etc.
Marsha Sabus, Fallbrook, CA

⅓ cup German-style mustard
2 tsp. coarsely ground black pepper
2 bay leaves
¼ tsp. ground cloves
⅓ cup flour
1 cup water

1. Brown roast on both sides in oil in skillet. Transfer to slow cooker.
2. Distribute carrots, onions, pickles and celery around roast in slow cooker.
3. Combine wine, mustard, pepper, bay leaves, and cloves in a bowl. Pour over ingredients in slow cooker.
4. Cover. Cook on Low 6-7 hours, or until meat and vegetables are tender but not dry or mushy.
5. Remove meat and vegetables to large platter. Cover to keep warm.
6. Mix flour with 1 cup water in bowl until smooth. Turn cooker to High. Stir in flour-water paste, stirring continually until broth is smooth and thickened. Serve with broth alongside.

Serving suggestion: Try serving this over ***noodles*** *or* ***spaetzle****.*

Sauerbraten

Leona M. Slabaugh
Apple Creek, OH

Makes 8-10 servings

Prep. Time: 10-20 minutes
Marinating Time: 8 hours, or overnight
Cooking Time: 5-7 hours
Ideal slow cooker size: 6-qt.

1 cup cider vinegar
¾ cup red wine vinegar
2 tsp. salt
½ tsp. black pepper
6 whole cloves
2 bay leaves
1 Tbsp. mustard seeds
3½-lb. boneless top round roast, tied
20 gingersnaps (about 5 oz.), crushed

1. Combine vinegars, salt, pepper, cloves, bay leaves, and mustard seeds in a large bowl.
2. Place roast in bowl. Spoon marinade over it.
3. Cover roast in marinade and refrigerate overnight, turning once.
4. Place roast and marinade in slow cooker.
5. Cover. Cook on High 5 hours or on Low 7 hours, or until meat is tender but not dry.
6. Remove roast to platter and keep warm.
7. Strain liquid from slow cooker. Stir crushed gingersnaps into liquid until well blended.
8. Slice roast and serve with sauce alongside.

Beef Pot Roast

Nancy Wagner Graves
Manhattan, KS

Makes 6-8 servings

Prep. Time: 10 minutes
Cooking Time: 6-7 hours
Ideal slow cooker size: 4-qt.

4-5-lb. beef chuck roast
1 garlic clove, cut in half
salt to taste
pepper to taste
1 carrot, chopped
1 rib celery, chopped
1 small onion, sliced
¾ cup sour cream
3 Tbsp. flour
½ cup dry white wine

1. Rub roast with garlic. Season with salt and pepper. Place in slow cooker.
2. Add carrots, celery, and onion.
3. Combine sour cream, flour, and wine in a small bowl. Pour into slow cooker.
4. Cover. Cook on Low 6-7 hours.

Pot-Roast Complete

Naomi E. Fast, Hesston, KS

Makes 6-8 servings

Prep. Time: 15 minutes • Cooking Time: 6½-7½ hours
Ideal slow cooker size: 4-qt.

3-3½-lb. arm roast, boneless
2 large onions, sliced
½ cup brown sugar
⅓ cup soy sauce
⅓ cup cider vinegar
2 bay leaves
2-3 garlic cloves, minced
1 tsp. grated fresh ginger, *or* **¼ tsp. ground ginger**
1 cup julienned carrots, matchstick size, *or* **baby carrots**
2 cups sliced button mushrooms
2-3 cups fresh spinach leaves, *or* **2 10-oz. pkgs. frozen spinach, thawed and squeezed dry**
2 Tbsp. cornstarch

1. Place meat in slow cooker. Top with onions.
2. Combine brown sugar, soy sauce, and vinegar in a small bowl. Spoon over beef.
3. Scatter bay leaves, garlic, and ginger over roast.
4. Cover. Cook on Low 6-7 hours.
5. Spread carrots, mushrooms, and spinach over beef.
6. Cover. Cook on High 20 minutes.
7. In small bowl, mix cornstarch with ½ cup broth from slow cooker. Return to slow cooker.
8. Cover. Cook 10 minutes more.

Serving suggestion: Serve over ***rice****.*

Note:
I can't count how many times I have used this recipe over the last 15-20 years as a guest meal.

Spicy Short Ribs

Joan Terwilliger
Lebanon, PA

Makes 4-6 servings

Prep Time: 30 minutes
Cooking Time: 6 hours
Ideal slow-cooker size: 4- to 6-qt.

8 bone-in beef short ribs
15-oz. can crushed tomatoes
3 Tbsp. tomato paste
2-3 Tbsp. hot pepper jam, *or* **horseradish jam**
6 cloves garlic, peeled
¾ tsp. dried rosemary, crushed
1 Tbsp. dried minced onions
½ tsp ground ginger
¼ cup dry red wine

1. Broil ribs 6 inches from heat until browned, 5-10 minutes per side.
2. Place ribs in slow cooker.
3. Combine remaining ingredients in mixing bowl. Pour over ribs. (If you've had to stack them, lift the top layer and spoon sauce over bottom layer.)
4. Cover. Cook on Low 6 hours.
5. Spoon off fat before serving.

Slow-Cooked Short Ribs

Jean A. Shaner
York, PA
Barbara L. McGinnis
Jupiter, FL

Makes 12 servings

Prep. Time: 35 minutes
Cooking Time: 9-10 hours
Ideal slow cooker size: 6-qt.

⅔ cup flour
2 tsp. salt
½ tsp. pepper
4-4½ lbs. boneless beef short ribs, *or* **6-7 lbs. bone-in beef short ribs**
oil, *or* **butter**
1 large onion, chopped
1½ cups beef broth
¾ cup wine, *or* **cider vinegar**
½-¾ cup packed brown sugar, according to your taste preference
½ cup chili sauce
⅓ cup ketchup
⅓ cup Worcestershire sauce
5 garlic cloves, minced
1½ tsp. chili powder

1. Combine flour, salt, and pepper in plastic bag. Add ribs, a few at a time, and shake to coat.
2. Brown meat in small amount of oil, or in butter, in batches in skillet. Transfer to slow cooker. Reserve drippings in skillet.
3. Combine remaining ingredients in skillet. Cook, stirring up browned drippings, until mixture comes to a boil. Pour over ribs.
4. Cover. Cook on Low 9-10 hours.
5. Debone and serve.

Serving suggestion: Serve over ***rice*** *or* ***noodles.***

Tip:
It is ideal to cook these ribs one day in advance of serving. Refrigerate for several hours or overnight. Remove layer of congealed fat before serving.

Beef Ribs with Sauerkraut

Rosaria Strachan
Fairfield, CT

Makes 8-10 servings

Prep. Time: 10 minutes
Cooking Time: 3-8 hours
Ideal slow cooker size: 6-qt.

3-4 lbs. beef short ribs
32-oz. bag, *or* **27-oz. can, sauerkraut, drained**
2 Tbsp. caraway seeds
¼ cup water

1. Put ribs in 6-qt. slow cooker.
2. Place sauerkraut and caraway seeds on top of ribs.
3. Pour in water.
4. Cover. Cook on High 3-4 hours or on Low 7-8 hours.

Serving suggestion: These need ***mashed potatoes*** *to complete the meal!*

Variation:
If you really enjoy sauerkraut, double the amount of sauerkraut, and divide the recipe between 2 4- or 5-qt. cookers.

Christmas is all year for me. Most of the gifts I give are homemade. This year I made six kinds of jelly, apple butter, chow-chow, and bread-and-butter pickles. This works well for people like me who are on a limited income. Plus I can be done early and share gifts from the heart.
Janet Batdorf, Harrisburg, PA

Ribs and Limas

Miriam Friesen
Staunton,VA

Makes 6 servings

Prep. Time: 25 minutes
Cooking Time: 5½-12½ hours
Ideal slow cooker size: 6-qt.

3 lbs. beef short ribs
2 Tbsp. oil
1 onion, chopped
4 carrots, sliced
¼ cup packed brown sugar
2 Tbsp. flour
2 tsp. dry mustard
1½ tsp. salt
¼ tsp. pepper
1¼ cups water
¼ cup cider vinegar
1 large bay leaf, broken in half
10-oz. pkg. frozen lima beans, *or* **peas**

1. Cut ribs into serving-size pieces. Brown ribs in large skillet in batches in oil.
2. Place onions and carrots in slow cooker. Add ribs.
3. In a mixing bowl, combine brown sugar, flour, mustard, salt, and pepper. Stir in water and vinegar until smooth. Pour over ribs. Push bay leaf pieces into liquid.
4. Cover. Cook on High 5-6 hours or on Low 10-12 hours.
5. Stir in lima beans.
6. Cover. Cook on High 20-30 minutes.
7. Remove bay leaf before serving.

Serving suggestion: We like this with a ***citrus salad*** *and* ***crusty rolls****.*

Tender Texas-Style Steaks

Janice Muller
Derwood, MD

Makes 4-6 servings

Prep. Time: 5 minutes
Cooking Time: 6 hours
Ideal slow cooker size: 3-qt.

6 ½-¾-lb. steaks, *or* **chops**
1 cup brown sugar
1 cup ketchup
salt to taste
pepper to taste
few dashes of Worcestershire sauce

1. Lay steaks in bottom of slow cooker.
2. Combine brown sugar and ketchup in a mixing bowl. Pour over steaks
3. Sprinkle with salt and pepper and a few dashes of Worcestershire sauce.
4. Cover. Cook on High 3 hours and on Low 3 hours, or until meat is fork tender but not dry.

Serving suggestion: Serve with ***wide egg noodles, green beans,*** *and* ***applesauce****.*

Tip:
I spoon some of the juice from the cooker over the noodles. Sometimes I stir 2-4 Tbsp. flour into the hot broth (after lifting the meat onto a platter) until it becomes smooth. By cooking it a few more minutes, the broth thickens into a gravy.

Swiss Steak

Marie Shank
Harrisonburg, VA

Makes 6-8 servings

Prep. Time: 5 minutes
Cooking Time: 3-10 hours
Ideal slow cooker size: 4-qt.

2-lb. round steak, cut into serving pieces
1 tsp. salt
½ tsp. pepper
1 large onion, sliced, *or* **1 pkg. dry onion soup mix**
16-oz. can tomatoes

1. Combine all ingredients in slow cooker.
2. Cover. Cook on Low 6-10 hours or on High 3-4 hours, just until meat is fork tender.

Tip:
You may want to omit the salt if you use the onion soup mix.

Savory Pepper Steak

Grace W. Yoder
Harrisonburg, VA

Makes 6 servings

Prep. Time: 15 minutes
Cooking Time: 8-10 hours
Ideal slow cooker size: 4-qt.

1½-lb. beef round steak, cut ½" thick
¼ cup flour
½ tsp. salt
⅛ tsp. pepper
1 medium onion, chopped, *or* **sliced**
1 garlic clove, minced
2 large green bell peppers, sliced in ½" strips, *divided*
29-oz. can whole tomatoes
1 Tbsp. beef flavor base, *or* **1 beef bouillon cube**
1 Tbsp. soy sauce
2 tsp. Worcestershire sauce
3 Tbsp. flour
3 Tbsp. water

1. Cut beef into strips about 1" wide.
2. In a large bowl, combine ¼ cup flour, salt, and pepper. Toss with beef until well coated. Place in slow cooker.
3. Add onions, garlic, and half the green pepper slices. Mix well.
4. In the large bowl, combine tomatoes, beef base, soy sauce, and Worcestershire sauce. Pour into slow cooker.
5. Cover. Cook on Low 8-10 hours.
6. One hour before serving, turn to High and stir in remaining green pepper strips.
7. Combine 3 Tbsp. flour and water in a small bowl to make a smooth paste. Stir into slow cooker. Cover. Cook until thickened, about 10 minutes.

Serving suggestion: This is a good topping for ***cooked rice.***

Three-Pepper Steak

Renee Hankins
Narvon, PA

Makes 10 servings

Prep. Time: 30 minutes
Cooking Time: 5-8 hours
Ideal slow cooker size: 4- to 5-qt.

3 bell peppers—one red, one orange, and one yellow pepper (or any combination of colors), cut into ¼"-thick slices
2 garlic cloves, sliced
1 large onion, sliced
1 tsp. ground cumin
½ tsp. dried oregano
1 bay leaf
3½-lb. beef flank steak, cut in ¼-½"-thick slices across the grain
salt to taste
14½-oz. can diced tomatoes in juice
jalapeño chilies, sliced, *optional*

1. Place sliced peppers, garlic, onion, cumin, oregano, and bay leaf in slow cooker. Stir gently to mix.
2. Put steak slices on top of vegetable mixture. Season with salt.
3. Spoon tomatoes with juice over top. Sprinkle with jalapeño pepper slices if you wish. Do not stir.
4. Cover. Cook on Low 5-8 hours, depending on your slow cooker. Check after 5 hours to see if meat is tender. If not, continue cooking until tender but not dry.

Serving suggestion: We love this served over ***noodles, rice,*** *or torn* ***tortillas.***

Stuffed Flank Steak

Renee Baum
Chambersburg, PA

Makes 6 servings

Prep. Time: 30 minutes
Cooking Time: 4½-5½ hours
Ideal slow cooker size: 4- to 5-qt.

8-oz. pkg. crushed cornbread stuffing
1 cup chopped onion
1 cup chopped celery
¼ cup minced fresh parsley
2 eggs
1¼ cups beef broth
5⅓ Tbsp. (⅓ cup) butter, melted
½ tsp. seasoned salt, *optional*
½ tsp. pepper
1½ lbs. flank steak

1. Combine stuffing, onion, celery, and parsley in large bowl.
2. In a small bowl, beat eggs. Stir in broth and butter. Pour over stuffing mixture. Sprinkle with seasoned salt if you wish, and pepper. Stir well.
3. Pound steak to ¼"- thickness.
4. Spread 1½ cups stuffing mixture over steak. Roll up, starting with short side. Tie with string.
5. Place steak in slow cooker.
6. Wrap remaining stuffing tightly in foil and place on top of rolled steak.
7. Cover. Cook on Low 4½-5½ hours, or until meat thermometer reaches 165 degrees.
8. Remove string before slicing.

Note:
If you have a helpful butcher, ask him/her to pound the steak for you.

Sometime between Christmas and New Year's we have a neighborhood dinner which we follow with singing hymns or Christmas songs. One neighbor brings her autoharp and another brings her accordion.

Sara Kinsinger, Stuarts Draft, VA

Fruited Flank Steak

Ruth A. Feister
Narvon, PA

Makes 6 servings

Prep. Time: 10 minutes
Cooking Time: 6-8 hours
Ideal slow cooker size: 3-qt.

1½-2-lb. flank steak
salt to taste
pepper to taste
14½-oz. can mixed fruit, *or* **your choice of canned fruit**
1 Tbsp. salad oil
1 Tbsp. lemon juice
¼ cup teriyaki sauce
1 tsp. vinegar
1 garlic clove, minced

1. Sprinkle steak with salt and pepper. Place in slow cooker.
2. Drain fruit, saving ¼ cup syrup. Set fruit aside.
3. In a small bowl, combine ¼ cup reserved syrup with remaining ingredients. Pour over steak.
4. Cover. Cook on Low 6-8 hours, or just until meat is tender but not dry.
5. Add drained fruit during last 15 minutes of cooking time.
6. Lift meat from cooker onto platter. Using sharp knife slice across the grain, making thin slices. Spoon fruit over meat.

Serving suggestion: Top off this meal by serving the steak and fruit with ***baked rice****.*

Slow Cooker Beef with Mushrooms

Grace W. Yoder, Harrisonburg, VA

Makes 6 servings

Prep. Time: 10 minutes
Cooking Time: 7-8 hours
Ideal slow cooker size: 3-qt.

2 medium onions, thinly sliced
½ lb. mushrooms, sliced, *or* **2 4-oz. cans sliced mushrooms, drained**
2½-lb. beef flank, *or* **round, steak**
salt to taste
pepper to taste
1 Tbsp. Worcestershire sauce
1 Tbsp. oil
paprika to taste

1. Place sliced onions and mushrooms in slow cooker.
2. Score top of meat about ½" deep in diamond pattern.
3. Season with salt and pepper. Rub in Worcestershire sauce and oil. Sprinkle top with paprika.
4. Place meat on top of onions.
5. Cover. Cook on Low 7-8 hours, or until meat is tender but not dry.
6. To serve, cut beef across grain in thin slices. Top with mushrooms and onions.

Variation:
Add 1 Tbsp. lemon juice to Worcestershire sauce and oil in Step 3.

Genelle Taylor
Perrysburg, OH

Barbecued Chuck Steak

Rhonda Burgoon
Collingswood, NJ

Makes 4 servings

Prep. Time: 10 minutes
Cooking Time: 3-5 hours
Ideal slow cooker size: 3-qt.

1½-lb. boneless chuck steak, 1½" thick
1 clove garlic, minced
¼ cup wine vinegar
1 Tbsp. brown sugar
1 tsp. paprika
2 Tbsp. Worcestershire sauce
½ cup ketchup
1 tsp. salt
1 tsp. prepared mustard
¼ tsp. black pepper

1. Cut beef on diagonal across the grain into 1"-thick slices. Place in slow cooker.
2. Combine remaining ingredients in a bowl. Pour over meat. Stir to mix.
3. Cover. Cook on Low 3-5 hours.

Pigs in Blankets

Linda Sluiter
Schererville, IN

Makes 4-6 servings

Prep. Time: 15 minutes
Cooking Time: 8 hours
Ideal slow cooker size: 4-qt.

2-3-lb. round steak, cut about 1" thick
1 lb. bacon
1 cup ketchup
¾ cup brown sugar
1 cup water
half a yellow onion, chopped

1. Cut steak into strips 1" thick x 3" long.
2. Lay a bacon strip down, then a strip of beef on top of the bacon slice. Roll up and secure with toothpick. Place in slow cooker.
3. Combine remaining ingredients in a bowl. Pour over meat roll-ups.
4. Cover. Cook on High 8 hours.

Corned Beef

Elaine Vigoda
Rochester, NY

Makes 8 servings

Prep. Time: 15 minutes
Cooking Time: 7-12 hours
Ideal slow cooker size: 5- to 6-qt.

3 large carrots, cut into chunks
1 cup chopped celery
1 tsp. salt
½ tsp. pepper
1 cup water
3-4-lb. corned beef
1 large onion, cut into pieces
half a small head of cabbage, cut in wedges
4 potatoes, peeled and chunked

1. Place carrots, celery, seasonings, and water in slow cooker. Stir together.
2. Add beef. Cover with onions.
3. Cover. Cook on Low 8-10 hours or on High 5-6 hours.
4. Lift corned beef out of cooker and add cabbage and potatoes, pushing them to bottom of slow cooker. Return beef to cooker.
5. Cover. Cook on High 2 hours, or until vegetables are as tender as you like them.
6. Remove corned beef. Cool and slice on the diagonal.
7. Serve surrounded by vegetables.

Variations:

1. Scatter 10-12 peppercorns over corned beef and onions in Step 2.

Rosaria Strachan
Fairfield, CT

2. In a bowl, mix together 1 cup water, ½ cup brown sugar, 1 Tbsp. prepared mustard, and a dash of ground cloves. Spread over beef in Step 4, just before cooking on High 2 more hours.

Shirley Sears
Tiskilwa, IL

Apple and Brown Sugar Corned Beef

Mary Seielstad
Sparks, NV

Makes 8-10 servings

Prep. Time: 10 minutes
Cooking Time: 6-12 hours
Ideal slow cooker size: 6-qt. or 2 4- to 5-qt. cookers

2½-3-lb. corned beef brisket
8 small red potatoes
3 medium carrots, peeled and sliced
1 large onion, cut in 6-8 pieces
1 small head cabbage, cut in chunks
1 qt. apple juice
1 cup brown sugar
1 Tbsp. prepared mustard

1. Place meat, potatoes, carrots, onion, and cabbage in 6-qt. slow cooker, or divide between 2 4- to 5-qt. cookers.
2. Combine apple juice, brown sugar, and mustard in a bowl. Pour into slow cooker(s).
3. Cover. Cook on High 6-6½ hours or on Low 10-12 hours, or until vegetables and meat are tender.
4. Remove meat and vegetables from slow cooker. Thinly slice meat across the grain. Serve topped with vegetables.

Serving suggestion: We love to eat this with ***cornbread****.*

Tip:

If potatoes are not small, quarter them before placing in slow cooker.

Home-Style Beef Cubes

Dorothy Horst
Tiskilwa, IL

Makes 8-10 servings

Prep. Time: 10 minutes
Cooking Time: 7-12 hours
Ideal slow cooker size: 5-qt.

½ cup flour
1 tsp. salt
⅛ tsp. pepper
4 lbs. beef cubes
½ cup chopped shallots, *or* **green onions**
2 4-oz. cans sliced mushrooms, drained, *or* **½ lb. fresh mushrooms, sliced**

14½-oz. can beef broth
1 tsp. Worcestershire sauce
2 tsp. ketchup
¼ cup water
3 Tbsp. flour

1. In a large bowl, combine ½ cup flour, salt, and pepper. Toss beef in flour mixture to coat. Place in slow cooker.
2. Cover with onions and mushrooms.
3. Combine broth, Worcestershire sauce, and ketchup in a bowl. Pour into slow cooker. Mix everything together well.
4. Cover. Cook on Low 7-12 hours, or until beef is as tender as you like.
5. One hour before serving, make a smooth paste of water and 3 Tbsp. flour in a small bowl. Stir into slow cooker. Cover and continue cooking until broth thickens.

Serving suggestion: This is a treat served over hot ***buttered noodles****.*

Fruited Beef Tagine

Naomi E. Fast
Hesston, KS

Makes 6-8 servings

Prep. Time: 20 minutes
Cooking Time: 5-6 hours
Ideal slow cooker size: 4-qt.

2 lbs. beef, cut into 2" cubes
1 Tbsp. oil
4 cups sliced onions
2 tsp. ground coriander
1½ tsp. ground cinnamon
¾ tsp. ground ginger
14½-oz. can beef broth, plus enough water to equal 2 cups
16 ozs. pitted prunes
salt to taste
fresh ground pepper to taste
juice of one lemon

1. Brown beef cubes in oil in skillet. Do in batches so beef browns and doesn't steam. As you finish browning, place beef in slow cooker. Reserve drippings.
2. Sauté onions in drippings until lightly browned, adding more oil if needed. Add to slow cooker.
3. Add remaining ingredients, except lemon juice.
4. Simmer on Low 5-6 hours, adding lemon juice during the last 10 minutes.

Serving suggestion: This recipe, accompanied with a tossed ***green salad*** *and* ***rolls****, makes a complete meal.*

Variations:

1. Mix in a few very thin slices of lemon rind to add flavor and eye appeal.
2. You can substitute lamb cubes for the beef.

Salsa Beef

Sarah Niessen
Akron, PA

Makes 5-6 servings

Prep. Time: 15 minutes
Cooking Time: 6-8 hours
Ideal slow cooker size: 5- to 6-qt.

2-2½ lbs. beef, cut in bite-sized cubes
1 Tbsp. oil
16-oz. jar salsa
8-oz. can tomato sauce
2 garlic cloves, minced
2 Tbsp. brown sugar
1 Tbsp. soy sauce
1 cup canned tomatoes

1. Brown beef in skillet in oil. Do it in batches so beef browns and doesn't steam. As you finish a batch, place browned cubes in slow cooker.
2. Stir in remaining ingredients.
3. Cover. Cook on Low 6-8 hours.

Serving suggestion: I usually serve this over ***rice****.*

Variation:

For added flavor, use Italian tomato sauce.

Beef Mushroom Casserole

Susan Stephani Smith
Monument, CO

Makes 12 servings

Prep. Time: 10 minutes
Cooking Time: 4½-5½ hours
Ideal slow cooker size: 5-qt.

4 lbs. lean beef sirloin, cut into 1" cubes
2 10¾-oz. cans cream of mushroom soup
2 pkgs. dry onion soup mix
¼-1 tsp. pepper, according to your taste preference
½ tsp. salt
1-2 cups red Burgundy wine, *optional*
1½ lbs. fresh mushrooms, quartered
¼ cup sour cream, *optional*

1. Combine all ingredients except wine, mushrooms, and sour cream in slow cooker.
2. Cover. Cook on Low 4-5 hours, stirring occasionally if you're home and able to do so.
3. Stir in mushrooms and wine. Cook 30 minutes longer.
4. Ten minutes before end of cooking time, stir in sour cream if you wish.

Serving suggestion: This is a treat served over ***egg noodles****.*

Easy Stroganoff

Vicki Dinkel
Sharon Springs, KS

Makes 6-8 servings

Prep. Time: 5 minutes
Cooking Time: 6½-8½ hours
Ideal slow cooker size: 4-qt.

10¾-oz. can cream of mushroom soup
14½-oz. can beef broth
1 lb. beef stewing meat, *or* **round steak, cut in 1" pieces**
1 cup sour cream
2 cups cooked noodles

1. Combine soup and broth in slow cooker.
2. Stir in meat.
3. Cover. Cook on High 3-4 hours. Reduce heat to Low and cook 3-4 hours, or just until beef is fork tender.
4. Stir in sour cream.
5. Stir in noodles.
6. Cook on High 20 minutes, or just until Stroganoff is hot throughout.

Serving suggestion: A ***vegetable*** *or* ***salad*** *and some crispy* ***French bread*** *make good additions to the meal.*

Note:
Since I'm in school part-time and work two part-time jobs, this nearly complete meal is great to come home to. It smells wonderful when I open the door.

Garlic Beef Stroganoff

Sharon Miller
Holmesville, OH

Makes 6-8 servings

Prep. Time: 10-15 minutes
Cooking Time: 7-8 hours
Ideal slow cooker size: 4-qt.

2 tsp. beef bouillon granules
2 4½-oz. jars sliced mushrooms, drained, with juice reserved
1 cup mushroom juice, with boiling water added to make a full cup
10¾-oz. can cream of mushroom soup
1 large onion, chopped
3 garlic cloves, minced
1 Tbsp. Worcestershire sauce
1½-2-lb. boneless round steak, cut into thin strips
2 Tbsp. oil
8-oz. pkg. cream cheese, cubed and softened

1. Dissolve bouillon in mushroom juice/water mixture in slow cooker.
2. Stir in mushrooms, soup, onion, garlic, and Worcestershire sauce.
3. Sauté beef in oil in skillet. Transfer to slow cooker and stir into sauce.
4. Cover. Cook on Low 7-8 hours. Turn off heat.
5. Stir in cream cheese until smooth.

Serving suggestion: You'll love this served over ***noodles****.*

Beef Burgundy

Joyce Kaut, Rochester, NY

Makes 6 servings

Prep. Time: 30 minutes • Cooking Time: 3¼-4¼ hours
Ideal slow cooker size: 3- to 4-qt.

2 slices bacon, cut in squares
2 lbs. sirloin tip, *or* **round, steak, cubed**
¼ cup flour
½ tsp. salt
¼ tsp. seasoning salt
¼ tsp. dried marjoram
¼ tsp. dried thyme
¼ tsp. pepper
1 garlic clove, minced
1 beef bouillon cube, crushed
1 cup burgundy wine
¼ lb. fresh mushrooms, sliced
1-1½ cups ketchup
2 Tbsp. cornstarch, *optional*
2 Tbsp. cold water, *optional*

1. Cook bacon in skillet until crisp and browned. Remove bacon, reserving drippings.
2. Coat beef with flour and brown on all sides in bacon drippings. (Don't crowd the skillet so the beef browns rather than steams.)
3. Combine steak, bacon drippings, bacon, seasonings and herbs, garlic, bouillon, and wine in slow cooker.
4. Cover. Cook on Low 4 hours (or 3 hours, if you've browned the beef well in Step 2), or until beef is just tender.
5. Stir in mushrooms and ketchup.
6. Dissolve cornstarch in water in a small bowl. Stir into slow cooker—if sauce is not as thick as you wish.
7. Cover. Cook on High 15 minutes, until sauce thickens.

Serving suggestion: Try serving this over ***noodles****.*

Italian Beef Stew

Kathy Hertzler
Lancaster, PA

Makes 4-6 servings

Prep. Time: 30 minutes
Cooking Time: 6½ hours
Ideal slow cooker size: 4-qt.

2 Tbsp. flour
2 tsp. chopped fresh thyme
1 tsp. salt
¼-½ tsp. freshly ground pepper
2¼ lbs. beef stewing meat, cubed
3 Tbsp. olive oil
1 onion, chopped
1 cup tomato sauce
1 cup beef stock
1 cup red wine
3 garlic cloves, minced
2 Tbsp. tomato paste
2 cups frozen peas, thawed but not cooked
1 tsp. sugar

1. Spoon flour into small dish. Season with thyme, salt, and pepper. Add beef cubes and coat evenly.
2. Heat oil in slow cooker on High. Add floured beef and brown on all sides.
3. Stir in remaining ingredients except peas and sugar.
4. Cover. Cook on Low 6 hours.
5. Add peas and sugar. Cook an additional 30 minutes, or until beef is tender and peas are warm.

Dawn's Mushroom Beef Stew

Dawn Day
Westminster, CA

Makes 8-10 servings

Prep. Time: 20 minutes
Cooking Time: 6-7½ hours
Ideal slow cooker size: 3- to 4-qt.

1 lb. sirloin, cubed
2 Tbsp. flour
oil
1 large onion, chopped
2 garlic cloves, minced
½ lb. button mushrooms, sliced
2 ribs celery, sliced
2 carrots, sliced
3-4 large potatoes, cubed
2 tsp. seasoning salt
14½-oz. can beef stock, *or* **2 bouillon cubes dissolved in 1⅔ cups water**
½-1 cup good red wine

1. Dredge sirloin in flour and brown in oil in skillet. Reserve drippings. Place meat in slow cooker.
2. Sauté onion, garlic, and mushrooms in drippings just until soft. Add to meat.
3. Stir in all remaining ingredients.
4. Cover. Cook on Low 6 hours. Test to see if vegetables are tender. If not, continue cooking on Low for another 1-1½ hours.

Tempting Beef Stew

Patricia Howard
Albuquerque, NM

Makes 10-12 servings

Prep. Time: 10 minutes
Cooking Time: 10-12 hours
Ideal slow cooker size: 5-qt.

2-3 lbs. beef stewing meat
3 carrots, sliced thin
1-lb. pkg. frozen green peas with onions
1-lb. pkg. frozen green beans
16-oz. can whole, *or* **stewed, tomatoes**
½ cup beef broth
½ cup white wine
½ cup brown sugar
4 Tbsp. instant tapioca
½ cup bread crumbs
2 tsp. salt
1 bay leaf
pepper to taste

1. Combine all ingredients in slow cooker.
2. Cover. Cook on Low 10-12 hours, or until meat and vegetables are as tender as you wish.

Serving suggestion: Serve over ***noodles, rice, couscous,*** *or* ***biscuits.***

Tip:
Prepare this Tempting Beef Stew before your guests arrive. Give yourself time to relax instead of panicking in a last-minute rush.

Variation:
In place of tapioca, thicken stew with ¼ cup flour dissolved in ⅓-½ cup water. Mix in and turn cooker to High. Cover and cook for 15-20 minutes.

Beef Stew with Wine

Andrea O'Neil
Fairfield, CT

Makes 8-10 servings

Prep. Time: 20 minutes
Cooking Time: 9-10 hours
Ideal slow cooker size: 4-qt.

1 lb. stewing meat, cubed
oil
2 onions, quartered
4 carrots, sliced
4-5 potatoes, cubed
28-oz. can crushed tomatoes
½ cup wine
1 pkg. dry onion soup mix
1 cup water
2 tsp. salt
¾ tsp. pepper
3 Tbsp. cornstarch
¼ cup water

1. Brown beef cubes in skillet in oil.
2. Place browned beef in slow cooker. Add all other ingredients except cornstarch and ¼ cup water. Stir to combine.
3. Cover. Cook on Low 9-10 hours.
4. Ten minutes before

Beef Stew with Shiitake Mushrooms

Kathy Hertzler, Lancaster, PA

Makes 4-6 servings

Prep. Time: 10 minutes • Cooking Time: 8-9 hours
Ideal slow cooker size: 5-qt.

12 new potatoes, cut into quarters
½ cup chopped onions
8-oz. pkg. baby carrots
3-4-oz. pkg. fresh shiitake mushrooms, sliced, *or* **2 cups regular white mushrooms, sliced**
16-oz. can whole tomatoes
14½-oz. can beef broth
½ cup flour
1 Tbsp. Worcestershire sauce
1 tsp. salt
1 tsp. sugar
1 tsp. dried marjoram leaves
¼ tsp. pepper
1 lb. beef stewing meat, cubed

1. Combine all ingredients except beef in slow cooker.
2. Stir in beef.
3. Cover. Cook on Low 8-9 hours. Stir well before serving.

serving, stir cornstarch into water in a small bowl until smooth. Stir into hot Stew.

Variation:

For added zest, add ½ tsp. Old Bay Seasoning and 1 rib celery, diced, in Step 2.

Best Ever Beef Stew

Barbara Walker
Sturgis, SD

Makes 6 servings

Prep. Time: 15 minutes
Cooking Time: 6-7 hours
Ideal slow cooker size: 4- to 5-qt.

2 cups water
1 pkg. beef stew mix
2 lbs. stewing meat, cubed
3 15-oz. cans whole new potatoes, *or* **3 lbs. fresh new potatoes**
1 cup sliced celery
10-12 small white onions, peeled
1-1½ cups sliced carrots
8 oz. fresh mushrooms, whole, *or* **sliced**

1. Combine water and beef stew mix in slow cooker.
2. Place meat in slow cooker.
3. Stir in remaining ingredients.
4. Cover. Cook on High 6-7 hours, or until meat and vegetables are as tender as you like.

I put up a small tree in my kitchen and decorate it with my mother's old cookie cutters and some of her recipe cards. I enjoy it while I'm in the kitchen during the holidays—which is a lot of time!

Carol L. Miller, Lockport, NY

Tomato-y Beef Stew

Janie Steele
Moore, OK

Makes 6-8 servings

Prep. Time: 15 minutes
Cooking Time: 8 hours
Ideal slow cooker size: 5- to 6-qt.

5 lbs. stewing meat, cubed
2 onions, chopped
14½-oz. can chopped tomatoes
10¾-oz. can tomato soup
5-6 carrots, sliced
5-6 potatoes, peeled and cubed
1 cup sliced celery
1 bell pepper, sliced
2 tsp. salt
½ tsp. pepper
2 cloves minced garlic

1. Combine all ingredients in slow cooker.
2. Cover. Cook on Low 8 hours.

Serving suggestion: Since this is a nearly complete meal, I usually add only warm ***bread*** *or* ***cornbread*** *to round it out.*

Tip:
This recipe is very adaptable. You can reduce the amount of meat and increase the vegetables as you wish.

After-Work Stew

Vera M. Kuhns
Harrisonburg, VA

Makes 5 servings

Prep. Time: 15-20 minutes
Cooking Time: 8-9 hours
Ideal slow cooker size: 3- to 4-qt.

1½ lbs. beef, cut into 1½" cubes
oil
3 medium-sized potatoes, pared and cubed
4 medium-sized carrots, quartered
2 celery ribs, sliced
2 medium-sized onions, sliced
2 tsp. salt
½ tsp. dried basil
½ tsp. pepper
10¾-oz. can tomato soup
half a soup can water

1. Brown beef cubes in oil in skillet. Do in batches so that beef browns and doesn't steam. Drain off drippings. Return beef to skillet.
2. Meanwhile, layer potatoes, carrots, celery, and onions in slow cooker.
3. Mix browned beef in skillet with salt, basil, and pepper, stirring up any browned bits in the skillet.
4. Place seasoned beef on top of vegetables.
5. Combine soup and water in a bowl. Pour over ingredients in slow cooker.
6. Cover. Cook on Low 8-9 hours, or just until vegetables and meat are tender.

Easy Beef Stew

Janie Steele
Moore, OK

Makes 14-18 servings

Prep. Time: 25 minutes
Cooking Time: 10-11 hours
Ideal slow cooker size: 2 4-qt. cookers

2-3 lbs. beef, cubed
16-oz. pkg. frozen green beans, *or* **mixed vegetables**
16-oz. pkg. frozen corn
2 lbs. carrots, chopped
1 large onion, chopped
4 medium potatoes, peeled and chopped
10¾-oz. can tomato soup
10¾-oz. can celery soup
10¾-oz. can mushroom soup
bell pepper chopped, *optional*
16-oz. pkg. frozen peas

1. Combine all ingredients except peas in 2 4-qt. slow cookers. This is a very large recipe.
2. Cover. Cook on Low 10-11 hours, or until beef and vegetables are as tender as you like them.
3. Fifteen minutes before end of cooking time, stir in peas.

New Mexico Stew

Helen Kenagy
Carlsbad, NM

Makes 8 servings

Prep. Time: 15 minutes
Cooking Time: 8½-10½ hours
Ideal slow cooker size: 5-qt.

salt to taste
pepper to taste
2 lbs. stewing meat, *or* **steak, cubed,** *divided*
1 Tbsp. oil
5-6 potatoes, cubed, *divided*
6-8 carrots, diced, *divided*
other vegetables of your choice, diced, *divided*
1-2 4¼-oz. cans chopped green chilies, undrained, *divided*
1½ lbs. raw pork sausage, crumbled, *divided*

1. Salt and pepper stewing meat. Brown in oil in skillet.
2. Place half the stewing meat in bottom of slow cooker. Sprinkle with salt and pepper.
3. Layer half the vegetables and chilies over beef. Sprinkle with salt and pepper.
4. Crumble half the sausage over top. Sprinkle with salt and pepper.
5. Repeat layering until all ingredients are used.
6. Cover. Cook on High until ingredients begin to boil. Then turn cooker to Low for 8-10 hours. Do not lift lid and do not stir during cooking.

Serving suggestion: With such a complete dish, all you need to add is a ***green salad*** *and* ***fresh bread*** *if you wish.*

Hungarian Beef Stew

Esther Becker
Gordonville, PA

Makes 6 servings

Prep. Time: 15 minutes
Cooking Time: 10-12 hours
Ideal slow cooker size: 4-qt.

2 lbs. beef cubes
1 onion, chopped
2 medium potatoes, peeled and cubed
2 carrots, sliced
10-oz. pkg. frozen lima beans
2 tsp. parsley
½ cup beef broth
2 tsp. paprika
1 tsp. salt
16-oz. can diced tomatoes

1. Combine beef, onion, potatoes, carrots, lima beans, and parsley in slow cooker.
2. Combine remaining ingredients in a bowl. Pour into slow cooker.
3. Cover. Cook on Low 10-12 hours.

Serving suggestion: This is a great meal, especially when served with a ***tossed salad*** *and* ***homemade rolls****.*

Hungarian Barley Stew

Naomi E. Fast
Hesston, KS

Makes 8 servings

Prep. Time: 20 minutes
Cooking Time: 5 hours
Ideal slow cooker size: 5-qt.

1½ lbs. beef cubes
2 Tbsp. oil
2 large onions, diced
1 medium-sized green bell pepper, chopped
28-oz. can whole tomatoes
½ cup ketchup
⅔ cup dry small pearl barley
1 tsp. salt
½ tsp. pepper
1 Tbsp. paprika
10-oz. pkg. frozen baby lima beans
3 cups water
1 cup sour cream

1. Brown beef cubes in oil in skillet. Add onions and green peppers. Sauté until no longer crispy. Pour into slow cooker.
2. Stir in remaining ingredients except sour cream.
3. Cover. Cook on High 5 hours.
4. Stir in sour cream before serving.

Serving suggestion: This goes well with ***cabbage slaw****.*

Wash-Day Stew

Naomi E. Fast
Hesston, KS

Makes 8-10 servings

Prep. Time: 10 minutes
Cooking Time: 6-7 hours
Ideal slow cooker size: 5-qt.

1½-2 lbs. lean lamb, *or* **beef, cubed**
2 15-oz. cans garbanzo beans, drained
2 15-oz. cans white beans, drained
2 medium onions, peeled and quartered
1 qt. water
1 tsp. salt
1 tomato, peeled and quartered
1 tsp. turmeric
3 Tbsp. fresh lemon juice
8-10 pita bread pockets

1. Combine all ingredients except pita bread in slow cooker.
2. Cover. Cook on High 6-7 hours.
3. Lift stew from cooker with a strainer spoon and stuff in pita bread pockets.

Note:

I learned to prepare this nutritious meal from a student from Iran, who was attending graduate school at the University of Nebraska. Fatimeh explained to me that her family prepared this dish every wash day.

Very early in the morning, they made a fire in a large rock-lined pit outside. Then they placed a large covered kettle, filled with the above ingredients, over the coals to cook slowly all day. At the end of a day of doing laundry, the food was ready with a minimum of preparation.

Of course, they started with dry garbanzos and white beans, presoaked the night before.

They served this Wash-Day Stew spooned into pita bread and ate it with their hands.

Potluck Beef Barbecue Sandwiches

Carol Sommers
Millersburg, OH

Makes 16 servings

Prep. Time: 5-10 minutes
Cooking Time: 6½-8¾ hours
Ideal slow cooker size: 5-qt.

4-lb. beef chuck roast
1 cup brewed coffee, *or* **water**
1 Tbsp. apple cider, *or* **red-wine, vinegar**
1 tsp. salt
½ tsp. pepper
14-oz. bottle ketchup
15-oz. can tomato sauce
1 cup sweet pickle relish
2 Tbsp. Worcestershire sauce
¼ cup brown sugar

1. Place roast, coffee, vinegar, salt, and pepper in slow cooker.
2. Cover. Cook on High 6-8 hours, or until meat is very tender.
3. Pour off cooking liquid. Shred meat with two forks.
4. Add remaining ingredients. Stir well.
5. Cover. Cook on High 30-45 minutes. Reduce heat to Low for serving.

Barbara Jean's Junior Beef

Barbara Jean Fabel
Wausau, WI

Makes 8 servings

Prep. Time: 10 minutes
Cooking Time: 5-6 hours
Ideal slow cooker size: 4-qt.

3½-5-lb. beef roast
½ tsp. salt
½ tsp. cayenne pepper
½ tsp. black pepper
1 tsp. seasoned salt
1 medium onion, chopped
1 qt. dill pickle juice
4 dill pickles, chopped
8 hamburger rolls
½ lb. fresh mushrooms, sliced and sautéed
2 cups grated cheddar, *or* **Swiss, cheese**

1. Combine all ingredients except rolls, mushrooms, and cheese in slow cooker.
2. Cover. Cook on High 4-5 hours.
3. Shred meat using two forks. Reduce heat to Low and cook 1 hour, or until meat is very tender.

4. Serve on hamburger buns with sautéed, sliced, fresh mushrooms and grated cheddar or Swiss cheese.

Ranch Hand Beef

Sharon Timpe
Mequon, WI

Makes 10-12 servings

Prep. Time: 10 minutes
Cooking Time: 4-9 hours
Ideal slow cooker size: 4-qt.

3-3½-lb. boneless beef chuck roast
1 cup thinly sliced onions
10¾-oz. can cream of celery soup
4-oz. can sliced mushrooms, drained
12-oz. can beer
½ cup ketchup
1 large bay leaf
½ tsp. salt
¼ tsp. lemon pepper
2 Tbsp. chopped fresh parsley, *or* **1½ tsp. dried parsley**

1. Place roast in slow cooker.
2. Combine remaining ingredients in a large bowl. Pour over roast.
3. Cover. Cook on Low 7-9 hours or on medium setting 4-6 hours, until meat is tender.
4. Remove bay leaf.
5. Shred roast with two forks. Mix meat through sauce.

Serving suggestion: This works well two ways: served on ***buns*** *as sandwiches, or over cooked* ***noodles****.*

Or, to give this dish a Mexican theme, serve the beef over ***tortilla chips*** *or* ***fritos*** *and have bowls of shredded* ***lettuce****, diced* ***avocado****, sliced* ***green onions****, sliced ripe* ***olives****,* ***sour cream****, diced* ***tomatoes****, and shredded* ***cheese*** *for garnishing the meat.*

Variation:

If you prefer a thicker sauce, stir 2 Tbsp. cornstarch into ¼ cup water. When smooth, stir into hot sauce in cooker, 15 minutes before serving.

Beef Barbecue Sandwiches

Melba Eshleman
Manheim, PA

Makes 12-16 servings

Prep. Time: 10 minutes
Refrigeration Time: 8-10 hours
Cooking Time: 10-12 hours
Ideal slow cooker size: 4-qt.

3-4-lb. beef roast (bottom round or rump is best)
½ cup water
½ cup ketchup
1 tsp. chili powder
1½ Tbsp. Worcestershire sauce
2 Tbsp. vinegar
1 tsp. salt
1 Tbsp. sugar
1 tsp. dry mustard
1 medium onion, finely chopped
½ cup water

1. The night before serving, place roast in slow cooker with ½ cup water.
2. Cover. Cook on Low 10-12 hours.
3. Also the night before serving, combine remaining ingredients (except rolls) and refrigerate 8-10 hours.
4. In the morning, shred roast with fork and return to cooker. Pour remaining ingredients over top. Mix together.
5. Heat on Low until lunch or suppertime.

Serving suggestion: Serve on ***kaiser rolls****.*

Easy Roast Beef Barbecue

Rose Hankins
Stevensville, MD

Makes 12-16 servings

Prep. Time: 10 minutes
Cooking Time: 12 hours
Ideal slow cooker size: 4-qt.

3-4-lb. beef roast
12-oz. bottle barbecue sauce
½ cup water
½ cup ketchup
½ cup chopped onions
½ cup chopped green pepper

1. Combine ingredients in slow cooker.
2. Cover. Cook on Low 12 hours.
3. Shred meat using 2 forks. Mix thoroughly through sauce.

Serving suggestion: This is enough Barbecue to serve on 12-16 ***sandwich rolls****. Offer* ***cole slaw*** *as a side dish, or as an additional sandwich filler.*

Herby Beef Sandwiches

Jean A. Shaner
York, PA

Makes 10-12 servings

Prep. Time: 5 minutes
Cooking Time: 7-8 hours
Ideal slow cooker size: 4-qt.

3-4-lb. boneless beef chuck roast
3 Tbsp. fresh basil, *or* **1 Tbsp. dried basil**
3 Tbsp. fresh oregano, *or* **1 Tbsp. dried oregano**
1½ cups water
1 pkg. dry onion soup mix

1. Place roast in slow cooker.
2. Combine basil, oregano, and water in a bowl. Pour over roast.
3. Sprinkle with onion soup mix.
4. Cover. Cook on Low 7-8 hours.
5. Shred meat with fork. Stir sauce through shredded meat.

Serving suggestion: I like to serve these on crusty ***Italian rolls****. This amount of beef fills 10-12 rolls.*

Hot Beef Sandwiches

Evelyn L. Ward
Greeley, CO

Makes 10 servings

Prep. Time: 5-10 minutes
Cooking Time: 8-10 hours
Ideal slow cooker size: 4-qt.

3 lbs. beef chuck roast
1 large onion, chopped
¼ cup vinegar
1 clove garlic, minced
1-1½ tsp. salt
¼-½ tsp. pepper

1. Place meat in slow cooker. Top with onions.
2. Combine vinegar, garlic, salt, and pepper in a bowl. Pour over meat, but don't disturb the onions.
3. Cover. Cook on Low 8-10 hours.
4. Drain broth but save for dipping.
5. Shred meat.

Note:

I volunteer with Habitat for Humanity. I don't do construction, but I provide lunch sometimes for work crews. These sandwiches are a favorite. I make the most colorful tossed salad that I can and serve seasonal fresh fruit and pie along with the sandwiches.

Middle Eastern Sandwiches (for a crowd)

Esther Mast
East Petersburg, PA

Makes 10-16 sandwiches

Prep. Time: 50 minutes
Cooking Time: 6¼-8¼ hours
Ideal slow cooker size: 4-qt.

4 lbs. boneless beef, *or* **venison, cut in ½" cubes**
4 Tbsp. cooking oil
2 cups chopped onions
2 garlic cloves, minced
1 cup dry red wine
6-oz. can tomato paste
1 tsp. dried oregano
1 tsp. dried basil
½ tsp. dried rosemary
2 tsp. salt
dash of pepper
¼ cup cornstarch
¼ cup cold water
pita pocket breads
2 cups shredded lettuce
1 large tomato, seeded and diced
1 large cucumber, seeded and diced
8-oz. carton plain yogurt

1. Brown meat, 1 lb. at a time, in skillet in 1 Tbsp. oil. As you finish one batch, place browned beef in slow cooker. Reserve drippings.
2. Sauté onions and garlic in drippings until tender. Add to meat.
3. Stir in wine, tomato paste, oregano, basil, rosemary, salt, and pepper.
4. Cover. Cook on Low 6-8 hours.
5. Turn cooker to High. Combine cornstarch and water in small bowl until smooth. Stir into meat mixture. Cook until bubbly and thickened, stirring occasionally.
6. Split pita breads to make pockets. Fill each with meat mixture, lettuce, tomato, cucumber, and yogurt.

Serving suggestion: All you need to top this off is ***salad*** *or* ***applesauce.***

Ground Beef Stroganoff

Janie S. Canupp
Millersville, MD

Makes 5-6 servings

Prep. Time: 30 minutes
Cooking Time: 3 hours
Ideal slow cooker size: 5-qt.

2 lbs. ground beef
2 medium onions, chopped
2 cloves garlic, minced
4-oz. can sliced mushrooms, drained
1-1½ tsp. salt
¼ tsp. black pepper
1 cup beef broth, *or* **1 bouillon cube dissolved in 1 cup water**
3 Tbsp. tomato paste, *or* **ketchup**
1½ cups sour cream
¼ cup flour

1. Brown beef in large skillet. Stir frequently to break up clumps.
2. When meat is no longer pink, add onions, garlic, and mushrooms. Sauté until onion is tender. Put mixture into slow cooker.
3. In a small bowl, mix together salt, pepper, broth, and tomato paste. Stir into beef mixture in slow cooker.
4. Cover. Cook on Low 2½ hours.
5. Meanwhile, combine sour cream and flour in a small bowl until well blended. Stir into slow cooker.
6. Cover. Cook 30 more minutes, or until Stroganoff is thickened and bubbly.

Serving suggestion: Serve over buttered ***noodles*** *or* ***rice.***

Variation:

Instead of beef broth or bouillon cube dissolved in water, use 10¾-oz. can cream of chicken soup in Step 3.

Bonnie L. Miller
Louisville, OH

Christmas Meat Loaf

Wafi Brandt
Manheim, PA

Makes 4-6 servings

Prep. Time: 25 minutes
Cooking Time: 4 hours
Ideal slow cooker size: 4-qt.

Meat Loaf:

2 eggs
1 envelope dry onion soup mix
½ cup seasoned bread crumbs
¼ cup chopped dried cranberries
1 tsp. parsley
1½ lbs. ground beef

Sauce:

16-oz. can whole berry cranberry sauce
¾ cup ketchup
½ cup beef broth
3 Tbsp. brown sugar
3 Tbsp. finely chopped onion
2 tsp. cider vinegar

1. Mix all Meat Loaf ingredients together in a good-sized bowl. Shape into loaf and place in lightly greased slow cooker.
2. Mix Sauce ingredients together in another bowl. Pour over meat.
3. Cover. Cook on High 4 hours.
4. Allow to stand 10 minutes before lifting out of cooker and slicing.

Tip from Tester:

After slicing and arranging the Meat Loaf on a platter, I ladled the Sauce over the slices. There was more Sauce than fit on the platter, so I put the remainder in a dish to pass. Then individuals could add more to their slices as a condiment. We loved it!

Meat Loaf

Colleen Heatwole
Burton, MI

Makes 8 servings

Prep. Time: 15 minutes
Cooking Time: 4-10 hours
Ideal slow cooker size: 4-qt.

2 lbs. ground beef
2 eggs
⅔ cup dry quick oats
1 envelope dry onion soup mix
½-1 tsp. liquid smoke
1 tsp. ground mustard
½ cup ketchup, *divided*

1. Combine ground beef, eggs, dry oats, dry soup mix, liquid smoke, ground mustard, and all but 2 Tbsp. ketchup in large bowl. Shape into loaf and place in slow cooker.
2. Top with remaining ketchup.
3. Cover. Cook on Low 8-10 hours or on High 4-6 hours.

Variation:

For a special topping for the Meat Loaf, make your own Sauce:

26-oz. can, *or* **2 10¾-oz. cans, mushroom soup**
6-10 fresh mushrooms, diced
1 Tbsp. onion flakes
half soup can water
¼ tsp. salt
⅛ tsp. pepper

Combine Sauce ingredients in a bowl. Pour over Meat Loaf in Step 2 instead of ketchup.

Betty B. Dennison
Grove City, PA

Magic Meat Loaf

Carolyn Baer
Conrath, WI

Makes 6 servings

Prep. Time: 20 minutes
Cooking Time: 9-11 hours
Ideal slow cooker size: 4-qt.

1 egg, beaten
¼ cup milk
1½ tsp. salt
2 slices bread, crumbled
1½ lbs. ground beef
half a small onion, chopped
2 Tbsp. chopped green bell peppers
2 Tbsp. chopped celery
ketchup
green pepper rings
4-6 potatoes, cubed
3 Tbsp. butter, melted

1. Combine egg, milk, salt, and bread crumbs in large bowl. Allow bread crumbs to soften.
2. Add meat, onions, green peppers, and celery. Shape into loaf and place off to the side in slow cooker.
3. Top with ketchup and green pepper rings.
4. Toss potatoes with melted butter in a good sized bowl. Spoon into cooker alongside meat loaf.
5. Cover. Cook on High 1 hour, and then on Low 8-10 hours, or until meat and vegetables are as tender as you want them.

Gourmet Meat Loaf

Anne Townsend
Albuquerque, NM

Makes 8 servings

Prep. Time: 25 minutes
Cooking Time: 8-12 hours
Ideal slow cooker size: 4-qt.

2 medium potatoes, cut in strips

Meat loaf:
2 lbs. ground beef
½ lb. bulk sausage
1 onion, finely chopped
2-3 cloves garlic, minced, according to your taste preference
½ cup ketchup
¾ cup crushed saltines
2 eggs
2 tsp. Worcestershire sauce
2 tsp. seasoning salt
¼ tsp. pepper

Sauce:
½ cup ketchup
¼ cup brown sugar
1½ tsp. dry mustard
½ tsp. ground nutmeg

1. Place potatoes in bottom of slow cooker.
2. Combine Meat Loaf ingredients in a large bowl. Form into loaf and place on top of potatoes.
3. Combine Sauce ingredients in a separate bowl. Spoon over Meat Loaf.
4. Cover. Cook on Low 8-12 hours.

Tip:
The potatoes take longer to cook than the meat so make sure you allow enough time.

Note:
My husband has this at the top of his list of favorite Meat Loaf recipes.

Our out-of-state relatives always bring gifts specifically made in their states to share with others.
Annie C. Boshart, Lebanon, PA

Cheese Meat Loaf

Mary Sommerfeld
Lancaster, PA

Makes 8 servings

Prep. Time: 15 minutes
Cooking Time: 6-8 hours
Ideal slow cooker size: 4-qt.

2 lbs. ground chuck, *or* **ground beef**
2 cups shredded sharp cheddar, *or* **American, cheese**
1 tsp. salt
1 tsp. dry mustard
¼ tsp. pepper
½ cup chili sauce
2 cups crushed cornflakes
2 eggs
½ cup milk

1. Combine all ingredients in a large bowl. Shape into loaf. Place in greased slow cooker.
2. Cover. Cook on Low 6-8 hours.

Serving suggestion: Slice and serve with your favorite ***tomato sauce*** *or* ***ketchup****.*

Variation:
Before baking, surround meat loaf with quartered potatoes, tossed lightly in oil.

Festive Meatballs

Jean Butzer
Batavia, NY

Makes 5-7 servings

Prep. Time: 20 minutes
Cooking Time: 2¾-3¾ hours
Ideal slow cooker size: 4-qt.

1½ lbs. ground beef
4½-oz. can deviled ham
⅔ cup evaporated milk
2 eggs, beaten slightly
1 Tbsp. grated onion
2 cups soft bread crumbs
1 tsp. salt
¼ tsp. allspice
¼ tsp. pepper
¼ cup flour
¼ cup water
1 Tbsp. ketchup
2 tsp. dill weed
1 cup sour cream

1. Combine beef, ham, milk, eggs, onion, bread crumbs, salt, allspice, and pepper in large bowl. Shape into 2" meatballs. As you finish making a ball, place it in the slow cooker.
2. Cover. Cook on Low 2½-3½ hours. Turn to High.
3. In a bowl, dissolve flour in water until smooth. Stir in ketchup and dill weed. Add to meatballs, stirring gently.
4. Cook on High 15-20 minutes, or until slightly thickened.
5. Turn off heat. Stir in sour cream.

*Serving suggestion: Serve over **rice** or **pasta**.*

Easy Meatballs

Carlene Horne
Bedford, NH

Makes 10-12 servings

Prep. Time: 5 minutes
Cooking Time: 4-5 hours
Ideal slow cooker size: 5-qt.

2 10¾-oz. cans cream of mushroom soup
2 8-oz. pkgs. cream cheese, softened
4-oz. can sliced mushrooms, undrained
1 cup milk
2-3 lbs. frozen meatballs

1. Combine soup, cream cheese, mushrooms, and milk in slow cooker.
2. Stir in meatballs.
3. Cover. Cook on Low 4-5 hours.

*Serving suggestion: Serve over **noodles**.*

Swedish Meat Balls

Zona Mae Bontrager
Kokomo, IN

Makes 6-8 servings

Prep. Time: 35 minutes
Cooking Time: 4¼-5¼ hours
Ideal slow cooker size: 4- to 5-qt.

1 lb. ground beef
½ lb. ground pork
½ cup minced onions
¾ cup fine dry bread crumbs
1 Tbsp. minced parsley
1 tsp. salt
⅛ tsp. pepper
½ tsp. garlic powder
1 Tbsp. Worcestershire sauce
1 egg
½ cup milk
¼ cup oil

Gravy:
¼ cup flour
¼ tsp. salt
¼ tsp. garlic powder
⅛ tsp. pepper
1 tsp. paprika
2 cups boiling water
¾ cup sour cream

1. In a large bowl, combine meats, onions, bread crumbs, parsley, salt, pepper, garlic powder, Worcestershire sauce, egg, and milk.
2. Shape into balls the size of a walnut. Brown in batches in oil in skillet. As you finish a batch, place browned Meatballs in slow cooker. Reserve drippings in skillet.
3. Cover. Cook on High 10-15 minutes.
4. Meanwhile, make Gravy by stirring flour, salt, garlic powder, pepper, and paprika into hot drippings in skillet.
5. Stir in water and sour cream, stirring continually over medium heat until Gravy thickens. Pour over meatballs.
6. Cover. Reduce heat to Low. Cook 4-5 hours.

*Serving suggestion: Serve over **rice** or **noodles**.*

Italian Meatball Subs

Bonnie Miller
Louisville, OH

Makes 6-7 servings

Prep. Time: 45 minutes
Cooking Time: 4-6 hours
Ideal slow cooker size: 4- to 5-qt.

2 eggs, beaten
¼ cup milk
½ cup dry bread crumbs
2 Tbsp. grated Parmesan cheese
1 tsp. salt
¼ tsp. pepper
⅛ tsp. garlic powder
1 lb. ground beef
½ lb. bulk pork sausage

Sauce:
15-oz. can tomato sauce
6-oz. can tomato paste
1 small onion, chopped
½ cup chopped green bell pepper
½ cup red wine, *or* **beef broth**
⅓ cup water
2 garlic cloves, minced
1 tsp. dried oregano
1 tsp. salt
½ tsp. pepper
½ tsp. sugar

1. Make Meatballs by combining eggs and milk in a large bowl. Add bread crumbs, cheese, and seasonings. Add meats.
2. Mix well. Shape into 1" balls. Broil or sauté in batches until brown in non-stick skillet. As you finish a batch, place Meatballs in slow cooker.
3. Combine Sauce ingredients in a good-sized bowl. Pour over Meatballs. (Make sure Meatballs on the bottom of the cooker are covered with Sauce, too.)
4. Cover. Cook on Low 4-6 hours.

Serving suggestion: Serve on ***rolls****, along with* ***creamy red potatoes, salad,*** *and* ***dessert****.*

We enjoy gathering for a simple meal with friends. We roast hot dogs in the fire place and everyone brings something they have on hand. The meal usually ends up well balanced even though unplanned.

Karen Sauder, Adamstown, PA

Arlene's BBQ Meatballs

Arlene Groff
Lewistown, PA

Makes 12 servings

Prep. Time: 35 minutes
Cooking Time: 4 hours
Ideal slow cooker size: 5-qt.

2 lbs. ground beef
2 eggs
1 small onion, chopped
¼ cup milk
1½ cup crushed crackers (equal to one packaged column of saltines)
1 tsp. prepared mustard
1 tsp. salt
½ tsp. pepper
oil
1½ cups tomato juice
⅓ cup vinegar
1 Tbsp. soy sauce
1 Tbsp. Worcestershire sauce
¾ cup brown sugar
2 Tbsp. cornstarch
1 tsp. prepared mustard

1. Combine beef, eggs, onion, milk, crackers, 1 tsp. mustard, salt, and pepper in a large bowl. Form into small balls.
2. Brown in batches in oil in skillet. As you finish a batch, place Meatballs in slow cooker.
3. Combine remaining ingredients in a good-sized bowl. Pour over Meatballs, making sure that all are covered with sauce.
4. Cover. Cook on Low 2 hours. Stir well. Cook an additional 2 hours on Low.

Cocktail Meatballs

Kathy Purcell
Dublin, OH

Makes 10-12 servings

Prep. Time: 50 minutes
Cooking Time: 3-4 hours
Ideal slow cooker size: 5- to 6-qt.

3 lbs. ground beef
1 envelope dry onion soup mix
14-oz. can sweetened condensed milk

Sauce:
18-oz. bottle ketchup
½ cup brown sugar
¼ cup Worcestershire sauce

1. Combine beef, soup mix, and condensed milk in a large bowl. Form into about 3 dozen meatballs, each about 1½" around.
2. Place meatballs on baking sheet. Brown in 350° oven for 30 minutes. Remove from oven and drain. Place meatballs in slow cooker.
3. Combine Sauce ingredients in a good-sized bowl. Pour over meatballs, making sure all are covered.
4. Cover. Cook on Low 3-4 hours.

Note:
I have made these meatballs for many different parties and events, and they are always a big hit. Everyone asks for the recipe.

Easy Meatballs for a Group

Penny Blosser
Beavercreek, OH

Makes 10-12 main-dish servings

Prep. Time: 5 minutes
Cooking Time: 4 hours
Ideal slow cooker size: 5- to 6-qt.

80-100 frozen small meatballs
16-oz. jar barbecue sauce
16-oz. jar apricot jam

1. Fill slow cooker with meatballs.
2. Combine sauce and jam in a bowl. Pour over meatballs, making sure that all are covered with sauce.
3. Cover. Cook on Low 4 hours, stirring occasionally if you're home and able to do so.

Serving suggestion: This works well as an appetizer (served with picks), or as a main dish over ***rice****.*

Sweet 'n' Tangy Meatballs

Donna Lantgen
Rapid City, SD

Makes 8 servings

Prep. Time: 45 minutes
Cooking Time: 5 hours
Ideal slow cooker size: 4-qt.

1½ lbs. ground beef
¼ cup plain dry bread crumbs
3 Tbsp. prepared mustard
1 tsp. Italian seasoning
¾ cup water
¼ cup ketchup
2 Tbsp. honey
1 Tbsp. red-hot cayenne pepper sauce
¾-oz. pkg. brown gravy mix

1. Combine ground beef, bread crumbs, mustard, and Italian seasoning in a large bowl. Shape into 1" balls.
2. Bake or microwave until browned. Drain. Place Meatballs in slow cooker.
3. Cover. Cook on Low 3 hours.
4. Combine remaining ingredients in saucepan. Cook for 5 minutes. Pour over meatballs, making sure that all are covered.
5. Cover cooker. Cook 2 more hours on Low.

Variation:
For a fuller flavor, use orange juice instead of water in sauce.

Meatballs and Spaghetti Sauce

Carol Sommers
Millersburg, OH

Makes 6-8 servings

Prep. Time: 35 minutes
Cooking Time: 6-8 hours
Ideal slow cooker size: 4-qt.

Meatballs:

1½ lbs. ground beef
2 eggs
1 cup bread crumbs
oil

Sauce:

28-oz. can tomato purée
6-oz. can tomato paste
10¾-oz. can tomato soup
¼-½ cup grated Romano, *or* **Parmesan, cheese**
1 tsp. oil
1 garlic clove, minced
sliced mushrooms, either canned, *or* **fresh,** *optional*

1. Combine ground beef, eggs, and bread crumbs in a large bowl. Form into 16 Meatballs.
2. Brown in batches in oil in skillet.
3. Meanwhile, combine Sauce ingredients in slow cooker.
4. Add Meatballs to slow cooker as you finish browning a batch. Stir gently into Sauce.
5. Cover. Cook on Low 6-8 hours.
6. Add mushrooms 1-2 hours before sauce is finished.

Serving suggestion: Serve over cooked ***spaghetti.***

Snappy Meatballs

Clara Newswanger
Gordonville, PA

Makes 6-8 main-dish servings, or 25 appetizer servings

Prep. Time: 35 minutes
Cooking Time: 4 hours
Ideal slow cooker size: 4-qt.

Meatballs:

2 lbs. ground beef
½ cup chopped onions
1 cup bread crumbs
2 eggs
1 tsp. salt
oil

Sauce:

3½ cups tomato juice
1 cup brown sugar
¼ cup vinegar
1 tsp. grated onion
12 gingersnap cookies, crushed

1. Combine Meatball ingredients in a large bowl. Shape into balls.
2. Brown in batches in skillet in oil. As you finish a batch, drain Meatballs and place in slow cooker.
3. Combine Sauce ingredients in large bowl. Pour over meatballs. Mix gently.
4. Cover. Cook on Low 4 hours.

Note:

Our son married a woman from the West Coast. He brought his new bride "home" on their honeymoon. We held an informal reception for friends who could not attend their wedding. Served with a light lunch, this recipe brought raves! Now we think of our children 3,000 miles away whenever we make these Meatballs.

Meatballs and Peppers

Frances L. Kruba
Dundalk, MD

Makes 6-8 servings

Prep. Time: 10-15 minutes
Cooking Time: 4-6 hours
Ideal slow cooker size: 4- to 5-qt.

2 28-oz. cans diced tomatoes with basil, garlic, and oregano, undrained
6-oz. can tomato paste
1½ lbs. (about 48) frozen meatballs
14-oz. pkg. frozen pepper strips

1. Combine tomatoes, tomato paste, meatballs, and pepper strips in slow cooker.
2. Cover. Cook on Low 4-6 hours.

Sweet and Sour Meatballs

Alice Miller
Stuarts Draft, VA

Makes 4 servings

Prep. Time: 35 minutes
Cooking Time: 3-4 hours
Ideal slow cooker size: 4-qt.

Meatballs:

1 lb. ground beef
½ cup dry bread crumbs
¼ cup milk
1 tsp. salt
1 egg, beaten
2 Tbsp. finely chopped onions
½ tsp. Worcestershire sauce
oil

Sauce:

½ cup packed brown sugar
2 Tbsp. cornstarch
13¼-oz. can pineapple chunks, undrained
⅓ cup vinegar
1 Tbsp. soy sauce
1 green bell pepper, chopped

1. Combine Meatball ingredients in a large bowl. Shape into 1½" balls.
2. Brown in batches in oil in skillet. As you finish a batch, drain well and place in slow cooker.
3. Add brown sugar and cornstarch to drippings in skillet. Stir in remaining Sauce ingredients.
4. Heat to boiling, stirring constantly. Pour over meatballs. Make sure all are covered with Sauce.
5. Cover cooker. Cook on Low 3-4 hours.

Variation:

If you like pineapples, use a 20-oz. can of chunks, instead of a 13¼-oz. can.

Asian Meatballs

Evelyn L. Ward
Greeley, CO

Makes 6 servings

Prep. Time: 40 minutes
Cooking Time: 3 hours
Ideal slow cooker size: 3-qt.

1 lb. ground beef
1 egg
5 Tbsp. cornstarch, *divided*
½ tsp. salt
2 Tbsp. minced onions
2 cups pineapple juice
2 Tbsp. soy sauce
½ cup wine vinegar
¾ cup water
½ cup sugar
1 green bell pepper, cut in strips
1 can water chestnuts, drained

1. Combine beef, egg, 1 Tbsp. cornstarch, salt, and onions in bowl. Mix well.
2. Shape into 1" Meatballs. Place on baking sheet. Brown on all sides under broiler.
3. Mix remaining cornstarch with pineapple juice in saucepan. When smooth, mix in soy sauce, vinegar, water, and sugar. Bring to boil. Simmer, stirring until thickened.
4. Combine Meatballs and Sauce in slow cooker.
5. Cover. Cook on Low 2 hours.
6. Stir in green peppers and water chestnuts.
7. Cover. Cook 1 hour on Low.

Serving suggestion: Serve over ***chow mein noodles*** *and garnish with* ***pineapple slices****.*

Applesauce Meatballs

Mary E. Wheatley
Mashpee, MA

Makes 6 servings

Prep. Time: 40 minutes
Cooking Time: 4-6 hours
Ideal slow cooker size: 3-qt.

¾ lb. ground beef
¼ lb. ground pork
1 egg
¾ cup soft bread crumbs
½ cup unsweetened applesauce
¾ tsp. salt
¼ tsp. pepper
oil
¼ cup ketchup
¼ cup water

1. Combine beef, pork, egg, bread crumbs, applesauce, salt, and pepper in bowl. Form into 1½" balls.
2. Brown in oil in batches in skillet. Transfer meat

to slow cooker as a batch browns, reserving drippings.

3. Combine ketchup and water in skillet. Stir up browned drippings and mix together well. Spoon over meatballs, making sure that all are covered.

4. Cover. Cook on Low 4-6 hours.

Serving suggestion: Serve with ***steamed rice*** *and* ***green salad.***

Holiday Meatballs

Jean Robinson
Cinnaminson, NJ

Makes 20 servings

Prep. Time: 10 minutes
Cooking Time: 3½-6½ hours
Ideal slow cooker size: 5-qt.

2 15-oz. bottles ketchup (spicy, if you can find it)
2 cups blackberry wine
2 12-oz. jars apple jelly
2 lbs. frozen, precooked meatballs, *or* **your own favorite meatballs, cooked**

1. Heat ketchup, wine, and jelly in slow cooker on High.

2. When hot, stir in frozen meatballs.

3. Cover. Cook on High 4-6 hours. (If the meatballs are not frozen, cook on High 3-4 hours.)

Variations:

1. For those who like it hotter and spicier, put a bottle of hot sauce on the table to add to their individual servings.

2. If you prefer a less wine-y flavor, use 1 cup water and only 1 cup wine.

Meatballs with Bounce

Arlene Leaman Kliewer
Lakewood, CO

Makes 8-10 servings, or 60 very small meatballs

Prep. Time: 1 hour
Ideal slow cooker size: 4-qt.

Meatballs:

2 lbs. ground beef
2 eggs, slightly beaten
1 cup bread crumbs
2 tsp. salt
¼ tsp. pepper

Sauce:

12-oz. bottle chili sauce
10-oz. jar grape jelly
½ cup ketchup
1 tsp. Worcestershire sauce

1. Combine ground beef, eggs, bread crumbs, salt, and pepper in bowl. Form into 60 small balls. Place on baking sheet.

2. Bake at 400° for 15-17 minutes. Place in slow cooker.

3. Combine Sauce ingredients in saucepan. Heat and stir until jelly melts. Pour over Meatballs.

4. Heat on Low until ready to serve.

Note:

We often make this recipe for our family's Christmas evening snack.

Variations:

1. Liven up the Meatballs by adding ⅔ cup chopped onions, 2 Tbsp. snipped fresh parsley, and 1 tsp. Worcestershire sauce in Step 1.

Joan Rosenberger
Stephens City, VA

2. Add juice of half a lemon to the Sauce in Step 3.

Linda Sluiter
Schererville, IN

3. Use ½ cup crushed cornflakes in place of 1 cup bread crumbs in Meatball mixture.

Add 1 Tbsp. bottled lemon juice to Sauce in Step 3.

Alice Miller
Stuarts Draft, VA

Meatball-Barley Casserole

Marjorie Y. Guengerich
Harrisonburg, VA

Makes 6 servings

Prep. Time: 40 minutes
Cooking Time: 4-8 hours
Ideal slow cooker size: 4-qt.

⅔ cup pearl barley
1 lb. ground beef
½ cup soft bread crumbs
1 small onion, chopped
¼ cup milk
¼ tsp. pepper
1 tsp. salt
oil
½ cup thinly sliced celery
½ cup finely chopped sweet peppers
10¾-oz. can cream of celery soup
⅓ cup water
paprika

1. Cook barley as directed on package. Set aside.
2. Combine beef, bread crumbs, onion, milk, pepper, and salt in a bowl. Shape into 20 balls.
3. Brown in batches on all sides in oil in skillet. Drain off drippings as you finish a batch, and place Meatballs in slow cooker.
4. Stir in barley, celery, and peppers.
5. Combine soup and water in a bowl. Pour into slow cooker. Mix all together gently.
6. Sprinkle with paprika.
7. Cover. Cook on Low 6-8 hours or on High 4 hours.

Sloppy Beef Sandwiches

Colleen Konetzni
Rio Rancho, NM

Makes 6 servings

Prep. Time: 30 minutes
Cooking Time: 3-4 hours
Ideal slow cooker size: 3- to 4-qt.

1½ lbs. lean ground beef
1 onion, chopped
½ cup water
1 small can sliced black olives, drained
1 jar salsa

1. Cook beef and onion in skillet with ½ cup water until meat is no longer pink. Stir with wooden spoon to break up clumps. Drain off drippings.
2. Place beef mixture into slow cooker. Add olives and salsa. Mix well.
3. Cover. Cook on Low 3-4 hours.

*Serving suggestion: Divide sandwich meat among **buns** and sprinkle with 2 cups shredded **cheese** and ½ cup chopped **lettuce**.*

Barbecue Sauce and Hamburgers

Dolores Kratz
Souderton, PA

Makes 6 servings

Prep. Time: 25 minutes
Cooking Time: 2-3 hours
Ideal slow cooker size: 4-qt.

14¾-oz. can beef gravy
½ cup ketchup
½ cup chili sauce
1 Tbsp. Worcestershire sauce
1 Tbsp. prepared mustard
6 grilled hamburger patties

1. Combine all ingredients except hamburger patties in slow cooker.
2. Add hamburger patties.
3. Cover. Cook on Low 2-3 hours.

*Serving suggestion: Serve in **buns**, each topped with a slice of **cheese** if you like.*

Tips:

1. Freeze leftover sauce for future use.
2. This is both a practical and a tasty recipe for serving a crowd (picnics, potlucks, etc.). You can grill the patties early in the day, rather than at the last minute when your guests are arriving.

No-More-Bottled Barbecue Sauce

Lauren Eberhard
Seneca, IL

Makes 2-2½ cups sauce

Prep. Time: 10 minutes
Cooking Time: 3 hours
Ideal slow cooker size: 1½-qt.

1 cup finely chopped onions
¼ cup oil
6-oz. can tomato paste
½ cup water
¼ cup brown sugar
¼ cup lemon juice (freshly squeezed juice is best)
3 Tbsp. Worcestershire sauce
2 Tbsp. prepared mustard
2 tsp. salt
¼ tsp. pepper

1. Combine all ingredients in slow cooker.
2. Cover. Cook on Low 3 hours.
3. Use on hamburgers, sausage, pork chops, ribs, steaks, chicken, turkey, or fish.

Note:
Sauce will keep in refrigerator for up to 2 weeks.

Pizzaburgers

Deborah Swartz
Grottoes, VA

Makes 4-6 servings

Prep. Time: 20 minutes
Cooking Time: 1-2 hours
Ideal slow cooker size: 4-qt.

1 lb. ground beef
½ cup chopped onions
¼ tsp. salt
⅛ tsp. pepper
8 oz. pizza sauce
10¾-oz. can cream of mushroom soup
2 cups shredded cheddar cheese

1. Brown ground beef and onion in skillet. Drain off drippings. Place in slow cooker.
2. Stir in remaining ingredients. Mix well.
3. Cover. Cook on Low 1-2 hours.

Serving suggestion: Serve on ***hamburger buns****.*

Yum-Yums

Evelyn L. Ward
Greeley, CO

Makes 12 servings

Prep. Time: 35 minutes
Cooking Time: 4-6 hours
Ideal slow cooker size: 4-qt.

3 lbs. ground beef
2 onions, chopped
10¾-oz. can cream of chicken soup
1½ cups tomato juice
1 tsp. prepared mustard
1 tsp. Worcestershire sauce
1 tsp. salt
¼ tsp. pepper

1. Brown beef and onions in skillet. Drain off drippings. Place in slow cooker.
2. Stir in remaining ingredients.
3. Cover. Cook on Low 4-6 hours.

Serving suggestion: Serve on ***hamburger buns****.*

Note:
This is a great recipe for serving a crowd. A club I am a part of serves it when we do fund-raisers. Our menu is Yum-Yums, marinated bean salad, and strawberry short cake. We make the food in our homes and carry it to the meeting site.

Don't apologize if your house is not spotless. Your guests will feel more relaxed when they invite you.
Karen Sauder, Adamstown, PA

Dianna's Barbecue

Lauren Eberhard
Seneca, IL

Makes 12 servings

Prep. Time: 30 minutes
Cooking Time: 1-4 hours
Ideal slow cooker size: 5-qt.

4 lbs. ground beef
oil
24-oz. bottle ketchup
¼ cup prepared mustard
2 Tbsp. vinegar
¼ cup sugar
¾ cup water
1 tsp. pepper
1 Tbsp. paprika
1 cup chopped celery
1 cup chopped onion

1. Brown ground beef in large skillet, in oil if needed. Drain off drippings. Place beef in slow cooker.
2. Stir in all other ingredients.
3. Cover. Cook on High 1-2 hours or on Low 4 hours.

Serving suggestion: Serve in 12 ***sandwich rolls****.*

Chili Spaghetti

Clara Newswanger
Gordonville, PA

Makes 8-10 servings

Prep. Time: 25 minutes
Cooking Time: 2-3 hours
Ideal slow cooker size: 4-qt.

1½ lbs. ground beef
12-oz. dry spaghetti
½ cup diced onions
2 cups tomato juice
2 tsp. chili powder
1 tsp. salt
¾ cup grated mild cheese

1. Brown beef in skillet, stirring frequently to break up clumps. When no longer pink, place in slow cooker.
2. Meanwhile, cook spaghetti until just softened in large stockpot. Drain and add to slow cooker.
3. Add all remaining ingredients to slow cooker. Mix together gently and well.
4. Cover. Cook on Low 2-3 hours. Check mixture about halfway through the cooking time. If it's becoming dry, stir in an additional cup of tomato juice.

Variations:

1. Add 8-oz. can sliced mushrooms to Step 3.
2. Use 2 Tbsp. chili powder instead of 2 tsp. chili powder for added flavor.

Dawn's Spaghetti and Meat Sauce

Dawn Day
Westminster, CA

Makes 6-8 servings

Prep. Time: 30 minutes
Cooking Time: 4 hours
Ideal slow cooker size: 4-qt.

1 lb. ground beef
1 Tbsp. oil, if needed
½ lb. fresh mushrooms, sliced
1 medium onion, chopped
3 garlic cloves, minced
½ tsp. dried oregano
½ tsp. salt
¼ cup grated Parmesan, *or* **Romano, cheese**
6-oz. can tomato paste
2 15-oz. cans tomato sauce
15-oz. can chopped, *or* **crushed, tomatoes**

1. Brown ground beef in skillet, in oil if needed. Stir frequently, breaking up clumps. Continue cooking until meat is no longer pink. Reserve drippings and transfer meat to slow cooker.
2. Sauté mushrooms, onion, and garlic in drippings until onions are transparent. Add to slow cooker.
3. Mix remaining ingredients into cooker.
4. Cover. Cook on Low 4 hours.

Serving suggestion: Serve with ***pasta*** *and* ***garlic bread****.*

Tip:

This recipe freezes well.

Quick and Easy Spaghetti

Beverly Getz
Warriors Mark, PA

Makes 8 servings

Prep. Time: 30 minutes
Cooking Time: 3-4 hours
Ideal slow cooker size: 4-qt.

1½ lbs. ground beef
2 onions, chopped
26-oz. jar spaghetti sauce with mushrooms
10¾-oz. can tomato soup
1, *or* **2, 14½-oz. cans stewed tomatoes, depending on the consistency you prefer**
8-oz. can mushrooms, undrained
½ tsp. garlic powder
½ tsp. garlic salt
½ tsp. minced dried garlic
½ tsp. onion salt
½ tsp. Italian seasoning

1. Brown beef and onions in skillet, stirring frequently to break up clumps. When meat is no longer pink, drain off drippings. Place meat and onions into slow cooker.
2. Stir in all remaining ingredients.
3. Cover. Cook on Low 3-4 hours.

Serving suggestion: Serve over 1 lb. ***cooked spaghetti.***

Spaghetti Sauce for a Crowd

Sue Pennington
Bridgewater, VA

Makes 18 cups

Prep. Time: 25 minutes
Cooking Time: 4-6 hours
Ideal slow cooker size: 6-qt.

1 lb. ground beef
1 lb. ground turkey
1 Tbsp. oil
5 15-oz. cans tomato sauce
3 6-oz. cans tomato paste
1 cup water
½ cup minced fresh, *or* **3 Tbsp. dried, parsley**
½ cup minced fresh, *or* **3 Tbsp. dried, oregano**
4 tsp. salt

1. Brown meat in oil in skillet. Stir frequently to break up clumps. When meat is no longer pink, drain off dripping. Place meat in 6-qt. slow cooker. (A 5-qt. cooker will work, but it will be brimful.)
2. Stir in remaining ingredients. Mix together thoroughly.
3. Cover. Cook on Low 4-6 hours.

Notes:

1. Add 1 medium onion, chopped, and/or 3 cloves garlic, minced, to Step 1, browning along with the meat.
2. Add 1 can crushed tomatoes, or 2 cups cut-up fresh tomatoes, to Step 2 to add a fresh-tomato taste. (This will make your cooker even fuller, so you may want to switch to two 4- or 5-qt. cookers.)
3. Make the sauce without meat if you prefer.
4. Use as a pizza sauce, especially if you make it meatless.
5. Sauce can be refrigerated for a week, or frozen up to 3 months.

Have a balance of meat and no-meat appetizers/dishes so you're not worried about vegetarian preferences. Veggie and fruit options allow dieters to enjoy the party as well.
Susan Tjon, Austin, TX

Beef and Sausage Spaghetti Sauce

Sherri Grindle
Goshen, IN

Makes 10-12 servings

Prep. Time: 30 minutes
Cooking Time: 6-8 hours
Ideal slow cooker size: 5-qt.

1 lb. ground beef
1 lb. Italian sausage, bulk, *or* **cut in thin slices**
1 large onion, chopped
3 Tbsp. oil, if needed
5 lbs., *or* **3 28-oz. cans, tomato purée**
6 cloves garlic, minced
2 Tbsp. parsley
1 Tbsp. salt
¼ rounded tsp. pepper
3 bay leaves
1 Tbsp. dried oregano
crushed red pepper, *optional*

1. Brown meat and onion in skillet in oil, unless they produce enough of their own drippings. Stir frequently to break up clumps. When meat is no longer pink, drain off drippings and place meat in slow cooker.
2. Combine all remaining ingredients in slow cooker with meat and onions.
3. Cover. Cook on Low 6-8 hours.

Serving suggestion: Serve over your favorite ***pasta****.*

Variation:
Add 1 box uncooked spaghetti 1 hour before serving. Cook on High for last hour.

Spaghetti Sauce with a Kick

Andrea O'Neil
Fairfield, CT

Makes 4-6 servings

Prep. Time: 25 minutes
Cooking Time: 4-6 hours
Ideal slow cooker size: 4-qt.

1 lb. ground beef
1 onion, chopped
2 28-oz. cans crushed tomatoes
16-oz. can tomato sauce
1-lb. Italian sausage, cut in chunks
3 cloves garlic, crushed
1 Tbsp. Italian seasoning
2 tsp. dried basil
red pepper flakes to taste

1. Brown beef and onions in skillet. Stir frequently to break up clumps. When meat is no longer pink, drain off drippings and place in slow cooker.
2. Stir remaining ingredients into slow cooker.
3. Cover. Cook on Low 4-6 hours.

Serving suggestion: Serve over your favorite ***pasta****.*

Variation:
Add 1-2 tsp. salt and 1-2 Tbsp. brown sugar or honey to Step 2, if you wish.

Slow Cooker Lasagna

Crystal Brunk
Singers Glen, VA

Makes 6-8 servings

Prep. Time: 20 minutes
Cooking Time: 4-8 hours
Ideal slow cooker size: 4-qt.

1 lb. ground beef
oil
4-5 cups spaghetti sauce, depending upon how firm *or* **how juicy you want the finished lasagna**
1 egg
24-oz. container cottage cheese
8-10 uncooked lasagna noodles, *divided*
2-3 cups mozzarella cheese, *divided*

1. Brown ground beef in skillet, in oil if needed. Stir frequently to break up clumps. When meat is no longer pink, drain off drippings.
2. Stir spaghetti sauce into beef in skillet.
3. Combine egg and cottage cheese in a bowl.
4. Layer half of ground beef mixture into slow cooker.
5. Layer in half the dry noodles (break to fit if you need to), half the cottage cheese mixture, and half the mozzarella cheese in slow cooker. Repeat layers.
6. Cover. Cook on High 4-5 hours or on Low 6-8 hours.

Variations:

1. Use ricotta instead of cottage cheese.
2. Add 2 Tbsp. chopped fresh parsley to Step 3.
3. Add 2 Tbsp. grated Parmesan cheese to Step 3, and sprinkle 2 Tbsp. grated Parmesan cheese over top before cooking in Step 5.

Elaine Rineer
Lancaster, PA

Now That's Lasagna

Shirley Unternahrer
Wayland, IA

Makes 10 servings

Prep. Time: 20 minutes
Cooking Time: 4 hours
Ideal slow cooker size: 6-qt.

1 lb. sausage, *or* **ground beef (if ground beef, add 1 tsp. dried basil, ½ tsp. salt, and ¼ tsp. pepper)**
1 small onion, chopped
1 small bell pepper, chopped
1 qt. tomato juice, *divided*
15 lasagna noodles, uncooked, *divided*
12 oz. cottage cheese, *divided*
3 cups grated mozzarella cheese
28-oz. jar spaghetti sauce of your choice, *divided*
6 oz. sliced pepperoni
3 cups grated mozzarella cheese

1. Brown sausage or hamburger in skillet. Drain off half the drippings.
2. Add chopped onions and peppers to skillet. Sauté 3 minutes in drippings with meat.
3. Pour 1 cup tomato juice into slow cooker as first layer.
4. Add a layer of 5 uncooked lasagna noodles. Break to fit inside curved edges of slow cooker.
5. Spread with half of cottage cheese as next layer.
6. Spoon half of meat/veggie mix over cottage cheese.
7. Sprinkle with 1 cup mozzarella cheese
8. Spoon half of spaghetti sauce over grated cheese.
9. Add another layer of 5 lasagna noodles.
10. Add remaining cottage cheese, followed by a layer of remaining meat/veggie mix.
11. Add remaining 5 noodles.
12. Top with pepperoni slices, remaining spaghetti sauce, and half of remaining mozzarella cheese.
13. Pour rest of tomato juice slowly around edge of cooker and its ingredients.
14. Cover. Cook on High 3½ hours.
15. Remove lid and top with remaining mozzarella cheese. Cook another 15 minutes.
16. Allow Lasagna to rest 15-20 minutes before serving.

Easy Ravioli

Karen Sauder
Adamstown, PA

Makes 4 servings

Prep. Time: 5 minutes
Cooking Time: 4 hours
Ideal slow cooker size: 3- to 4-qt.

25-oz. bag frozen beef ravioli
45-oz. jar spaghetti sauce of your choice
1 cup Monterey Jack, *or* **mozzarella, cheese, grated**

1. Place all of ravioli into slow cooker.
2. Pour in spaghetti sauce. Stir to distribute sauce evenly.
3. Sprinkle with cheese.
4. Cover. Cook on Low 4 hours.

Note:

This is my favorite recipe for a potluck or fellowship meal, or supper on a busy day.

Slow Cooker Almost Lasagna

Jeanette Oberholtzer
Manheim, PA

Makes 8-10 servings

Prep. Time: 40 minutes
Cooking Time: 4-6 hours
Ideal slow cooker size: 6-qt.

1 box rotini, *or* **ziti, cooked**
2 Tbsp. olive oil
2 28-oz. jars pasta sauce with tomato chunks
2 cups tomato juice
½ lb. ground beef
½ lb. bulk sausage, crumbled, *or* **links cut into ¼" slices**
2 cups grated Parmesan cheese, *divided*
½ cup Italian bread crumbs
3 eggs, *divided*
2 cups mozzarella cheese, *divided*
2 cups ricotta cheese
1½ tsp. parsley flakes
¾ tsp. salt
¼ tsp. pepper

1. In large bowl, toss pasta with olive oil. Add pasta sauce and tomato juice and mix well. Set aside.
2. Brown beef and sausage together in skillet. Stir frequently to break up clumps. When meat is no longer pink, drain off drippings. Remove skillet from heat; keep meat in skillet.
3. Stir 1 cup Parmesan cheese, bread crumbs, 1 egg, and 1 cup mozzarella cheese into meat in skillet. Set aside.
4. In separate bowl, beat together ricotta cheese, 2 eggs, 1 cup Parmesan cheese, parsley, salt, and pepper. Set aside.
5. Pour half of pasta-sauce mixture into slow cooker.
6. Spread entire ricotta mixture over pasta. Top with entire meat-cheese mixture. Cover with remaining pasta-sauce mixture.
7. Sprinkle with remaining 1 cup mozzarella cheese.
8. Cover. Cook on Low 4-6 hours.

Meat Loaf Burgers

Lafaye M. Musser
Denver, PA

Makes 6 servings

Prep. Time: 25 minutes
Cooking Time: 7-9 hours
Ideal slow cooker size: 4-qt.

1 large onion, sliced
1 rib celery, chopped
2 lbs. ground beef
1 tsp. salt
1¼ tsp. pepper
2 cups tomato juice
4 garlic cloves, minced
1 Tbsp. ketchup
1 tsp. Italian seasoning
½ tsp. salt

1. Place onion and celery in slow cooker.
2. Combine beef, salt, and pepper. Shape into 6 patties. Arrange in slow cooker.
3. In a good-sized mixing bowl, combine tomato juice, garlic, ketchup, Italian seasoning, and salt. Pour over patties.
4. Cover. Cook on Low 7-9 hours.

Serving suggestion: This makes enough to serve on 6 ***hamburger buns****.*

Barbecued Hamburgers

Martha Hershey
Ronks, PA

Makes 4 serving

Prep. Time: 20 minutes
Cooking Time: 2-6 hours
Ideal slow cooker size: 3-qt.

1 lb. ground beef
¼ cup chopped onions
3 Tbsp. ketchup
1 tsp. salt
1 egg, beaten
¼ cup seasoned bread crumbs
oil
18-oz. bottle of your favorite barbecue sauce

1. Combine beef, onions, ketchup, salt, egg, and bread crumbs in a good-sized bowl. Form into 4 patties.
2. Brown both sides lightly in oil in skillet. Arrange browned burgers in slow cooker.
3. Cover with barbecue sauce.

4. Cover. Bake on High 2-3 hours or on Low 5-6 hours.

Note:
We first had Barbecued Hamburgers at a 4-H picnic, and they have been a family favorite ever since.

Tip:
Mix the hamburger patties, brown them, and freeze them in advance, and you'll have little to do at the last minute.

Hamburger-Potato Slow Cooker Dinner

Lafaye M. Musser
Denver, PA

Makes 6-8 servings

Prep. Time: 30 minutes
Cooking Time: 3-8 hours
Ideal slow cooker size: 4-qt.

1 lb. ground beef
1 cup water
½ tsp. cream of tartar
6 medium potatoes, thinly sliced
1 onion, chopped
¼ cup flour
½ tsp. salt
¼ tsp. pepper
1 cup grated cheddar cheese, *divided*
¼ stick (2 Tbsp.) butter
10¾-oz. can cream of mushroom soup

1. Brown ground beef in skillet, using oil if necessary. Drain off drippings. Set aside.
2. In separate bowl, combine water and cream of tartar. Toss potatoes in water. Drain.
3. In another bowl, mix together onion, flour, salt, pepper, and half of cheese.
4. Place browned beef in bottom of cooker. Top with sliced potatoes. Add onion-cheese mixture.
5. Dot top with butter.
6. Pour soup over all.
7. Cover. Cook on Low 6-8 hours or on High 3-4 hours.
8. Sprinkle remaining cheese over top, 30 minutes before serving.

Variation:
Spread 2 4¼-oz. cans chopped green chilies, undrained, over potatoes in Step 4.

Colleen Konetzni
Rio Rancho, NM

1-2-3-4 Casserole

Betty K. Drescher
Quakertown, PA

Makes 8 servings

Prep. Time: 35 minutes
Cooking Time: 7-9 hours
Ideal slow cooker size: 4-qt.

1 lb. ground beef
2 onions, sliced
3 carrots, thinly sliced
½ tsp. salt
⅛ tsp. pepper
½ tsp. cream of tartar
1 cup cold water
4 potatoes, thinly sliced
10¾-oz. can cream of mushroom soup
¼ cup milk
½ tsp. salt
⅛ tsp. pepper

1. Layer in greased slow cooker in this order: ground beef, onions, carrots, ½ tsp. salt, and ⅛ tsp. pepper.
2. Dissolve cream of tartar in water in large bowl. Toss sliced potatoes with water. Drain off water.
3. Combine soup and milk in bowl with potatoes. Stir in remaining salt and pepper.
4. Arrange potatoes in slow cooker over top vegetables.
5. Cover. Cook on Low 7-9 hours, or until meat is cooked through and vegetables are as tender as you like them.

Variations:
1. Substitute sour cream for the milk.
2. Top potatoes with ½ cup shredded cheese.

Hamburger Potato Casserole

Sue Pennington
Bridgewater, VA

Makes 6-10 servings

Prep. Time: 30 minutes
Cooking Time: 8-10 hours
Ideal slow cooker size: 4-qt.

1 lb. ground beef, *divided*
1 Tbsp. oil
6-8 potatoes, peeled and sliced, *divided*
4-6 carrots, sliced, *divided*
2 medium onions, sliced, *divided*
1 cup grated cheddar cheese, *divided*
1 tsp. salt , *divided*
¼ tsp. pepper, *divided*
10-oz. can cream of chicken soup
1 cup peas

1. Brown ground beef in oil in skillet. Drain off drippings.
2. Layer half of beef, potatoes, carrots, onions, and cheese in cooker. Sprinkle with half of salt and pepper.
3. Repeat layers.
4. Pour cream of chicken soup over top.
5. Cover. Cook on Low 8-10 hours.
6. Fifteen minutes before end of cooking time, stir in 1 cup peas.

Note:

My husband came up with this recipe. Our family loves it and often requests it when I ask them what they want to eat.

Hamburger Casserole

Kelly Evenson
Pittsboro, NC

Makes 6-8 servings

Prep. Time: 30 minutes
Cooking Time: 8 hours
Ideal slow cooker size: 4-qt.

2 large potatoes, sliced
2-3 medium carrots, sliced
3 medium onions, sliced
2 celery ribs, sliced
garlic salt to taste
pepper to taste
salt to taste
1 lb. ground beef
oil
10¾-oz. can tomato soup
1 soup can of water
1 cup frozen peas, thawed and drained

1. Layer potatoes, carrots, onions, and celery in order given into slow cooker.
2. Sprinkle each layer with garlic salt, pepper, and salt.
3. Brown ground beef in oil in skillet. Stir frequently to break up clumps. When meat is no longer pink, drain off drippings.
4. Place meat on top of celery.
5. Combine soup and water in bowl. Pour over all.
6. Cover. Cook on Low 8 hours, or until vegetables are as tender as you like them.
7. Fifteen minutes before end of cooking time, stir in peas.

Serving suggestion: Serve this nearly complete meal with ***applesauce.***

Wholesome Hamburger Dinner

Reba Rhodes
Bridgewater, VA

Makes 6-8 servings

Prep. Time: 25 minutes
Cooking Time: 3-6 hours
Ideal slow cooker size: 4-qt.

1 lb. ground beef
1 cup sliced carrots
1 cup coarsely chopped celery
1 medium onion, sliced
1 cup green beans
1 tsp. salt
¼ tsp. pepper
2 tsp. sugar
2-3 cups tomato juice
½ lb. grated cheese

1. Brown ground beef in skillet. Stir frequently to break up clumps. Continue browning until pink no longer appears.
2. Drain off drippings. Place meat in bottom of slow cooker.
3. Layer remaining ingredients, except cheese, over ground beef in order given.
4. Cover. Cook on High 3-4 hours or on Low 5-6 hours, or until vegetables are done to your liking.
5. Thirty minutes before end of cooking time, layer cheese on top. Cover and resume cooking.

Serving suggestion: Serve with ***cornbread.***

Tip:

You can double all vegetable amounts, if you wish.

If you do so, increase cooking time to 5-6 hours on High or 9-11 hours on Low, or until vegetables are as tender as you like.

Stuffed Baked Topping

Fannie Miller
Hutchinson, KS

Makes 12 servings

Prep. Time: 35 minutes
Cooking Time: 1 hour
Ideal slow cooker size: 6- to 7-qt.

3 lbs. ground beef
1 cup chopped green bell peppers
½ cup chopped onions
¾ stick (6 Tbsp.) butter
¼ cup flour
3 cups milk
½ cup pimento, *or* **chopped sweet red peppers**
¾ lb. cheddar cheese, grated
¾ lb. your favorite mild cheese, grated
½ tsp. hot pepper sauce
¼ tsp. dry mustard
salt to taste

1. Brown ground beef, green peppers, and onions in butter in large skillet. Transfer mixture to slow cooker, reserving drippings.
2. Stir flour into drippings in skillet. Slowly add milk. Stir continually over medium heat until smooth and thickened.
3. Stir pimento, cheeses, and seasonings into white sauce in skillet. Continue stirring until cheese melts and sauce is smooth.
4. Pour sauce over ingredients in slow cooker.
5. Cover. Heat on Low for 1 hour.

Serving suggestion: Serve over ***baked potatoes****, each one split open on an individual dinner plate.*

Ground Beef Stew

Ruth Ann Hoover
New Holland, PA
Kim Stoltzfus
New Holland, PA

Makes 8-10 servings

Prep. Time: 25 minutes
Cooking Time: 4½-5 hours
Ideal slow cooker size: 4-qt.

1 lb. ground beef
oil
6 medium potatoes, peeled if you wish, and cubed
16-oz. pkg. baby carrots
3 cups water
3 Tbsp. dry onion soup mix
1 garlic clove, minced
1½ tsp. Italian seasoning
1-1½ tsp. salt
½ tsp. garlic powder
¼ tsp. pepper
10¾-oz. can tomato soup
6-oz. can Italian tomato paste

1. Brown beef in skillet, in oil if needed. Stir frequently, breaking up clumps. Continue cooking until all pink disappears.
2. Remove beef from drippings and place in slow cooker.
3. Combine all remaining ingredients in cooker, except tomato soup and tomato paste.
4. Cover. Cook on High 3½-4 hours, or until carrots are nearly tender.
5. Stir in soup and tomato paste.
6. Cover. Cook on High 1 hour more.

Variation:
If you'd like to add color and more vegetables to the stew, stir in 1½ cups frozen peas in Step 5.

Prompt

Mary Martins
Fairbank, IA

Makes 6-8 servings

Prep. Time: 20 minutes
Cooking Time: 1½-2 hours
Ideal slow cooker size: 4-qt.

4-6 medium-sized potatoes, sliced
½-¾ cup uncooked minute rice
1 onion, sliced
1½ lbs. ground beef
1 diced green bell pepper, *optional*
1 qt. tomatoes with juice
salt to taste
pepper to taste

1. Layer ingredients in order given in greased slow cooker. Salt and pepper each layer to taste.
2. Cover. Cook on High 1½-2 hours.

Variation:
You may substitute 1 qt. V-8 juice for the quart of tomatoes with juice.

Cheeseburger Casserole

Erma Kauffman
Cochranville, PA

Makes 6 servings

Prep. Time: 20 minutes
Cooking Time: 3 hours
Ideal slow cooker size: 3-qt.

1 lb. ground beef
1 small onion, chopped
1 tsp. salt
dash of pepper
½ cup bread crumbs
1 egg
tomato juice to moisten
4½ cups mashed potatoes (leftover mashed potatoes work well)
9 slices your favorite cheese

1. Combine beef, onions, salt, pepper, bread crumbs, egg, and tomato juice in a large bowl.
2. Place one-third of mixture in slow cooker.
3. Spread with one-third of mashed potatoes and 3 slices cheese.
4. Repeat layering 2 times.
5. Cover. Cook on Low 3 hours.

Hamburger/ Green Bean Dish

Hazel L. Propst
Oxford, PA

Makes 4-5 servings

Prep. Time: 25 minutes
Cooking Time: 5-6 hours
Ideal slow cooker size: 4-qt.

1 lb. ground beef
1 onion, chopped
1 qt. green beans, *or* **2 lbs. frozen green beans,** *or* **2 15-oz. cans green beans**
10¾-oz. can tomato soup
¾ tsp. salt
¼ tsp. pepper
6-7 cups mashed potatoes
1 egg, beaten

1. Brown meat and onion in skillet. Stir frequently to break up clumps. When meat is no longer pink, drain off drippings and discard.
2. Place meat in slow cooker. Stir in beans, soup, and seasonings.
3. Combine mashed potatoes with egg in large bowl. Spread over meat-vegetable mixture in slow cooker.
4. Cover. Cook on Low 5-6 hours, or until beans are tender.

Have a recycled Christmas. All gifts can be either handmade or bought from a boutique specializing in used items. All wrappings can be either reused gift bags or homemade gift wrap, using brown paper bags or the comics papers.
Katrina Eberly, Wernersville, PA

Meal-in-One

Melanie L. Thrower
McPherson, KS

Makes 6-8 servings

Prep. Time: 25 minutes
Cooking Time: 4 hours
Ideal slow cooker size: 4- to 5-qt.

2 lbs. ground beef
1 onion, diced
1 green bell pepper, diced
1 tsp. salt
¼ tsp. pepper
1 large bag frozen hash brown potatoes, *divided*
16-oz. container sour cream, *divided*
24-oz. container cottage cheese, *divided*
1 cup Monterey Jack cheese, shredded

1. Brown ground beef, onion, and green pepper in skillet. Stir frequently to break up clumps. Continue cooking until meat is no longer pink. Drain off drippings and discard.
2. Season meat and vegetable mixture with salt and pepper.
3. In slow cooker, layer one-third of potatoes, then one-third of meat mixture, one-third of sour cream, and one-third of cottage cheese.
4. Repeat layers twice.
5. Cover. Cook on Low 4 hours, sprinkling Monterey Jack cheese over top during last hour.

Serving suggestion: Serve with ***red*** *or* ***green salsa****.*

Variation:

For a cheesier dish, prepare another cup of shredded cheese and sprinkle ½ cup over first layer of potatoes, meat, sour cream, and cottage cheese, and another ½ cup over second layer of those ingredients.

Cedric's Casserole

Kathy Purcell
Dublin, OH

Makes 4-6 servings

Prep. Time: 30 minutes
Cooking Time: 3-4 hours
Ideal slow cooker size: 3-qt.

1 medium onion, chopped
3 Tbsp. butter
1 lb. ground beef
½-¾ tsp. salt
¼ tsp. pepper
3 cups shredded cabbage, *divided*
10¾-oz. can tomato soup

1. Sauté onion in skillet in butter.
2. Add ground beef and brown. Stir frequently, breaking up clumps until pink no longer appears.
3. Season meat and onions with salt and pepper.
4. Layer half of cabbage in slow cooker, followed by half of meat mixture.
5. Repeat layers again.
6. Pour soup over top.
7. Cover. Cook on Low 3-4 hours.

Serving suggestion: Serve with ***garlic bread*** *and* ***canned fruit****.*

Note:

I grew up with this recipe and remember my mother serving it often. It makes a wonderful potluck take-a-long.

Beef and Macaroni

Esther J. Yoder
Hartville, OH

Makes 4-5 servings

Prep. Time: 20 minutes
Cooking Time: 2-2½ hours
Ideal slow cooker size: 3-qt.

1 lb. ground beef
1 small onion, chopped
half a green bell pepper, chopped
1 cup cooked macaroni
½ tsp. dried basil
½ tsp. dried thyme
1 tsp. Worcestershire sauce
1 tsp. salt
10¾-oz. can cheddar cheese soup

1. Brown beef, onions, and green pepper in skillet. Stir frequently to break up clumps. Cook until no more pink appears in meat. Drain off drippings.
2. Place meat and vegetables in slow cooker.
3. Combine all ingredients in cooker.
4. Cover. Cook on High 2-2½ hours, stirring once or twice, if you're home and able to do so.

Serving suggestion: Serve with ***broccoli*** *and* ***applesauce****.*

Plenty More in the Kitchen

Jean Robinson
Cinnaminson, NJ

Makes 12-16 servings

Prep. Time: 30 minutes
Cooking Time: 5¼ hours
Ideal slow cooker size: 6-qt.

3 lbs. ground beef
1 cup chopped onions
1 Tbsp. oil
26-oz. jar tomato sauce, *or* **spaghetti sauce**
1 tsp. salt
2 tsp. chili powder
1 tsp. pepper
2 Tbsp. dark brown sugar
16-oz. can whole-kernel corn
2 14½-oz. cans beef broth
8-oz. pkg. uncooked elbow macaroni
1 cup grated sharp cheese

1. Brown beef and onion in oil in skillet. Stir frequently, breaking up clumps. Continue cooking until meat is no longer pink. Drain off drippings.
2. Place meat in cooker, along with all other ingredients except cheese.
3. Cover. Cook on High 1 hour. Turn to Low and cook 4 more hours.
4. Sprinkle with cheese and cook 10 minutes more.

Variation:
You can change the balance of ingredients by using only 1-1½ lbs. ground beef and adding another ½-1 cup uncooked macaroni.

Note:
This is a tried and true recipe adapted from an old 1984 Pennsylvania Grange cookbook. It's an easy meal to carry outside to the picnic table or to take to a Little League game.

Cheese and Pasta in a Pot

Cathy Boshart
Lebanon, PA

Makes 8 servings

Prep. Time: 35-40 minutes
Cooking Time: 2-3 hours
Ideal slow cooker size: 5-qt.

2 lbs. ground beef
1 Tbsp. oil
2 medium onions, chopped
1 garlic clove, minced
14-oz. jar spaghetti sauce
16-oz. can stewed tomatoes
4-oz. can sliced mushrooms, undrained
8 oz. dry shell macaroni, cooked al dente, *divided*
1½ pints sour cream, *divided*
½ lb. provolone cheese, sliced
½ lb. mozzarella cheese, sliced thin, *or* **shredded**

1. Brown ground beef in oil in large skillet or Dutch oven. Stir frequently to break up clumps. Continue cooking

until all pink disappears. Drain off all but 2 Tbsp. drippings.

2. Add onions, garlic, spaghetti sauce, stewed tomatoes, and undrained mushrooms to beef and remaining drippings in skillet. Mix well.

3. Simmer 10-15 minutes in skillet, or until onions are soft.

4. Pour half of macaroni into slow cooker.

5. Cover with half tomato-meat sauce.

6. Spread half sour cream over sauce.

7. Top with provolone cheese.

8. Repeat macaroni and tomato-meat sauce layers.

9. Top with mozzarella cheese.

10. Cover. Cook on High 2 hours or on Low 3 hours.

Hamburger Rice Casserole

Shari Mast
Harrisonburg, VA

Makes 6-8 servings

Prep. Time: 25 minutes
Cooking Time: 4 hours
Ideal slow cooker size: 4-qt.

½ lb. ground beef
1 onion, chopped
1 cup diced celery
1 tsp. dried basil
1 tsp. dried oregano
10¾-oz. can cream of mushroom soup
1 soup can water
4 cups cooked rice, *divided*
4-oz. can mushroom pieces, drained, *divided*
Velveeta cheese slices

1. Brown ground beef, onion, and celery in skillet. Stir frequently to break clumps of meat. Continue browning until no pink remains in meat. Drain off drippings.

2. Season meat in skillet with basil and oregano.

3. Combine soup and water in bowl.

4. In well greased slow cooker, layer half of rice, half of mushrooms, half of ground-beef mixture, and half of soup mixture.

5. Repeat layers.

6. Cover. Cook on High 4 hours.

7. Top with cheese 30 minutes before serving.

Serving suggestion: This casserole, served with ***corn-bread*** *and* ***applesauce****, makes a well-rounded meal that is quick and easy to prepare and well-received by children and adults.*

Hearty Rice Casserole

Dale Peterson
Rapid City, SD

Makes 12-16 servings

Prep. Time: 25 minutes
Cooking Time: 6-7 hours
Ideal slow cooker size: 4-qt.

1 lb. ground beef
1 lb. loose pork sausage
10¾-oz. can cream of mushroom soup
10¾-oz. can creamy onion soup
10¾-oz. can cream of chicken soup
1 cup water
1 large onion, chopped
1 large green bell pepper, chopped
1½ cups uncooked long-grain rice
shredded cheese, *optional*

1. Brown beef and sausage in large skillet. Stir frequently to break up clumps. Continue cooking until no more pink remains. Drain off drippings.

2. Place browned meat in slow cooker.

3. Add all ingredients except cheese to slow cooker. Mix well.

4. Cover. Cook on Low 6-7 hours, or until rice is fully cooked.

5. Sprinkling with cheese during last hour if you wish.

Beef and Pepper Rice

Liz Ann Yoder
Hartville, OH

Makes 4-6 servings

Prep. Time: 20 minutes
Cooking Time: 3-6 hours
Ideal slow cooker size: 3-qt.

1 lb. ground beef
2 green bell peppers, *or* **1 green and 1 red bell pepper, coarsely chopped**
1 cup chopped onions
1 cup uncooked brown rice
2 beef bouillon cubes, crushed
3 cups water
1 Tbsp. soy sauce

1. Brown beef in skillet. Stir frequently to break up clumps. Continue cooking until meat is no longer pink. Drain off drippings.
2. Place meat in slow cooker.
3. Add all remaining ingredients to slow cooker. Mix well.
4. Cover. Cook on Low 5-6 hours or on High 3 hours, or until rice is tender and liquid is absorbed.

Stuffed Green Peppers

Patricia Howard
Albuquerque, NM

Makes 6 servings

Prep. Time: 40 minutes
Cooking Time: 4-5 hours
Ideal slow cooker size: 6- to 7-qt.

6 green bell peppers
1 lb. ground beef
¼ cup chopped onions
1 tsp. salt
¼ tsp. pepper
1¼ cups cooked rice
1 Tbsp. Worcestershire sauce
8-oz. can tomato sauce
¼ cup beef broth

1. Cut stem ends from peppers. Carefully remove seeds and membrane without breaking pepper apart. Parboil in water for 5 minutes. Drain. Set aside.
2. Brown ground beef and onions in skillet. Stir frequently to break up clumps. Continue cooking until meat is no longer pink. Drain off drippings.
3. Place meat and onions in mixing bowl.
4. Add seasonings, rice, and Worcestershire sauce to meat and combine well.
5. Stuff green peppers with mixture. Stand stuffed peppers upright in large slow cooker.
6. Mix together tomato sauce and beef broth in a bowl. Pour over peppers.
7. Cover. Cook on Low 4-5 hours.

Variation:
Add ½-¾ cup grated cheddar cheese to Step 4.
Rosaria Strachan
Fairfield, CT

Ask for help. It's okay to ask someone to bring a dish, bread, or beverage. It's okay to ask your children to pick up toys and be a "pre-host or hostess," especially if your get-together is for families with children. Have your family help to decorate. I know this can take longer, but if you keep things simple, you will be enjoying family time together and broader ownership of the event. Next time it will be easier for all, and you will have begun traditions that can be carried to the next generation.
Carol Findling, Carol Stream, IL

Spanish Stuffed Peppers

Katrine Rose
Woodbridge, VA

Makes 4 servings

Prep. Time: 20 minutes
Cooking Time: 8-10 hours
Ideal slow cooker size: 6- to 7-qt.

1 lb. ground beef
7-oz. pkg. Spanish rice mix
1 egg
¼ cup chopped onions
4 medium-sized green bell peppers, halved lengthwise, cored, and seeded
28-oz. can stewed, *or* **crushed, tomatoes**
10¾-oz. can tomato soup
1 cup water
shredded cheese, *optional*

1. Combine beef, rice mix (reserving seasoning packet), egg, and onions in large bowl.
2. Divide meat mixture among pepper halves.
3. Pour tomatoes into slow cooker. Arrange pepper halves over tomatoes.
4. Combine tomato soup, rice-mix seasoning packet, and water in bowl. Pour over peppers.
5. Cover. Cook on Low 8-10 hours.
6. Twenty minutes before end of the cooking time, top stuffed peppers with cheese if you wish.

Haystacks

Judy Buller
Bluffton, OH

Makes 10-12 servings

Prep. Time: 20 minutes
Cooking Time: 1-3 hours
Ideal slow cooker size: 5-qt.

2 lbs. ground beef
oil
1 small onion, chopped
2 8-oz. cans tomato sauce
2 15-oz. cans chili beans with chili gravy, *or* **red beans**
2 10-oz. cans mild enchilada sauce, *or* **mild salsa**
½ tsp. chili powder
1 tsp. garlic salt
pepper to taste

Condiments:
raisins
chopped apples
shredded lettuce
chopped tomatoes
shredded cheese
corn chips
rice, *or* **baked potatoes**

1. Brown beef in skillet, in oil if needed, stirring frequently to break up clumps. Continue cooking until meat is no longer pink. Drain off drippings.
2. Combine beef, onion, tomato sauce, chili beans, enchilada sauce, chili powder, garlic salt, and pepper in slow cooker.
3. Cover. Bake on Low 2-3 hours or on High 1 hour.
4. Serve over baked potatoes or rice and pass dishes of condiments so everyone can choose their own toppings.

Note:
Because this recipe offers such a wide choice of toppings, all diners are sure to find something they like. Haystacks are easy to serve buffet-style. The wide array of condiments sparks conversation—and becomes an adventure in eating. Members of my family like a little of each topping over the chili.

Guests are often surprised to see how large their haystacks are when they're finished serving themselves. They frequently fill their entire plates!

The atmosphere can be comfortable when everything is prepared ahead. And with this recipe, the serving time can vary to meet uncertain schedules.

Don't forget to do the rice or baked potatoes in a second slow cooker.

Mexican Goulash

Sheila Plock
Boalsburg, PA

Makes 8-10 servings

Prep. Time: 45 minutes
Cooking Time: 3-4 hours
Ideal slow cooker size: 5-qt.

1½-2 lbs. ground beef
2 onions, chopped
1 green bell pepper, chopped
½ cup celery, chopped
1 garlic clove, minced
28-oz. can whole tomatoes, cut up
6-oz. can tomato paste
4¼-oz. can sliced black olives, drained
14½-oz. can green beans, drained
15¼-oz. can Mexicorn, drained
15-oz. can dark red kidney beans, rinsed and drained
diced jalapeño peppers to taste
1 tsp. salt
¼ tsp. pepper
1 Tbsp. chili powder
3 dashes Tabasco sauce
grated cheddar cheese

1. Brown ground beef in skillet, stirring frequently to break up clumps. Continue cooking until meat is no longer pink. Reserve drippings and transfer beef to slow cooker.
2. Sauté onions, pepper, celery, and garlic in drippings in skillet. Transfer to slow cooker.
3. Add remaining ingredients except cheese to slow cooker. Mix well.
4. Cover. Cook on Low 3-4 hours.
5. Sprinkle individual servings with grated cheese.

Serving suggestion: Serve with ***tortilla chips.***

Tortilla Bake

Kelly Evenson
Pittsboro, NC

Makes 6-8 servings

Prep. Time: 20 minutes
Cooking Time: 3-4 hours
Ideal slow cooker size: 3-qt.

1½ lbs. ground beef, *divided*
oil
10¾-oz. can cheddar cheese soup
1½-oz. pkg. dry taco seasoning mix
8 corn tortillas, *divided*
3 medium tomatoes, coarsely chopped, *divided*

Toppings:
sour cream
grated cheese
thinly sliced green onions
cut-up bell peppers
diced avocado
shredded lettuce

1. Brown ground beef in skillet, in oil if needed. Stir frequently to break up clumps. Continue cooking until no pink remains in meat. Drain off drippings. Set aside meat in skillet.
2. Combine soup and taco seasoning in bowl.
3. Cut each tortilla into 6 wedges.
4. Spoon one-quarter of ground beef into slow cooker.
5. Top with one-quarter of all tortilla wedges.
6. Spoon one-quarter of soup mixture over tortillas.
7. Top with one-quarter of tomatoes.
8. Repeat layers 3 times.
9. Cover. Cook on Low 3-4 hours.
10. To serve, spoon onto plates and offer toppings as condiments.

We call the local assisted-living facility and ask for names and a list of gift ideas for 3 people who live in the facility but who don't usually get visitors at Christmas-time. Then on Christmas Day, our family delivers the gifts and visits with each person. Our kids are learning that Christmas is not all about them.

Kendra Dreps, Liberty, PA

Three-Bean Burrito Bake

Darla Sathre
Baxter, MN

Makes 6 servings

Prep. Time: 30 minutes
Cooking Time: 4-5 hours
Ideal slow cooker size: 4-qt.

1 onion, chopped
1 green bell pepper, chopped
2 garlic cloves, minced
1 Tbsp. oil
16-oz. can pinto beans, drained
16-oz. can kidney beans, drained
15-oz. can black beans, drained
4-oz. can sliced black olives, drained
4-oz. can green chilies, undrained
2 15-oz. cans diced tomatoes, undrained
1 tsp. chili powder
1 tsp. ground cumin
6-8 6" flour tortillas, *divided*
2 cups shredded Colby Jack cheese, *divided*

1. Sauté onions, green peppers, and garlic in large skillet in oil.
2. Add beans, olives, chilies, tomatoes, chili powder, and cumin to skillet. Stir together well.
3. In greased slow cooker, layer ¾ cup vegetables, followed by a tortilla, followed by ⅓ cup cheese.
4. Repeat layers until all those ingredients are used, ending with vegetable sauce on top.
5. Cover. Cook on Low 4-5 hours.

Serving suggestion: Serve with dollops of ***sour cream*** *on individual servings.*

Taco Casserole

Marcia S. Myer
Manheim, PA

Makes 6 servings

Prep. Time: 25 minutes
Cooking Time: 3-4 hours
Ideal slow cooker size: 3-qt.

1½ lbs. ground beef
oil
14½-oz. can diced tomatoes with chilies
10¾-oz. can cream of onion soup
1 envelope dry taco seasoning mix
¼ cup water
6 corn tortillas, cut in ½" strips
½ cup sour cream
1 cup shredded cheddar cheese
2 green onions, sliced, *optional*

1. Brown beef in skillet, in oil if needed. Stir frequently, breaking up clumps. Continue cooking until no pink remains in meat. Drain off drippings.
2. Place beef in slow cooker.
3. Stir in tomatoes, soup, seasoning mix, and water in slow cooker. Mix together well.
4. Stir in tortilla strips.
5. Cover. Cook on Low 3-4 hours.
6. Spread sour cream over casserole. Sprinkle with cheese.
7. Cover. Let stand 5 minutes until cheese melts.
8. Remove cover. Garnish with green onions. Allow to stand 15 more minutes before serving.

Casserole Verde

Julia Fisher
New Carlisle, OH

Makes 6 servings

Prep. Time: 35 minutes
Cooking Time: 2-3 hours
Ideal slow cooker size: 4-qt.

1 lb. ground beef
1 small onion, chopped
⅛ tsp. garlic powder
oil
8-oz. can tomato sauce
⅓ cup chopped black olives
4-oz. can sliced mushrooms, drained
8-oz. container sour cream
8-oz. container cottage cheese
4¼-oz. can chopped green chilies, drained
12-oz. pkg. tortilla chips, *divided*
8 oz. Monterey Jack cheese, grated, *divided*

1. Brown ground beef, onions, and garlic in skillet, in oil if needed. Stir frequently to break up clumps. Continue cooking until no pink remains in meat. Drain off drippings.
2. Add tomato sauce, olives, and mushrooms to meat in skillet.
3. In a separate bowl, combine sour cream, cottage cheese, and green chilies.
4. In slow cooker, layer in one-third of chips, followed by half the ground beef mixture.
5. Follow with a layer of half the sour cream mixture and half the shredded cheese.
6. Repeat all layers, except reserve last third of chips to add just before serving.
7. Cover. Cook on Low 2-3 hours.
8. Ten minutes before serving time, scatter reserved chips over top and continue cooking, uncovered.

Tiajuana Tacos

Helen Kenagy
Carlsbad, NM

Makes 6 servings

Prep. Time: 20 minutes
Cooking Time: 2 hours
Ideal slow cooker size: 3½-qt.

3 cups thinly sliced uncooked beef steak
oil
1-lb. can refried beans
½ cup chopped onions
½ cup chopped green bell peppers
½ cup chopped ripe olives
8-oz. can tomato sauce
3 tsp. chili powder
1 Tbsp. Worcestershire sauce
½ tsp. garlic powder
¼ tsp. pepper
¼ tsp. paprika
⅛ tsp. celery salt
⅛ tsp. ground nutmeg
¾ cup water
1 tsp. salt
1 cup crushed corn chips
6 taco shells
shredded lettuce
chopped tomatoes
grated cheddar cheese

1. Sauté beef lightly in skillet, in oil if needed. Drain off drippings.
2. Place in slow cooker, along with all ingredients except corn chips, taco shells, lettuce, chopped tomatoes, and grated cheese.
3. Cover. Cook on Low 2 hours.
4. Just before serving, fold in corn chips.
5. Spoon mixture into taco shells.

Serving suggestion: Top with ***lettuce, tomatoes,*** *and* ***cheese.***

Pork and Ham Main Dishes

Barbecued Ribs

Virginia Bender
Dover, DE

Makes 6 servings

Prep. Time: 10 minutes
Cooking Time: 8-10 hours
Ideal slow cooker size: 6-qt.

4 lbs. pork ribs
½ cup brown sugar
12-oz. jar chili sauce
¼ cup balsamic vinegar
2 Tbsp. Worcestershire sauce
2 Tbsp. Dijon mustard
1 tsp. hot sauce

1. Place ribs in slow cooker.
2. Combine remaining ingredients in a good-sized bowl.
3. Pour half of sauce over ribs.
4. Cover. Cook on Low 8-10 hours.
5. Serve with remaining sauce.

Sweet and Sour Ribs

Cassandra Ly
Carlisle, PA

Makes 8-10 servings

Prep. Time: 15 minutes
Cooking Time: 8-10 hours
Ideal slow cooker size: 6-qt.

3-4 lbs. boneless country-style pork ribs
20-oz. can pineapple tidbits, drained
2 8-oz. cans tomato sauce
½ cup thinly sliced onions
½ cup thinly sliced green bell peppers
½ cup packed brown sugar
¼ cup cider vinegar
¼ cup tomato paste
2 Tbsp. Worcestershire sauce
1 garlic clove, minced
1 tsp. salt
½ tsp. pepper

1. Place ribs in slow cooker.
2. Combine remaining ingredients in a good-sized bowl. Pour over ribs.
3. Cover. Cook on Low 8-10 hours.

*Serving suggestion: Serve over **rice**.*

Give a basket filled with a recipe, the ingredients to make it, decorative potholders or towels, and a special utensil for preparing the recipe. Maryann Markano, Wilmington, DE

1-2-3 Barbecued Country Ribs

Barbara Walker
Sturgis, SD

Makes 4 servings

Prep. Time: 10 minutes
Cooking Time: 8-10 hours
Ideal slow cooker size: 5-qt.

18-oz. bottle prepared barbecue sauce
4 lbs. spareribs, *or* **3 lbs. country-style ribs, cut in serving-size pieces**

1. Pour a little sauce into slow cooker. Put in a layer of ribs, meaty side up. Cover with barbecue sauce.
2. Continue layering until all ribs are in the pot. Submerge them as much as possible in sauce.
3. Cover. Cook on Low 8-10 hours.

Note:
No need to precook the ribs if they're lean. If they're fattier than you like, parboil in water in stockpot before placing in cooker, to cook off some of the grease. Drain and place in slow cooker. Follow Steps 1-3.

Tender 'n' Tangy Ribs

Sherri Grindle, Goshen, IN

Makes 2-3 servings

Prep. Time: 20 minutes • Cooking Time: 4-6 hours
Ideal slow cooker size: 4-qt.

¾-1 cup vinegar
½ cup ketchup
2 Tbsp. sugar
2 Tbsp. Worcestershire sauce
1 clove garlic, minced
1 tsp. ground mustard
1 tsp. paprika
½-1 tsp. salt
⅛ tsp. pepper
2 lbs. pork spareribs, *or* **country-style ribs**
1 Tbsp. oil

1. Combine first nine ingredients in slow cooker.
2. Cut ribs into serving-size pieces. Brown in batches in oil in skillet. Don't crowd the skillet or the ribs will steam and not brown. Transfer to slow cooker as you finish browning them.
3. Stir sauce through ribs.
4. Cover. Cook on Low 4-6 hours.

Serving suggestion: Serve the ribs with ***baked potatoes*** *or* ***rice.***

Note: *I often use this recipe if I am having company for Sunday lunch.*

Country-Style Ribs and Sauerkraut

Rhonda Burgoon
Collingswood, NJ

Makes 4-6 servings

Prep. Time: 15 minutes
Cooking Time: 8-10 hours
Ideal slow cooker size: 5-qt.

16-oz. bag sauerkraut, rinsed and drained
1 onion, diced
1 red-skinned apple, chopped
2-3 lbs. country-style pork ribs
1 cup beer

1. Combine sauerkraut, onion, and apple in slow cooker.
2. Layer ribs over sauerkraut mixture.
3. Pour beer over ribs just before turning on cooker.
4. Cover. Cook on Low 8-10 hours.

Serving suggestion: You'll love this served with homemade ***cornbread*** *and* ***mashed potatoes****, or deboned on* ***kaiser rolls.***

Sauerkraut & Pork Ribs

Annabelle Unternahrer
Shipshewana, IN

Makes 6-8 servings

Prep. Time: 15-25 minutes
Cooking Time: 6 hours
Ideal slow cooker size: 3- to 4-qt.

2 lbs. country pork ribs
oil
32-oz. jar sauerkraut
1 large apple, chopped
1 cup shredded carrots
1½ cups tomato juice
3 Tbsp. brown sugar
2 tsp. caraway seeds, *optional*

1. Cut ribs in 2"-thick pieces. Brown in skillet with small amount of oil.
2. Combine sauerkraut, apple, carrots, juice, brown sugar, and caraway seeds if you wish, in a bowl.
3. Put half of sauerkraut mixture in bottom of slow cooker.
4. Top with browned ribs.
5. Cover with remainder of sauerkraut mixture.
6. Cover cooker. Cook on Low 6 hours, or until meat leaves the bone when pulled with a fork.

Barbara Jean's Whole Pork Tenderloin

Barbara Jean Fabel
Wausau, WI

Makes 6-8 servings

Prep. Time: 25 minutes
Cooking Time: 3-5 hours
Ideal slow cooker size: 4- to 5-qt.

½ cup sliced celery
¼ lb. fresh mushrooms, quartered
1 medium onion, sliced
half a stick (4 Tbsp.) butter, melted
2 1¼-lb. pork tenderloins
1 Tbsp. butter
2 tsp. salt
¼ tsp. pepper
1 Tbsp. butter
½ cup beef broth
1 Tbsp. flour

1. Place celery, mushrooms, onion, and half a stick melted butter in slow cooker.
2. Brown tenderloins in skillet in 1 Tbsp. butter. Layer browned meat over vegetables in slow cooker.
3. Sprinkle with salt and pepper.
4. Combine broth and flour in small bowl until smooth. Pour over tenderloins.
5. Cover. Cook on High 3 hours or on Low 4-5 hours.

Autumn Harvest Pork Loin

Stacy Schmucker Stoltzfus
Enola, PA

Makes 4-6 servings

Prep. Time: 30 minutes
Cooking Time: 5-6 hours
Ideal slow cooker size: 5-qt.

1 cup cider, *or* **apple juice**
1½-2-lb. pork loin
salt
pepper
2 large Granny Smith apples, peeled and sliced
1½ whole butternut squashes, peeled and cubed
½ cup brown sugar
¼ tsp. cinnamon
¼ tsp. dried thyme
¼ tsp. dried sage

1. Heat cider in hot skillet. Sear pork loin on all sides in cider.
2. Sprinkle meat with salt and pepper on all sides. Place in slow cooker, along with pan juices.
3. In a good-sized bowl, combine apples and squash. Sprinkle with sugar and herbs. Stir. Spoon around pork loin in cooker.
4. Cover. Cook on Low 5-6 hours.
5. Remove pork from cooker. Let stand 10-15 minutes. Slice into ½"-thick slices.
6. Serve topped with apples and squash.

Cranberry Pork

Barbara Walker
Sturgis, SD
Donna Treloar
Muncie, IN

Makes 9-12 servings

Prep. Time: 15 minutes
Cooking Time: 6¼-8¼ hours
Ideal slow cooker size: 5-qt.

3-4-lb. boneless rolled pork loin roast
2 Tbsp. canola oil
14-oz. can whole berry cranberry sauce
¾ cup sugar
¾ cup cranberry juice
1 tsp. ground mustard
1 tsp. pepper
¼ tsp. ground cloves
¼ cup cornstarch
¼ cup cold water
salt to taste

1. In Dutch oven, brown roast in oil on all sides over medium-high heat. You may need to cut roast in half to fit into your Dutch oven and/or your slow cooker.
2. Place browned roast in slow cooker.
3. In a medium-sized bowl, combine cranberry sauce, sugar, cranberry juice, mustard, pepper, and cloves. Pour over roast.
4. Cover. Cook on Low 6-8 hours, or until a meat thermometer reads 160 degrees in center of roast. Remove roast and keep warm. Keep sauce on Low in slow cooker.
5. In a small bowl, combine cornstarch, water, and salt until smooth.
6. Turn cooker to High. Stir cornstarch-water mixture into cooking juices. Bring to a boil. Cook and stir until sauce thickens. Serve with slices of pork roast.

Variations:

1. In place of sugar, use ¼ cup honey.
2. Instead of ¼ tsp. ground cloves, use ⅛ tsp. ground cloves and ⅛ tsp. ground nutmeg.
3. Add 1 tsp. grated orange peel to Step 3.

Renee Baum
Chambersburg, PA

4. Create a whole different twist to the Cranberry Pork Loin by dropping the sugar, cranberry juice, ground mustard, pepper, and cloves. Instead, add 2 Tbsp. Dijon mustard, 1 Tbsp. grated horseradish, and 1 cup chicken stock to the cranberry sauce. Continue with Steps 4-6.

Susan Kasting
Jenks, OK

Pork Loin with Spiced Fruit Sauce

Maricarol Magill
Freehold, NJ

Makes 4 servings

Prep. Time: 25-40 minutes
Cooking Time: 4-6 hours
Ideal slow cooker size: 5- to 6-qt.

8-oz. pkg. dried mixed fruit (including plums and apricots), chopped
¼ cup golden raisins
2 tsp. minced fresh ginger
1 small onion, chopped
⅓ cup brown sugar
2 Tbsp. cider vinegar
¾ cup water
¼ tsp. ground cinnamon
¼ tsp. curry powder
½ tsp. salt, *divided*
½ tsp. pepper, *divided*
2¼-lb. boneless pork loin roast, trimmed of fat
¾ lb. fresh green beans, ends nipped off
1 Tbsp. Dijon mustard
1 Tbsp. cornstarch
1 Tbsp. cold water

1. In slow cooker, combine dried fruit, raisins, ginger, onion, sugar, vinegar, water, cinnamon, curry powder, and ¼ tsp. each of salt and pepper. Stir.
2. Season pork with remaining ¼ tsp. salt and pepper. Place pork on top of fruit mixture in slow cooker. Cover. Cook on High 2 hours or on Low 3 hours.
3. Layer green beans over pork. Cover.

4. Cook for 2 more hours on High or for 3 more hours on Low—or until meat is tender and beans are done to your liking.
5. When meat and beans are tender but not dry, remove to separate plates. Cover and keep warm.
6. Stir mustard into sauce in cooker.
7. In a small bowl, mix cornstarch with 1 Tbsp. cold water until smooth. Stir into sauce.
8. Cover. Turn cooker to High and let sauce cook a few minutes until thickened.
9. Slice pork and serve with sauce and green beans.

Note:

We discovered this to be a great Christmas dinner one year when we were remodeling and had limited kitchen facilities. I put the ingredients in the slow cooker, and we played Scrabble all day while it cooked. I served it with microwaved rice pilaf. It was my most stress-free Christmas ever!

No Fuss Sauerkraut

Vera M. Kuhns
Harrisonburg, VA

Makes 12 servings

Prep. Time: 10-15 minutes
Cooking Time: 4-5 hours
Ideal slow cooker size: 5-qt.

3-lb. pork roast
3 2-lb. pkgs. sauerkraut (drain off juice from 1 pkg.)
2 apples, peeled and sliced
½ cup brown sugar
1 cup apple juice

1. Place meat in large slow cooker.
2. Place sauerkraut on top of meat.
3. Add apples and brown sugar. Add juice.
4. Cover. Cook on High 4-5 hours.

Serving suggestion: I think this is made to be eaten with ***mashed potatoes****.*

Tip:

If your slow cooker isn't large enough to hold all the ingredients, cook one package of sauerkraut and half the apples, brown sugar, and apple juice in another cooker. Mix the ingredients of both cookers together before serving.

Variations:

1. Replace brown sugar with ¼ cup honey.
2. Sprinkle 2 Tbsp. dried basil over contents of slow cooker at end of Step 3.

Jean Harris Robinson
Pemberton, NJ

Flautas with Pork Filling

Donna Lantgen
Rapid City, SD

Makes 6-8 servings

Prep. Time: 20 minutes
Cooking Time: 4-6 hours
Ideal slow cooker size: 3½-qt.

1-lb. pork roast, *or* **chops, cubed**
¼ cup chopped onions
4-oz. can diced green chilies, drained
7-oz. can green chile salsa, *or* **chile salsa**
1 tsp. cocoa powder
16-oz. can chili

1. Brown cubed pork in non-stick skillet. Drain off any drippings. Place in slow cooker.
2. Stir in remaining ingredients except chili.
3. Cover. Cook on Low 2-3 hours.
4. Add chili. Cook on Low 2-3 hours longer.

Tip:

This is especially good served on spinach-herb tortillas with guacamole dip.

Pork Chops and Gravy

Barbara Walker
Sturgis, SD

Makes 6 servings

Prep. Time: 15-20 minutes
Cooking Time: 2-2½ hours
Ideal slow cooker size: 4-qt.

½ cup flour
½ tsp. salt
½ tsp. garlic powder
1½ tsp. dry mustard
6 1"-thick lean pork chops
10¾-oz can condensed chicken broth
2 Tbsp. vegetable oil

1. Mix first 4 ingredients in a shallow dish. Dredge pork chops in flour mixture then set aside.
2. Combine remaining flour mixture and chicken broth in slow cooker until thoroughly mixed.
3. Pour oil into large skillet. Place over medium-high heat until hot. Cook chops in hot oil just until browned on both sides. Place in cooker, pushing them down into broth.
4. Cover. Cook on High 2-2½ hours, or just until chops are tender.

Pork Chops

Linda Sluiter
Schererville, IN

Makes 4 servings

Prep. Time: 10 minutes
Cooking Time: 5-8 hours
Ideal slow cooker size: 3-qt.

4 boneless pork chops, 1"-thick
½ tsp. dry mustard
¼ cup flour
½ tsp. sugar
1 tsp. vinegar
½ cup water
½ cup ketchup
½ tsp. salt

1. Place pork chops in slow cooker.
2. Combine remaining ingredients in a bowl. Pour over pork chops.
3. Cover. Cook on High 2-3 hours, and then on Low 3-4 hours, or cook on Low 8 hours—just until chops are fork-tender but not dry.
4. Spoon sauce over chops to serve.

Barbecued Pork Chops

LaVerne A. Olson
Lititz, PA

Makes 6-8 servings

Prep. Time: 15 minutes
Cooking Time: 2-3 hours
Ideal slow cooker size: 5-qt.

6-8 thin pork chops
½ cup ketchup
1 tsp. salt
1 tsp. celery seed
½ tsp. ground nutmeg
⅓ cup vinegar
½ cup water
1 bay leaf

1. Lightly brown chops on both sides in non-stick skillet. Do it in several batches so chops brown and don't steam each other.
2. Place browned chops in slow cooker.
3. Combine remaining ingredients in a small bowl. Pour over chops.
4. Cover. Cook on Low 2-3 hours, or until chops are tender.
5. Remove bay leaf before serving. Top chops with sauce.

Pork Chops Pierre

Genelle Taylor
Perrysburg, OH

Makes 6 servings

Prep. Time: 30-40 minutes
Cooking Time: 4½-6½ hours
Ideal slow cooker size: 3-qt.

6 pork chops, each ½"-thick
½ tsp. salt, *optional*
⅛ tsp. pepper
2 medium onions, chopped
2 ribs celery, chopped
1 large green bell pepper, sliced
14-oz. can stewed tomatoes
½ cup ketchup
2 Tbsp. cider vinegar
2 Tbsp. brown sugar
2 Tbsp. Worcestershire sauce
1 Tbsp. lemon juice
1 beef bouillon cube
2 Tbsp. cornstarch
2 Tbsp. water

1. Place chops in slow cooker. Sprinkle with salt and pepper.
2. Place onions, celery, green pepper, and tomatoes over chops.
3. In a small bowl, combine ketchup, vinegar, sugar, Worcestershire sauce, lemon juice, and bouillon cube. Pour over vegetables.
4. Cover. Cook on Low 4-6 hours, just until chops are tender but not dry.
5. Remove chops to a platter and keep warm.
6. In a small bowl, mix together cornstarch and water until smooth. Stir into liquid in slow cooker.
7. Cover. Cook on High 30 minutes or until sauce thickens.

Serving suggestion: Serve over cooked ***rice*** *if you wish.*

Choose a large vase and stick a small pine branch down into it head first. Sprinkle a handful of cranberries or holly berries on top. Fill the vase with a mixture of evergreens stuck in stem first. Lay a few miniature pine cones and cranberries or holly berries around the foot of the vase. Lay some smaller branches around the base, too, if you like.
Juanita Weaver, Johnsonville, IL

Pork Chops and Potatoes

Sherry H. Kauffman
Minot, ND

Makes 6 servings

Prep. Time: 25 minutes
Cooking Time: 3½-4½ hours
Ideal slow cooker size: 5-qt.

10¾-oz. can cream of mushroom soup
¼ cup chicken broth
¼ cup country-style Dijon mustard
1 garlic clove, minced
½ tsp. dried thyme
¼-½ tsp. salt, according to your taste preference
¼ tsp. pepper
6 medium red potatoes, sliced
1 medium onion, thinly sliced
6 5-oz. boneless pork loin chops

1. In slow cooker, combine soup, broth, mustard, garlic, thyme, salt, and pepper.
2. Stir in potatoes and onion slices.
3. Top with pork chops. Push down into sauce as much as possible.
4. Cover. Cook on Low 3½-4½ hours, or until meat and potatoes are tender.

Pork Chops on Rice

Hannah D. Burkholder
Bridgewater, VA

Makes 4 servings

Prep. Time: 30 minutes
Cooking Time: 4-9 hours
Ideal slow cooker size: 5-qt.

⅔ cup uncooked converted white rice
½ cup uncooked brown rice
half a stick (4 Tbsp.) butter
½ cup chopped onions
4-oz. can sliced mushrooms, drained
½ tsp. dried thyme
½ tsp. sage
½ tsp. salt
¼ tsp. black pepper
4 boneless pork chops, ¾"-1" thick
10½-oz. can beef consommé
2 Tbsp. Worcestershire sauce
½ tsp. dried thyme
½ tsp. paprika
¼ tsp. ground nutmeg

1. Sauté white and brown rice in butter in skillet until rice is golden brown.
2. Remove from heat and stir in onions, mushrooms, thyme, sage, salt, and pepper. Pour into greased slow cooker.
3. Arrange chops over rice.
4. Combine consommé and Worcestershire sauce in a bowl. Pour over chops.
5. Combine thyme, paprika, and nutmeg in a small bowl. Sprinkle over chops.
6. Cover. Cook on Low 7-9 hours or on High 4-5 hours.

Baked Beans and Chops

John D. Allen
Rye, CO

Makes 6 servings

Prep. Time: 10 minutes
Cooking Time: 4-6 hours
Ideal slow cooker size: 5-qt.

2 16½-oz. cans baked beans
6 rib pork chops, ½" thick
1½ tsp. prepared mustard
1½ Tbsp. brown sugar
1½ Tbsp. ketchup
6 onion slices, ¼" thick

1. Pour baked beans into bottom of greased slow cooker.
2. Layer pork chops over beans.
3. Spread mustard over pork chops. Sprinkle with brown sugar and drizzle with ketchup.
4. Top with onion slices.
5. Cover. Cook on High 4-6 hours.

Pork Chops in Orange Sauce

Kelly Evenson
Pittsboro, NC

Makes 4 servings

Prep. Time: 25 minutes
Cooking Time: 5¼-6¼ hours
Ideal slow cooker size: 5-qt.

4 thick, center-cut pork chops
salt to taste
pepper to taste
1 Tbsp. oil
1 orange
¼ cup ketchup
¾ cup orange juice
1 Tbsp. orange marmalade
1 Tbsp. cornstarch
¼ cup water

1. Season pork chops on both sides with salt and pepper.
2. Brown chops lightly on both sides in skillet in oil. Transfer to slow cooker. Reserve 2 Tbsp. drippings and discard the rest.
3. Grate ½ tsp. orange zest from top or bottom of orange (in order to preserve the main part of the orange for later use). Combine zest with ketchup, orange juice, and marmalade in skillet with reserved drippings. Simmer 1 minute, stirring constantly.
4. Pour sauce over chops.
5. Cover. Cook on Low 5-6 hours. Remove chops and keep warm on a platter.
6. In a small bowl, dissolve cornstarch in water. Stir into

Oxford Canal Chops Deluxe

Willard E. Roth, Elkhart, IN

Makes 6 servings

Prep. Time: 25 minutes • Cooking Time: 4 hours
Ideal slow cooker size: 5-qt.

6 6-oz. boneless pork chops
¼ cup flour
1 tsp. powdered garlic
1 tsp. sea salt
1 tsp. black pepper
1 tsp. dried basil and/or dried oregano
2 medium onions, sliced
2 Tbsp. oil
1 cup burgundy wine
14½-oz. can beef broth
1 soup can water
6-oz. can tomato sauce
8 oz. dried apricots
½ lb. fresh mushroom caps

1. Shake chops in bag with flour and seasonings.
2. Glaze onions in oil in medium hot skillet. Add chops and brown on both sides.
3. Pour any remaining flour over chops in skillet.
4. In large bowl mix together wine, broth, water, and tomato sauce. Pour over meat. Bring to boil.
5. Remove chops from skillet and place in cooker.
6. Layer in apricots and mushrooms. Pour heated broth over top.
7. Cover. Cook on Low 2½ hours, and then on High 1½ hours, or until chops are just tender.

*Serving suggestion: This is a great dish to serve with the Celtic speciality Bubble and Squeak—**Irish potatoes mashed with green cabbage or brussels sprouts**.*

Note:

My favorite memory with this recipe was the time I prepared it in the tiny kitchen of a houseboat on the Oxford Canal and then shared it with five friends. It was a hit!

sauce in slow cooker until it becomes smooth. Cook on High 15 minutes, or until sauce thickens.

7. Serve chops with orange sauce on top, along with slices of fresh orange.

Pork Chop Slow Cooker Casserole

Janice Crist
Quinter, KS

Makes 5 servings

Prep. Time: 15 minutes
Cooking Time: 4-6 hours
Ideal slow cooker size: 5-qt.

4-5 medium potatoes, quartered or sliced
10¾-oz. can cream of chicken soup
10¾-oz. can cream of celery soup
2 15-oz. cans green beans, drained
5 pork chops

1. Layer potatoes in slow cooker.
2. In a medium-sized bowl, combine 2 soups until smooth. Spread over potatoes.
3. Cover with green beans.
4. Place chops on top of beans.
5. Cover. Cook on Low 5-6 hours or on High 4 hours.

Variations:

1. Cover soup layer with 4 slices of your favorite cheese.
2. Sprinkle chops with garlic salt.

Cheryl Hagner
Montague, MI

Teriyaki Pineapple Pork Chops

Kayla Snyder
North East, PA

Makes 4 servings

Prep. Time: 10-15 minutes
Cooking Time: 4-5 hours
Ideal slow cooker size: 2- to 3-qt.

4 8-oz. bone-in pork loin chops
1 Tbsp. minced fresh rosemary, *or* **1 tsp. dried rosemary, crushed**
1 tsp. garlic powder
½ tsp. salt
¼ tsp. pepper
1 cup unsweetened pineapple juice
½ cup teriyaki sauce

1. Put chops in slow cooker.
2. Mix remaining ingredients in a small bowl. Pour over chops. If you've stacked the chops, lift up the top ones and ladle sauce over bottom ones, too.
3. Cover. Cook on High 4-5 hours, or until chops are tender but still juicy.

Tip:
For added flavor, marinate chops in sauce 2-3 hours before cooking.

Apples, Sauerkraut, and Chops

Carol Sherwood
Batavia, NY

Makes 4 servings

Prep. Time: 25 minutes
Cooking Time: 4-8 hours
Ideal slow cooker size: 5-qt.

1 onion, sliced and separated into rings, *divided*
⅛ tsp. garlic flakes, *or* **garlic powder,** *divided*
3 cups sauerkraut, drained, *divided*
1 cup unpeeled apple slices, *divided*
1½ tsp. caraway seeds, *divided*
¼ tsp. salt, *divided*
¼ tsp. dried thyme, *divided*
¼ tsp. pepper, *divided*
4 ½"-thick pork chops
¾ cup apple juice

1. Place half of onion rings, garlic flakes, sauerkraut, apple slices, and caraway seeds in slow cooker.
2. Season with half the salt, thyme, and pepper.
3. Brown chops in large non-stick skillet over high heat on both sides. This takes only a few minutes since you're browning and not cooking.
4. Place pork chops on top of ingredients in slow cooker.
5. Layer remaining ingredients in order given.
6. Pour apple juice over all.
7. Cover. Cook on Low 6-8 hours or on High 4 hours.

Pork Chops with Stuffing

Erma Kauffman
Cochranville, PA

Makes 2 servings

Prep. Time: 15 minutes
Cooking Time: 4-5 hours
Ideal slow cooker size: 1½-qt.

4 slices bread, cubed
1 egg
¼ cup grated, *or* **finely chopped, celery**
¼-½ tsp. salt
⅛ tsp. pepper
2 thick pork chops
1 cup water

1. Combine bread cubes, egg, celery, salt, and pepper in a good-sized bowl.
2. Cut pork chops part way through their thick sides, creating a pocket. Fill with stuffing, dividing the stuffing between them.
3. Pour water into slow cooker. Add chops.
4. Cover. Cook on Low 4-5 hours, or until chops are tender but not dry.

Pork Chops and Stuffing with Curry

Mary Martins
Fairbank, IA

Makes 3-4 servings

Prep. Time: 10 minutes
Cooking Time: 6-7 hours
Ideal slow cooker size: 4-qt.

1 box stuffing mix
1 cup water
10¾-oz. can cream of mushroom soup
1 tsp., *or* **more, curry powder, according to your taste preference**
3-4 pork chops

1. Combine stuffing mix and water in a large mixing bowl. Place half in bottom of slow cooker.
2. In another bowl, combine soup and curry powder. Pour half over stuffing.
3. Place pork chops on top.
4. Spread remaining stuffing over pork chops. Pour rest of soup on top.
5. Cover. Cook on Low 6-7 hours, or just until chops are tender.

Moo Shu Pork

Gwendolyn Chapman
Gwinn, MI

Makes 12 servings

Prep. Time: 20 minutes
Cooking Time: 2-5 hours
Ideal slow cooker size: 4- to 5-qt.

½ cup hoisin sauce
3 large cloves garlic, minced
2 Tbsp. dark Asian sesame oil
2 Tbsp. soy sauce
1 Tbsp. cornstarch
16-oz. bag shredded cole slaw mix
half a 10-oz. bag shredded carrots
1 lb. boneless pork loin chops
12 6" flour tortillas
scallion strips, *optional*

1. In small bowl, stir together hoisin sauce, garlic, sesame oil, soy sauce, and cornstarch. Set aside.
2. Place cole slaw and carrots into slow cooker.
3. Cut pork into ⅛"-thick slices. Then cut each slice in half lengthwise. Scatter over top of cabbage mixture in slow cooker.
4. Drizzle with ¼ cup hoisin sauce mixture.
5. Cover. Cook on High 2-3 hours or on Low 4-5 hours, or just until vegetables and meat are as tender as you like them.
6. Remove cover. Stir in remaining ½ cup hoisin sauce mixture.
7. Heat tortillas according to package directions.
8. Place ½ cup pork mixture in center of each tortilla. Top with scallion strips if you wish and roll up.

Tip from Tester:
The Moo Shu mixture is also great served over rice instead of rolling it into tortillas.

Give the gift of time. Give certificates for a trip to the movies, a day at the mall, or a visit to a local historical site, with you, of course. Also, find ways to spread gift-giving throughout the holidays, rather than just on one overwhelming Christmas Day.

Sandra Haverstraw, Hummelstown, PA

Pork Roast with Applesauce "Pulled Pork"

Colleen Heatwole
Burton, MI

Makes 8-10 servings

Prep. Time: 30 minutes
Cooking Time: 10-12 hours
Ideal slow cooker size: 5- to 6-qt.

4-6-lb. pork roast, visible fat removed
24-oz. jar unsweetened applesauce
18-24-oz. bottle barbecue sauce of your choice

1. Place meat in slow cooker.
2. Spread applesauce over top.
3. Spoon barbecue sauce over top of applesauce, being careful not to disturb it.
4. Cover. Cook on Low 10-12 hours, or until roast is very tender but not dry.
5. Remove from slow cooker onto platter. Pull apart with forks.
6. Put shredded meat in bowl. Add some of cooking broth so meat is somewhat juicy but not swimming in sauce.

Serving suggestion: Serve on sandwich or hamburger ***buns.***

Tip from Tester:
I cooked rice in the leftover sauce. I mixed some water with it; the proportion of the liquid was about ⅔ roast-pork sauce and ⅓ water. It was delicious rice!

Zesty Pulled Pork

Sheila Plock
Boalsburg, PA

Makes 10 servings

Prep. Time: 5-10 minutes
Cooking Time: 4½-10¾ hours
Ideal slow cooker size: 4-qt.

2½-3½ lbs. boneless pork shoulder roast, *or* **pork sirloin roast**
salt to taste
pepper to taste
½ cup water
3 Tbsp. cider vinegar
2 Tbsp. Worcestershire sauce
1 tsp. cumin
18-oz. bottle barbecue sauce of your choice

1. Trim fat from roast. Fit roast into slow cooker.
2. Season meat with salt and pepper.
3. In a small bowl, combine water, vinegar, Worcestershire sauce, and cumin. Spoon over roast, being careful not to wash off the seasonings.
4. Cover. Cook on Low 8-10 hours or on High 4-5 hours, just until pork is very tender but not dry.
5. Remove meat onto a platter. Discard liquid.
6. Shred meat using 2 forks. Return to slow cooker.
7. Stir in 1-2 cups barbecue sauce to taste.
8. Cover. Cook on High 30-45 minutes.

Serving suggestion: Serve on split hamburger ***buns.***

Note:
This is a great recipe when having friends over to watch Christmas and New Year's Bowl games.

Pulled Pork BBQ

Marsha Sabus
Fallbrook, CA

Makes 4-6 servings

Prep. Time: 20 minutes
Cooking Time: 8 hours
Ideal slow cooker size: 3- to 4-qt.

2 tsp. salt
2 tsp. pepper
1 Tbsp. paprika
2-lb. pork butt
2 Tbsp. olive oil
1 large onion, chopped
12-oz. can beer
1 bottle Sweet Baby Ray's Hickory and Brown Sugar BBQ Sauce
½ cup ketchup
3-4 drops hot pepper sauce

1. Rub or pat salt, pepper, and paprika on pork butt.
2. In large skillet, brown each side of meat in olive oil. Place browned butt in slow cooker.
3. Add onion to skillet. Sauté just until tender. Add to slow cooker.
4. Mix remaining ingredients in a good-sized bowl. Pour over pork in slow cooker.
5. Cover. Cook on High 2 hours. Turn to Low and cook 6 more hours.

6. Remove pork from slow cooker to platter. Shred meat with 2 forks.
7. Return pulled pork to slow cooker. Mix thoroughly with sauce.

Serving suggestion: Serve the meat on toasted ***buns*** *with* ***cole slaw****—either inside the rolls, or alongside.*

Note:
This recipe can easily be doubled for a large group.

Rob's Sweet and Sour Joe

Sue Hamilton
Minooka, IL

Makes 12 servings

Prep. Time: 10 minutes
Cooking Time: 3-4 hours
Ideal slow cooker size: 3- to 4-qt.

1 lb. ground lean pork
8 oz. cocktail sauce
8 oz. orange marmalade
¼ tsp. Chinese five spice
½ tsp. garlic powder
2 cups cole slaw mix, *or* **shredded cabbage**
ground black pepper to taste

1. Brown pork in saucepan, stirring frequently to break up clumps. Drain off drippings. Place meat in slow cooker.
2. Add sauce, marmalade, spice, garlic powder, cole slaw mix, and pepper. Mix well.
3. Cover. Cook on High 3-4 hours, or until heated through.

Serving suggestion: This makes enough to fill 12 ***sandwich rolls****.*

Tip:
If you can't find Chinese 5 spice in your grocery store, you can make your own:

2 tsp. fresh peppercorns
1 star anise
½ Tbsp. ground cloves
1 Tbsp. ground cinnamon
1 Tbsp. fennel seeds

Grind all together in a coffee or spice grinder until fine.
Use only ¼ tsp. in Rob's Sweet and Sour Joe, but store the rest in a tightly covered container for the next time.

Savory Sausage Sandwiches

Mary Jane Musser
Manheim, PA

Makes 8 servings

Prep. Time: 25 minutes
Cooking Time: 3-6 hours
Ideal slow cooker size: 3½-qt.

2 lbs. fresh sausage, cut into bun-length pieces
2 pkgs. dry spaghetti sauce mix
12-oz. can tomato paste
3 cups water
½ cup brown sugar
¼ cup vinegar

1. Cook sausage in skillet in water for 10 minutes.* Drain. Place in slow cooker.
2. Combine remaining ingredients in saucepan. Simmer 5 minutes. Pour over sausage.
3. Cover. Cook on High 3 hours or Low 6 hours.

Serving suggestion: Serve in ***rolls*** *topped with grated* ***cheese****.*

*You can skip this step. But pre-cooking the sausages lightly in this way cooks off much of their grease.

Variation:
Use 1 qt. spaghetti sauce, either homemade or bought, instead of sauce mix, tomato paste, and water.

Italian Sausage

Lauren Eberhard
Seneca, IL

Makes 15 servings

Prep. Time: 40 minutes
Cooking Time: 6-7 hours
Ideal slow cooker size: 6-qt., or 2 4-qt. cookers

5 lbs. Italian sausage in casing
4 large green bell peppers, sliced
3 large onions, sliced
1, *or* 2, garlic cloves, minced
28-oz. can tomato purée
14-oz. can tomato sauce
12-oz. can tomato paste
1 Tbsp. dried oregano
1 Tbsp. dried basil
½ tsp. garlic powder
1½ tsp. salt
2 tsp. sugar

1. Cut sausage into 4″ or 5″ pieces and brown on all sides in batches in skillet.
2. Sauté peppers, onions, and garlic in drippings.
3. Combine tomato purée, sauce, and paste in bowl. Stir in seasonings and sugar.
4. Layer half of sausage, onions, and peppers in 6-qt. slow cooker, or in 2 4-qt. cookers. Cover with half the tomato mixture. Repeat layers.
5. Cover. Cook on High 1 hour and then on Low 5-6 hours.

*Serving suggestion: Serve over **pasta**, or dip mixture with a straining spoon onto **Italian sandwich rolls**.*

Dawn's Sausage and Peppers

Dawn Day
Westminster, CA

Makes 8-10 servings

Prep. Time: 25-30 minutes
Cooking Time: 6 hours
Ideal slow cooker size: 5-qt.

3 medium onions, sliced
1 sweet red pepper, sliced
1 sweet green pepper, sliced
1 sweet yellow pepper, sliced
4 garlic cloves, minced
1 Tbsp. oil
28-oz. can chopped tomatoes
1 tsp. salt
½ tsp. crushed red pepper flakes
2-3 lbs. sweet Italian sausage, cut into 3″ pieces

1. Sauté onions, peppers, and garlic in oil in skillet. When just softened, place in slow cooker. (Or skip this step, but check that the vegetables are cooked to your liking at the end of the 6-hour cooking time.)
2. Add tomatoes, salt, and crushed red pepper. Mix well.
3. Add sausage links.
4. Cover. Cook on Low 6 hours.

*Serving suggestion: Serve on **rolls**, or over **pasta** or **baked potatoes**.*

Variation:
For a thicker sauce, stir 2 Tbsp. cornstarch into 2 Tbsp. water in a small bowl until smooth. Fifteen minutes before end of cooking time, stir into slow cooker, stirring until well mixed. Cover and cook 15 minutes.

Super-Simple Sausage and Sauerkraut

Eileen Lehman
Kidron, OH

Makes 12 servings

Prep. Time: 10 minutes
Cooking Time: 4-8 hours
Ideal slow cooker size: 4-qt.

2-3 lbs. fresh sausage, cut in 3″-lengths, or removed from casings
3 32-oz. cans sauerkraut

1. Brown sausage in large non-stick skillet. (Don't crowd the skillet or the sausages will steam and not brown.)
2. Combine sausage and sauerkraut in slow cooker.
3. Cover. Cook on Low 4-8 hours, or until meat is fully cooked.

Note:
It is traditional to serve sauerkraut with mashed potatoes on New Year's Day in Kidron!

Bratwurst in Sauce

Joyce Shackelford
Green Bay, WI

Makes 6-10 servings

Prep. Time: 20 minutes
Cooking Time: 6-10 hours
Ideal slow cooker size: 4-qt.

2-3 lbs. uncooked bratwursts
6-oz. can tomato paste
½ cup ketchup
12-oz. can beer
½ small onion, chopped fine
2 cloves garlic, minced

1. Place bratwursts in saucepan. Barely cover with water. Bring to a boil and cook 5-10 minutes. Drain well. Cut into bite-size pieces.
2. Combine tomato paste, ketchup, beer, onion, and garlic in slow cooker. Add partially cooked brats.
3. Cover. Cook on Low 6-10 hours, or until brats are cooked through and as hot as you like them.

*Serving suggestion: Serve over cooked **rice** or **pasta**. Or serve with wooden picks, accompanied with a good **dark bread**.*

Brats and Spuds

Kathi Rogge
Alexandria, IN

Makes 6 servings

Prep. Time: 35 minutes
Cooking Time: 4-6 hours
Ideal slow cooker size: 4-qt.

5-6 bratwurst links, cut into 1" pieces
5 medium-sized potatoes, peeled and cubed
27-oz. can sauerkraut, rinsed and drained
1 medium-sized tart apple, chopped
1 small onion, chopped
⅓-½ cup packed brown sugar
½ tsp. salt

1. Brown bratwurst on all sides in skillet.
2. Combine remaining ingredients in slow cooker. Stir in bratwurst and pan drippings.
3. Cover. Cook on High 4-6 hours, or until potatoes and apples are tender.

Variation:
Add a small amount of caraway seeds or crisp bacon pieces, just before serving.

Sausage and Scalloped Potatoes

Carolyn Baer
Conrath, WI

Makes 5 servings

Prep. Time: 25 minutes
Cooking Time: 5-10 hours
Ideal slow cooker size: 4-qt.

2½ lbs. potatoes, sliced ¼" thick, *divided*
1 lb. fully cooked smoked sausage links, sliced ½" thick, *divided*
2 medium onions, chopped, *divided*
10¾-oz. can cheddar cheese soup, *divided*
10¾-oz. can cream of celery soup, *divided*

1. Layer one-third of potatoes, one-third of sausage, one-third of onions, one-third of cheddar cheese soup, and one-third of celery soup into slow cooker.
2. Repeat 2 times.
3. Cover. Cook on Low 10 hours or on High 5 hours, or until vegetables are as tender as you like them.

*Serving suggestion: Serve with **peas**, a **salad**, and **dessert**.*

Note:
I like to prepare this delicious dish when I will be gone for the day, but know I will have guests for the evening meal. When I get home, the meat and potatoes are already cooked.

Sausage-Potato Slow Cooker Dinner

Deborah Swartz
Grottoes, VA

Makes 6-8 servings

Prep. Time: 25-30 minutes
Cooking Time: 3-9 hours
Ideal slow cooker size: 4-qt.

¾ lb. sausage, casings removed, *divided*
1 cup water
½ tsp. cream of tartar
6 medium potatoes, thinly sliced, peeled or not, *divided*
1 onion, chopped, *divided*
¼ cup flour, *divided*
salt to taste
pepper to taste
1½ cups grated cheddar cheese, *divided*
¼ stick (2 Tbsp.) butter
10¾-oz. can cream of mushroom soup

1. Brown sausage in skillet. Drain off drippings.
2. Combine water and cream of tartar in a good-sized mixing bowl. Place potatoes in water as you slice them. When finished slicing, toss potatoes in water to keep them from turning brown. Drain off water.
3. Layer half of potatoes, sausage, onion, flour, a sprinkling of salt and pepper, and half of cheddar cheese in slow cooker.
4. Repeat layers of potatoes, sausage, onion, flour, salt and pepper until completely used.
5. Dot butter over top. Pour soup over all.
6. Cover. Cook on Low 7-9 hours or on High 3-4 hours, or until potatoes and onions are tender.
7. Sprinkle reserved cheese over top just before serving.

As Christmas comes near, my husband and I spend seven different evenings with each one of our seven married children. It's so special to see their reactions as they open their gifts. On Christmas Day we all gather together to eat and sing. Mary B. Sensenig, New Holland, PA

Sausage and Sweet Potatoes

Ruth Hershey
Paradise, PA

Makes 4-6 servings

Prep. Time: 25 minutes
Cooking Time: 4-10 hours
Ideal slow cooker size: 4-qt.

1 lb. bulk sausage
2 sweet potatoes, peeled and sliced
3 apples, peeled and sliced
2 Tbsp. brown sugar
1 Tbsp. flour
¼ tsp. ground cinnamon
¼ tsp. salt
¼ cup water

1. Brown sausage in skillet. Drain off drippings.
2. Layer sausage, sweet potatoes, and apples in slow cooker.
3. Combine remaining ingredients in a small bowl. Stir until well mixed.
4. Pour over ingredients in slow cooker.
5. Cover. Cook on Low 8-10 hours or on High 4 hours.

Harvest Kielbasa

Christ Kaczynski
Schenectady, NY

Makes 6 servings

Prep. Time: 20 minutes
Cooking Time: 4-8 hours
Ideal slow cooker size: 5-qt.

2 lbs. smoked kielbasa
3 cups unsweetened applesauce
½ cup brown sugar
3 medium onions, sliced

1. Slice kielbasa into ¼" slices. Brown in skillet. Drain off drippings.
2. Combine applesauce and brown sugar in a good-sized mixing bowl.
3. Layer kielbasa, onions, and applesauce mixture in slow cooker.
4. Cover. Cook on Low 4-8 hours.

Note:
The longer it cooks, the better the flavor.

Kielbasa Stew

Fannie Miller
Hutchinson, KS

Makes 6-8 servings

Prep. Time: 40-45 minutes
Cooking Time: 8-10 hours
Ideal slow cooker size: 5-qt.

6 strips of bacon
1 onion, chopped
1-1½ lbs. smoked, fully cooked kielbasa, thinly sliced
2 15½-oz. cans great northern beans, drained
2 8-oz. cans tomato sauce
4¼-oz. can chopped green chilies, undrained
2 medium carrots, thinly sliced
1 medium green bell pepper, chopped
½ tsp. Italian seasoning
½ tsp. dried thyme
½ tsp. black pepper

1. Fry bacon in skillet until crisp. Crumble bacon and place in large slow cooker.
2. Add onions and sausage to drippings in skillet. Cook until onions are soft. Drain off drippings.
3. Transfer onions and sausage to slow cooker.
4. Add all remaining ingredients to cooker and stir together well.
5. Cover. Cook on Low 8-10 hours, or until vegetables are as tender as you like them.

Kielbasa and Cabbage

Mary Ann Lefever
Lancaster, PA

Makes 4 servings

Prep. Time: 10-15 minutes
Cooking Time: 8 hours
Ideal slow cooker size: 4- to 5-qt.

1 lb. kielbasa cut into 4 chunks
4 large white potatoes, cut into chunks
1-lb. head green cabbage, shredded
1 qt. whole tomatoes (strained if you don't like seeds)
onion, thinly sliced, *optional*

1. Layer kielbasa, then potatoes, and then cabbage into slow cooker.
2. Pour tomatoes over top.
3. Top with sliced onions if you wish.
4. Cover. Cook on High 8 hours, or until meat is cooked through and vegetables are as tender as you like them.

Rice and Beans—and Sausage

Marcia S. Myer
Manheim, PA

Makes 8 servings

Prep. Time: 25 minutes
Cooking Time: 4-6 hours
Ideal slow cooker size: 5-qt.

3 celery ribs, chopped
1 onion, chopped
2 garlic cloves, minced
1¾ cups tomato juice
2 16-oz. cans kidney beans, drained
¾ tsp. dried oregano
¾ tsp. dried thyme
¼ tsp. red pepper flakes
¼ tsp. pepper
½ lb. (*or* more) fully cooked smoked turkey sausage, *or* kielbasa, cut into ¼"-thick slices

1. Combine all ingredients in slow cooker.
2. Cover. Cook on Low 4-6 hours.

Serving suggestion: Serve over ***rice****. Garnish with* ***shredded cheese*** *if you wish.*

Election Lunch

Alix Nancy Botsford
Seminole, OK

Makes 6-12 servings

Prep. Time: 30 minutes
Cooking Time: 2-4 hours
Ideal slow cooker size: 6-qt., or 2 4-qt. cookers

1 large onion, chopped
1 lb. sausage, cut into thin slices, *or* with casings removed and meat crumbled
1 rib celery, sliced
1 Tbsp. Worcestershire sauce
1½ tsp. dry mustard
¼ cup honey
10-oz. can tomatoes with green chili peppers
1-lb. can lima, *or* butter, beans, drained, with liquid reserved
1-lb. can red kidney beans, drained, with liquid reserved
1-lb. can garbanzo beans, drained, with liquid reserved

1. Brown onion and sausage in skillet. Stir frequently. Continue cooking until pink disappears from meat. Drain off drippings.
2. Place meat and onions in 6-qt. slow cooker, or divide between 2 4-qt. cookers.
3. Stir in all other ingredients, combining well. Add reserved juice from lima, kidney, and garbanzo beans if there's enough room in the cooker(s).
4. Cover. Cook on Low 2-4 hours.

Note:

I mixed up this hearty stew the night before an Election Day and took it to the voting site the next morning. I plugged it in, and all day long we could smell the Lunch cooking. I work at a very sparsely populated, country poling place and ended up giving out the recipe in little water-cup samples to many voters!

I have four different sizes of slow cookers. One is very tiny, with only an on and off switch, for keeping cheese sauce hot. One I use for heating gravy. Another I often use to keep mashed potatoes warm.

Sausage Pasta Stew

Betty K. Drescher
Quakertown, PA

Makes 8 servings

Prep. Time: 30-35 minutes
Cooking Time: 7¼-9¼ hours
Ideal slow cooker size: 6-qt.

1 lb. Italian sausage, casings removed
4 cups water
26-oz. jar meatless spaghetti sauce
16-oz. can kidney beans, rinsed and drained
1 medium yellow summer squash, cut in 1" pieces
2 medium carrots, cut in ¼" slices
1 medium red, *or* green, sweet pepper, diced
⅓ cup chopped onions
1½ cups uncooked spiral pasta
1 cup frozen peas
1 tsp. sugar
½ tsp. salt
¼ tsp. pepper

1. Sauté sausage in skillet until no longer pink. Drain off drippings. Place sausage in slow cooker.
2. Add water, spaghetti sauce, kidney beans, squash, carrots, pepper, and onions. Mix well.
3. Cover. Cook on Low 7-9 hours, or until vegetables are tender.
4. Add remaining ingredients. Mix well.
5. Cover. Cook on High 15-20 minutes, or until pasta is tender.

Note:
Add 1 Tbsp. tapioca in Step 5 if you like a thicker stew.

Golden Autumn Stew

Naomi E. Fast, Hesston, KS

Makes 8-10 servings

Prep. Time: 30-40 minutes • Cooking Time: 6 hours
Ideal slow cooker size: 5-qt.

2 cups cubed Yukon gold potatoes
2 cups cubed, peeled sweet potatoes
2 cups cubed, peeled butternut squash
1 cup cubed, peeled rutabaga
1 cup diced carrots
1 cup sliced celery
1 lb. smoked sausage
2 cups apple juice, *or* cider
1 tart apple, thinly sliced
salt to taste
pepper to taste
1 Tbsp. sugar, *or* honey

1. Combine vegetables in slow cooker.
2. Place ring of sausage on top. Or arrange sausage links or pieces over top of vegetables.
3. Pour in apple juice. Place apple slices over top.
4. Cover. Cook on High 2 hours, and then on Low 4 hours, or until vegetables are tender. Do not stir.
5. To prepare to serve, remove sausage and keep warm. Season vegetables with salt, pepper, and sugar as desired. Place vegetables in bowl. Slice meat into pieces and place on top.

*Serving suggestion: I like to serve the Stew with hot **baking-powder biscuits** and **honey**, and a **green salad** or **cole slaw**.*

Tip:
Don't omit the rutabaga! Get acquainted with its rich uniqueness. It will surprise and please your taste buds.

Chili Casserole

Sharon Miller
Holmesville, OH

Makes 6 servings

Prep. Time: 20-25 minutes
Cooking Time: 7 hours
Ideal slow cooker size: 5-qt.

1 lb. bulk pork sausage
2 cups water
15½-oz. can chili beans, drained
14½-oz. can diced tomatoes
¾ cup uncooked brown rice
¼ cup chopped onions
1 Tbsp. chili powder
1 tsp. Worcestershire sauce
1 tsp. prepared mustard
¾ tsp. salt
⅛ tsp. garlic powder
1 cup shredded cheddar cheese

1. Brown sausage in skillet. Stir frequently to break up clumps. When meat is no longer pink, drain off drippings.
2. Spoon meat into slow cooker.
3. Add all other ingredients, except cheese, to slow cooker.
4. Cover. Cook on Low 7 hours.
5. Stir in cheese during last 10 minutes of cooking time.

Pizza Rigatoni

Tina Snyder
Manheim, PA

Makes 6-8 servings

Prep. Time: 25 minutes
Cooking Time: 4 hours
Ideal slow cooker size: 5-qt.

1½ lbs. bulk sausage, *divided*
3 cups rigatoni, lightly cooked, *divided*
4 cups shredded mozzarella cheese, *divided*
10¾-oz. can cream of mushroom soup, *divided*
1 small onion, sliced, *divided*
15-oz. can pizza sauce, *divided*
8-oz. can pizza sauce, *divided*
3½-oz. pkg. sliced pepperoni, *divided*
6-oz. can sliced ripe olives, drained, *divided*

1. Brown sausage in skillet. Drain off drippings.
2. Place half the sausage in the slow cooker.
3. Place half of pasta, cheese, soup, onion, pizza sauce, pepperoni, and olives in layers over sausage. Repeat layers.
4. Cover. Cook on Low 4 hours.

Tip:
If your store doesn't carry 8-oz. cans pizza sauce, substitute an 8-oz. can tomato sauce with basil, garlic, and oregano.

Slow-Cooker Pizza

Sharon Miller
Holmesville, OH

Makes 6 servings

Prep. Time: 25 minutes
Cooking Time: 6-8 hours
Ideal slow cooker size: 5-qt.

1½ lbs. bulk sausage, *divided*
1 small onion, chopped, *divided*
1-lb. pkg. pasta, *or* **noodles, uncooked,** *divided*
28-oz. jar spaghetti sauce
16-oz. can tomato sauce
¾ cup water
4-oz. can mushrooms, drained
8-oz. pkg. pepperoni, chopped
16-oz. pkg. shredded mozzarella cheese

1. Brown sausage and onion in skillet. Drain.
2. Place one-third of mixture in slow cooker.
3. Layer in one-third of uncooked pasta.
4. Combine spaghetti sauce, tomato sauce, water, and mushrooms in a good-sized bowl. Ladle one-third of that mixture over noodles.
5. Repeat the above layers 2 more times.
6. Top with pepperoni. Top pepperoni with shredded cheese.
7. Cover. Cook on Low 6-8 hours, or until pasta is cooked to your liking and pizza is hot throughout.

Ham in Foil

Jeanette Oberholtzer
Manheim, PA
Vicki Dinkel
Sharon Springs, KS
Janet Roggie
Lowville, NY

Makes 8 servings

Prep. Time: 5 minutes
Cooking Time: 7 hours
Ideal slow cooker size: 5-qt.

½ cup water
3-4-lb. precooked ham
liquid smoke

1. Pour water into slow cooker.
2. Sprinkle ham with liquid smoke. Wrap in foil. Place in slow cooker.
3. Cover. Cook on High 1 hour, and then on Low 6 hours.
4. Cut into thick chunks or ½"-thick slices and serve.

Easy and Elegant Ham

Lorraine Pflederer
Goshen, IN

Makes 18-20 servings

Prep. Time: 10 minutes
Cooking Time: 6-7 hours
Standing Time: 10-15 minutes
Ideal slow cooker size: 5-qt.

2 20-oz. cans sliced pineapple, *divided*
1 fully cooked boneless ham (about 6 lbs.), halved
6-oz. jar cherries, well drained
12-oz. jar orange marmalade

1. Drain pineapple, reserving juice. Set juice aside.
2. Place half of pineapple in ungreased slow cooker.
3. Top with ham. Add cherries, remaining pineapple, and reserved juice.
4. Spoon marmalade over ham.
5. Cover. Cook on Low 6-7 hours or until heated through. Remove to serving platter and let stand for 10-15 minutes before slicing.
6. Serve pineapple and cherries over sliced ham.

Honey-Dijon Holiday Ham

Robin Schrock
Millersburg, OH

Makes 10 servings

Prep. Time: 15 minutes
Cooking Time: 8 hours
Ideal slow cooker size: 6-qt.

5-lb. bone-in fully cooked smoked ham
⅓ cup apple juice
¼ cup packed brown sugar
1 Tbsp. honey
1 Tbsp. Dijon mustard

1. Place ham in slow cooker.
2. In a small bowl, mix juice, brown sugar, honey, and mustard together. Spread over ham.
3. Cover. Cook on Low 8 hours or until ham is hot through.
4. Slice ham and serve.
5. Pass sauce to top ham slices.

We ask the youngest child present on Christmas Eve to place baby Jesus in the crib or nativity as we all sing "Away in a Manger" and other Christmas carols.

Donna Treloar, Muncie, IN

Glazed Ham in a Bag

Eleanor J. Ferreira
North Chelmsford, MA

Makes 12 servings

Prep. Time: 10 minutes
Cooking Time: 6-8 hours
Ideal slow cooker size: 6-qt.

5-lb. cooked ham
3 Tbsp. orange juice
1 Tbsp. Dijon mustard

1. Rinse meat.
2. Combine orange juice and mustard. Spread over ham.
3. Place in cooking bag. Seal bag with twist tie. Poke 4 holes in top of bag. Place in slow cooker.
4. Cover. Cook on Low 6-8 hours.
5. To serve, remove ham from bag, reserving juices. Slice ham and spoon juices over.

Tip:
Serve additional juice with ham in small pitcher.

Raspberry-Glazed Ham

Gloria Frey
Lebanon, PA

Makes 16-20 servings

Prep Time: 10-15 minutes
Cooking Time: 4 hours
Ideal slow-cooker size: 6-qt.

8-10-lb. boneless ham, fully cooked
¼ cup apple juice
2 Tbsp. lemon juice
2 tsp. cornstarch
⅓ cup seedless raspberry jam, *divided*
1 Tbsp. butter

1. Place ham in slow cooker. Cover. Cook on Low 2 hours.
2. While ham is cooking, blend apple juice, lemon juice, and cornstarch together in saucepan.
3. Stir in about half of jam after liquid is well blended.
4. Cook and stir until hot and bubbly. Add butter. Stir in remaining jam.
5. Spoon glaze over ham after it has cooked 2 hours.
6. Cover. Cook 2 more hours on Low.
7. Slice ham and serve.

Tip:
If you wish, double the amount of glaze. Place half in a serving bowl. Pass alongside ham slices so individuals can add more glaze to the meat if they wish.

Ham with Pineapple Sauce

Kayla Snyder
North East, PA

Makes 14-16 servings

Prep. Time: 20-30 minutes
Cooking Time: 3 hours
Ideal slow cooker size: 5-qt.

20-oz. can crushed pineapple, undrained
1 tsp. vinegar
1 Tbsp. lemon juice
½ tsp. salt
2 cups brown sugar
¾ tsp. dry mustard
4 Tbsp. flour
7-8-lb. ham, precooked and sliced in ¼"-thick slices

1. Mix together pineapple, vinegar, lemon juice, salt, brown sugar, mustard, and flour in a saucepan. Bring to boil. Cook, stirring frequently until slightly thickened.
2. Layer several slices of ham into slow cooker. Ladle some of sauce over top of each slice. Continue layering until all ham and sauce are stacked in slow cooker.
3. Cover. Cook on High 3 hours, or until heated through.

Note:
We served this recipe at our wedding, so it is especially special to us.

New England Boiled Dinner

Leona M. Slabaugh
Apple Creek, OH

Makes 4 servings

Prep. Time: 30 minutes
Cooking Time: 3-6 hours
Ideal slow cooker size: 3- to 5-qt.

2 lbs. boneless smoked ham piece
1 lb. potatoes, halved
1-lb. bag baby carrots
1 lb. cabbage, cut in wedges
¼ cup water

1. Place meat in slow cooker. Fit vegetables around meat.
2. Add water
3. Cover. Cook on Low 6 hours or on High 3 hours, or just until meat and vegetables are as tender as you like.

Ham, Bean, and Potato Dish

Hazel L. Propst
Oxford, PA

Makes 6-8 servings

Prep. Time: 10 minutes
Cooking Time: 6-8 hours
Ideal slow cooker size: 5-qt.

8-10 small potatoes
3-4 cans string beans, undrained
ham hock, *or* **leftover ham**
salt to taste
pepper to taste

1. Place potatoes in bottom of slow cooker.
2. Alternate layers of beans and ham over potatoes. Sprinkle with salt and pepper.
3. Cover. Cook on Low 8 hours if using ham hock; 6 hours if using leftover ham, or until meat and potatoes are tender but not dry or mushy.

Schnitz und Knepp

Jean Robinson
Cinnaminson, NJ

Makes 6 servings

Prep. Time: 20 minutes
Soaking Time: 2-3 hours
Cooking Time: 5¼ hours
Ideal slow cooker size: 4-qt.

Schnitz:

¾-1 lb. dried sweet apples (also known as "schnitz")
3 lbs. ham slices, cut into 2" cubes
2 Tbsp. brown sugar
1 cinnamon stick

Knepp (dumplings):

2 cups flour
4 tsp. baking powder
1 egg, well beaten
3 Tbsp. melted butter
scant ½ cup milk
1 tsp. salt
¼ tsp. pepper

1. Cover apples with water in large bowl and let soak for a few hours.
2. Place ham cubes in slow cooker. Cover with water.
3. Cover cooker. Cook on High 2 hours.
4. Add apples and water in which they have been soaking.
5. Add brown sugar and cinnamon stick. Mix until sugar dissolves.
6. Cover. Cook on Low 3 hours.
7. Combine dumpling ingredients in bowl. Drop into hot liquid in cooker by tablespoonfuls.
8. Turn cooker to High. Cover. Do not lift lid for 15 minutes.
9. Serve piping hot on a large platter.

Note:

This was my grandmother's recipe and she had no slow cooker. I was allowed to drop in the dumplings. Schnitz und Knepp cooked on the back of the woodstove while Grandma quilted.

Ham with Sweet Potatoes and Oranges

Esther Becker, Gordonville, PA

Makes 4 servings

Prep. Time: 15 minutes • Cooking Time: 7-8 hours
Ideal slow cooker size: 3-qt.

2-3 sweet potatoes, peeled and sliced ¼" thick
1 large ham slice
3 seedless oranges, peeled and sliced
3 Tbsp. orange juice concentrate
3 Tbsp. honey
½ cup brown sugar
2 Tbsp. cornstarch

1. Place sweet potato slices in slow cooker.
2. Arrange ham and orange slices on top of potatoes.
3. Combine remaining ingredients in a small bowl. Drizzle over ham and oranges.
4. Cover. Cook on Low 7-8 hours.

Serving suggestion: Delicious served with a ***fruit salad.***

Ham and Hash Browns

Evelyn Page, Riverton, WY
Anna Stoltzfus, Honey Brook, PA

Makes 6-8 servings

Prep. Time: 15 minutes
Cooking Time: 6-8 hours
Ideal slow cooker size: 5-qt.

28-oz. pkg. frozen hash brown potatoes
2½ cups cubed cooked ham
2-oz. jar pimentos, drained and chopped
10¾-oz. can cheddar cheese soup
¾ cup half-and-half, *or* **milk**
dash of pepper
salt to taste

1. Combine potatoes, ham, and pimentos in slow cooker.
2. In a bowl, combine soup, half-and-half, and seasonings. Pour over potatoes and ham. Stir well.
3. Cover. Cook on Low 6-8 hours. (If you turn the cooker on when you go to bed, you'll have a wonderfully tasty breakfast in the morning.)

Variation:

Add a 4-oz. can of mushrooms, drained, *or* ¼ lb. sliced fresh mushrooms, to Step 1.

Creamy Ham Topping (for baked potatoes)

Judy Buller
Bluffton, OH

Makes 6 servings

Prep. Time: 15 minutes
Cooking Time: 1-2 hours
Ideal slow cooker size: 3½-qt.

half a stick (¼ cup) butter
¼ cup flour
2 cups milk
¼ cup half-and-half
1 Tbsp. chopped parsley
1 Tbsp. chicken bouillon granules
½ tsp. Italian seasoning
2 cups diced cooked ham
¼ cup Romano cheese, grated
1 cup sliced mushrooms
baked potatoes
shredded cheese
sour cream

1. Melt butter in saucepan over medium heat. Stir in flour. Add milk and half-and-half.
2. Continue stirring until sauce thickens and becomes smooth.
3. Stir in remaining ingredients (except baked potatoes, shredded cheese, and sour cream). Pour into slow cooker.
4. Cover. Cook on Low 1-2 hours.
5. Serve over baked potatoes. Top with shredded cheese and sour cream.

Ham and Lima Beans

Charlotte Shaffer
East Earl, PA

Makes 6 servings

Prep. Time: 15 minutes
Soaking Time: 8 hours, or overnight
Cooking Time: 4-7 hours
Ideal slow cooker size: 4-qt.

1 lb. dry lima beans
1 onion, chopped
1 bell pepper, chopped
1 tsp. dry mustard
1 tsp. salt
1 tsp. pepper
½ lb. ham, finely cubed
1 cup water
10¾-oz. can tomato soup

1. Cover beans with water. Soak 8 hours or overnight. Drain.
2. Combine all ingredients in slow cooker.
3. Cover. Cook on Low 7 hours or on High 4 hours, or until vegetables are as tender as you like them.
4. If mixture begins to dry out, add ½ cup water or more and stir well.

Serving suggestion: We think this is delicious served with hot ***cornbread****.*

Black Beans with Ham

Colleen Heatwole
Burton, MI

Makes 8-10 servings

Prep. Time: 20 minutes
Soaking Time: 8 hours or overnight
Cooking Time: 10-12 hours
Ideal slow cooker size: 5-qt.

4 cups dry black beans
1-2 cups diced ham
1 tsp. salt, *optional*
1 tsp. cumin
½-1 cup minced onion
2 garlic cloves, minced
3 bay leaves
1 qt. diced tomatoes
1 Tbsp. brown sugar

1. Cover black beans with water and soak 8 hours, or overnight, in slow cooker.
2. Drain and pour beans back into slow cooker.
3. Add all remaining ingredients. Stir well. Cover with water.
4. Cover cooker. Cook on Low 10-12 hours, or until beans are as tender as you like them.

Note:
This is our favorite black bean recipe. We usually serve it over rice. It's good any time of the year, but we make it especially frequently in the winter.

Ham 'n' Cabbage Stew

Dede Peterson
Rapid City, SD

Makes 4-5 servings

Prep. Time: 25-30 minutes
Cooking Time: 4-6 hours
Ideal slow cooker size: 4-qt.

½ lb. cooked ham, cubed
½ cup diced onions
1 garlic clove, minced
4-oz. can sliced mushrooms, undrained
4 cups shredded cabbage
2 cups sliced carrots
¼ tsp. pepper
¼ tsp. caraway seeds
⅔ cup beef broth
1 Tbsp. cornstarch
2 Tbsp. water

1. Combine all ingredients except cornstarch and water in slow cooker.
2. Cover. Cook on Low 4-6 hours, or until vegetables are cooked as you like them.
3. In a small bowl, mix cornstarch into water until smooth. Stir into slow cooker during last hour to thicken Stew slightly.

Ham and Corn Slow-Cooker Casserole

Vicki Dinkel
Sharon Springs, KS

Makes 8 servings

Prep. Time: 30 minutes
Cooking Time: 4-8 hours
Ideal slow cooker size: 4-qt.

1 stick (8 Tbsp.) butter
1 small green bell pepper, chopped
1 medium onion, chopped
½ cup flour
½ tsp. paprika
½ tsp. salt
½ tsp. pepper
¼ tsp. dried thyme
1 tsp. dry mustard
4 cups milk
8-oz. can cream-style corn
2 cups diced, slightly cooked potatoes
4 cups diced cooked ham
1 cup shredded cheddar cheese

1. Sauté green pepper and onion in butter in skillet.
2. Stir in flour and seasonings.
3. Gradually stir in milk and cook over medium heat. Stir continually until thickened. Pour into slow cooker.
4. Stir in remaining ingredients.
5. Cover. Cook on Low 8 hours or on High 4 hours.

Cheesy Ham and Broccoli

Dolores Kratz
Souderton, PA

Makes 6 servings

Prep. Time: 25-30 minutes
Cooking Time: 6-7 hours
Ideal slow cooker size: 4- to 5-qt.

1 bunch fresh broccoli
1½ cups chopped ham
¾ cup uncooked rice
4-oz. can mushrooms, drained
1 small onion, chopped
10¾-oz. can cheddar cheese soup
¾ cup water
¼ cup half-and-half, *or* **milk**
dash of pepper
½-1 can chow mein noodles

1. Cut broccoli into pieces and steam for 4 minutes in microwave. Place in slow cooker.
2. Add remaining ingredients to slow cooker except noodles. Mix well.
3. Cover. Cook on Low 6-7 hours.
4. Just before serving, sprinkle with noodles.

Serving suggestion: This is a good main dish, with a ***tossed salad*** *or* ***applesauce*** *as a go-along.*

Broccoli Casserole

Rebecca Meyerkorth
Wamego, KS

Makes 4 servings

Prep. Time: 20 minutes
Cooking Time: 4-5 hours
Ideal slow cooker size: 4- to 5-qt.

16-oz. pkg. frozen broccoli cuts, thawed and drained
2-3 cups cubed, cooked ham
10¾-oz. can cream of mushroom soup
4 oz. of your favorite mild cheese, cubed
1 cup milk
1 cup instant rice, uncooked
1 rib celery, chopped
1 small onion, chopped

1. Combine broccoli and ham in slow cooker.
2. In a medium-sized bowl, combine soup, cheese, milk, rice, celery, and onion. Stir into broccoli and ham.
3. Cover. Cook on Low 4-5 hours.

Ham and Broccoli

Dede Peterson
Rapid City, SD

Makes 6-8 servings

Prep. Time: 20 minutes
Cooking Time: 3¼-4¼ hours
Ideal slow cooker size: 5-qt.

¾ lb. fresh broccoli, chopped, *or* **10-oz. pkg.**

frozen chopped broccoli
10¾-oz. can cream of mushroom soup
8-oz. jar cheese sauce
2½ cups milk
1¼ cups long-grain rice, uncooked
1 rib celery, sliced
⅛ tsp. pepper
3 cups cooked and cubed ham
8-oz. can water chestnuts, drained and sliced
½ tsp. paprika

1. Combine all ingredients except ham, water chestnuts, and paprika in slow cooker.
2. Cover. Cook on High 3-4 hours.
3. Stir in ham and water chestnuts. Cook 15-20 minutes, or until heated through. Let stand 10 minutes before serving.
4. Sprinkle with paprika just before serving.

Underground Ham and Cheese

Carol Sommers
Millersburg, OH

Makes 12-16 servings

Prep. Time: 30-40 minutes
Cooking Time: 3-4 hours
Ideal slow cooker size: 2 4- to 5-qt. cookers

half a stick (4 Tbsp.) butter
½ cup chopped onions
4 cups cooked ham, cut into chunks
1 Tbsp. Worcestershire sauce
2 10¾-oz. cans cream of mushroom soup
1 cup milk
2 cups Velveeta cheese, cubed
4 qts. mashed potatoes
1 pt. sour cream
browned and crumbled bacon

1. Combine butter and onions in saucepan. Cook until onions are tender.
2. Place sautéed onions, ham, and Worcestershire sauce in large slow cooker, or divide between 2 4- or 5-qt. cookers.
3. In saucepan, heat together soup, milk, and cheese until cheese melts. Pour into cooker(s).
4. In a large bowl, fold mashed potatoes and sour cream together. Spread over mixture in slow cooker(s).
5. Sprinkle with bacon.
6. Cover. Cook on Low 3-4 hours, or until cheese mixture comes to top when done (hence, the name "Underground").

Verenike (or Creamy Lasagna)

Jennifer Yoder Sommers
Harrisonburg, VA

Makes 8-10 servings

Prep. Time: 10-15 minutes
Cooking Time: 5-6 hours
Ideal slow cooker size: 5-qt.

24 ozs. cottage cheese
3 eggs
1 tsp. salt
½ tsp. pepper
1 cup sour cream
2 cups evaporated milk
2 cups cubed cooked ham
7-9 uncooked lasagna noodles

1. Combine all ingredients except noodles in a good-sized mixing bowl.
2. Place half of creamy ham mixture in bottom of cooker.
3. Stack in uncooked noodles. Break them to fit if you need to.
4. Cover with remaining half of creamy ham sauce. Push noodles down so that they are fully submerged in the sauce.
5. Cover. Cook on Low 5-6 hours, or until noodles are tender but not mushy.

*Serving suggestion: Serve it with **green salad**, **peas**, and **zwiebach** (a favorite Mennonite food), or small **dinner rolls**.*

Note:
This is an easy way to make the traditional Russian Mennonite dish—verenike.

Shepherd's Pie

Melanie Thrower
McPherson, KS

Makes 3-4 servings

Prep. Time: 30-40 minutes
Cooking Time: 3 hours
Ideal slow cooker size: 4-qt.

1 lb. ground pork
1 Tbsp. vinegar
1 tsp. salt
¼ tsp. hot pepper
1 tsp. paprika
¼ tsp. dried oregano
¼ tsp. black pepper
1 tsp. chili powder
1 small onion, chopped
15-oz. can whole-kernel corn, drained
3 large potatoes
¼ cup milk
1 tsp. butter
¼ tsp. salt
dash of pepper
shredded cheese

1. Combine pork, vinegar, and seasonings in skillet. Cook until meat browns.
2. Add onions and cook until they begin to glaze.
3. Spread mixture into slow cooker.
4. Spread corn over meat.
5. Cook potatoes in water on stovetop until soft. Mash with milk, butter, ¼ tsp. salt, and dash of pepper.
6. Spread mashed potatoes over meat and corn.
7. Cover. Cook on Low 3 hours.
8. Sprinkle top with cheese a few minutes before serving.

Variation:
You can substitute ground beef for the pork.

Note:
This is my 9-year-old son's favorite dish!

Ham Balls

Jo Haberkamp
Fairbank, IA

Makes 12-16 servings

Prep. Time: 30 minutes
Cooking Time: 4-5 hours
Ideal slow cooker size: 6-qt.

Ham Balls:
3 eggs
3 cups crushed graham crackers
2 cups milk
1 tsp. salt
1 tsp. onion salt
¼ tsp. pepper
2 lbs. ground ham
1½ lbs. ground beef
1½ lbs. ground pork

Topping:
½ cup ketchup
¼ cup water
1 cup brown sugar
¼ cup, plus 2 Tbsp., apple cider vinegar
½ tsp. dry mustard

1. Beat eggs slightly in large bowl. Add graham crackers, milk, salt, onion salt, pepper, and ground meats. Mix well.
2. Form into 24 balls, using ½-cup measuring cup for each ball.
3. In a separate bowl, combine Topping ingredients.
4. Layer Ham Balls and Topping in greased slow cooker. Make sure each layer of Ham Balls is well covered with Topping.
5. Cover. Cook on High 1 hour. Reduce heat to Low and cook 3-4 hours more, or until meat is cooked through but not dried out.

Ham Loaf or Balls

Michelle Strite
Goshen, IN

Makes 8-10 servings

Prep. Time: 30 minutes
Cooking Time: 4-6 hours
Ideal slow cooker size: 4- to 5-qt.

Ham Loaf or Balls:
1 lb. ground ham
1 lb. ground pork, *or* **ground beef**
1 cup soft bread crumbs
2 eggs, slightly beaten
1 cup milk
2 Tbsp. minced onions

Beside each dish of food on the buffet, place a stack of cards with its recipe written on them. Then guests can take the recipe if they wish. — *Anita Troyer, Fairview, MI*

1¼ tsp. salt
⅛ tsp. pepper

Glaze:
¾ cup brown sugar
1 tsp. dry mustard
1 Tbsp. cornstarch
¼ cup vinegar
½ cup water

1. Combine ingredients for Ham Loaf or Ham Balls. Form into Loaf or Balls and place in slow cooker.
2. Combine dry ingredients for Glaze in bowl. Mix in vinegar and water until smooth.
3. Pour Glaze into saucepan. Cook uncovered until slightly thickened.
4. Pour over meat.
5. Cover. Cook on High 4-6 hours, or until meat is cooked through.

Variations:
1. For a firmer Loaf, or Balls, use dry bread crumbs instead of soft. Use only ¾ cup milk instead of 1 cup.
2. Form meat mixture into 1" balls. Brown lightly by baking on cookie sheet in 400° oven for 5-10 minutes. Place browned Balls in slow cooker. Pour cooked Glaze over Balls. Cover. Cook on High 2-4 hours.

Julia A. Fisher
New Carlisle, OH

Pork Barbecue

Barbara L. McGinnis
Jupiter, FL

Makes 6 servings

Prep. Time: 5-10 minutes
Cooking Time: 8 hours
Ideal slow cooker size: 5-qt.

3-4-lb. pork loin
2 cups cider vinegar
salt to taste
pepper to taste
2 tsp. sugar
½ cup ketchup
crushed red pepper to taste
Tabasco sauce to taste
sandwich rolls

1. Place pork in slow cooker.
2. Pour vinegar over meat. Sprinkle salt, pepper and sugar over top.
3. Cover. Cook on Low 8 hours.
4. Remove pork from cooker and shred meat. Reserve drippings.
5. In large mixing bowl, stir together ketchup, red pepper, Tabasco sauce, and ½ cup vinegar-sugar drippings from slow cooker. Stir in shredded meat.
6. Serve on sandwich rolls.

Serving suggestion: ***Cole slaw*** *is a good accompaniment to these sandwiches. Serve it either alongside them, or pile it into the rolls with the meat.*

Variation:
To increase the tang, add 1 tsp. dry mustard in Step 5. Use ¼ cup ketchup and ¼ cup orange juice, instead of ½ cup ketchup.

Barbecued Pork and Beef Sandwiches

Sherry L. Lapp
Lancaster, PA

Makes 6-8 sandwiches

Prep. Time: 15 minutes
Cooking Time: 8 hours
Ideal slow cooker size: 4-qt.

1½ lbs. cubed pork
1 lb. stewing beef, cubed
6-oz. can tomato paste
¼ cup vinegar
½ cup brown sugar
1 tsp. salt
1 Tbsp. chili powder
1 large onion, chopped
1 green bell pepper, chopped

1. Combine ingredients in slow cooker.
2. Cover. Cook on Low 8 hours.
3. Shred meat with fork before serving on rolls.

Serving suggestion: Bring to the table with ***sandwich rolls*** *and creamy* ***cole slaw****.*

Ham Barbecue

Amber Swarey
Honea Path, SC

Makes 10-12 servings

Prep. Time: 10 minutes
Cooking Time: 4-5 hours
Ideal slow cooker size: 3-qt.

2 lbs. thinly sliced deli ham
1 cup water
1 cup ketchup
¼ cup packed brown sugar
¼ cup Worcestershire sauce
2 Tbsp. white vinegar
2 tsp. prepared mustard

1. Place ham in greased slow cooker.
2. In bowl, combine water, ketchup, brown sugar, Worcestershire sauce, vinegar, and mustard. Pour over ham and stir well.
3. Cover. Cook on Low 4-5 hours, or until heated through.

Serving suggestion: This Ham Barbecue will fill 12 ***hamburger buns****. They're especially good if you've split and toasted them.*

Super-Bowl Little Smokies

Mary Sommerfeld
Lancaster, PA
Alicia Denlinger
Lancaster, PA

Makes 9-10 main-dish servings, or 15-20 appetizer servings

Prep. Time: 5 minutes
Cooking Time: 2 hours
Ideal slow cooker size: 4-qt.

3 1-lb. pkgs. Little Smokies
8-oz. bottle Catalina dressing
splash of liquid smoke

1. Combine all ingredients in slow cooker.
2. Cover. Cook on Low 2 hours.
3. Use toothpicks to serve. Or pile into sandwich rolls for a lunch or supper.

Note:
These are always a hit at parties, whether it's Christmas, New Year's, or the Super Bowl. They are good any time that you'd like to serve food beyond dessert, but you don't want to have a formal sit-down meal.

Cranberry Franks

Loretta Krahn
Mountain Lake, MN

Makes 15-20 servings

Prep. Time: 10 minutes
Cooking Time: 1-2 hours
Ideal slow cooker size: 3-qt.

2 pkgs. cocktail wieners, *or* **little smoked sausages**
16-oz. can jellied cranberry sauce
1 cup ketchup
3 Tbsp. brown sugar
1 Tbsp. lemon juice

1. Combine all ingredients in slow cooker.
2. Cover. Cook on High 1-2 hours.

Note:
Great picnic, potluck, or buffet food.

I have a few antique Christmas ornaments, but they tend to get lost on the tree with everything else. So I put them in a glass bowl with evergreens, and they are noticed and appreciated much more.

Carol L. Miller, Lockport, NY

Chicken Main Dishes

Sunday Roast Chicken

Ruth A. Feister, Narvon, PA

Makes 4-5 servings

Prep. Time: 30-35 minutes
Cooking Time: 6 hours
Ideal slow cooker size: 6- to 7-qt.

Seasoning Mix:

1 Tbsp. salt
2 tsp. paprika
1½ tsp. onion powder
1½ tsp. garlic powder
1½ tsp. dried basil
1 tsp. dry mustard
1 tsp. cumin
2 tsp. pepper
½ tsp. dried thyme
½ tsp. savory

¼ stick (2 Tbsp.) butter
2 cups chopped onions
1 cup chopped green bell pepper
1 roasting chicken
¼ cup flour
1-2 cups chicken stock

1. Combine Seasoning Mix ingredients in small bowl.
2. Melt butter over high heat in skillet. When butter starts to sizzle, add chopped onions and peppers, and 3 Tbsp. seasoning mix.
3. Cook until onions are golden brown. Cool.
4. Stuff cavity of chicken with cooled vegetables.
5. Sprinkle outside of chicken with 1 Tbsp. seasoning mix. Rub in well so it sticks.
6. Place chicken in large slow cooker.
7. Cover. Cook on Low 6 hours.
8. Empty vegetable stuffing and juices into saucepan. Whisk in flour and 1 cup stock from slow cooker.
9. Cook over high heat until thickened. Add more stock if you prefer a thinner gravy.

Note:

The first time I served this dish was when we had family visiting us from Mississippi. We had a wonderful time sitting around a large table, sharing many laughs and catching up on the years since our last visit.

Old-Fashioned Stewed Chicken

Bonnie Goering
Bridgewater, VA

Makes 6-8 servings

Prep. Time: 20 minutes
Cooking Time: 8¼ hours
Ideal slow cooker size: 5-qt.

3-4-lb. chicken, cut up
1 small onion, cut into wedges
1 rib celery, sliced
1 carrot, sliced
1 Tbsp. chopped fresh parsley, *or* **1 tsp. dried parsley**
1 Tbsp. chopped fresh thyme, *or* **1 tsp. dried thyme**
1 Tbsp. chopped fresh rosemary, *or* **1 tsp. dried rosemary**
3 tsp. salt
¼ tsp. pepper
3-4 cups hot water
⅓ cup flour

1. Place chicken in slow cooker. Scatter vegetables, herbs, and seasonings around it and over top. Pour water down along interior wall of cooker so as not to disturb the other ingredients.
2. Cover. Cook on Low 8 hours.
3. Remove chicken from cooker. When cool enough to handle, debone. Set aside and keep warm.
4. In small bowl, stir ⅓ cup flour into 1 cup chicken broth from slow cooker.
5. When smooth, stir back into slow cooker. Continue cooking on Low until broth thickens, stirring occasionally to prevent lumps from forming.
6. When gravy is bubbly and thickened, stir in chicken pieces.

Serving suggestion: Serve with ***mashed potatoes*** *or* ***noodles*** *and* ***creamed peas.***

Note:
I cook every Thursday afternoon for a 93-year-old woman who lives by herself. She taught me how to cook with fresh herbs from her garden. I've found they make food taste so much better that I've started an herb garden. And I dry some herbs to use during the winter.

One-Pot Easy Chicken

Jean Robinson
Cinnaminson, NJ

Makes 6 servings

Prep. Time: 25-30 minutes
Cooking Time: 6 hours
Ideal slow cooker size: 6-qt.

6-8 potatoes, quartered
1-2 large onions, sliced
3-5 carrots, cubed
5-lbs. chicken, skin removed (quarters, or legs and thighs work well)
1 small onion, chopped
1 tsp. black pepper
1 Tbsp. whole cloves, *optional*
1 Tbsp. garlic salt
1 Tbsp. chopped fresh oregano
1 tsp. dried rosemary
½ cup lemon juice, *or* **chicken broth**

1. Layer potatoes, sliced onions, and carrots in bottom of slow cooker.
2. Rinse and pat chicken dry. In shallow dish with sides mix together chopped onions, pepper, cloves, and garlic salt.
3. Dredge chicken in seasonings. Place in cooker over vegetables. Spoon any remaining seasonings over chicken.
4. Sprinkle with oregano and rosemary. Pour lemon juice around chicken.
5. Cover. Cook on Low 6 hours.

Note:
This is a lifesaver when the grandchildren come for a weekend. I get to play with them, and dinner is timed and ready when we are.

Chicken Cacciatore with Spaghetti

Phyllis Pellman Good, Lancaster, PA

Makes 4-5 servings

Prep. Time: 15 minutes • Cooking Time: 4 hours
Ideal slow cooker size: 4- to 5-qt.

2 onions, sliced
2½-3 lbs. chicken legs and thighs, skin removed
2 garlic cloves, minced
16-oz. can stewed tomatoes
8-oz. can tomato sauce
1 tsp. salt
¼ tsp. pepper
1-2 tsp. dried oregano
½ tsp. dried basil
1 bay leaf
¼ cup white wine

1. Place onions in bottom of slow cooker.
2. Lay chicken over onions.
3. Combine remaining ingredients in a good-sized bowl. Pour over chicken.
4. Cover. Cook on Low 4 hours, or until chicken is tender but not dry.
5. Remove bay leaf before serving.

Serving suggestion: Serve over hot ***buttered spaghetti, linguini,*** *or* ***fettucini.***

Chicken Cacciatore

Eleanor J. Ferreira
North Chelmsford, MA

Makes 8 servings

Prep. Time: 40 minutes
Cooking Time: 4-5 hours
Ideal slow cooker size: 6- to 6½-qt., or 2 4-qt. cookers

2 chickens, cut into pieces
1 cup flour
2 tsp. salt
½ tsp. pepper
olive oil
2 4-oz. cans sliced mushrooms, drained
3 medium onions, sliced
2 celery ribs, chopped
4 large green bell peppers, cut into 1" strips
28-oz. can tomatoes
28-oz. can tomato purée
½ tsp. dried basil
½ tsp. dried oregano
½ tsp. salt
¼ tsp. pepper
½ tsp. dried parsley

1. Shake chicken pieces, one at a time, in bag with flour, salt, and pepper. When well coated, brown chicken pieces on both sides in skillet in oil.
2. Place chicken in large slow cooker, or in two medium-sized cookers, reserving drippings.
3. Sauté mushrooms, onions, celery, and peppers in drippings from chicken. Spread over chicken in cooker.
4. Mix remaining ingredients together in bowl and pour over chicken and vegetables.
5. Cover. Cook on Low 4-5 hours.

Serving suggestion: Serve over hot ***spaghetti.***

Chicken and Sausage Cacciatore

Joyce Kaut
Rochester, NY

Makes 4-6 servings

Prep. Time: 25-35 minutes
Cooking Time: 3-4 hours
Ideal slow cooker size: 5-qt.

1 lb. Italian sausage, cut in ½"-thick slices
1 lb. skinless, boneless chicken breasts, cut into 1" pieces
oil
1 large green bell pepper, sliced in 1" strips
1 cup sliced fresh mushrooms
1 medium onion, sliced in rings
½ tsp. dried oregano
½ tsp. dried basil
1½ cups Italian-style tomato sauce

1. Lightly brown sausage and chicken breast pieces in skillet, in oil if needed. Drain off drippings.
2. Layer vegetables into slow cooker.
3. Top with meat.
4. Sprinkle with oregano and basil.
5. Top with tomato sauce.
6. Cover. Cook on Low 3-4 hours.
7. Remove cover during last 30 minutes of cooking time to allow sauce to cook off and thicken.

*Serving suggestion: Serve over cooked **spiral pasta**.*

Basil Chicken

Sarah Niessen, Akron, PA

Makes 4-6 servings

Prep. Time: 15 minutes • Cooking Time: 7-10 hours
Ideal slow cooker size: 5-qt.

1 lb. baby carrots
2 medium onions, sliced
1-2 cups celery slices and leaves
3-lb. chicken, cut-up
½ cup chicken broth, *or* **white cooking wine**
2 tsp. salt
½ tsp. black pepper
1 tsp. dried basil

1. Place carrots, onions, and celery in bottom of slow cooker.
2. Add chicken.
3. Pour broth over chicken.
4. Sprinkle with salt, pepper, and basil.
5. Cover. Cook on Low 7-10 hours, or until chicken and vegetables are tender.

Con Pollo

Dorothy Van Deest
Memphis, TN

Makes 4-6 servings

Prep. Time: 10 minutes
Cooking Time: 3-5 hours
Ideal slow cooker size: 5-qt.

3-4-lb. chicken, cut-up
salt to taste
pepper to taste
paprika to taste
garlic salt to taste
6-oz. can tomato paste
½ cup beer
3-oz. jar stuffed olives with liquid

1. Wash chicken. Sprinkle all over with salt, pepper, paprika, and garlic salt. Place in slow cooker.
2. Combine tomato paste and beer in small bowl. Pour over chicken.
3. Scatter olives over chicken. Pour liquid into cooker.
4. Cover. Cook on Low 5 hours or on High 3 hours.

*Serving suggestion: Serve over **rice** or **noodles**, along with **salad** and **cornbread**, and **sherbet** for dessert.*

Note:
This is chicken with a Spanish flair. This easy supper is quick, too, by slow-cooker standards, if you use the high temperature. Let your slow cooker be the chef.

Dad's Spicy Chicken Curry

Tom & Sue Ruth
Lancaster, PA

Makes 8 servings

Prep. Time: 25 minutes
Cooking Time: 6-8 hours
Ideal slow cooker size: 6- to 7-qt.

4 lbs. chicken pieces, with bones in
water
2 onions, diced
10-oz. pkg. frozen chopped spinach, thawed and squeezed dry
1 cup plain yogurt
2-3 diced red potatoes
3 tsp. salt
1 tsp. garlic powder
1 tsp. ground ginger
1 tsp. ground cumin
1 tsp. ground coriander
1 tsp. pepper
1 tsp. ground cloves
1 tsp. ground cardamom
1 tsp. ground cinnamon
½ tsp. chili powder
1 tsp. red pepper flakes
3 tsp. turmeric

1. Place chicken in large slow cooker. Cover with water.
2. Cover. Cook on High 2 hours, or until tender.
3. Drain chicken. Remove from slow cooker. Cool briefly and cut/shred into small pieces.
4. Return chicken to slow cooker.
5. Stir in all remaining ingredients.
6. Cover. Cook on Low 4-6 hours, or until potatoes are tender.

*Serving suggestion: Serve on **rice**. Accompany with **fresh mango slices** or **mango chutney**.*

Variation:
Substitute 5 tsp. curry powder for the garlic powder, ginger, cumin, coriander, and pepper.

Delicious Chicken with Curried Cream Sauce

Jennifer J. Gehman
Harrisburg, PA

Makes 4-6 servings

Prep. Time: 25 minutes
Cooking Time: 3-5 hours
Ideal slow cooker size: 4-qt.

4-6 boneless, skinless, chicken breasts, *or* **legs and thighs**
oil
salt to taste
pepper to taste
10¾-oz. can cream of chicken soup
½ cup mayonnaise
1-2 Tbsp. curry powder
½ tsp. salt
⅛ tsp. pepper
1 lb. fresh, *or* **15-oz. can, asparagus spears**
½-1 cup shredded cheddar cheese

1. Brown chicken on all sides in skillet in oil. Season with salt and pepper. Place in slow cooker.
2. Combine soup, mayonnaise, curry powder, salt, and pepper in bowl. Pour over chicken.
3. Cover. Cook on High 3 hours or on Low 5 hours.
4. If using fresh asparagus, steam lightly until just tender. If using canned asparagus, drain asparagus.
5. Place asparagus in bottom of serving dish.
6. Cover asparagus with chicken and sauce.
7. Sprinkle with cheese.

*Serving suggestion: Serve with **egg noodles** or **white rice**. Add another **cooked vegetable**, along with **fruit salad**, **applesauce**, or **mandarin oranges**, as side dishes.*

Curried Chicken

Marlene Bogard
Newton, KS

Makes 5 servings

Prep. Time: 20 minutes
Cooking Time: 4¼-6¼ hours
Ideal slow cooker size: 5-qt.

2½-3½-lb. fryer chicken, cut up
salt to taste
pepper to taste
1 Tbsp. curry powder
1 garlic clove, crushed *or* **minced**
1 Tbsp. melted butter
½ cup chicken broth, *or* **1 chicken bouillon cube dissolved in ½ cup water**
2 Tbsp. onion, chopped fine
29-oz. can sliced peaches
½ cup pitted prunes
3 Tbsp. cornstarch
3 Tbsp. cold water

1. Sprinkle chicken with salt and pepper. Arrange in slow cooker.
2. Combine curry, garlic, butter, broth, and onions in bowl.
3. Drain peaches, reserving syrup. Add ½ cup syrup to curry mixture. Pour over chicken.
4. Cover. Cook on Low 4-6 hours.
5. Remove chicken pieces from cooker to platter. Keep warm.
6. Turn cooker on High. Stir in prunes.
7. Dissolve cornstarch in cold water in small bowl. Stir into hot sauce in cooker.
8. Cover. Cook on High 10 minutes, or until thickened.
9. Stir in peaches and cooked chicken.

Serving suggestion: Serve over ***rice****. Offer* ***peanuts, shredded coconut,*** *and* ***fresh pineapple chunks*** *as condiments.*

Lemon Chicken

Judy Newman
St. Mary's, Ontario Canada

Makes 10-12 servings

Prep. Time: 25 minutes
Cooking Time: 3-4 hours
Ideal slow cooker size: 5-qt.

¼-½ cup flour
1 tsp. salt
5-6 lbs. chicken, cut into pieces
2-4 Tbsp. oil, *divided*
1 can frozen lemonade concentrate, thawed
3 Tbsp. brown sugar
1 Tbsp. ketchup
1 Tbsp. vinegar
2 Tbsp. cold water
2 Tbsp. cornstarch

1. Combine flour and salt in a shallow bowl. Dredge chicken pieces in it, one at a time.
2. Place 2 Tbsp. oil in large skillet. Brown several pieces of chicken in oil at a time. Be careful not to crowd the skillet, or the chicken will steam and not brown. Continue until all pieces are browned on both sides, adding more oil as necessary.
3. As you finish browning pieces of chicken, place them in slow cooker.
4. In a mixing bowl, whisk together lemonade concentrate, brown sugar, ketchup, and vinegar. Pour over chicken.
5. Cover. Cook on High 3-4 hours.
6. Remove chicken, place on platter, cover with foil, and keep warm.
7. In a small bowl, blend cold water into cornstarch.
8. Stir into juices in slow cooker until well blended. Cover and continue cooking juices several minutes, until thickened and bubbly.
9. Spoon some of thickened juice over chicken to serve.
10. Place remaining juices in serving bowl and pass as topping for chicken and cooked rice.

Tip:
Put this in the slow cooker and then go wrap your gifts without concern!

Garlic Lime Chicken

Loretta Krahn
Mountain Lake, MN

Makes 5 servings

Prep. Time: 10 minutes
Cooking Time: 4-8 hours
Ideal slow cooker size: 4-qt.

5 skinless chicken breast halves
½ cup soy sauce
¼-⅓ cup lime juice, according to your taste preference
1 Tbsp. Worcestershire sauce
2 garlic cloves, minced, *or* **1 tsp. garlic powder**
½ tsp. dry mustard
½ tsp. ground pepper

1. Place chicken in slow cooker.
2. Combine remaining ingredients in a bowl. Pour over chicken.
3. Cover. Cook on High 4-6 hours or on Low 6-8 hours, or until chicken is tender but not dry.

Herbed Chicken

LaVerne A. Olson
Lititz, PA

Makes 8 serving

Prep. Time: 10 minutes
Cooking Time: 6¼-8¼ hours
Ideal slow cooker size: 6- to 7-qt.

4 whole chicken breasts, halved, with skin removed
10¾-oz. can cream of mushroom, *or* **chicken, soup**
¼ cup soy sauce
¼ cup oil
¼ cup wine vinegar
¾ cup water
½ tsp. minced garlic
1 tsp. ground ginger
½ tsp. dried oregano
1 Tbsp. brown sugar

1. Arrange chicken in slow cooker.
2. Combine remaining ingredients in bowl. Pour over chicken.
3. Cover. Cook on Low 6-8 hours, or until tender but not dry.
4. Uncover and cook 15 minutes more.

Serving suggestion: Serve with ***rice****.*

Note:
A favorite with our whole family, even the grandchildren. The gravy is delicious!

Teriyaki Chicken

Colleen Konetzni
Rio Rancho, NM

Makes 6 servings

Prep. Time: 10 minutes
Cooking Time: 6-7 hours
Ideal slow cooker size: 4-qt.

6-8 skinless chicken thighs
½ cup soy sauce
2 Tbsp. brown sugar
2 Tbsp. grated fresh ginger
2 garlic cloves, minced

1. Wash and dry chicken. Arrange in slow cooker.
2. Combine remaining ingredients in bowl. Pour over chicken.
3. Cover. Cook on High 1 hour. Reduce heat to Low and cook 5-6 hours, or until chicken is fork-tender.

Serving suggestion: Serve over ***rice*** *with a* ***fresh salad****.*

Barbecued Chicken

Gladys Longacre
Susquehanna, PA

Makes 4-6 servings

Prep. Time: 20-25 minutes
Cooking Time: 3½-6 hours
Ideal slow cooker size: 5-qt.

3-4 lbs. boneless, skinless, chicken breasts
oil
1 onion, chopped
¼ cup chopped green bell pepper
1 cup ketchup
1-2 Tbsp. hickory-smoked barbecue sauce
1 Tbsp. prepared mustard
1 Tbsp. Worcestershire sauce
1 Tbsp. lemon juice
2 Tbsp. vinegar
3 Tbsp. brown sugar
¼ cup water
½ tsp. salt
⅛ tsp. pepper

1. Lightly brown chicken in oil in skillet. Drain off drippings. Arrange chicken in slow cooker.
2. Layer onions and green pepper over chicken.
3. Combine remaining ingredients in bowl. Pour over chicken.
4. Cover. Cook on Low 6 hours or on High 3½-4 hours, or just until chicken is tender but still moist.

*Serving suggestion: Serve chicken and sauce over cooked **rice**.*

Barbecued Chicken with Peppers, Onions, and Celery

Joanne Kennedy
Plattsburgh, NY

Makes 4 servings

Prep. Time: 15 minutes
Cooking Time: 2½-6 hours
Ideal slow cooker size: 4-qt.

2 whole boneless, skinless chicken breasts, cubed
1 medium onion, sliced
1 green bell pepper, sliced
1 cup chopped celery
2 Tbsp. Worcestershire sauce
2 Tbsp. brown sugar
1½ cups ketchup
1½ cups water
½ tsp. pepper

1. Combine all ingredients in slow cooker.
2. Cover. Cook on Low 5-6 hours or on High 2½-3 hours, or until chicken is tender but not dry.

*Serving suggestion: Serve over **rice** with a **tossed salad**.*

Hawaiian Chicken

Leona M. Slabaugh
Apple Creek, OH

Makes 6-8 servings

Prep. Time: 30 minutes
Cooking Time: 3-8 hours
Ideal slow cooker size: 3- to 5-qt.

3 lbs. boneless, skinless chicken breast halves
16-oz. can pineapple slices, drained
15-oz. can mandarin oranges, drained
2 Tbsp. cornstarch
3 Tbsp. brown sugar, packed
2 tbsp. lemon juice
¼ tsp. salt
¼ tsp. ground ginger

1. Combine all ingredients in slow cooker. Stir well.
2. Cover. Cook on Low 6-8 hours or on High 3 hours, or until meat is tender but not dry.

On Christmas Eve we visit our neighbors, just to say "Merry Christmas." If you set aside 30 minutes per house, you can visit six to eight in no time. Those visits really can make a difference during the year if problems arise (like dogs barking or where to shovel unwanted snow).

Rose Hankins, Stevensville, MD

Chicken Stew with Peppers and Pineapples

Judi Manos
West Islip, NY

Makes 4 servings

Prep. Time: 20 minutes
Cooking Time: 2¾-6¼ hours
Ideal slow cooker size: 4-qt.

1 lb. boneless, skinless chicken breasts, cut in 1½" cubes
4 medium carrots, sliced into 1" pieces
½ cup chicken broth
2 Tbsp. gingerroot, chopped
1 Tbsp. brown sugar
2 Tbsp. soy sauce
½ tsp. ground allspice
½ tsp. hot pepper sauce
8-oz. can pineapple chunks, drained, with juice reserved
1 Tbsp. cornstarch
1 medium sweet green pepper, cut in 1" pieces

1. Combine chicken, carrots, chicken broth, gingerroot, sugar, soy sauce, allspice, and red pepper sauce in slow cooker.
2. Cover. Cook on Low 5-6 hours or on High 2½-3 hours, or until chicken is tender.
3. Combine pineapple juice and cornstarch in bowl until smooth. Stir into chicken mixture.
4. Add pineapple chunks and green pepper.
5. Cover. Cook on High 15 minutes, or until sauce is slightly thickened.

*Serving suggestion: Serve over cooked **rice**.*

Variation:
Add 1 cut-up fresh tomato 30 minutes before end of cooking time.

Pineapple-Glazed Chicken with Sweet Potatoes

Katrina Eberly
Wernersville, PA

Makes 4 servings

Prep. Time: 25-30 minutes
Cooking Time: 3½-4 hours
Ideal slow cooker size: 4- to 5-qt.

3 medium sweet potatoes, peeled and sliced into 1" chunks
⅔ cup, plus 3 Tbsp., flour, *divided*
1 tsp. salt
1 tsp. onion powder
1 tsp. ground nutmeg
1 tsp. ground cinnamon
1 tsp. pepper
4 5-oz. boneless skinless chicken breast halves
¼ stick (2 Tbsp.) butter
10¾-oz. can cream of chicken soup
¾ cup pineapple juice
2 tsp. brown sugar
1 tsp. grated orange peel

1. Layer sweet potatoes into slow cooker.
2. In a large resealable plastic bag, combine ⅔ cup flour and seasonings. Add chicken, one piece at a time, and shake to coat.
3. In a large skillet over medium heat, cook chicken in butter for 3 minutes on each side, or until lightly browned. (Don't crowd the skillet or the chicken will steam rather than brown.) Arrange browned chicken over sweet potatoes.
4. Place remaining flour in a medium-sized mixing bowl. Stir in soup, pineapple juice, brown sugar, and orange peel until blended. Pour over chicken.
5. Cover. Cook on Low 3½-4 hours, or until potatoes are soft and chicken is cooked through but not dry.

*Serving suggestion: Serve over **rice** if you wish.*

Maui Chicken

John D. Allen, Rye, CO

Makes 6 servings

Prep. Time: 20 minutes • Cooking Time: 3-4 hours
Ideal slow cooker size: 4- to 5-qt.

6 boneless, skinless chicken breast halves
2 Tbsp. oil
14½-oz. can chicken broth
20-oz. can pineapple chunks
¼ cup vinegar
2 Tbsp. brown sugar
2 tsp. soy sauce
1 garlic clove, minced
1 medium green bell pepper, chopped
3 Tbsp. cornstarch
¼ cup water

1. Brown chicken in oil in skillet until lightly browned. Transfer chicken to slow cooker.
2. Combine remaining ingredients, except cornstarch and water, in bowl. Pour over chicken.
3. Cover. Cook on High 3-4 hours, or just until chicken is tender.
4. Ten minutes before end of cooking time, dissolve cornstarch in water in a small bowl. When smooth, stir into slow cooker until dissolved. Continue cooking until sauce thickens.

*Serving suggestion: Serve over **rice**.*

Chicken in a Hurry

Yvonne Boettger
Harrisonburg, VA

Makes 4-5 servings

Prep. Time: 10 minutes
Cooking Time: 3-7 hours
Ideal slow cooker size: 4- to 5-qt.

2½-3 lbs. skinless chicken drumsticks
½ cup ketchup
¼ cup water
¼ cup brown sugar
1 envelope dry onion soup mix

1. Arrange chicken in slow cooker.
2. Combine remaining ingredients in a bowl. Pour over chicken.
3. Cover. Cook on High 3-4 hours or on Low 6-7 hours, or just until chicken is tender.

Tender Barbecued Chicken

Betty Stoltzfus
Honeybrook, PA

Makes 4-6 servings

Prep. Time: 10 minutes
Cooking Time: 6-8 hours
Ideal slow cooker size: 6-qt.

3-4-lb. broiler chicken, whole, or cut up
1 medium onion, thinly sliced
1 medium lemon, thinly sliced
18-oz. bottle barbecue sauce
¾ cup cola-flavored soda

1. Place chicken in slow cooker.
2. Top with onion and lemon.
3. Combine barbecue sauce and cola in bowl. Pour into slow cooker.
4. Cover. Cook on Low 6-8 hours, or until chicken juices run clear.
5. Cut into serving-sized pieces and serve with barbecue sauce.
6. Slice any leftovers and use in sandwiches.

Spicy Sweet Chicken

Carolyn Baer
Conrath, WI

Makes 4 servings

Prep. Time: 25 minutes
Cooking Time: 3½-6¾ hours
Ideal slow cooker size: 4-qt.

2½-3 lbs. chicken breasts, thighs, and/or legs, skinned
1 Tbsp. oil
16-oz. can whole cranberry sauce, *divided*
¼ cup spicy-sweet Catalina salad dressing
2 Tbsp. dry onion soup mix
1 Tbsp. cornstarch

1. Rinse chicken. Pat dry. Brown in hot oil in skillet. Arrange in slow cooker.
2. In a bowl, combine half of cranberry sauce and all of salad dressing and soup mix. Pour over chicken.
3. Cover. Cook on Low 6 hours or on High 3 hours.
4. Stir cornstarch into remaining cranberry sauce in bowl. Stir into chicken mixture.
5. Turn slow cooker to High. Cover and cook 30-45 minutes more, or until thickened and bubbly.

Serving suggestion: Serve over cooked ***noodles*** *or* ***rice****.*

Chicken with Applesauce

Kelly Evenson
Pittsboro, NC

Makes 4 servings

Prep. Time: 20 minutes
Cooking Time: 2-3 hours
Ideal slow cooker size: 4-qt.

4 boneless, skinless chicken breast halves
salt to taste
pepper to taste
2 Tbsp. oil
2 cups applesauce
¼ cup barbecue sauce
½ tsp. poultry seasoning
2 tsp. honey
½ tsp. lemon juice

1. Season chicken with salt and pepper. Brown in oil in skillet for 5 minutes per side.
2. Allow chicken to cool. Then cut up into 1" chunks. Transfer to slow cooker.
3. Combine remaining ingredients in medium-sized bowl. Pour over chicken and mix together well.
4. Cover. Cook on High 2-3 hours, or just until chicken is tender.

Serving suggestion: Serve over ***rice*** *or* ***noodles****.*

Saucy Apricot Chicken

Anna Stoltzfus
Honey Brook, PA

Makes 6 servings

Prep. Time: 5-10 minutes
Cooking Time: 4-5 hours
Ideal slow cooker size: 4-qt.

6 boneless, skinless chicken breast halves
2 12-oz. jars apricot preserves
1 pkg. dry onion soup mix

1. Arrange chicken in slow cooker.
2. Combine preserves and onion soup mix in separate bowl. Spoon over chicken.
3. Cover. Cook on Low 4-5 hours.

Serving suggestion: Serve over ***rice****.*

I put a tea kettle with water, cinnamon, and apple peels on top of my woodstove. It makes the house smell great.
Kendra Dreps, Liberty, PA

Chicken ala Orange

Carlene Horne
Bedford, NH

Makes 8 servings

Prep. Time: 10 minutes
Cooking Time: 6-7 hours
Ideal slow cooker size: 4-qt.

8 boneless, skinless chicken breast halves
½ cup chopped onion
12-oz. jar orange marmalade
½ cup Russian dressing
1 Tbsp. dried parsley, *or* **to taste**

1. Arrange chicken and onion in slow cooker.
2. Combine marmalade and dressing in bowl. Pour over chicken.
3. Sprinkle with parsley.
4. Cover. Cook on Low 6-7 hours, or until chicken is just tender.

Serving suggestion: Serve with ***rice****.*

Scrumptious Chicken

Kathi Rogge
Alexandria, IN

Makes 8 servings

Prep. Time: 10 minutes
Cooking Time: 6-7 hours
Ideal slow cooker size: 6-qt.

8 skinned chicken breast halves
10¾-oz. can cream of mushroom, *or* **cream of chicken, soup**
16 ozs. sour cream
1 envelope dry onion soup mix
fresh basil, *or* **oregano, chopped**

1. Arrange chicken in slow cooker.
2. Combine all remaining ingredients, except fresh herbs, in good-sized mixing bowl. Pour over chicken.
3. Cover. Cook on Low 6-7 hours, or until chicken is fork-tender. (If convenient for you, stir after 3 hours of cooking.)
4. Sprinkle with fresh herbs just before serving.

Serving suggestion: Serve with ***brown and wild rice, mixed****, or* ***couscous****.*

Variation:

1. Cut up 4 lightly cooked chicken breast halves. Place in slow cooker.
2. Add 8 ozs. sour cream, 1 envelope dry onion soup mix, and a 10¾-oz. can cream of mushroom soup. Mix together well.
3. Cover and cook on Low 3-4 hours.

Sherry Conyers
McPherson, KS

Angel Chicken Pasta

Lena Sheatfer
Port Matilda, PA

Makes 4 servings

Prep. Time: 10 minutes
Cooking Time: 5-6 hours
Ideal slow cooker size: 4- to 5-qt.

half a stick (4 Tbsp.) butter
1 pkg. dry Italian-style salad-dressing mix
½ cup white wine
10¾-oz. can condensed golden mushroom soup
half an 8-oz. pkg. cream cheese with chives
4 boneless skinless chicken breast halves

1. In large saucepan, melt butter over low heat. Stir in salad-dressing mix. Blend in wine and soup. Mix in cream cheese and stir until smooth. Do not boil.
2. Arrange chicken in slow cooker. Pour sauce over top.
3. Cover. Cook on Low 5-6 hours, or just until chicken is tender but not dry.

Serving suggestion: When ready to eat, cook ***pasta****. Serve chicken and sauce over pasta.*

Sunday Chicken

Leona M. Slabaugh
Apple Creek, OH

Makes 6 servings

Prep. Time: 30-45 minutes
Cooking Time: 2-5 hours
Ideal slow cooker size: 3- to 5-qt.

10½-oz. can cream of celery soup
½ cup white wine, *or* **chicken broth**
3½ lbs. chicken, cut-up, *divided*
paprika
salt
pepper

1. Combine soup and wine in a small bowl.
2. Rinse chicken in cold water. Pat dry.
3. Sprinkle chicken with paprika, salt, and pepper.
4. Place half of chicken in slow cooker.
5. Pour half of soup mixture over chicken.
6. Repeat layers.
7. Cover. Cook on Low 4-5 hours or on High 2-3 hours, or until chicken is tender but not dry.

Creamy Chicken Breasts

Judy Buller
Bluffton, OH

Makes 6-8 servings

Prep. Time: 5-10 minutes
Cooking Time: 6 hours
Ideal slow cooker size: 6-qt.

6-8 skinless chicken breast halves
salt to taste
pepper to taste
paprika to taste
10¾-oz. can cream of mushroom soup
½ cup sour cream

1. Season chicken breasts with salt, pepper, and paprika. Arrange in slow cooker.
2. Combine mushroom soup and sour cream in bowl. Pour over chicken.
3. Cover. Cook on Low 6 hours, or just until tender but not dry.

Serving suggestion: Serve with ***rice, noodles,*** *or* ***mashed potatoes.***

Miriam's Chicken

Arlene Leaman Kliewer
Lakewood, CO

Makes 6 servings

Prep. Time: 10 minutes
Cooking Time: 5-6 hours
Ideal slow cooker size: 4-qt.

4 boneless, skinless chicken breast halves, cut into 1" chunks
8-oz. pkg. cream cheese, cubed
2 10¾-oz. cans cream soup, your favorite, *or* **a combination of your favorites**

1. Place chicken in slow cooker.
2. Combine cream cheese and soups in bowl.
3. Pour over chicken. Stir.
4. Cover. Cook on Low 5-6 hours, or until chicken is cooked through and tender.

Serving suggestion: Serve over ***croissants*** *split in half. Sprinkle with* ***paprika*** *and* ***parsley.***

Involve your guests, whether family or friends, in making your holiday meals. It's a great way to spend time together, learn different cooking tips and tricks from each other, and share recipes. — *Moreen Weaver, Bath, NY*

Elegant Chicken with Gravy

Leesa Lesenski, South Deerfield, MA

Makes 6 servings

Prep. Time: 10 minutes • Cooking Time: 3-6 hours
Ideal slow cooker size: 4-qt.

6 boneless, skinless chicken breast halves
10¾-oz. can cream of broccoli, *or* **broccoli cheese, soup**
10¾-oz. can cream of chicken soup
½ cup white wine
4-oz. can sliced mushrooms, undrained, *optional*

1. Arrange chicken breasts in slow cooker.
2. In bowl mix together soups, wine, and mushroom slices if you wish.
3. Pour over chicken.
4. Cover. Cook on High 3 hours or on Low 6 hours, or until chicken is tender but not dry.

Serving suggestion: Serve over ***rice*** *or* ***noodles****.*

Janie's Chicken a La King

Lafaye M. Musser
Denver, PA

Makes 4 servings

Prep. Time: 20 minutes
Cooking Time: 3½-4½ hours
Ideal slow cooker size: 4-qt.

10¾-oz. can cream of chicken soup
3 Tbsp. flour
½ tsp. salt
¼ tsp. pepper
dash cayenne pepper
1 lb. boneless chicken thighs, uncooked and cut in pieces
1 rib celery, chopped
½ cup chopped green bell pepper
¼ cup chopped onions
9-oz. bag frozen peas, thawed

1. Combine soup, flour, salt, pepper, and cayenne pepper in slow cooker.
2. Stir in chicken, celery, green pepper, and onion.
3. Cover. Cook on Low 3-4 hours, or until chicken and vegetables are as tender as you like them.
4. Stir in peas.
5. Cover. Cook 30 minutes longer.

Serving suggestion: Serve in ***pastry cups*** *or over* ***rice, waffles,*** *or* ***toast****.*

Savory Chicken, Meal #1

Shari Mast
Harrisonburg, VA

Makes 8-10 servings

Prep. Time: 10 minutes
Cooking Time: 4-5 hours
Ideal slow cooker size: 5-qt.

4 boneless, skinless chicken breast halves
4 skinless chicken quarters
10¾-oz. can cream of chicken soup
1 Tbsp. water
¼ cup chopped sweet red peppers
1 Tbsp. chopped fresh parsley, *or* **1 tsp. dried parsley**
1 Tbsp. lemon juice
½ tsp. paprika

1. Layer chicken in slow cooker.
2. Combine remaining ingredients in bowl. Pour over chicken.
3. Cover. Cook on High 4-5 hours, or until chicken is tender.

Savory Chicken, Meal #2

Shari Mast
Harrisonburg, VA

Makes 8-10 servings

Prep. Time: 30 minutes
Cooking Time: 3¼-4¼ hours
Ideal slow cooker size: 4- to 5-qt.

leftover chicken and broth from Savory Chicken, Meal #1
2 carrots
1 rib celery
2 medium-sized onions
2 Tbsp. flour *or* **cornstarch**
¼ cup cold water

1. For a second Savory Chicken Meal, pick leftover chicken off bone. Set aside.
2. Return remaining broth to slow cooker. Stir in thinly sliced carrots and celery, and onions cut up in chunks.
3. Cover. Cook 3-4 hours on High.
4. In small bowl, mix flour or cornstarch with cold water. When smooth, stir into hot broth.
4. Stir in cut-up chicken. Heat 15-20 minutes, or until broth thickens and chicken is hot.

Serving suggestion: Serve over ***rice*** *or* ***pasta****.*

Creamy Chicken and Vegetables

Dawn M. Propst
Levittown, PA

Makes 4 servings

Prep. Time: 10 minutes
Cooking Time: 5-6 hours
Ideal slow cooker size: 4-qt.

10¾-oz. can cream of mushroom soup, *divided*
4 boneless, skinless chicken breast halves
16-oz. pkg. frozen vegetable medley (broccoli, cauliflower, and carrots), thawed and drained
½ tsp. salt
⅛-¼ tsp. pepper
1 cup shredded cheddar cheese, *divided*

1. Pour small amount of soup in bottom of slow cooker.
2. Add chicken breasts, vegetables, and seasonings.
3. Mix in ½ cup cheddar cheese. Stir in remaining soup.
4. Cover. Cook on Low 5-6 hours, or until vegetables are cooked and chicken is no longer pink.
5. Sprinkle with remaining cheese 10-15 minutes before serving.

Chicken Alfredo

Dawn M. Propst
Levittown, PA

Makes 4-6 servings

Prep. Time: 20 minutes
Cooking Time: 6 hours
Ideal slow cooker size: 4-qt.

16-oz. jar Alfredo sauce, *divided*
4-6 boneless, skinless chicken breast halves
8 ozs. dry noodles, cooked
4-oz. can mushroom pieces and stems, drained
1 cup shredded mozzarella cheese, *or* **½ cup grated Parmesan cheese**

1. Pour about one-third of Alfredo sauce in bottom of slow cooker.
2. Add chicken and cover with remaining sauce.
3. Cover. Cook on Low 6 hours, or until chicken is tender but not dry.
4. Fifteen minutes before serving, add noodles and mushrooms to cooker ingredients, mixing well.
5. Sprinkle top with cheese. Dish is ready to serve when cheese is melted.

Serving suggestion: Serve with ***green salad*** *and* ***Italian bread****.*

Creamy Chicken and Noodles

Rhonda Burgoon
Collingswood, NJ

Makes 4-6 servings

Prep. Time: 25 minutes
Cooking Time: 4¼-9¼ hours
Ideal slow cooker size: 4-qt.

2 cups sliced carrots
1½ cups chopped onions
1 cup sliced celery
2 Tbsp. snipped fresh parsley
bay leaf
3 medium-sized chicken legs and thighs (about 2 lbs.), skin removed
2 10¾-oz. cans cream of chicken soup
½ cup water
1 tsp. dried thyme
1 tsp. salt
¼ tsp. pepper
1 cup peas

1. Place carrots, onions, celery, parsley, and bay leaf in slow cooker.
2. Arrange chicken on top of vegetables.
3. Combine soup, water, thyme, salt, and pepper in bowl. Pour over chicken and vegetables.
4. Cover. Cook on Low 8-9 hours or on High 4-4½ hours.
5. Remove chicken from slow cooker. Cool slightly.
6. Debone chicken, cut into bite-sized pieces, and return to slow cooker.
7. Remove and discard bay leaf.
8. Stir peas into mixture in slow cooker. Cook 5-10 minutes.

Serving suggestion: Pour over 12-oz. pkg. cooked ***noodles****. Toss gently to combine. Serve with* ***crusty bread*** *and a* ***salad****.*

Szechwan-Style Chicken and Broccoli

Jane Meiser, Harrisonburg, VA

Makes 4 servings

Prep. Time: 20 minutes • Cooking Time: 1-3 hours
Ideal slow cooker size: 4-qt.

2 whole boneless, skinless chicken breasts
oil
½ cup picante sauce
2 Tbsp. soy sauce
½ tsp. sugar
½ Tbsp. quick-cooking tapioca
1 medium onion, chopped
2 garlic cloves, minced
½ tsp. ground ginger
2 cups broccoli florets
1 medium red bell pepper, cut into pieces

1. Cut chicken into 1" cubes. Brown lightly in oil in skillet. Place meat in slow cooker.
2. Stir in remaining ingredients.
3. Cover. Cook on High 1-1½ hours or on Low 2-3 hours.

Chicken Gumbo

Virginia Bender
Dover, DE

Makes 6-8 servings

Prep. Time: 25 minutes
Cooking Time: 2½-6 hours
Ideal slow cooker size: 4-qt.

1 large onion, chopped
3-4 garlic cloves, minced
1 green bell pepper, diced
2 cups okra, sliced
2 cups tomatoes, chopped
4 cups chicken broth
1 lb. chicken breast, cut into 1" pieces
2 tsp. Old Bay Seasoning

1. Combine all ingredients in slow cooker.
2. Cover. Cook on Low 5-6 hours or on High 2½-3 hours.

Serving suggestion: Serve over ***rice****.*

Gourmet Chicken Breasts

Sharon Swartz Lambert
Dayton, VA
Deborah Santiago
Lancaster, PA

Makes 4-6 servings

Prep. Time: 15 minutes
Cooking Time: 6-8 hours
Ideal slow cooker size: 4-qt.

6-8 slices thinly sliced dried beef
4-6 boneless, skinless chicken breast halves
2-3 slices bacon, cut in half lengthwise
10¾-oz. cream of mushroom soup
8 oz. sour cream
½ cup flour

1. Line bottom of slow cooker with dried beef.
2. Roll up each chicken breast half and wrap with a half-slice of bacon. Place in slow cooker.
3. Combine remaining ingredients in bowl. Pour over breasts.
4. Cover. Cook on Low 6-8 hours, or until chicken and bacon are fully cooked but not dry.

*Serving suggestion: Serve with **cooked noodles**, **rice**, or **mashed potatoes**.*

Creamy Nutmeg Chicken

Amber Swarey
Honea Path, SC

Makes 6 servings

Prep. Time: 25 minutes
Cooking Time: 3-4 hours
Ideal slow cooker size: 4-qt.

6 boneless, skinless chicken breast halves
oil
¼ cup chopped onions
¼ cup minced parsley
2 10¾-oz. cans cream of mushroom soup
½ cup sour cream
½ cup milk
1 Tbsp. ground nutmeg
¼ tsp. sage
¼ tsp. dried thyme
¼ tsp. crushed rosemary

1. Brown chicken in skillet in oil. Reserve drippings and place chicken in slow cooker.
2. Sauté onions and parsley in drippings until onions are tender.
3. Stir in remaining ingredients. Mix well. Pour over chicken.
4. Cover. Cook on Low 3-4 hours, or until juices run clear.

*Serving suggestion: Serve over **mashed** or **fried potatoes**, or **rice**.*

Slow Cooker Creamy Chicken Italian

Sherri Grindle
Goshen, IN

Makes 8 servings

Prep. Time: 10-15 minutes
Cooking Time: 5-6 hours
Ideal slow cooker size: 4- to 5-qt.

8 boneless, skinless chicken breast halves
1 envelope dry Italian salad dressing mix
¼ cup water
8-oz. pkg. cream cheese, softened
10¾-oz. can cream of chicken soup
4-oz. can mushrooms, drained

1. Place chicken in greased slow cooker.
2. Combine salad-dressing mix and water in bowl. Pour over chicken.
3. Cover. Cook on Low 4-5 hours.
4. In saucepan, combine cream cheese and soup. Heat slightly to melt cream cheese. Stir in mushrooms. Pour over chicken.
5. Cover. Cook 1 additional hour on Low.

*Serving suggestion: Serve over **noodles** or **rice**.*

Variation:
Add frozen vegetables along with the mushrooms in Step 4.

Mushroom Chicken in Sour Cream Sauce

Lavina Hochstedler
Grand Blanc, MI
Joyce Shackelford
Green Bay, WI

Makes 6 servings

Prep. Time: 15 minutes
Cooking Time: 3-7 hours
Ideal slow cooker size: 6-qt.

1½ tsp. salt
¼ tsp. pepper
½ tsp. paprika
¼ tsp. lemon pepper
1 tsp. garlic powder
6 skinless, bone-in chicken breast halves
10¾-oz. can cream of mushroom soup
8 oz. sour cream
½ cup dry white wine, *or* **chicken broth**
½ lb. fresh mushrooms, sliced

1. Combine salt, pepper, paprika, lemon pepper, and garlic powder in a small bowl. Rub over chicken. Place meat in slow cooker.
2. Combine soup, sour cream, and wine or broth in bowl. Stir in mushrooms. Spoon over chicken, being careful not to disturb rub.
3. Cover. Cook on Low 5-7 hours or on High 3 hours, or until chicken is fully cooked but not dry.

Serving suggestion: Serve over ***potatoes, rice,*** *or* ***couscous****. Delicious accompanied with* ***broccoli-cauliflower salad*** *and* ***applesauce****.*

Indonesian Peanut Chicken

Naomi Ressler
Harrisonburg, VA

Makes 6 servings

Prep. Time: 15-20 minutes
Cooking Time: 4 hours
Ideal slow cooker size: 4-qt.

1½ lbs. boneless, skinless chicken breasts, cut into chunks
⅓ cup chopped onions
⅓ cup water
¼ cup creamy, *or* **chunky, peanut butter**
3 Tbsp. chili sauce
¼ tsp. salt
¼ tsp. pepper
¼ tsp. cayenne pepper
cooked rice, *or* **soba noodles**
6 Tbsp. chopped peanuts
6 Tbsp. chopped sweet red peppers

1. Place chicken in slow cooker.
2. In a small bowl, combine onions, water, peanut butter, chili sauce, salt, and peppers. Pour over chicken.
3. Cover. Cook on Low 4 hours, or until chicken is tender.
4. Serve over rice or soba noodles. Sprinkle with peanuts and red peppers.

Chicken Cashew Dish

Dorothy Horst
Tiskilwa, IL

Makes 6 servings

Prep. Time: 15 minutes
Cooking Time: 2-4 hours
Ideal slow cooker size: 3-qt.

14-oz. can bean sprouts, drained
3 Tbsp. butter, melted
4 green onions, chopped
4-oz. can mushroom pieces, drained
10¾-oz. can cream of mushroom soup
1 cup sliced celery
12½-oz. can chunk chicken breast, *or* **1 cup cooked chicken, cubed**
1 Tbsp. soy sauce
1 cup cashew nuts

1. Combine all ingredients except nuts in slow cooker.
2. Cover. Cook on Low 3-4 hours or on High 2-2½ hours.
3. Stir in cashew nuts before serving.

Serving suggestion: Serve over ***rice****.*

Note:
I teach English as a Second Language to Vietnamese women. Occasionally they invite us to join them for dinner on Vietnamese New Year. We enjoy the fellowship and Vietnamese traditions immensely. They always have a "Lucky Tree," a tree with yellow flowers which blooms in

Vietnam on New Year's. They decorate the tree by hanging red envelopes in it. Each contains a money gift; one is given to each unmarried person present, including the babies.

Chicken Azteca

Katrine Rose
Woodbridge, VA

Makes 10-12 servings

Prep. Time: 15-20 minutes
Cooking Time: 2½-6½ hours
Ideal slow cooker size: 6- to 7-qt.

2 15-oz. cans black beans, drained
4 cups frozen corn kernels
2 garlic cloves, minced
¾ tsp. ground cumin
2 cups chunky salsa, *divided*
10 boneless, skinless chicken breast halves
2 8-oz. pkgs. cream cheese, cubed

1. Combine beans, corn, garlic, cumin, and half of salsa in slow cooker.
2. Arrange chicken breasts over top. Pour remaining salsa over top.
3. Cover. Cook on High 2-3 hours or on Low 4-6 hours, or until chicken is tender but not dry.
4. Remove chicken and cut into bite-sized pieces. Return to cooker.
5. Stir in cream cheese. Cook on High until cream cheese melts.

Serving suggestion: Spoon chicken and sauce over cooked ***rice****. Top with* ***shredded cheese****.*

Tamale Chicken

Jeanne Allen
Rye, CO

Makes 6 servings

Prep. Time: 45 minutes
Cooking Time: 3-4 hours
Ideal slow cooker size: 4-qt.

1 medium onion, chopped
4-oz. can chopped green chilies, drained
2 Tbsp. oil
10¾-oz. can cream of chicken soup
2 cups sour cream
1 cup sliced ripe olives
1 cup chopped stewed tomatoes
2 cups shredded cheddar cheese
8 boneless, skinless chicken breast halves, cooked* and chopped
16-oz. can beef tamales, chopped
1 tsp. chili powder
1 tsp. pepper
½ cup shredded cheddar cheese, *divided*

1. Sauté onion and chilies in oil in skillet. Place in slow cooker.
2. Combine all remaining ingredients, except ½ cup shredded cheese, in slow cooker.
3. Top with remaining cheese.
4. Cover. Cook on High 3-4 hours.

Serving suggestion: Pass chopped fresh ***tomatoes****,* ***shredded lettuce****,* ***sour cream****,* ***salsa****, and* ***guacamole*** *so guests can top their Tamale Chicken with these condiments.*

*You can cook the chicken breasts by placing them in your slow cooker. Sprinkle generously with salt and pepper. Pour 3-4 cups water into cooker, along its interior side so as not to wash the seasonings off the meat. Cover. Cook on Low 6 hours or so, until chicken is fork-tender but not dry.

Choose a country that has special meaning for your family and plan a holiday menu around the foods of that country. For example, our children grew up in Honduras where tamales were served on Christmas and New Year's Eve. These foods bring back special memories.

Elena Yoder, Albuquerque, NM

Tex-Mex Chicken and Rice

Kelly Evenson
Pittsboro, NC

Makes 8 servings

Prep. Time: 25 minutes
Cooking Time: 4-4½ hours
Ideal slow cooker size: 5-qt.

1 cup uncooked converted white rice
28-oz. can diced peeled tomatoes
6-oz. can tomato paste
3 cups hot water
1 envelope dry taco seasoning mix
4 whole boneless, skinless chicken breasts, uncooked and cut into ½" cubes
2 medium onions, chopped
1 green bell pepper, chopped
4-oz. can diced green chilies
1 tsp. garlic powder
½ tsp. pepper

1. Combine all ingredients except chilies and seasonings in large slow cooker.
2. Cover. Cook on Low 4-4½ hours, or until rice is tender and chicken is cooked.
3. Stir in green chilies and seasonings and serve.

*Serving suggestion: Serve with **mixed green leafy salad** and **refried beans**.*

Red Pepper Chicken

Sue Graber
Eureka, IL

Makes 4 servings

Prep. Time: 10 minutes
Cooking Time: 4-6 hours
Ideal slow cooker size: 4-qt.

4 boneless, skinless chicken breast halves
15-oz. can black beans, drained
12-oz. jar roasted red peppers, undrained
14½-oz. can Mexican stewed tomatoes, undrained
1 large onion, chopped
½ tsp. salt
pepper to taste

1. Place chicken in slow cooker.
2. Combine beans, red peppers, stewed tomatoes, onion, salt, and pepper in a good-sized mixing bowl. Pour over chicken.
3. Cover. Cook on Low 4-6 hours, or until chicken is tender and no longer pink.

*Serving suggestion: Serve over **rice**.*

Chicken and Seafood Gumbo

Dianna Milhizer
Brighton, MI

Makes 12 servings

Prep. Time: 40-45 minutes
Cooking Time: 8-10 hours
Ideal slow cooker size: 6-qt.

1 cup chopped celery
1 cup chopped onions
½ cup chopped green bell peppers
¼ cup olive oil
¼ cup, plus 1 Tbsp., flour
6 cups chicken stock
2 lbs. chicken, skin removed and cut up
3 bay leaves
1½ cups sliced okra
12-oz. can diced tomatoes
1 tsp. Tabasco sauce
salt to taste
pepper to taste
1 lb. ready-to-eat shrimp
½ cup snipped fresh parsley

1. Sauté celery, onions, and peppers in oil in skillet.
2. Blend in flour and chicken stock until smooth. Cook 5 minutes. Pour into slow cooker.
3. Stir remaining ingredients, except seafood and parsley, into slow cooker.
4. Cover. Cook on Low 8-10 hours, or until chicken is tender but not dry.
5. One hour before serving add shrimp and parsley.
6. Remove bay leaves before serving.

*Serving suggestion: Serve over **white rice**.*

Chicken Rice Special

Jeanne Allen
Rye, CO

Makes 6-8 servings

Prep. Time: 40 minutes
Cooking Time: 4-6 hours
Ideal slow cooker size: 4-qt.

1 lb. pork, *or* turkey, sausage
6 chicken breast halves, cooked* and chopped (save 4 cups broth)
half a large sweet green pepper, chopped
1 medium onion, chopped
4 ribs celery, chopped
1 cup uncooked rice
2-oz. pkg. dry noodle-soup mix
½ cup sliced almonds
1-2 oz. jar pimentos, chopped

1. Brown sausage in skillet. Drain off any drippings. Place meat in slow cooker.
2. Add all other ingredients, except almonds and pimentos, to slow cooker. Stir well.
3. Top with almonds and pimentos.
4. Cover. Cook on High 4-6 hours, or until rice is done and liquid has been absorbed.
5. Stir well 1 hour before serving.

*See page 175, at end of recipe for Tamale Chicken, for instructions about cooking chicken in your slow cooker.

Company Casserole

Vera Schmucker
Goshen, IN

Makes 4-6 servings

Prep. Time: 15-20 minutes
Cooking Time: 3-8 hours
Ideal slow cooker size: 5-qt.

1¼ cups uncooked long-grain rice
1 stick (8 Tbsp.) butter, melted
3 cups chicken broth
3-4 cups cut-up cooked chicken breast
2 4-oz. cans sliced mushrooms, drained
⅓ cup soy sauce
12-oz. pkg. shelled frozen shrimp, thawed
8 green onions, chopped, 2 Tbsp. reserved
⅔ cup slivered almonds

1. Combine rice and butter in slow cooker. Stir to coat rice well.
2. Add remaining ingredients, except almonds and 2 Tbsp. green onions.
3. Cover. Cook on Low 6-8 hours or on High 3-4 hours, until rice is tender.
4. Thirty minutes before end of cooking time, stir in thawed shrimp.
5. Sprinkle almonds and green onions over top before serving.

*Serving suggestion: Serve with **green beans**, **tossed salad**, and **fruit salad**.*

Chicken Broccoli Rice Casserole

Gloria Julien
Gladstone, MI

Makes 4-6 servings

Prep. Time: 30 minutes
Cooking Time: 2-3 hours
Ideal slow cooker size: 5-qt.

1 onion, chopped
3 Tbsp. oil
2-3 cups uncooked chicken, cut in 1" pieces
10¾-oz. can cream of chicken soup
12-oz. can evaporated milk
2 cups cubed Velveeta cheese
3 cups cooked rice
2 cups frozen broccoli cuts, thawed
¼ tsp. pepper
4-oz. can mushrooms, drained

1. Sauté onion in oil in skillet.
2. Add chicken and sauté until no longer pink.
3. Combine all ingredients in slow cooker.
4. Cover. Cook on Low 2-3 hours.

Notes:

1. This is an ideal dish for people who are not big meat-eaters.

2. This is good carry-in for potluck or fellowship meals. I put the ingredients together the night before.

Baked Chicken and Rice

Fannie Miller
Hutchinson, KS

Makes 10-12 servings

Prep. Time: 15 minutes
Cooking Time: 4-6 hours
Ideal slow cooker size: 6- to 7-qt.

2 cups dry instant rice
10¾-oz. can cream of chicken soup
10¾-oz. can cream of mushroom soup
10¾-oz. can cream of celery soup
1 stick (8 Tbsp.) butter
1 soup can water
10 skinless chicken breast halves, *or* **1 large chicken, cut into 10-12 pieces**
1 envelope dry onion soup mix

1. Place rice in large slow cooker.
2. Combine soups, butter, and water in large bowl. Pour half over rice.
3. Lay chicken over rice. Pour remaining soup mixture over chicken.
4. Sprinkle with dry onion soup mix.
5. Cover. Cook on Low 4-6 hours, or until chicken is done but not dry, and rice is tender but not mushy.

Chicken Pasta

Evelyn L. Ward
Greeley, CO

Makes 4 servings

Prep. Time: 25-30 minutes
Cooking Time: 4 hours and 20 minutes
Ideal slow cooker size: 4-qt.

1½-lb. boneless, skinless chicken breast
1 large zucchini, diced
1 envelope chicken gravy mix
2 Tbsp. water
2 Tbsp. evaporated milk, *or* **cream**
1 large tomato, chopped
4 cups cooked macaroni
8 ozs. smoked Gouda cheese, grated

1. Cut chicken into 1″ cubes. Place in slow cooker.
2. Add zucchini, gravy mix, and water, and stir together.
3. Cover. Cook on Low 4 hours.
4. Add milk and tomato. Cook an additional 20 minutes.
5. Stir in pasta. Top with cheese. Serve immediately.

Our Favorite Chicken and Stuffing

Kim Stoll
Abbeville, SC

Makes 6 servings

Prep. Time: 10-15 minutes
Cooking Time: 3-5 hours
Ideal slow cooker size: 5-qt.

6 boneless, skinless chicken breast halves
6 slices Swiss cheese
¼ cup milk
10¾-oz. can cream of mushroom, *or* **chicken, soup**
2 cups stuffing mix
1 stick (8 Tbsp.) butter, melted

1. Grease slow cooker with nonstick cooking spray.
2. Top each breast half with slice of cheese. Arrange cheese-covered chicken in slow cooker.
3. In a mixing bowl, combine milk and soup until smooth. Pour over chicken. (If you've stacked the breasts, lift the ones on top to make sure the ones on the bottom are topped with sauce, too.)

Depending on the number of guests you may do formal or informal. Thanksgiving with 40 has me using disposables. Christmas with seven adults calls for fine china and crystal at our house. Colleen Heatwole, Burton, MI evenly over sauced chicken, including those on the bottom.

5. Drizzle with melted butter.

6. Cover. Cook on High 3 hours or on Low 5 hours, or just until meat is tender but not dry.

Variation:

Use cornbread stuffing instead of regular stuffing mix.

Betty Moore
Plano, IL

Chicken Dressing

Lydia A. Yoder
London, ON

Makes 20 servings

Prep. Time: 40-45 minutes
Cooking Time: 3-4 hours
Ideal slow cooker size: 6-qt.

1½ sticks (12 Tbsp.) butter
1 cup chopped onions
2 cups chopped celery
2 Tbsp. parsley flakes
1½ tsp. salt
½ tsp. pepper
3½-4 cups chicken broth
12-14 cups dried bread cubes
4 cups cut-up, cooked chicken*
2 eggs, beaten
1 tsp. baking powder

1. Sauté onion and celery in butter in skillet.

2. Combine seasonings and broth in large bowl. Mix in bread cubes.

3. Fold in chicken and sautéed onions and celery.

4. Add eggs and baking powder.

5. Lightly pack into large slow cooker.

6. Cover. Cook on Low 3-4 hours.

Serving suggestion: Serve with ***turkey*** *or* ***chicken, mashed potatoes****, a* ***vegetable****, and* ***lettuce salad****.*

*For instructions about how to cook chicken in your slow cooker, see page 175, at end of recipe for Tamale Chicken. (Or use leftover chicken.)

Tip:

The longer the dressing cooks, the drier it will become. Keep that in mind if you do not care for moist stuffing.

Chicken and Stuffing Dinner

Trudy Kutter
Corfu, NY

Makes 4-6 servings

Prep. Time: 20 minutes
Cooking Time: 6¾-7 hours
Ideal slow cooker size: 6-qt.

4-6 skinless chicken breast halves
10¾-oz. can cream of chicken, *or* **celery, soup**
4-6 potatoes, peeled and sliced
6-oz. pkg. stuffing mix
1¼ cups water
¼ stick (2 Tbsp.) melted butter
1-1½ cups frozen green beans, thawed

1. Arrange chicken in slow cooker.

2. Spoon soup over chicken.

3. Top with potatoes.

4. Combine stuffing mix, water, and butter in bowl. Spoon over potatoes.

5. Cover. Cook on Low 6 hours.

6. Sprinkle green beans over stuffing.

7. Cover. Cook on Low 45-60 minutes, or until beans are just tender.

Serving suggestion: Serve with a ***salad****.*

Chicken and Dumplings

Bonnie Miller
Louisville, OH

Makes 4 servings

Prep. Time: 20 minutes
Cooking Time: 3½-8½ hours
Ideal slow cooker size: 4-qt.

2 lbs. boneless, skinless chicken breast halves
1¾ cups chicken broth
2 chicken bouillon cubes
2 tsp. salt
1 tsp. pepper
1 tsp. poultry seasoning
2 celery ribs, cut into 1" pieces
6 small carrots, cut into 1" chunks

Biscuits:
2 cups buttermilk biscuit mix
½ cup, plus 1 Tbsp., milk
1 tsp. parsley

1. Arrange chicken in slow cooker.
2. Dissolve bouillon in broth in bowl. Stir in salt, pepper, and poultry seasoning.
3. Pour over chicken.
4. Spread celery and carrots over top.
5. Cover. Cook on Low 6-8 hours or on High 3-3½ hours, or until chicken is tender but not dry.
6. Combine Biscuit ingredients in a bowl until just moistened. Drop by spoonfuls over steaming chicken.
7. Cover. Cook on High 35 minutes. Do not remove cover while dumplings are cooking. Serve immediately.

Scalloped Chicken

Brenda Joy Sonnie
Newton, PA

Makes 4-6 servings

Prep. Time: 15-30 minutes
Cooking Time: 2-3 hours
Ideal slow cooker size: 5-qt.

4 cups cooked chicken*
1 box stuffing mix for chicken
2 eggs
1 cup water
1½ cups milk
1 cup frozen peas

1. In large bowl, combine chicken and dry stuffing mix. Place in slow cooker.
2. In same bowl, beat together eggs, water, and milk. Pour over chicken and stuffing.
3. Cover. Cook on High 2-3 hours.
4. Add frozen peas during last hour of cooking.

Variation:
For more flavor use chicken broth instead of water.

*If you don't have leftover cooked chicken, turn to page 175, at end of recipe for Tamale Chicken, for instructions about how to cook chicken in your slow cooker.

Brunswick Stew

Violette Denney
Carrollton, GA

Makes 8-10 servings

Prep. Time: 30-60 minutes
Cooking Time: 4 hours
Ideal slow cooker size: 8-qt.

3 lbs. boneless, skinless chicken breasts
reserved chicken broth (from cooking chicken breasts)
2 lbs. lean ground beef
2 cans creamed corn
1 can whole-kernel corn, drained
2 cups ketchup
1 cup mild barbecue sauce
2 Tbsp. Worcestershire sauce
2 large sweet onions, chopped
15-oz. can English peas, drained
1 qt. stewed tomatoes
salt and pepper to taste

1. In good-sized stockpot, cook chicken in 2" of water. Cover and cook slowly, just until meat is tender but not at all dry.
2. Remove chicken to platter and allow to cool. (Reserve broth.) When cool enough to handle, cut chicken into small chunks.
3. Meanwhile, brown ground beef in large skillet. Stir occasionally with wooden spoon, breaking up clumps. Brown until meat is no longer pink.
4. Place 1 cup chicken

broth in slow cooker. (Reserve rest of broth.)

5. Drain drippings off browned ground beef. Add beef to slow cooker.

6. Stir all other ingredients into slow cooker.

7. Cover. Cook on Low 4 hours.

Notes:

1. Add more broth if the Stew gets thicker than you like. Use canned broth if you need to.

2. If you have leftovers, this Stew freezes well and is welcome on any cold day when you want something hot.

3. Serve this as soup, or over pasta as a topping.

Hot Chicken Sandwiches

Glenna Fay Bergey
Lebanon, OR

Makes 6-8 servings

Prep. Time: 5 minutes
Cooking Time: 6-7 hours
Ideal slow cooker size: 6-qt.

1 large chicken, whole or cut up
1 cup water

1. Place chicken in slow cooker. Add water.

2. Cover. Cook on Low 6-7 hours.

3. Debone chicken. Mix cut-up chicken with broth.

4. Spoon into dinner rolls with straining spoon to make small hot sandwiches.

Serving suggestion: Top with your favorite ***condiments****.*

Tip:

This is also a great way to prepare cooked chicken for soups or casseroles. Save the broth if you think you might make soup.

Barbecued Chicken Sandwiches

Brittany Miller
Millersburg, OH

Makes 10 servings

Prep. Time: 25-30 minutes
Cooking Time: 6 hours
Ideal slow cooker size: 5-qt.

3 lbs. boneless, skinless chicken thighs
1 cup ketchup
1 small onion, chopped
¼ cup water
¼ cup cider vinegar
2 Tbsp. Worcestershire sauce
1 Tbsp. brown sugar
1 garlic clove, minced
1 bay leaf
2 tsp. paprika
1 tsp. dried oregano
1 tsp. chili powder
½ tsp. salt
½ tsp. pepper

1. Place chicken in slow cooker.

2. In a medium-sized mixing bowl, combine ketchup, onion, water, vinegar, Worcestershire sauce, brown sugar, garlic, bay leaf, and seasonings. Pour over chicken.

3. Cover. Cook on Low 5 hours, or until meat is tender.

4. Discard bay leaf.

5. Remove chicken to large bowl. Shred meat with 2 forks. Return chicken to slow cooker.

6. Stir shredded chicken and sauce together thoroughly.

7. Cover. Cook on Low 30 minutes. Remove lid. Continue cooking 30 more minutes, allowing sauce to cook off and thicken.

Serving suggestion: This is enough chicken and sauce to fill up to 10 ***sandwich rolls****.*

Levi's Sesame Chicken Wings

Shirley Unternahrer
Wayland, IA

Makes 16 appetizer servings, or 6-8 main-dish servings

Prep. Time: 35-40 minutes
Cooking Time: 2½-5 hours
Ideal slow cooker size: 4-qt.

3 lbs. chicken wings
salt to taste
pepper to taste
1¾ cups honey
1 cup soy sauce
½ cup ketchup
2 Tbsp. canola oil
2 Tbsp. sesame oil
2 garlic cloves, minced
toasted sesame seeds

1. Rinse wings. Cut at joint. Sprinkle with salt and pepper. Place on broiler pan.
2. Broil 5 inches from broiler flame, 10 minutes on each side. Place chicken in slow cooker.
3. Combine remaining ingredients in bowl, except sesame seeds. Pour over chicken.
4. Cover. Cook on Low 5 hours or on High 2½ hours.
5. Sprinkle sesame seeds over top just before serving.
6. Serve as appetizer, or with white or brown rice and shredded lettuce to turn this appetizer into a meal.

Note:

My husband and his co-workers have a pot-luck-lunch at work. It's a good way to break the monotony of the week or month. And it gives them a chance to share with each other.

What better way to have the food ready than in a slow cooker!

A loaf of homemade bread is an excellent gift. What comfort comes from a warm loaf, knowing that someone slowed down enough to make it and share it. My mother did this often. Her baking was a way of making the kitchen a comfortable place to be. She was so encouraging when teaching me to bake or cook.

Shirley Unternahrer, Wayland, IA

Chicken Wings Colorado

Nancy Rexrode Clark
Woodstock, MD

Makes 6-8 servings

Prep. Time: 40 minutes
Cooking Time: 6½-7½ hours
Ideal slow cooker size: 4-qt.

1½ cups sugar
¼ tsp. salt
1 chicken bouillon cube
1 cup cider vinegar
½ cup ketchup
2 Tbsp. soy sauce
12-16 chicken wings
¼ cup cornstarch
½ cup cold water
red hot sauce to taste, *optional*

1. Combine sugar, salt, bouillon cube, vinegar, ketchup, and soy sauce in slow cooker. Turn to High and bring sauce to a boil.
2. Add chicken wings, pushing them down into sauce.
3. Cover. Cook on Low 6-7 hours.
4. Combine cornstarch and cold water in small bowl. Stir into slow cooker.
5. Cover. Cook on High until liquid thickens, about 30 minutes.
6. Season with red hot sauce, or let each diner add to his or her own serving.

Turkey Main Dishes

Herb-Roasted Turkey Breast

Kristi See
Weskan, KS

Makes 6 servings

Prep. Time: 15 minutes
Cooking Time: 4-6 hours
Ideal slow cooker size: 5- to 6-qt.

5 tsp. lemon juice
1 Tbsp. olive oil
1-2 tsp. pepper
1 tsp. dried rosemary, crushed
1 tsp. dried thyme
1 tsp. garlic salt
6-7-lb. bone-in turkey breast
1 medium onion, cut into wedges
1 celery rib, cut into 2"-thick pieces
½ cup white wine, *or* **chicken broth**

1. Spray slow cooker with nonstick cooking spray.

2. In a small bowl, combine lemon juice and olive oil. In another bowl, combine pepper, rosemary, thyme, and garlic salt.

3. With your fingers, carefully loosen skin from both sides of breast. Brush oil mixture under skin. Rub herb-seasoning mixture under and on top of skin.

4. Arrange onion and celery in slow cooker. Place turkey breast, skin-side up, on top of vegetables.

5. Pour wine around breast.

6. Cover. Cook on Low 4-6 hours, or until meat is tender but not dry.

Note:

I made this turkey recipe for our first Thanksgiving after we were married. We really enjoyed the taste. Clean-up was easy, and because I prepared the turkey in the slow cooker, I wasn't short on oven space.

Variations:

1. Add carrot chunks to Step 4 to add more flavor to the turkey broth.

2. Reserve broth for soups, or thicken with flour-water paste and serve as gravy over sliced turkey.

3. Freeze broth in pint-sized containers for future use.

4. Debone turkey and freeze in pint-sized containers for future use. Or freeze any leftover turkey.

Liz Ann Yoder
Hartville, OH

5. See Turkey Cacciatore, page 188, for a great dish with cut-up cooked turkey!

Turkey Breast with Orange Sauce

Jean Butzer
Batavia, NY

Makes 4-6 servings

Prep. Time: 10 minutes
Cooking Time: 7-8 hours
Ideal slow cooker size: 6-qt.

1 large onion, chopped
3 garlic cloves, minced
1 tsp. dried rosemary
½ tsp. pepper
2-3-lb. boneless, skinless turkey breast
1½ cups orange juice

1. Place onions in slow cooker.
2. Combine garlic, rosemary, and pepper in a small bowl.
3. Make gashes in turkey, about ¾ of the way through at 2″ intervals. Stuff with herb mixture. Place turkey in slow cooker.
4. Pour juice over turkey.
5. Cover. Cook on Low 7-8 hours, or until turkey is no longer pink in center.

Note:
This very easy, impressive-looking and -tasting recipe is perfect for company.

Turkey Slow Cooker

Arlene Leaman Kliewer
Lakewood, CO

Makes 8 servings

Prep. Time: 5 minutes
Cooking Time: 8 hours
Ideal slow cooker size: 6-qt.

5-lb. turkey breast
1 envelope dry onion soup mix
16-oz. can whole cranberry sauce

1. Place turkey in slow cooker.
2. Combine soup mix and cranberry sauce in bowl. Spread over turkey.
3. Cover. Cook on Low 8 hours.

Before guests are scheduled to arrive I take the lids off whatever's cooking and allow the fragrances to fill the kitchen. Very inviting! Barbara Yoder, Angola, IN

Stuffed Turkey Breast

Jean Butzer
Batavia, NY

Makes 8 servings

Prep. Time: 25 minutes
Cooking Time: 7-9 hours
Ideal slow cooker size: 6-qt.

half a stick (¼ cup) butter, melted
1 small onion, finely chopped
½ cup finely chopped celery
2½-oz. pkg. croutons with real bacon bits
1 cup chicken broth
2 Tbsp. fresh minced parsley
½ tsp. poultry seasoning
1 whole uncooked turkey breast, *or* **2 halves, about 5 lbs. total**
salt to taste
pepper to taste
24″ x 26″ piece of cheesecloth for each breast half
dry white wine

1. Combine butter, onion, celery, croutons, broth, parsley, and poultry seasoning in a bowl.
2. Cut turkey breast in thick slices from breastbone to rib cage, leaving slices attached to bone (crosswise across breast).
3. Sprinkle turkey with salt and pepper.
4. Soak cheesecloth in wine. Place turkey on cheese-

cloth. Stuff bread mixture into slits between turkey slices.

5. Fold one end of cheesecloth over the other to cover meat. Place on metal rack or trivet in 6-qt. slow cooker.

6. Cover. Cook on Low 7-9 hours or until tender. Pour additional wine over turkey during cooking.

7. Remove turkey from cooker and remove cheesecloth immediately. (If you prefer a browner result, remove from cooker, discard cheesecloth, and brown turkey in 400° oven for 15-20 minutes.)

8. Let turkey stand 10 minutes before slicing through and serving.

9. Thicken the drippings, if you wish, for gravy. Mix together 3 Tbsp. cornstarch and ¼ cup cold water in small bowl.

10. When smooth, stir into broth (with turkey removed from cooker). Turn cooker to High and stir until cornstarch paste is dissolved. Allow to cook about 10 minutes, until broth is thickened and smooth.

Slow Cooker Turkey and Dressing

Carol Sherwood
Batavia, NY

Makes 4-6 servings

Prep. Time: 10-15 minutes
Cooking Time: 5-6 hours
Ideal slow cooker size: 5- to 6-qt.

8-oz. pkg., *or* **2 6-oz. pkgs., stuffing mix**
½ cup hot water
¼ stick (2 Tbsp.) butter, softened
1 onion, chopped
½ cup chopped celery
¼ cup dried cranberries
3-lb. boneless turkey breast
¼ tsp. dried basil
½ tsp. salt
½ tsp. pepper

1. Spread dry stuffing mix in greased slow cooker.

2. Add water, butter, onion, celery, and cranberries. Mix well.

3. Sprinkle turkey breast with basil, salt, and pepper. Place over stuffing mixture.

4. Cover. Cook on Low 5-6 hours, or until turkey is done but not dry.

5. Remove turkey. Slice and set aside.

6. Gently stir stuffing and allow to stand 5 minutes before serving.

7. Place stuffing on platter, topped with sliced turkey.

Zucchini and Turkey Dish

Dolores Kratz
Souderton, PA

Makes 6 servings

Prep. Time: 15 minutes
Cooking Time: 4-5 hours
Ideal slow cooker size: 4-qt.

3 cups zucchini, sliced
1 small onion, chopped
¼ tsp. salt
1 cup cubed cooked turkey
2 fresh tomatoes, sliced, *or* **14½-oz. can diced tomatoes**
½ tsp. dried oregano
1 tsp. dried basil
¼ cup grated Parmesan cheese
½ cup shredded provolone cheese
¾ cup dry stuffing mix

1. Combine zucchini, onion, salt, turkey, tomatoes, oregano, and basil in slow cooker. Mix well.

2. Top with cheeses and stuffing.

3. Cover. Cook on Low 4-5 hours.

Slow-Cooked Turkey Dinner

Miriam Nolt
New Holland, PA

Makes 4-6 servings

Prep. Time: 15 minutes
Cooking Time: 7½ hours
Ideal slow cooker size: 4-qt.

1 onion, diced
6 small red potatoes, quartered
2 cups sliced carrots
1½-2 lbs. boneless, skinless turkey thighs
¼ cup flour
2 Tbsp. dry onion soup mix
10¾-oz. can cream of mushroom soup
⅔ cup chicken broth, *or* **water**

1. Place vegetables in bottom of slow cooker.
2. Place turkey thighs over vegetables.
3. Combine remaining ingredients in bowl. Pour over turkey.
4. Cover. Cook on High 30 minutes. Reduce heat to Low and cook 7 hours, or until vegetables and meat are tender but not dry.

Variation:

Use 1 cup uncooked long-grain rice instead of potatoes.
Increase water to 1⅔ cups.
Increase dry onion soup to ¼ cup.
Continue with Step 4 above.

Turkey Thighs, Acorn Squash, and Apples

Mary E. Wheatley
Mashpee, MA

Makes 6-8 sevings

Prep. Time: 35 minutes
Cooking Time: 6-8 hours
Ideal slow cooker size: 6-qt.

2 lbs. acorn squash, peeled, seeded, and cut into 1"- thick rings
6 medium-sized Granny Smith, *or* **other tart, apples cored and cut into ½"-thick rings**
4 turkey thighs, skin and excess fat removed
salt and pepper to taste
1 shallot, *or* **small onion, chopped**
½ cup apple juice, *or* **cider**
1 Tbsp. apple brandy
3 Tbsp. brown sugar
1 tsp. ground cinnamon
½ tsp. ground allspice

1. Spray inside of slow cooker with non-stick spray. Layer in squash, followed by apple rings.
2. Place turkey thighs on top. Sprinkle with salt, pepper, and onion or shallot.
3. In a small bowl, combine apple juice, brandy, brown sugar, cinnamon, and allspice. Pour over turkey.
4. Cover. Cook on Low 6-8 hours, or just until turkey and squash are tender.

Barbecued Turkey Legs

Barbara Walker
Sturgis, SC

Makes 4-6 servings

Prep. Time: 10 minutes
Cooking Time: 4-6 hours
Ideal slow cooker size: 4- to 5-qt.

4 turkey drumsticks
1-2 tsp. salt
¼-½ tsp. pepper
⅓ cup molasses
¼ cup vinegar
½ cup ketchup
3 Tbsp. Worcestershire sauce
¾ tsp. hickory smoke
2 Tbsp. instant minced onion

1. Sprinkle turkey with salt and pepper. Place in slow cooker.
2. Combine remaining ingredients in bowl. Pour over turkey.
3. Cover. Cook on Low 4-6 hours, or until turkey is tender.

Turkey Barbecue

Mary B. Sensenig
New Holland, PA

Makes 8 servings

Prep. Time: 10-20 minutes
Cooking Time: 9 hours
Ideal slow cooker size: 3- to 4-qt.

4 cups boneless skinless turkey thighs, *uncooked*, cut in 1" lengths
½ cup chopped onion
½ cup chopped celery
1 cup ketchup
½ cup water
1 tsp. dried mustard
2 Tbsp. brown sugar
½ tsp. salt
2 Tbsp. vinegar
2 Tbsp. Worcestershire sauce

1. Mix all ingredients together in slow cooker.
2. Cover. Cook on High 1 hour.
3. Turn cooker to Low and cook 8 more hours.

Serving suggestion: This Barbecue will fill at least 8 ***sandwich rolls.***

Barbecued Turkey Cutlets

Maricarol Magill, Freehold, NJ

Makes 6-8 servings

Prep. Time: 10 minutes • Cooking Time: 3 hours
Ideal slow cooker size: 4- to 5-qt.

6-8 (1½-2 lbs.) turkey cutlets
¼ cup molasses
¼ cup cider vinegar
¼ cup ketchup
3 Tbsp. Worcestershire sauce
1 tsp. garlic salt
3 Tbsp. chopped onion
2 Tbsp. brown sugar
¼ tsp. pepper

1. Place turkey cutlets in slow cooker.
2. Combine remaining ingredients in bowl. Pour over turkey.
3. Cover. Cook on Low 3 hours.

Serving suggestion: Serve over ***white*** *or* ***brown rice.***

Fruited Turkey and Yams

Jean M. Butzer
Batavia, NY

Makes 4 servings

Prep. Time: 30-40 minutes
Cooking Time: 3-10 hours
Ideal slow cooker size: 5- to 6-qt.

¼ stick (2 Tbsp.) butter
2-3 lbs. (3-4) turkey thighs, cut in half lengthwise
2 medium (2 cups) yams, *or* **sweet potatoes, cut crosswise into ½"-thick slices**
1 cup mixed chopped dried fruit
1 tsp. chopped garlic
½ tsp. salt
¼ tsp. pepper
¾ cup orange juice
¼ cup chopped fresh parsley

1. Melt butter in 12-inch skillet. Add turkey thighs, skin-side down. Brown over medium-high heat, turning once. Drain off drippings.
2. Meanwhile, place yams in slow cooker. Top with turkey thighs.
3. Sprinkle with dried fruit, garlic, salt, and pepper.
4. Gently pour orange juice into cooker, being careful not to disturb fruit and seasonings.
5. Cover. Cook on Low 8-10 hours or on High 3-4 hours, just until turkey is tender.
6. Slice; then sprinkle with parsley before serving.

Turkey Fajitas

Carol Ambrose
McMinnville, OR

Makes 8 servings

Prep. Time: 10-15 minutes
Cooking Time: 3-4 hours
Ideal slow cooker size: 2½-qt.

2½ lbs. turkey tenderloins
1¼-oz. envelope taco seasoning mix
1 celery rib, chopped
1 onion, chopped
14½-oz. can mild diced tomatoes and green chilies, undrained
1 cup (4 oz.) shredded cheddar cheese
8 (7½") flour tortillas

Toppings:
lettuce
sour cream
sliced olives
chopped tomatoes

1. Cut turkey into 2½"-long strips. Place in zip-top plastic bag.
2. Add taco seasoning to bag. Seal and shake to coat meat.
3. Empty seasoned turkey into slow cooker. Add celery, onion, and tomatoes. Stir together gently.
4. Cover. Cook on High 3-4 hours, or just until turkey is cooked through and tender.
5. Stir in cheese.
6. Warm tortillas according to package directions. Spoon turkey mixture evenly into center of each tortilla, and roll up.
7. Serve with Toppings.

Tip:
Put this recipe in your cooker. Then take your kids or grandkids out to cut down the tree or to do their holiday shopping. When you get back, your meal is ready!

Turkey Sloppy Joes

Marla Folkerts
Holland, OH

Makes 6 servings

Prep. Time: 20 minutes
Cooking Time: 4½-6 hours
Ideal slow cooker size: 4-qt.

1 red onion, chopped
1 sweet pepper, chopped
1½ lbs. boneless turkey, finely chopped
1 cup chili sauce, *or* **ketchup**
¼ tsp. salt
1 garlic clove, minced
1 tsp. Dijon-style mustard
⅛ tsp. pepper

1. Place onion, sweet pepper, and turkey in slow cooker.
2. Add chili sauce, salt, garlic, mustard, and pepper to cooker. Mix together well.
3. Cover. Cook on Low 4½-6 hours, or until turkey and vegetables are tender.

Serving suggestion: Serve on thickly sliced ***homemade bread*** *or fill up 6* ***sandwich rolls****.*

Turkey Cacciatore

Dorothy VanDeest
Memphis, TN

Makes 6 servings

Prep. Time: 20 minutes
Cooking Time: 4 hours
Ideal slow cooker size: 4-qt.

2½ cups cut-up ***cooked*** **turkey**
1 tsp. salt
dash of pepper
1 Tbsp. dried onion flakes
1 green bell pepper, seeded and finely chopped
1 clove garlic, finely chopped
15-oz. can whole tomatoes, mashed
4-oz. can sliced mushrooms, drained
2 tsp. tomato paste
1 bay leaf
¼ tsp. dried thyme
2 Tbsp. finely chopped pimento

1. Combine all ingredients well in slow cooker.
2. Cover. Cook on Low 4 hours.

Serving suggestion: Serve over ***rice*** *or* ***pasta****. Or drain off most liquid and serve in* ***taco shells****.*

Turkey Lasagna

Rhoda Atzeff
Lancaster, PA

Makes 8-10 servings

Prep. Time: 20-30 minutes
Cooking Time: 5 hours
Ideal slow cooker size: 5-qt.

1 lb. lean ground turkey
1 onion, chopped
⅛ tsp. garlic powder
2 15-oz. cans tomato sauce
6-oz. can tomato paste
½-1 tsp. salt
1 tsp. dried oregano, *or*
½ tsp. dried oregano and
½ tsp. dried basil
12 oz. fat-free cottage cheese
½ cup grated Parmesan cheese
12 oz. shredded non-fat mozzarella cheese
12 oz. lasagna noodles, uncooked, *divided*

1. Brown ground turkey and onions in skillet. Drain off any drippings.
2. Stir garlic powder, tomato sauce, tomato paste, salt, and herbs into browned turkey in skillet.
3. In a good-sized mixing bowl, blend together cottage cheese, Parmesan cheese, and mozzarella cheese.
4. Spoon ⅓ of meat sauce into slow cooker.
5. Add ⅓ of uncooked lasagna noodles, breaking them to fit.
6. Top with ⅓ of cheese mixture. You may have to use a knife to spread it.
7. Repeat layers two more times.
8. Cover. Cook on Low 5 hours.
9. Allow to stand 10 minutes before serving.

Note:
I tried this on my brothers. It is a delicious dish, but I thought their raves were maybe a bit overdone. But it was a good feeling to know it pleased them. I overheard my one brother calling another brother in Virginia and telling him about it!

Savory Turkey Meatballs in Italian Sauce

Marla Folkerts
Holland, OH

Makes 8 servings

Prep. Time: 30 minutes
Cooking Time: 3-4 hours
Ideal slow cooker size: 4-qt.

28-oz. can crushed tomatoes
1 Tbsp. red wine vinegar
1 medium onion, finely chopped
2 garlic cloves, minced
¼ tsp. Italian herb seasoning
1 tsp. dried basil
1 lb. ground turkey
⅛ tsp. garlic powder
⅛ tsp. black pepper
⅓ cup dried parsley
2 egg whites
¼ tsp. dried minced onion
⅓ cup dry quick oats
¼ cup grated Parmesan cheese
¼ cup flour
oil

1. Combine tomatoes, vinegar, onions, garlic, Italian seasoning, and basil in slow cooker. Turn to Low.
2. Combine remaining ingredients, except flour and oil, in large bowl. Form into 1" balls.
3. Dredge each ball in flour.
4. Brown balls in batches in oil in skillet over medium heat. As you finish a batch, transfer it to slow cooker. Stir into sauce in cooker.
5. When all balls are browned and in cooker, cover. Cook on Low 3-4 hours, or until Meatballs are cooked through.

Serving suggestion: Serve over ***pasta*** *or* ***rice.***

Tip:
The meatballs and sauce freeze well.

Tricia's Cranberry Turkey Meatballs

Shirley Unternahrer
Wayland, IA

Makes 12 servings

Prep. Time: 25 minutes
Cooking Time: 3½ hours
Ideal slow cooker size: 3-qt.

16-oz. can jelled cranberry sauce
½ cup ketchup, *or* **barbecue sauce**
1 egg
1 lb. ground turkey
half a small onion, chopped
1 tsp. salt
¼ tsp. black pepper
1-2 tsp. grated orange peel, *optional*
oil

1. Combine cranberry sauce and ketchup in slow cooker.
2. Cover. Cook on High until cranberry sauce is melted and well blended with ketchup, about 30 minutes.
3. Combine remaining ingredients, except oil, in bowl. Shape into 24 balls.
4. Cook in batches over medium heat in skillet, in oil if you need it, for 8-10 minutes, or just until browned. As you finish a batch, add it to sauce in slow cooker.
5. Cover. Cook on Low 3 hours.

Serving suggestion: Serve with ***rice*** *and a* ***steamed vegetable****.*

Turkey Meatballs and Gravy

Betty Sue Good
Broadway, VA

Makes 8 servings

Prep. Time: 30 minutes
Cooking Time: 2-4 hours
Ideal slow cooker size: 4-qt.

2 eggs, beaten
¾ cup bread crumbs
½ cup finely chopped onions
½ cup finely chopped celery
2 Tbsp. chopped fresh parsley
¼ tsp. pepper
⅛ tsp. garlic powder
1 tsp. salt
2 lbs. ground raw turkey
1½ Tbsp. cooking oil
10¾-oz. can cream of mushroom soup
1 cup water
⅞-oz. pkg. turkey gravy mix
½ tsp. dried thyme
2 bay leaves

1. Combine eggs, bread crumbs, onions, celery, parsley, pepper, garlic powder, Shape into 1½" balls.
2. Brown meat balls in oil in skillet. Don't crowd skillet, or Meatballs will steam and not brown. As you finish a batch, drain off drippings. Place meatballs into slow cooker.
3. Combine soup, water, dry gravy mix, thyme, and bay leaves in bowl. Pour over browned Meatballs in cooker.
4. Cover. Cook on Low 4 hours or on High 2 hours.
5. Discard bay leaves before serving.

Serving suggestion: Serve over ***mashed potatoes*** *or* ***buttered noodles****.*

I'm beginning to notice more and more slow cookers at our family potluck gatherings. Old favorite recipes are being converted for slow-cooker use, and new ones are being introduced. Take a copy of the recipe you prepared, plus some blank cards, just in case you want to swap recipes with others.
Shirley Unternahrer, Wayland, IA

Meat and Bean Main Dishes

"Famous" Baked Beans

Katrine Rose
Woodbridge, VA

Makes 10 servings

Prep. Time: 20 minutes
Cooking Time: 3-6 hours
Ideal slow cooker size: 4-qt.

1 lb. ground beef
¼ cup minced onions
1 cup ketchup
4 15-oz. cans pork and beans
1 cup brown sugar
2 Tbsp. liquid smoke
1 Tbsp. Worcestershire sauce

1. Brown beef and onions in skillet. Stir frequently to break up clumps of meat. Continue cooking until no pink remains in meat. Drain off drippings.
2. Spoon meat and onions into slow cooker.
3. Add remaining ingredients and stir well.
4. Cover. Cook on High 3 hours or on Low 5-6 hours.

Note:
There are many worthy baked bean recipes, but these are both easy and absolutely delicious. The secret to this recipe is the liquid smoke. I get many requests for this recipe, and some friends have added the word "famous" to its name.

Barbecued Beans

Esther J. Yoder
Hartville, OH

Makes 10 servings

Prep. Time: 20 minutes
Cooking Time: 2-3 hours
Ideal slow cooker size: 3-qt.

1 lb. ground beef
½ cup chopped onions
½ tsp. salt
¼ tsp. pepper
28-oz. can pork and beans (your favorite variety)
½ cup ketchup
1 Tbsp. Worcestershire sauce
1 Tbsp. vinegar
¼ tsp. Tabasco sauce

1. Brown beef and onions together in skillet. Stir frequently to break up clumps of meat. Continue cooking until meat is no longer pink. Drain off drippings.
2. Spoon meat and onions into cooker.
3. Add all other ingredients to cooker.
4. Cover. Cook on High 2-3 hours, stirring once or twice, if you're home and able to do so.

Tip:
These beans' flavor gets better on the second and third days.

Cowboy Beans

Reba Rhodes
Bridgewater, VA

Makes 8 servings

Prep. Time: 20-25 minutes
Cooking Time: 1-2 hours
Ideal slow cooker size: 3-qt.

1 lb. ground beef
1 large onion, finely chopped
1 small green bell pepper, finely chopped
28-oz. can pork and beans
1½ cups ketchup
1 tsp. vinegar
3 Tbsp. brown sugar
2 tsp. prepared mustard
2 tsp. salt
1 tsp. pepper

1. Brown ground beef, onion, and bell pepper in skillet. Stir often to break up clumps of meat. Continue cooking until meat is no longer pink. Drain off drippings.
2. Spoon meat and vegetables into slow cooker.
3. Add all other ingredients to slow cooker. Mix well.
4. Cover. Cook on Low 1-2 hours.

Note:
This travels well to a potluck or holiday buffet.

Hamburger Beans

Joanne Kennedy
Plattsburgh, NY

Makes 6 servings

Prep. Time: 20-25 minutes
Cooking Time: 2-3 hours
Ideal slow cooker size: 3-qt.

1 lb. ground beef
1 onion, chopped
2 15-oz. cans pork and beans
15-oz. can butter beans, drained
15-oz. can kidney beans, drained
½ tsp. garlic powder
1 cup ketchup
¾ cup molasses
½ cup brown sugar

1. Brown ground beef and onion in skillet. Stir frequently to break up clumps. Continue cooking until meat is no longer pink. Drain off drippings.
2. Spoon beef and onion into slow cooker.
3. Add remaining ingredients. Mix well.
4. Cover. Cook on Low 2-3 hours.

Pasta Bean Pot

Donna Conto
Saylorsburg, PA

Makes 8 servings

Prep. Time: 10-15 minutes
Cooking Time: 4-5 hours
Ideal slow cooker size: 4-qt.

1 Tbsp. olive oil
1 medium onion, chopped
1 garlic clove, minced
½ tsp. vinegar
8 oz. uncooked elbow macaroni
28-oz. can stewed, *or* **diced, tomatoes**
15-oz. can cannellini beans, undrained
15-oz. can kidney beans, undrained
12-oz. can chicken broth
1 tsp. dried oregano
1 tsp. parsley
dash red pepper

1. Put all ingredients in slow cooker. Mix well.
2. Cover. Cook on Low 4-5 hours, or until macaroni are tender but not mushy.

Note:
I like to have this soup cooking as my granddaughter and I bake cookies. That frees us from worrying about making dinner.

Keep a bowl of ornaments by the door throughout the season and let guests help themselves when they leave.
Carol L. Miller, Lockport, NY

One-Pot Dinner

Vicki Dinkel
Sharon Springs, KS

Makes 4 servings

Prep. Time: 30 minutes
Cooking Time: 3-9 hours
Ideal slow cooker size: 4- to 5-qt.

½-1 lb. ground beef, according to your preference
½ lb. bacon, cut in pieces
1 cup chopped onions
2 31-oz. cans pork and beans
16-oz. can kidney beans, drained
1 cup ketchup
16-oz. can butter beans, drained
¼ cup brown sugar
1 Tbsp. liquid smoke
3 Tbsp. white vinegar
1 tsp. salt
dash of pepper

1. Brown ground beef in skillet. Stir frequently to break up clumps of meat. Continue cooking until meat is no longer pink. Drain off drippings.
2. Place beef in slow cooker.
3. Brown bacon and onions in same skillet. Stir frequently to brown evenly. Drain off drippings.
4. Add bacon and onions to slow cooker.
5. Stir remaining ingredients into cooker.
6. Cover. Cook on Low 5-9 hours or on High 3 hours.

Calico Beans

Mary Rogers
Waseca, MN

Makes 12-15 servings

Prep. Time: 30-40 minutes
Cooking Time: 3-4 hours
Ideal slow cooker size: 4- to 5-qt.

1 lb. bacon
1 lb. ground beef
½ cup chopped onions
½ cup chopped celery
½ cup ketchup
1 Tbsp. prepared mustard
16-oz. can kidney beans, undrained
16-oz. can great northern beans, undrained
½ cup brown sugar
1 Tbsp. vinegar
16-oz. can butter beans, undrained
28-oz. can Bush's Baked Beans

1. Cut bacon in small squares. Brown in skillet, stirring often to brown evenly. Drain off drippings.
2. Spoon bacon into slow cooker.
3. Brown ground beef in skillet, stirring frequently to break up clumps of meat. Continue cooking until meat is no longer pink.
4. Using a slotted spoon, lift beef from drippings and place in slow cooker. Reserve drippings.
5. Sauté onions and celery in drippings until soft. Place vegetables in cooker.
6. Combine all ingredients in slow cooker. Stir together well.
7. Cover. Simmer on Low 3-4 hours.

Note:
This is a favorite dish that we serve at neighborhood and family gatherings any time of the year. Our children especially enjoy it.

Trio Bean Casserole

Stacy Schmucker Stoltzfus
Enola, PA

Makes 4-6 servings

Prep. Time: 15-20 minutes
Cooking Time: 2-4 hours
Ideal slow cooker size: 3½-qt.

16-oz. can kidney beans, drained
16-oz. can green beans, drained
16-oz. can pork and beans with tomato sauce
½ cup chopped onions
½ cup brown sugar
½ cup ketchup
1 Tbsp. vinegar
1 tsp. prepared mustard
1 lb. bacon, fried and crumbled, *or* **1 lb. cooked ham, cubed**
1 Tbsp. barbecue sauce

1. Combine all ingredients in slow cooker. Stir well.
2. Cover. Cook on High 2 hours or on Low 3-4 hours.

Galloping Beans

Sharon Timpe
Mequon, WI

Makes 10-12 servings

Prep. Time: 15-20 minutes
Cooking Time: 3-7 hours
Ideal slow cooker size: 3½-qt.

6 slices bacon, cut in pieces
½ cup onions, chopped
1 garlic clove, minced
16-oz. can baked beans
16-oz. can kidney beans, drained
15-oz. can butter, *or* **pinto, beans, drained**
2 Tbsp. dill pickle relish, *or* **chopped dill pickles**
⅓ cup chili sauce, *or* **ketchup**
2 tsp. Worcestershire sauce
½ cup brown sugar
⅛ tsp. hot pepper sauce, *optional*

1. Lightly brown bacon, onions, and garlic in skillet. Stir frequently. Drain off drippings.
2. Lift bacon and vegetables into slow cooker with slotted spoon.
3. Add all other ingredients to slow cooker. Mix well.
4. Cover. Cook on Low 5-7 hours or on High 3-4 hours.

Deb's Baked Beans

Deborah Swartz
Grottoes, VA

Makes 4-6 servings

Prep. Time: 20 minutes
Cooking Time: 1½-2 hours
Ideal slow cooker size: 3-qt.

4 slices bacon
2 Tbsp. reserved drippings
½ cup chopped onions
2 15-oz. cans pork and beans
½ tsp. salt, *optional*
2 Tbsp. brown sugar
1 Tbsp. Worcestershire sauce
1 tsp. prepared mustard

1. Fry bacon in skillet until crisp. Drain off all but 2 Tbsp. drippings.
2. Remove bacon from skillet and crumble into cooker.
3. Cook onions in reserved drippings until just tender.
4. Add onions to slow cooker.
5. Mix in all additional ingredients.
6. Cover. Cook on High 1½-2 hours.

Lotsa-Beans Pot

Dorothy Van Deest
Memphis, TN

Makes 15-20 servings

Prep. Time: 30 minutes
Cooking Time: 3-4 hours
Ideal slow cooker size: 5-qt.

8 bacon strips, diced
2 onions, thinly sliced
1 cup packed brown sugar
½ cup cider vinegar
1 tsp. salt
1 tsp. ground mustard
½ tsp. garlic powder
28-oz. can baked beans
16-oz. can kidney beans, rinsed and drained
15½-oz. can pinto beans, rinsed and drained
15-oz. can lima beans, rinsed and drained
15½-oz. can black-eyed peas, rinsed and rained
1 cup ketchup
2 Tbsp. barbecue sauce
1 Tbsp. liquid smoke

1. Cook bacon in skillet until crisp. Remove bacon to paper towels.
2. Drain off drippings, reserving 2 Tbsp.
3. Sauté onions in drippings until tender.
4. Add brown sugar, vinegar, salt, mustard, and garlic powder to skillet. Bring to boil.
5. Combine beans and peas in slow cooker.
6. Add onion mixture, ketchup, barbecue sauce, liquid smoke, and bacon. Mix well.

Set your table early. Have ready any soup, salad or dessert plates. Clear well after each entrée. Do dishes the next day—enjoy your guests. Karen Cenevivo, Seymour, CT

7. Cover. Cook on High 3-4 hours.

Note:
This hearty bean concoction tastes especially yummy when the gang comes in from an evening of sledding or skating or Christmas carolling. Keep the beans warm to hot and serve them from the pot.

Auntie Ginny's Baked Beans

Becky Harder
Monument, CO

Makes 8 servings

Prep. Time: 15 minutes
Cooking Time: 4-5 hours
Ideal slow cooker size: 3-qt.

4 slices bacon, diced
28-oz. can pork and beans
1 tsp. dark molasses
1 Tbsp. brown sugar
1 cup dates, cut up
1 medium onion, chopped

1. Partially fry bacon in skillet. Drain off drippings.
2. Place bacon in slow cooker.
3. Add all other ingredients to slow cooker.
4. Cover. Cook on Low 4-5 hours.

Tip:
There are many varieties of canned baked beans available. Choose a flavor that fits your guests—from vegetarian (you'll want to leave out the bacon if this is important to your diners) to country-style to onion.

Note:
Written down at the bottom of my copy of this recipe is this note: "Harder picnic—1974." Notations like that help us remember special family get-togethers or reunions.

This recipe was shared almost 20 years ago as we gathered cousins and aunts together in our hometown. Today no one from our family lives in the hometown, and we cousins are scattered over six states, but one way to enjoy fond memories is to record dates or events on recipes we share with each other.

Creole Black Beans

Joyce Kaut
Rochester, NY

Makes 6-8 servings

Prep. Time: 30 minutes
Cooking Time: 4-8 hours
Ideal slow cooker size: 4-qt.

1½-2 lbs. smoked sausage, sliced in ½"-thick pieces
3 15-oz. cans black beans, drained
1½ cups chopped onions
1½ cups chopped green bell peppers
1½ cups chopped celery
4 garlic cloves, minced
2 tsp. dried thyme
1½ tsp. dried oregano
1½ tsp. pepper
1 chicken bouillon cube
3 bay leaves
8-oz. can tomato sauce
1 cup water

1. Brown sausage in non-stick skillet.
2. Place in slow cooker.
3. Stir in all other ingredients and mix well.
4. Cover. Cook on Low 8 hours or on High 4 hours.
5. Remove bay leaves before serving.

*Serving suggestion: Serve over **rice**, with a **salad** and **fresh fruit** for dessert.*

Variation:
You may substitute a 14½-oz. can of stewed tomatoes for the tomato sauce.

Pizza Beans

Kelly Evenson
Pittsboro, NC

Makes 6 servings

Prep. Time: 30 minutes
Cooking Time: 7-9 hours
Ideal slow cooker size: 4-qt.

16-oz. can pinto beans, drained
16-oz. can kidney beans, drained
2¼-oz. can ripe olives, sliced, drained
28-oz. can stewed, *or* **whole, tomatoes**
¾ lb. bulk Italian sausage
1 Tbsp. oil
1 green bell pepper, chopped
1 medium onion, chopped
1 garlic clove, minced
1 tsp. salt
1 tsp. dried oregano
1 tsp. dried basil
Parmesan cheese, grated

1. Combine beans, olives, and tomatoes in slow cooker.
2. Brown sausage in oil in skillet. Stir frequently, breaking up clumps of meat. Continue cooking until meat is no longer pink. Drain, reserving drippings.
3. Transfer sausage to slow cooker.
4. Sauté green pepper in drippings 1 minute, stirring constantly. Add onions and continue stirring until onions start to become translucent. Add garlic and cook 1 more minute. Transfer vegetables to slow cooker.
5. Stir in seasonings.
6. Cover. Cook on Low 7-9 hours.
7. To serve, sprinkle with Parmesan cheese.

Variation:

For a thicker dish, 20 minutes before serving remove ¼ cup liquid from cooker. Place in small bowl. Add 1 Tbsp. cornstarch to it. Stir until dissolved. Return to soup. Cook on High 15 minutes, or until thickened.

Pioneer Beans

Kay Magruder
Seminole, OK

Makes 4-6 servings

Prep. Time: 10 minutes
Soaking Time: 8 hours, or overnight
Cooking Time: 8-9 hours
Ideal slow cooker size: 4-qt.

1 lb. dry lima beans
1 bunch green onions, chopped
3 beef bouillon cubes
6 cups water
1 lb. smoked sausage, cut in ½"-thick slices
½ tsp. garlic powder
¾ tsp. Tabasco sauce

1. Place dry lima beans in slow cooker. Cover with water. Let soak 8 hours, or overnight.
2. Drain off water.
3. Add all other ingredients to beans in slow cooker. Mix together well.
4. Cover. Cook on Low 8-9 hours, or until beans are soft but not mushy.

Dawn's Special Beans

Dawn Day
Westminster, CA

Makes 8-10 servings

Prep. Time: 10-15 minutes
Cooking Time: 6 hours
Ideal slow cooker size: 4-qt.

16-oz. can kidney beans
16-oz. can small white beans
16-oz. can butter beans
16-oz. can small red beans
1 cup chopped onions
2 tsp. dry mustard
½ tsp. hickory-smoke flavoring
½ cup dark brown sugar
½ cup honey
1 cup barbecue sauce
2 Tbsp. apple cider vinegar

1. Combine all ingredients in slow cooker.
2. Cover. Cook on Low 6 hours.

Tip:

If you like soupy beans, do not drain the beans before adding them to the cooker. If you prefer a drier outcome, drain all beans before pouring into cooker.

Partytime Beans

Beatrice Martin
Goshen, IN

Makes 14-16 servings

Prep. Time: 15-20 minutes
Cooking Time: 5-7 hours
Ideal slow cooker size: 4-qt.

1½ cups ketchup
1 onion, chopped
1 green bell pepper, chopped
1 sweet red pepper, chopped
½ cup water
½ cup packed brown sugar
2 bay leaves
2-3 tsp. cider vinegar
1 tsp. ground mustard
⅛ tsp. pepper
16-oz. can kidney beans, rinsed and drained
15½-oz. can great northern beans, rinsed and drained
15-oz. can lima beans, rinsed and drained
15-oz. can black beans, rinsed and drained
15½-oz. can black-eyed peas, rinsed and drained

1. Combine first 10 ingredients in slow cooker. Mix well.
2. Add remaining ingredients. Mix well.
3. Cover. Cook on Low 5-7 hours, or until onion and peppers are tender.
4. Remove bay leaves before serving.

Red Beans and Pasta

Naomi E. Fast, Hesston, KS

Makes 6-8 servings

Prep. Time: 10-15 minutes • Cooking Time: 3½-4½ hours
Ideal slow cooker size: 5-qt.

3 15-oz. cans chicken, *or* **vegetable, broth**
½ tsp. ground cumin
1 Tbsp. chili powder
1 garlic clove, minced
8 oz. uncooked spiral pasta
half a large green bell pepper, diced
half a large red bell pepper, diced
1 medium onion, diced
15-oz. can red beans, rinsed and drained
chopped fresh parsley
chopped fresh cilantro

1. Combine broth, cumin, chili powder, and garlic in slow cooker.
2. Cover. Cook on High until mixture comes to boil.
3. Add pasta, vegetables, and beans. Stir together well.
4. Cover. Cook on Low 3-4 hours.
5. Add parsley and cilantro before serving.

Slow-Cooker Kidney Beans

Jeanette Oberholtzer
Manheim, PA

Makes 12 servings

Prep. Time: 10-15 minutes
Cooking Time: 6-7 hours
Ideal slow cooker size: 5-qt.

2 30-oz. cans kidney beans, rinsed and drained
28-oz. can diced tomatoes
2 medium-sized red bell peppers, chopped
1 cup ketchup
½ cup brown sugar
¼ cup honey
¼ cup molasses
1 Tbsp. Worcestershire sauce
1 tsp. dry mustard
2 medium red apples, cored, unpeeled, cut into pieces

1. Combine all ingredients, except apples, in slow cooker.
2. Cover. Cook on Low 4-5 hours.
3. Stir in apples.
4. Cover. Cook 2 more hours on Low.

Note:
Tasty, meatless eating!

Zesty Calico Beans

Gloria Julien
Gladstone, MI

Makes 10 servings

Prep. Time: 20-30 minutes
Cooking Time: 2-3 hours
Ideal slow cooker size: 5-qt.

1 lb. hamburger
½ cup chopped onion
½ lb. bacon
1 can kidney beans, drained
1 can great northern white beans, drained
1 cup brown sugar
1 cup ketchup
2 large cans baked beans, undrained
4 drops Tabasco sauce
2 tsp. dry mustard
1 tsp. chili powder

1. Brown hamburger and onion together in skillet. Stir frequently to break up clumps of meat. When meat is no longer pink, drain off drippings.
2. Spoon beef and onions into slow cooker.
3. Brown bacon in same skillet until crispy. Remove from drippings and drain. Place bacon in slow cooker.
4. Stir remaining ingredients into slow cooker until well mixed.
5. Cover. Cook on Low 2-3 hours.

Edna's Baked Beans

Sharon Easter
Yuba City, CA

Makes 6 servings

Prep. Time: 5-10 minutes
Cooking Time: 4 hours
Ideal slow cooker size: 3½-qt.

1 cup applesauce (not chunky)
¼ cup brown sugar
¼ cup ketchup
½ tsp. prepared mustard (or use small pkg. hot mustard from Chinese take-out)
21-oz. can pork & beans, *or* **2 15-oz. cans**
6 hot dogs, sliced ¼"-thick, *optional*

1. Stir all ingredients together in slow cooker.
2. Cover. Cook on Low 4 hours.

Variation:
Substitute ½ lb. thinly sliced smoked sausage for hot dogs.

Note from Tester:
This recipe was as good, if not better, the second day. Next time I'll double the recipe so we're sure to have leftovers!

Vegetarian Baked Beans

Janice Muller
Derwood, MD

Makes 4 servings

Prep. Time: 10-15 minutes
Cooking Time: 4-5 hours
Ideal slow cooker size: 4-qt.

1 cup picante sauce
¼ cup molasses
2 Tbsp. packed brown sugar
2 tsp. prepared mustard
1 tsp. onion powder
16-oz. can black beans, rinsed and drained
16-oz. can white beans, rinsed and drained
1 Tbsp. lime juice

1. Mix all ingredients together in slow cooker.
2. Cover. Cook on Low 4-5 hours.

Make more than enough food so you can send a small amount home with your guests. This is especially nice for older friends who find it hard to cook, but any guest will enjoy eating good leftovers.

Leona M. Slabaugh, Apple Creek, OH

Other Main Dish Favorites

Lamb Stew

Dottie Schmidt
Kansas City, MO

Makes 6 servings

Prep. Time: 35 minutes
Cooking Time: 8-10 hours
Ideal slow cooker size: 5-qt.

2 lbs. lamb, cubed
½ tsp. sugar
2 Tbsp. oil
2 tsp. salt
¼ tsp. pepper
¼ cup flour
2 cups water
¾ cup red wine
¼ tsp. powdered garlic
2 tsp. Worcestershire sauce
6-8 carrots, sliced
4 small onions, quartered
4 ribs celery, sliced
3 medium potatoes, diced

1. Sprinkle lamb with sugar. Brown in oil in skillet.
2. Remove lamb and place in cooker, reserving drippings. Stir salt, pepper, and flour into drippings until smooth. Stir in water and wine until smooth, stirring until broth simmers and thickens.
3. Pour into cooker. Add remaining ingredients and stir until well mixed.
4. Cover. Cook on Low 8-10 hours.

Serving suggestion: We like this served with ***crusty bread.***

Lamb Chops

Shirley Sears
Tiskilwa, IL

Makes 4-6 servings

Prep. Time: 10 minutes
Cooking Time: 4-6 hours
Ideal slow cooker size: 5-qt.

1 medium onion, sliced
1 tsp. dried oregano
½ tsp. dried thyme
½ tsp. garlic powder
¼ tsp. salt
⅛ tsp. pepper
8 loin lamb chops (1¾-2 lbs.)
2 garlic cloves, minced
¼ cup water

1. Place onion in slow cooker.
2. In a small bowl, combine oregano, thyme, garlic powder, salt, and pepper. Rub over lamb chops. Place chops in slow cooker.
3. Top chops with garlic.
4. Pour water down along side of cooker, so as not to disturb rub and garlic on chops.
5. Cover. Cook on Low 4-6 hours, or until Chops are tender but not dry.

Venison Roast

Colleen Heatwole
Burton, MI

Makes 6-8 servings

Prep. Time: 15 minutes
Marinating Time: at least 8 hours
Cooking Time: 8-12 hours
Ideal slow cooker size: 5-qt.

3-4-lb. venison roast
¼ cup vinegar
2 garlic cloves, minced
2 Tbsp. salt
½ cup chopped onions
15-oz. can tomato sauce
1 Tbsp. ground mustard
1 pkg. brown gravy mix
½ tsp. salt
¼ cup water

1. Place venison in deep bowl. Combine vinegar, garlic, and salt in a small bowl. Pour over venison.
2. Add enough cold water to cover venison. Cover. Marinate for at least 8 hours in refrigerator.
3. Rinse and drain venison. Place in slow cooker.
4. Combine remaining ingredients in a bowl. Pour over venison.
5. Cover. Cook on Low 8-12 hours, or until fork-tender but not dry.

*Serving suggestion: Serve this with a **green salad**, **potatoes**, and **rolls** to make complete meal.*

Notes:

1. The sauce on this Roast works well for any meat.
2. This is an easy meal to have for a Saturday dinner with guests or extended family. There is usually a lot of sauce, so make plenty of potatoes, noodles, or rice.

Venison in Sauce

Anona M. Teel
Bangor, PA

Makes 12 sandwiches

Prep. Time: 20 minutes
Marinating Time: 8 hours
Cooking Time: 8-10 hours
Ideal slow cooker size: 5-qt.

3-4-lb. venison roast
½ cup vinegar
2 garlic cloves, minced
2 Tbsp. salt
cold water
oil
large onion, sliced
half a green bell pepper, sliced
2 ribs celery, sliced
1-2 garlic cloves, minced
1½-2 tsp. salt
¼ tsp. pepper
½ tsp. dried oregano
¼ cup ketchup
1 cup tomato juice

1. Place venison in a large bowl. Combine vinegar, garlic cloves, and 2 Tbsp. salt, and pour over venison. Add water until meat is covered. Marinate 8 hours.
2. Cut meat into pieces. Brown in oil in skillet. Place in slow cooker.
3. Mix remaining ingredients together; then pour into cooker. Stir together well.
4. Cover. Cook on Low 8-10 hours.
5. Using two forks, pull meat apart and stir it through Sauce.

*Serving suggestion: Serve on **sandwich rolls**, or over **rice** or **pasta**.*

Beef-Venison Barbecue

Gladys Longacre
Susquehanna, PA

Makes 8 servings

Prep. Time: 25 minutes
Cooking Time: 1-3 hours
Ideal slow cooker size: 4-qt.

1½ lbs. ground beef
½ lb. ground venison
oil, if needed
1 onion, chopped
½ cup chopped green bell peppers
1 garlic clove, minced
1 tsp. salt
¼ tsp. pepper
½ tsp. dried thyme
1 tsp. dried oregano
1 tsp. dried basil
¼ cup brown sugar
¼ cup vinegar
1 Tbsp. dry mustard
1 cup ketchup
½-1 Tbsp. hickory-smoked barbecue sauce

1. Brown meat in skillet, in oil if needed. Drain off

drippings. Place meat in slow cooker.

2. Add remaining ingredients. Mix well.

3. Cover. Cook on High 1 hour or on Low 2-3 hours.

Serving suggestion: Serve Barbecue in ***hamburger rolls****.*

Tip:

This recipe can be made in larger quantities to freeze and then reheat when needed.

Note:

This Barbecue recipe was made in large quantities and served at the concession stand for our farm machinery sale in 1987. The servers used ice-cream dippers to scoop the meat into sandwich rolls.

Company Seafood Pasta

Jennifer Yoder Sommers
Harrisonburg, VA

Makes 4-6 servings

Prep. Time: 15 minutes
Cooking Time: 1-2 hours
Ideal slow cooker size: 4-qt.

2 cups sour cream
3 cups shredded Monterey Jack cheese
¼ stick (2 Tbsp.) butter, melted
½ lb. crabmeat, *or* **imitation flaked crabmeat**
⅛ tsp. pepper
½ lb. bay scallops, lightly cooked
1 lb. medium shrimp, cooked and peeled

1. Combine sour cream, cheese, and butter in slow cooker.

2. Stir in remaining ingredients.

3. Cover. Cook on Low 1-2 hours.

Serving suggestion: Serve immediately over ***linguine****. Garnish with* ***fresh parsley****.*

Oyster and Potato Filling Yuletide

Jane Geigley
Honey Brook, PA

Makes 3-4 servings

Prep. Time: 10 minutes if mashed potatoes are prepared; 50 minutes if you need to make the mashed potatoes
Cooking Time: 1½-3 hours
Ideal slow cooker size: 2-qt.

1 small onion, minced
½ cup celery, diced
¼ stick (2 Tbsp.) butter, melted
2 cups very moist mashed potatoes
1 egg, well beaten
1 Tbsp. minced parsley
1-1½ tsp. salt
dash of black pepper
1 qt. stale bread, cubed
1 doz. oysters with liquid milk, ***if needed***

1. Sauté onion and celery in butter in skillet.

2. Blend together mashed potatoes and egg in slow cooker. Pour in sautéed onion and celery. Mix together well.

3. Stir in parsley, salt, pepper, bread cubes, and oysters with their liquid. If mixture is stiff, add several Tbsp. milk.

4. Cover cooker.

5. Cook on High 1½ hours, or on Low 3 hours.

Invite an elderly person, or someone with limited mobility, to help you bake. If they are unable to stand for long periods they can use bar stools at the kitchen counter or even work at the table from a wheelchair. This offers great fellowship and conversation. Orpha Herr, Andover, NY

Curried Shrimp

Charlotte Shaffer
East Earl, PA

Makes 4-5 servings

Prep. Time: 5-10 minutes
Cooking Time: 2 hours
Ideal slow cooker size: 3-qt.

1 small onion, chopped
2 cups cooked shrimp
1 tsp. curry powder
10¾-oz. can cream of mushroom soup
1 cup sour cream

1. Place chopped onion in non-stick skillet over medium heat. Stir until onion wilts.
2. Place in slow cooker along with all other ingredients, except sour cream.
3. Cover. Cook on Low 2 hours.
4. Ten minutes before serving, stir in sour cream.

*Serving suggestion: Serve over **rice** or **puff pastry**.*

Variation:
Add another ½ tsp. curry for some added flavor.

Tuna Noodle Casserole

Ruth Hofstetter
Versailles, Missouri

Makes 8 servings

Prep. Time: 5-10 minutes
Cooking Time: 2-4 hours
Ideal slow cooker size: 3-qt.

2½ cups dry noodles
1 tsp. salt
½ cup finely chopped onion
6- *or* 12-oz. can tuna, according to your taste preference
10¾-oz. can cream of mushroom soup
half a soup can of water
¼ cup almonds, *optional*
½ cup shredded Swiss, *or* sharp cheddar, cheese
1 cup frozen peas

1. Combine all ingredients in slow cooker, except peas.
2. Cover. Cook on High 2-3 hours or on Low 4 hours, stirring occasionally.
3. Twenty minutes before end of cooking time, stir in peas and reduce heat to Low if cooking on High.

Macaroni and Cheese

Sherry L. Lapp
Lancaster, PA

Makes 8 servings

Prep. Time: 20 minutes
Cooking Time: 3 hours
Ideal slow cooker size: 4-qt.

8-oz. pkg. elbow macaroni, cooked al dente
12-oz. can evaporated milk
1 cup whole milk
half a stick (4 Tbsp.) butter, melted
2 large eggs, slightly beaten
4 cups grated sharp cheddar cheese, *divided*
¼-½ tsp. salt, according to your taste preference
⅛ tsp. white pepper
¼ cup grated Parmesan cheese

1. In slow cooker, combine lightly cooked macaroni, evaporated milk, whole milk, melted butter, eggs, 3 cups cheddar cheese, salt, and pepper.
2. Top with remaining cheddar and Parmesan cheeses.
3. Cover. Cook on Low 3 hours.

Variations:
1. Add 12-oz. can drained tuna in Step 1.

Janice Muller
Derwood, MD

2. Add ½ tsp. paprika and 2-4 Tbsp. minced onion in Step 1.

Kaye Taylor
Florissant, MO

I make a list of small jobs and ask each grandchild to do one of them. They love to help get everything on the table.
Carol Duree, Salina, KS

Slow and Easy Macaroni and Cheese

Janice Muller
Derwood, MD

Makes 6-8 servings

Prep. Time: 20 minutes
Cooking Time: 4¼ hours
Ideal slow cooker size: 3½-qt.

1 lb. dry macaroni
1 stick (8 Tbsp.) butter
2 eggs
12-oz. can evaporated milk
10¾-oz. can cheddar cheese soup
1 cup whole milk
4 cups shredded cheddar cheese, *divided*
⅛ tsp. paprika

1. Cook macaroni al dente. Drain off cooking water. Pour hot macaroni into slow cooker.
2. Slice butter into chunks and add to macaroni. Stir until melted.
3. In large mixing bowl, combine eggs, evaporated milk, soup, and whole milk. Add 3 cups cheese. Pour over macaroni and mix well.
4. Cover. Cook on Low 4 hours.
5. Sprinkle with remaining cheese. Cook 15 minutes, or until cheese melts.
6. Sprinkle with paprika before serving.

Variation:
Add 12-oz. can drained tuna in Step 3.

Easy Stuffed Shells

Rebecca Plank Leichty
Harrisonburg, VA

Makes 4-6 servings

Prep. Time: 5 minutes
Cooking Time: 3-8 hours
Ideal slow cooker size: 3½- to 4-qt.

20-oz. bag frozen stuffed shells
15-oz. can marinara, *or* **spaghetti, sauce**
15-oz. can green beans, drained

1. Place shells around inside edge of greased slow cooker.
2. Cover with marinara sauce.
3. Pour green beans in center.
4. Cover. Cook on Low 8 hours, or on High 3 hours.

Serving suggestion: Serve with ***garlic toast*** *and* ***salad*** *for a complete meal.*

Variation:
Reverse Steps 2 and 3. Double the amount of marinara sauce and pour over both shells and beans.

Cheese Souffle Casserole

Vicki Dinkel
Sharon Spring, KS

Makes 4 servings

Prep. Time: 15 minutes
Cooking Time: 4-6 hours
Ideal slow cooker size: 5-qt.

14 slices fresh bread, crusts removed, *divided*
3 cups grated sharp cheese, *divided*
¼ stick (2 Tbsp.) butter, melted, *divided*
6 eggs
3 cups milk, scalded
2 tsp. Worcestershire sauce
½ tsp. salt
paprika

1. Tear bread into small pieces. Place half in well-greased slow cooker.
2. Add half the grated cheese and half the butter. Repeat layers.
3. In a good-sized bowl, beat together eggs, milk, Worcestershire sauce, and salt.
4. Pour over bread and cheese. Push bread and cheese down into liquid. Sprinkle top with paprika.
5. Cover. Cook on Low 4-6 hours, or until Souffle sets up.

Arroz con Queso

Nadine L. Martinitz
Salina, KS

Makes 6-8 servings

Prep. Time: 15 minutes
Cooking Time: 6-9 hours
Ideal slow cooker size: 4-qt.

14½-oz. can whole tomatoes, mashed
15-oz. can Mexican-style beans, undrained
1½ cups uncooked long-grain rice
1 cup grated Monterey Jack cheese
1 large onion, finely chopped
1 cup cottage cheese
4¼-oz. can chopped green chili peppers, drained
1 Tbsp. oil
3 garlic cloves, minced
1 tsp. salt
1 cup grated Monterey Jack cheese

1. Combine all ingredients except final cup of cheese in well greased slow cooker.
2. Cover. Cook on Low 6-9 hours, or until rice is fully cooked but dish is not dry.
3. Sprinkle with remaining cheese before serving.

Serving suggestion: We eat this with ***salsa*** *on the side.*

Minestra Di Ceci

Jeanette Oberholtzer
Manheim, PA

Makes 4-6 servings

Prep. Time: 25 minutes
Soaking Time: 8 hours, or overnight
Cooking Time: 5½-6 hours
Ideal slow cooker size: 4-qt.

1 lb. dry chickpeas
1 sprig fresh rosemary
10 leaves fresh sage
2 Tbsp. salt
1-2 large garlic cloves, minced
olive oil
1 cup uncooked small pasta, your choice of shape, *or* **uncooked penne**

1. Wash chickpeas. Place in slow cooker. Cover with water. Stir in rosemary, sage, and salt. Soak 8 hours, or overnight.
2. Drain water. Remove herbs.
3. Refill slow cooker with peas and fresh water to 1" above peas.
4. Cover. Cook on Low 5 hours.
5. Sauté garlic in olive oil in skillet until clear.
6. Purée half of peas, along with several cups of broth from cooker, in blender. Return purée to slow cooker.
7. Add garlic and oil.
8. Boil pasta in saucepan until al dente, about 5 minutes. Drain. Add to beans.
9. Cover. Cook on High 30-60 minutes, or until pasta is tender and heated through, but not mushy.

Variation:
Add ½ tsp. black pepper in Step 1, if you like.

Easy Wheatberries

Elaine Vigoda
Rochester, NY

Makes 4-6 servings

Prep. Time: 10 minutes
Soaking Time: 2 hours
Cooking Time: 2 hours
Ideal slow cooker size: 4-qt.

1 cup uncooked wheatberries
1 cup couscous, *or* **small pasta like orzo**
14½-oz. can broth
½-1 broth can of water
½ cup dried craisins

1. Place wheatberries in slow cooker. Cover with water. Soak 2 hours before cooking.
2. Drain off soaking water. Add remaining ingredients to slow cooker. Stir together well.
3. Cover. Cook on Low until liquid is absorbed and berries are soft, about 2 hours.

Notes:
1. If craisins are unavailable, use raisins.
2. This is a satisfying vegetarian main dish, if you use vegetable broth.

Vegetables

Easy Flavor-Filled Green Beans

Paula Showalter
Weyers Cave, VA

Makes 10 servings

Prep. Time: 5-10 minutes
Cooking Time: 2-4 hours
Ideal slow cooker size: 3- to 3½-qt.

2 qts., *or* **4 14½-oz. cans, green beans, drained**
⅓ cup chopped onions
4-oz. can mushrooms, drained
2 Tbsp. brown sugar
3 Tbsp. butter
pepper to taste

1. Combine beans, onions, and mushrooms in slow cooker.
2. Sprinkle with brown sugar.
3. Dot with butter.
4. Sprinkle with pepper.
5. Cover. Cook on Low 2-4 hours, or until onions are tender.
6. Stir just before serving.

Creamy Green Bean Casserole

Jena Hammond
Traverse City, MI

Makes 10 servings

Prep. Time: 10 minutes
Cooking Time: 3 hours
Ideal slow cooker size: 5- to 6-qt.

3 qts., *or* **6 14½-oz. cans, green beans**
2 10¾-oz. cans mushroom soup
1 tsp. black pepper
1 tsp. Lawry's seasoned salt

Topping:
3-oz. can French-fried onions
1 cup Colby cheese, shredded

1. Drain half of liquid off green beans. (Find another use for it or discard.)
2. Mix beans, soup, pepper, and seasoned salt together in the slow cooker.
3. Cover. Cook on Low 3 hours.
4. Twenty minutes before serving, top beans with French-fried onions and shredded cheese.

Variations:

1. Instead of canned green beans, use 2 lbs. frozen French-cut green beans, thawed. Extend cooking time to 4-5 hours if you like soft green beans.

Rhonda Freed
Croghan, NY

2. Replace one can of mushroom soup with 16 oz. sour cream. Drop Topping above and replace with 2 cups cheddar cheese, shredded, and ½ cup crisp bacon pieces.

Jennifer A. Crouse
Mt. Crawford, VA

Green Bean Casserole

Jane Meiser
Harrisonburg, VA

Makes 4 servings

Prep. Time: 10-15 minutes
Cooking Time: 3-4 hours
Ideal slow cooker size: 3-qt.

14½-oz. can green beans, drained, *divided*
3½-oz. can French-fried onions, *divided*
1 cup grated cheddar cheese, *divided*
8-oz. can water chestnuts, drained, *divided*
10¾-oz. can cream of chicken soup
¼ cup white wine, *or* **water**
½ tsp. curry powder
¼ tsp. pepper

1. Alternate layers of half the beans, half the onions, half the cheese, and half the water chestnuts in slow cooker. Repeat.
2. Combine remaining ingredients in a bowl. Pour over vegetables in slow cooker.
3. Cover. Cook on Low 3-4 hours.

Au Gratin Green Beans

Donna Lantgen
Rapid City, SD

Makes 6 servings

Prep. Time: 10 minutes
Cooking Time: 3-4 hours
Ideal slow cooker size: 2-qt.

2 14½-oz. cans green beans, drained
¼ cup diced onions
½ cup cubed Velveeta cheese
¼ cup evaporated milk
1 tsp. flour
½ tsp. salt
dash of pepper
sliced almonds, *optional*

1. Combine all ingredients, except almonds, in slow cooker.
2. Cover. Cook on Low 3-4 hours.
3. Garnish with sliced almonds at serving time, if you wish.

Brookville Hotel Creamed Corn

Melanie Thrower
McPherson, KS

Makes 3-4 servings

Prep. Time: 10-15 minutes
Cooking Time: 3-8 hours
Ideal slow cooker size: 5-qt.

16-oz. pkg. frozen whole-kernel corn
¾ cup heavy cream
1 tsp. salt
dash of pepper
1 Tbsp. sugar
1 Tbsp. cornstarch

1. Combine all ingredients in slow cooker.
2. Cook on High 3-4 hours or on Low 6-8 hours.

Note:
The corn needs to boil to thicken.

A calendar made with family photos is my favorite gift. Seeing photos of my family and remembering them all year long is the most wonderful thing!

Ruth Schiefer, Vassar, MI

Super Creamed Corn

Ruth Ann Penner
Hillsboro, KS

Alix Nancy Botsford
Seminole, OK

Makes 8-12 servings

Prep. Time: 5-10 minutes
Cooking Time: 4 hours
Ideal slow cooker size: 3- to 4-qt.

2-3 lbs. frozen corn
8-oz. pkg. cream cheese, cubed
half a stick (4 Tbsp) butter, melted
2-3 Tbsp. sugar, *or* **honey**
2-3 Tbsp. water, *optional*

1. Combine all ingredients in slow cooker.
2. Cover. Cook on Low 4 hours.

Serving suggestion: Serve with ***meat loaf, turkey,*** *or* ***hamburgers.***

Variation:

1. Add ¼ lb. mild cheese, shredded to Step 1.

Marlene Weaver
Lititz, PA

Note:

A great addition to a holiday that is easy and requires no last-minute preparation. It also frees the stove and oven for other food preparation.

Baked Corn

Velma Stauffer, Akron, PA

Makes 8 servings

Prep. Time: 5-10 minutes • Cooking Time: 3¾ hours
Ideal slow cooker size: 2-qt.

1 qt. fresh, *or* **2 1-lb. bags frozen, corn**
2 eggs, beaten
1 tsp. salt
1 cup milk
⅛ tsp. pepper
2 tsp. oil
3 Tbsp. sugar
3 Tbsp. flour

1. Combine all ingredients well in greased slow cooker.
2. Cover. Cook on High 3 hours and then on Low 45 minutes.

Tip:

If you use home-grown sweet corn, you could reduce the amount of sugar.

Corn and Macaroni

Kristine Martin
Newmanstown, PA

Makes 3-4 servings

Prep. Time: 5 minutes
Cooking Time: 2½ hours
Ideal slow cooker size: 3-qt.

15½-oz. can whole-kernel corn, drained
15½-oz. can creamed corn
1 cup uncooked macaroni
1 cup mild cheese of your choice, shredded
1 stick (8 Tbsp.) butter, cut in pieces
1 Tbsp. onion powder
1 tsp. salt
¾ cup milk

1. Spray interior of slow cooker with cooking spray.
2. Mix all ingredients together in slow cooker.
3. Cover. Cook on High 2½ hours, or until macaroni is soft but not mushy.

Variation from Tester:

Add 1 cup of cubed, fully cooked ham to Step 2 to add flavor and substance.

Tip:

This helps children to eat their vegetables!

Dried Corn

Julia Burkholder
Robesonia, PA

Makes 20 servings

Prep. Time: 15 minutes
Chilling Time: 8 hours, or overnight
Cooking Time: 3-4 hours
Ideal slow cooker size: 4- to 5-qt.

22½ oz. dried corn*
half a stick (4 Tbsp.) butter, melted
1½ tsp. salt
¼ cup sugar
2 cups half-and-half
¾ cup water
5 cups whole milk

1. Mix all ingredients in slow cooker.
2. Cover. Refrigerate 8 hours, or overnight.
3. Cook on High 3-4 hours, or until corn is soft but not mushy. Stir occasionally.

*Found in canned vegetable section in 7½-oz. plastic bags.

Confetti Scalloped Corn

Rhoda Atzeff
Harrisburg, PA

Makes 6-8 servings

Prep. Time: 15 minutes
Cooking Time: 2-2½ hours
Ideal slow cooker size: 3-qt.

2 eggs, beaten
1 cup sour cream
half a stick (¼ cup) butter, melted
1 small onion, finely chopped, *or* **2 Tbsp. dried chopped onion**
11-oz. can Mexicorn, drained
14-oz. can cream-style corn
2-3 Tbsp. green jalapeño salsa, regular salsa, *or* **chopped green chilies**
8½-oz. pkg. cornbread mix

1. Combine all ingredients in lightly greased slow cooker.
2. Cover. Bake on High 2-2½ hours, or until corn is fully cooked.

Mexican Corn

Betty K. Drescher
Quakertown, PA

Makes 4-6 servings

Prep. Time: 10 minutes
Cooking Time: 2¾-4¾ hours
Ideal slow cooker size: 2-qt.

2 10-oz. pkgs. frozen corn, partially thawed
4-oz. jar chopped pimentos, drained
⅓ cup chopped green bell peppers
⅓ cup water
1 tsp. salt
¼ tsp. pepper
½ tsp. paprika
½ tsp. chili powder

1. Combine all ingredients in slow cooker.
2. Cover. Cook on High 45 minutes, and then on Low 2-4 hours. Stir occasionally if you're home and able to do so.

Variations:
For more fire, add ⅓ cup salsa to ingredients, and increase amounts of pepper, paprika, and chili powder to match your taste.

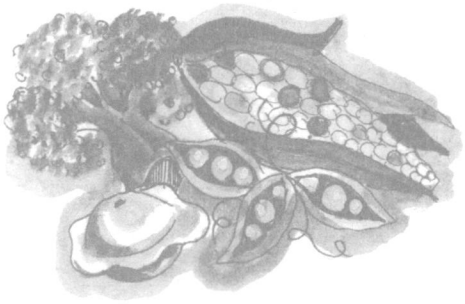

Spicy Corn Casserole

Beth Nafziger
Lowville, NY

Makes 10 servings

Prep. Time: 10-15 minutes
Cooking Time: 2-3 hours
Ideal slow cooker size: 4-qt.

1 stick (8 Tbsp.) butter
1 large onion, chopped
2 medium green bell peppers, chopped
¼ cup flour
2 cups fresh, *or* **frozen, corn**
2 cups cooked long-grain rice (I use brown rice)
14½-oz. can diced tomatoes with liquid
4 hard-cooked eggs, chopped
2½ cups shredded sharp cheese
2 Tbsp. Worcestershire sauce
2-3 tsp. hot pepper sauce
1 tsp. salt
½ tsp. pepper

1. In large skillet, melt butter. Sauté onion and pepper until tender.
2. Stir in flour and remove from heat.
3. Place sautéed vegetables in slow cooker. Add all remaining ingredients. Mix together gently.
4. Cover. Cook on Low 2-3 hours. If the corn becomes drier than I like while cooking, I add tomato juice.

Note:
I serve this casserole when I'm looking for a spicy, meatless meal. This recipe is a family favorite that we enjoy over and over and never tire of.

Cornbread Casserole

Arlene Groff
Lewistown, PA

Makes 8 servings

Prep. Time: 10 minutes
Cooking Time: 3¼-4 hours
Ideal slow cooker size: 3½- to 4-qt.

1 qt., or 2 14½-oz. cans, whole-kernel corn
1 qt., or 2 14½-oz. cans, creamed corn
1 pkg. corn muffin mix
1 egg
¼ stick (2 Tbsp.) butter
¼ tsp. garlic powder
2 Tbsp. sugar
¼ cup milk
½ tsp. salt
¼ tsp. pepper

1. Combine all ingredients in greased slow cooker.
2. Cover. Cook on Low 3½-4 hours, stirring once halfway through.

Variation:
You can replace 1 egg and ¼ cup milk with 8 oz. sour cream.

Kendra Dreps
Liberty, PA

Cheesy Hominy

Michelle Showalter
Bridgewater, VA

Makes 12-14 servings

Prep. Time: 10 minutes
Cooking Time: 3½-9 hours
Ideal slow cooker size: 5- to 6-qt.

2 cups dry cracked hominy
6 cups water
2 Tbsp. flour
1½ cups milk
4 cups sharp cheddar cheese, grated
1-2 tsp. salt
¼ tsp. pepper
half a stick (4 Tbsp.) butter, cut in chunks, or melted

1. Combine hominy and water in 5-6 qt. slow cooker.
2. Cover. Cook on High 3-4 hours or on Low 6-8 hours.
3. Stir in remaining ingredients.
4. Cover. Cook 30-60 minutes.

Note:
Cheesy Hominy is a nice change if you're tired of the same old thing. It's wonderful with ham, slices of bacon, or meatballs. Add a green vegetable and you have a lovely meal. Hominy is available at bulk-food stores.

Southwest Posole

Becky Harder
Monument, CO

Makes 6 servings

Prep. Time: 5-10 minutes
Soaking Time: 4-8 hours
Cooking Time: 5 hours
Ideal slow cooker size: 4-qt.

2 12-oz. pkgs. dry posole
1 garlic clove, minced
2 14-oz. cans vegetable, *or* **chicken, broth**
2 10-oz. cans Rotel Mexican diced tomatoes
4¼-oz. can diced green chilies, drained, *optional*
salt to taste

1. Place dry posole in slow cooker. Cover with water. Soak 4-8 hours.
2. Drain water.
3. Add all remaining ingredients to posole in slow cooker.
4. Cover. Cook on High 3 hours and then on Low 2 hours.

Serving suggestion: Serve with ***enchiladas, black beans, Spanish rice,*** *and chopped* ***lettuce*** *with* ***black olives*** *and* ***tomatoes.***

Tip:
Dry posole can be found in the Mexican food department of the grocery store. If you cannot find dry posole, you can used canned hominy and skip to Step 3.

Cheesy Broccoli Casserole

Dorothy Van Deest
Memphis, TN

Makes 3-4 servings

Prep. Time: 10-15 minutes
Cooking Time: 3-5 hours
Ideal slow cooker size: 3-qt.

10-oz. pkg. frozen chopped broccoli
6 eggs, beaten
24 oz. small-curd cottage cheese
6 Tbsp. flour
8 oz. mild cheese of your choice, diced
half a stick (4 Tbsp.) butter, melted
2 green onions, chopped
salt to taste

1. Place frozen broccoli in colander. Run cold water over it until it thaws. Separate into pieces. Drain well.
2. Combine broccoli and all other ingredients in greased slow cooker. Mix together gently but well.
3. Cover. Cook on High 1 hour. Stir well, then continue cooking on Low 2-4 hours.

Broccoli and Rice Casserole

Deborah Swartz
Grottoes, VA

Makes 4-6 servings

Prep. Time: 15-20 minutes
Cooking Time: 5-6 hours
Ideal slow cooker size: 3½-qt.

1 lb. chopped broccoli, fresh *or* **frozen, thawed**
1 medium onion, chopped
half a stick (4 Tbsp.) butter, cut in chunks
1 cup minute rice, uncooked, *or* **1½ cups cooked rice**
10¾-oz. can cream of chicken, *or* **mushroom, soup**
¼ cup milk
1⅓ cups Velveeta cheese, cubed, *or* **cheddar cheese, shredded**
1 tsp. salt

1. Combine all ingredients in lightly greased slow cooker.
2. Cover. Cook on Low 5-6 hours.

Don't forget your pastor and his or her family. They may enjoy being included in one of your holiday gatherings.
Leona M. Slabaugh, Apple Creek, OH

Quick Broccoli Fix

Willard E. Roth, Elkhart, IN

Makes 6 servings

Prep. Time: 15 minutes • Cooking Time: 5-6 hours
Ideal slow cooker size: 3½-qt.

1 lb. fresh, *or* **frozen, broccoli, cut up**
10¾-oz. can cream of mushroom soup
½ cup mayonnaise
½ cup plain yogurt
½ lb. sliced fresh mushrooms
1 cup shredded cheddar cheese, *divided*
1 cup crushed saltine crackers
sliced almonds, *optional*

1. Microwave broccoli for 3 minutes. Place in greased slow cooker.
2. Combine soup, mayonnaise, yogurt, mushrooms, and ½ cup cheese in mixing bowl. Pour over broccoli. Stir together gently but well
3. Cover. Cook on Low 5-6 hours.
4. Top with remaining cheese and crackers for last half hour of cooking time.
5. If you wish, top with sliced almonds, for a special touch, before serving.

Christmas Carrots

Lindsey Spencer
Marrow, OH

Makes 8 servings

Prep. Time: 10-15 minutes
Cooking Time: 3 hours
Ideal slow cooker size: 3-qt.

2 lbs. carrots
half a stick (4 Tbsp.) butter, melted
½ cup brown sugar
8-oz. can crushed pineapple, undrained
½ cup shredded coconut

1. Peel carrots and cut into strips ½" wide and 2" long.
2. For extra flavor, brown carrots in skillet in butter before placing in slow cooker. Or skip doing that and place carrots and butter straight into slow cooker.
3. Add all other ingredients to slow cooker. Mix together gently but well
4. Cover. Cook on Low 3 hours.
5. Add coconut as garnish to carrots when serving.

Orange-Glazed Carrots

Barbara Smith
Bedford, PA

Makes 3-4 servings

Prep. Time: 15 minutes
Cooking Time: 2½ -3½ hours
Ideal slow cooker size: 2½-qt.

3 cups thinly sliced carrots
2 cups water
¼ tsp. salt
2-3 Tbsp. butter
3 Tbsp. orange marmalade
2 Tbsp. chopped pecans, *optional*

1. Combine carrots, water, and salt in slow cooker.
2. Cover. Cook on High 2-3 hours, or until carrots are as tender as you like them.
3. Drain. Stir in butter and marmalade.
4. Cover. Cook on High 30 minutes.

Glazed Carrots

Sharon Timpe
Jackson, WI

Makes 6-8 servings

Prep. Time: 15-25 minutes
Cooking Time: 3-3½ hours
Ideal slow cooker size: 3½-qt.

18 small carrots, cleaned and peeled, *or* 2 lbs. baby carrots, cleaned
5⅔ Tbsp. (⅓ cup) butter
½ tsp. salt
⅓ cup sugar
½ tsp. cinnamon
⅓ cup water

1. Place carrots in slow cooker.
2. Heat butter, salt, sugar, cinnamon, and water together in a small pan.
3. Pour mixture over carrots in slow cooker. Mix together gently but well.
4. Cover. Cook on Low 3-3½ hours, or until carrots are tender.

Note:

I've often prepared these Glazed Carrots by baking them in the oven. One year my oven was full and whenever that happens, I bring out my slow cooker and quickly adapt the recipe to it. Slow cooker to the rescue!

One of our favorite holiday meals for guests includes these carrots, along with beef rouladen, riced boiled potatoes with gravy, and green beans with browned butter and basil.

Sweet-Sour Red Cabbage

Kaye Taylor
Florissant, MO

Makes 6-8 servings

Prep. Time: 30-45 minutes
Cooking Time: 3-4 hours
Ideal slow cooker size: 3½-qt.

4 slices bacon, diced
¼ cup brown sugar
2 Tbsp. flour
1 tsp. salt
⅛ tsp. pepper
½ cup water
¼ cup vinegar
1 medium head red cabbage shredded (6-8 cups)
1 small onion, finely chopped

1. Sauté bacon in skillet until crisp. Set bacon aside. Reserve 1 Tbsp. drippings.
2. Combine 1 Tbsp. bacon drippings in slow cooker with sugar, flour, salt, and pepper. Stir in water and vinegar.
3. Add cabbage and onion. Mix together well.
4. Cover. Cook on Low 3-4 hours, or until cabbage and onion are as tender as you like them.
5. Sprinkle cooked bacon on top just before serving.

Black-Eyed Peas and Ham

Susan Tjon
Austin, TX

Makes 6-8 servings

Prep. Time: 20 minutes
Soaking Time: 8 hours, or overnight
Cooking Time: 8-9 hours
Ideal slow cooker size: 5-qt.

1 lb. dry black-eyed peas
4 cups water
2 tsp. salt
¼ tsp. pepper
1 large onion, chopped
2 ribs celery, chopped
2 ham hocks

1. Place beans in cooker. Cover with water. Allow to soak overnight or for 8 hours.
2. Drain. Return beans to slow cooker.

Take your grandkids shopping for their parents and siblings, and then take them to lunch.

Carol Ambrose, McMinnville, OR

3. Add 4 cups water, salt, pepper, onion, and celery. Stir to combine.

4. Place ham hocks in cooker, pushing them down into liquid as much as possible.

5. Cover. Cook on Low 8-9 hours, or until peas are tender but not mushy and ham is tender but not dried out.

6. When finished cooking, remove ham hocks from cooker. Allow to cool until you can handle them without burning your fingers.

7. Debone ham and cut meat into small chunks. Stir into soup. Serve immediately, or turn cooker on High for 30 minutes, or until heated through.

Note:

We always serve this on New Year's Day. It's our good luck dish.

On Christmas Eve we always watch "Christmas Vacation" after dinner. Even if a family member is far away, we synchronize the movie start time, so we still feel like we're together.

Squash Medley

Evelyn Page
Riverton, WY

Makes 8 servings

Prep. Time: 20 minutes
Cooking Time: 4-6 hours
Ideal slow cooker size: 3½-qt.

8 summer squash, *or* **zucchini, each about 4" long, peeled or not, thinly sliced,** *divided*
½ tsp. salt
2 tomatoes, peeled and chopped, *or* **14½-oz. can diced tomatoes,** *divided*
¼ cup sliced green onions, *divided*
half a small sweet green pepper, chopped, *divided*
1 chicken bouillon cube
¼ cup hot water
4 slices bacon, fried and crumbled
¼ cup fine dry bread crumbs

1. Sprinkle squash with salt.

2. In slow cooker, layer half the squash, tomatoes, onions, and pepper.

3. Repeat layers.

4. Dissolve bouillon in hot water. Pour into slow cooker.

5. Top with bacon. Sprinkle bread crumbs over top.

6. Cover. Cook on Low 4-6 hours.

Variation:

For a sweeter touch, sprinkle 1 Tbsp. brown sugar over half the layered vegetables. Repeat over second half of layered vegetables.

Baked Acorn Squash

Dale Peterson
Rapid City, SD

Makes 4 servings

Prep. Time: 15 minutes
Cooking Time: 5-6 hours
Ideal slow cooker size: 5- to 6-qt., or 2 4- to 6-qt., depending on size of squash

2 acorn squash
⅔ cup cracker crumbs
½ cup coarsely chopped pecans
5⅓ Tbsp. (⅓ cup) butter, melted
4 Tbsp. brown sugar
½ tsp. salt
¼ tsp. ground nutmeg
2 Tbsp. orange juice

1. Cut squash in half through the middle. Remove seeds.

2. Combine remaining ingredients in a bowl. Spoon into squash halves.

3. Place squash halves in slow cooker side by side.

4. Cover. Cook on Low 5-6 hours, or until squash is tender.

Apple Walnut Squash

Michele Ruvola
Selden, NY

Makes 4 servings

Prep. Time: 15 minutes
Cooking Time: 3-4 hours
Ideal slow cooker size: 5- to 6-qt., or 2 4- to 6-qt., depending on size of squash

¼ cup water
2 small acorn squash
¼ cup packed brown sugar
half a stick (4 Tbsp.) butter, melted
3 Tbsp. apple juice
1½ tsp. ground cinnamon
¼ tsp. salt
1 cup toasted walnuts
1 apple, chopped

1. Pour water into slow cooker.
2. Cut squash in half through the middle. Remove seeds.
3. Combine brown sugar, butter, apple juice, cinnamon, and salt in bowl.
4. Spoon mixture into squash. Place in slow cooker, side by side.
5. Cover. Cook on High 3-4 hours, or until squash is tender.
6. Combine walnuts and chopped apple in bowl. Add spoonfuls to center of each squash half and mix lightly with sauce.

Stuffed Acorn Squash

Jean Butzer
Batavia, NY

Makes 6 servings

Prep. Time: 15 minutes
Cooking Time: 2½ hours
Ideal slow cooker size: 5- to 6-qt.

3 small carnival, *or* **acorn, squash**
5 Tbsp. instant brown rice, uncooked
3 Tbsp. dried cranberries
3 Tbsp. diced celery
3 Tbsp. minced onion
pinch of ground, *or* **dried, sage**
1 Tbsp. butter, *divided*
3 Tbsp. orange juice
½ cup water

1. Slice off points on bottoms of squash so they will stand in slow cooker. Slice off tops and discard. Scoop out seeds. Place squash side by side in slow cooker.
2. Combine rice, cranberries, celery, onion, and sage in bowl. Stuff into squash centers.
3. Dot with butter.
4. Pour 1 Tbsp. orange juice into each squash center.
5. Pour water into bottom of slow cooker.
6. Cover. Cook on Low 2½ hours.

Serving suggestion: Serve with cooked ***turkey breast*** *or* ***pork*** *or* ***ham****.*

Tip:
To make squash easier to slice, microwave whole squash on High 5 minutes to soften skin.

Tzimmes

Elaine Vigoda
Rochester, NY

Makes 6-8 servings

Prep. Time: 25-30 minutes
Cooking Time: 10 hours
Ideal slow cooker size: 6-qt. or 2 4- to 5-qt.

1-2 sweet potatoes, sliced
6 carrots, sliced
1 potato, peeled and diced
1 onion, chopped
2 apples, peeled and sliced
1 butternut squash, peeled and sliced
¼ cup dry white wine, *or* **apple juice**
½ lb. dried apricots
1 Tbsp. ground cinnamon
1 Tbsp. apple pie spice
1 Tbsp. maple syrup, *or* **honey**
1 tsp. salt
1 tsp. ground ginger

1. Combine all ingredients in large slow cooker, or mix all ingredients in large bowl and then divide between 2 4- or 5-qt. cookers.
2. Cover. Cook on Low 10 hours.

Note:
This is a special dish served primarily on Jewish holidays

such as Rosh Hashana and Passover. The sweetness of the vegetables and fruit signifies wishes for a sweet year.

Stewed Tomatoes

Michelle Showalter
Bridgewater, VA

Makes 10-12 servings

Prep. Time: 10 minutes
Cooking Time: 3-4 hours
Ideal slow cooker size: 3-qt.

2 qts. canned, *or* **4 14½-oz. cans diced** *or* **stewed, tomatoes**
⅓ cup sugar
1½ tsp. salt
dash of pepper
3 Tbsp. butter
2 cups soft bread cubes

1. Place tomatoes in slow cooker.
2. Sprinkle with sugar, salt, and pepper.
3. Lightly toast bread cubes in melted butter on baking sheet in oven, or in large skillet.
4. Spread over tomatoes.
5. Cover. Cook on High 3-4 hours.

Variation:

If you prefer bread that is less moist and soft, add bread cubes 15 minutes before serving and continue cooking without lid.

Stuffed Mushrooms

Melanie L. Thrower
McPherson, KS

Makes 4-6 servings

Prep. Time: 15-20 minutes
Cooking Time: 2-4 hours
Ideal slow cooker size: 5-qt.

8-10 large mushrooms
¼ tsp. minced garlic
1 Tbsp. oil
dash of salt
dash of pepper
dash of cayenne pepper
¼ cup grated Monterey Jack cheese

1. Remove stems from mushrooms and dice.
2. Heat oil in skillet. Sauté diced stems with garlic until softened. Remove skillet from heat.
3. Stir in seasonings and cheese. Stuff into mushroom caps.
4. Place in slow cooker.
5. Cover. Heat on Low 2-4 hours.

Variations:

1. Add 1 Tbsp. minced onion to Step 2.
2. Use Monterey Jack cheese with jalapeños.

Easy Olive Bake

Jean Robinson
Cinnaminson, NJ

Makes 8 servings

Prep. Time: 15 minutes
Cooking Time: 3 hours
Ideal slow cooker size: 3½-qt.

1 cup uncooked long-grain rice
2 medium onions, chopped
1 stick (8 Tbsp.) butter, melted
2 cups, or 1 14½-oz. can, stewed tomatoes
2 cups water
1 cup black olives, quartered
½-¾ tsp. salt
½ tsp. chili powder
1 Tbsp. Worcestershire sauce
4-oz. can mushrooms with juice
½ cup grated cheese of your choice

1. Place rice in slow cooker.
2. Add all remaining ingredients, except cheese. Mix well.
3. Cover. Cook on High 1 hour, and then on Low 2 hours, or until rice is tender but not mushy.
4. Stir in cheese just before serving.

Serving suggestion: This is a good accompaniment to ***baked ham.***

Caponata

Katrine Rose
Woodbridge, VA

Makes 8-10 servings

Prep. Time: 20 minutes
Cooking Time: 7-8 hours
Ideal slow cooker size: 3½- to 4-qt.

1 medium eggplant, peeled and cut into ½" cubes
14½-oz. can diced tomatoes
1 medium onion, chopped
1 red bell pepper, cut into ½" pieces
¾ cup salsa, your choice of heat
¼ cup olive oil
2 Tbsp. capers, drained
3 Tbsp. balsamic vinegar
3 garlic cloves, minced
1¼ tsp. dried oregano
⅓ cup chopped fresh basil, packed in measuring cup
toasted, sliced French bread

1. Combine all ingredients except basil and bread in slow cooker.
2. Cover. Cook on Low 7-8 hours, or until vegetables are tender.
3. Stir in basil. Serve on toasted bread.

Candied Sweet Potatoes

Jean M. Butzer
Batavia, NY

Makes 8 servings

Prep. Time: 5-10 minutes
Cooking Time: 2¼-3¼ hours
Ideal slow cooker size: 5-qt.

2 29-oz. cans cut sweet potatoes, drained
½ cup chopped pecans
¾ stick (6 Tbsp.) butter, cut in pieces
2 Tbsp. frozen orange juice concentrate, thawed
⅓ cup brown sugar
2 tsp. pumpkin pie spice
¼ tsp. cayenne pepper, *optional*
3 cups miniature marshmallows

1. Stir together sweet potatoes, pecans, butter, and orange juice concentrate in lightly greased slow cooker.
2. In a small bowl, combine brown sugar, pumpkin pie spice, and cayenne pepper if you wish. Sprinkle over sweet potato mixture and stir.
3. Cover. Cook on Low 2-3 hours, or until potatoes are heated through.
4. Sprinkle marshmallows over top of sweet potatoes.
5. Cover. Cook on Low 15 minutes, or until marshmallows are melted.

Orange Candied Sweet Potatoes

Robin Schrock
Millersburg, OH

Makes 10-12 servings

Prep. Time: 20-30 minutes
Cooking Time: 7¼ hours
Ideal slow cooker size: 4-qt.

4 lbs. (8-10) sweet potatoes, peeled and cut into 1" chunks
1½ sticks (¾ cup) butter, melted
2 cups brown sugar
½ cup orange juice
1 Tbsp. ground cinnamon
1 Tbsp. grated lemon peel
1½ tsp. salt
½ tsp. nutmeg
2½ cups miniature marshmallows

1. Place potato chunks in slow cooker.
2. Mix butter, brown sugar, juice, cinnamon, lemon peel, salt, and nutmeg together in small bowl. Pour over potatoes and stir to coat potatoes.
3. Cover. Cook on Low 7 hours, or until potatoes are tender.
4. Sprinkle marshmallows over mixture and cook on Low until marshmallows are melted, about 15 minutes.

Orange Yams

Gladys Longacre
Susquehanna, PA

Makes 6-8 servings

Prep. Time: 15 minutes
Cooking Time: 3 hours
Ideal slow cooker size: 3½-qt.

40-oz. can yams, *or* **sweet potatoes, drained**
2 apples, peeled if you wish and thinly sliced
3 Tbsp. butter, melted
2 tsp. orange zest
1 cup orange juice
2 Tbsp. cornstarch
½ cup brown sugar
1 tsp. salt
dash of ground cinnamon and/or nutmeg

1. Place yams and apples in slow cooker.
2. Stir in butter and orange zest.
3. Combine remaining ingredients in small bowl. Pour over yams and apples.
4. Cover. Cook on High 1 hour and on Low 2 hours, or until apples are tender.

Variation:
Substitute 6-8 medium-sized cooked sweet potatoes, or approximately 4 cups cubed butternut squash, for yams.

Sweet Potatoes That Can Wait

Alix Nancy Botsford
Seminole, OK

Makes 6-8 servings

Prep. Time: 15-20 minutes
Cooking Time: 3 hours
Ideal slow cooker size: 2-qt.

3-4 medium-sized sweet potatoes
½-¾ cup packed brown sugar, *or* **maple syrup**
half a stick (4 Tbsp.) butter, cut into pieces
¼-½ tsp. salt
1 cup apple juice, *or* **cider**

1. Peel and dice sweet potatoes. Put into slow cooker.
2. Add brown sugar, butter, and salt.
3. Pour apple juice or cider over all.
4. Cover. Cook on High 3 hours, or until potatoes are tender.

Notes:
When we lived in western New York, I liked to make this recipe with maple syrup from the local area.

For our 50th Anniversary, I cooked 6 large briskets. Our daughter and granddaughter made 3 large salads and tripled this potato dish. We fed our whole church that Sunday!

The great thing about making a Christmas meal in slow cookers is that when the meal is ready, it can wait until we're ready! There is no pressure. We can sit and visit and wait for the stragglers to arrive.

"Baked" Sweet Potatoes

Shari Mast
Harrisonburg, VA

Makes 6-8 servings

Prep. Time: 10 minutes
Cooking Time: 4-8 hours
Ideal slow cooker size: 5-qt.

6-8 medium-sized sweet potatoes

1. Scrub and prick sweet potatoes with fork. Wrap each in tin foil and arrange in slow cooker.
2. Cover. Cook on Low 6-8 hours or on High 4-5 hours, or until each potato is soft.
3. Remove from foil and serve with butter and salt.

Apples 'n' Yams

Rebecca Plank Leichty
Harrisonburg, VA

Makes 8-10 servings

Prep. Time: 20-25 minutes
Cooking Time: 4-6 hours
Ideal slow cooker size: 4- to 5-qt.

1 Tbsp. lemon juice, *or* **lemonade**
6 apples, peeled if you wish and sliced
6 large yams, *or* **sweet potatoes, peeled and thinly sliced**
¼ cup apple juice
1 Tbsp. butter, melted

1. Toss sliced apples and yams in lemon juice in lightly greased slow cooker.
2. Combine apple juice and butter in small bowl. Pour over apples and sweet potatoes. Mix well together.
3. Cover. Cook on High 4 hours or on Low 6 hours.

Note:

This is a tasty vegetable dish to add to a meal when serving children. The apples smell wonderful when cooking and truly moisten the potatoes when served together. It is a well-rounded and easy way to serve sweet potatoes.

Sweet Potatoes and Apples

Bernita Boyts
Shawnee Mission, KS

Makes 8-10 servings

Prep. Time: 10-15 minutes
Cooking Time: 6-8 hours
Ideal slow cooker size: 3-qt.

3 large sweet potatoes, peeled and cubed, *divided*
3 large tart and firm apples, peeled if you wish and sliced, *divided*
½-¾ tsp. salt
⅛-¼ tsp. pepper
1 tsp. sage
1 tsp. ground cinnamon
half a stick (4 Tbsp.) butter, melted
¼ cup maple syrup
toasted sliced almonds, *or* **chopped pecans,** *optional*

1. Place half the sweet potatoes in slow cooker. Layer in half the apple slices.
2. Mix together salt, pepper, sage, and cinnamon in a small bowl. Sprinkle half over apples.
3. Mix together butter and maple syrup in a small bowl. Spoon half over seasonings.
4. Repeat layers.
5. Cover. Cook on Low 6-8 hours, or until potatoes are soft, stirring occasionally if you're home and able to do so.
6. To add a bit of crunch, sprinkle with toasted almonds or pecans when serving if you wish.

Serving suggestion: Serve with pork or ***poultry.***

Sweet Potatoes with Applesauce

Judi Manos
West Islip, NY

Makes 6-8 servings

Prep. Time: 10 minutes
Cooking Time: 6-7 hours
Ideal slow cooker size: 3- to 3½-qt.

6 medium-sized sweet potatoes, *or* **yams**
1½ cups applesauce
⅔ cup packed brown sugar
3 Tbsp. butter, melted
1 tsp. ground cinnamon
½ cup chopped toasted nuts

1. Peel sweet potatoes and cut into ½" cubes. Place in slow cooker.
2. Combine remaining ingredients, except nuts, in a bowl. Stir into potatoes.
3. Cover. Cook on Low 6-7 hours, or until potatoes are very tender.
4. Sprinkle with nuts just before serving.

Variation:

If you prefer a less sweet dish, cut the sugar back to ⅓ cup.

Pineapple Sweet Potatoes

Renee Baum
Chambersburg, PA

Makes 12-14 servings

Prep. Time: 20-30 minutes, if potatoes are cooked already
Cooking Time: 4-5 hours
Ideal slow cooker size: 5-qt.

6-6½ cups mashed sweet potatoes, without milk and butter added
4 eggs
1 cup milk
1 stick (8 Tbsp.) butter, softened
1 tsp. vanilla
½ tsp. lemon extract
1 tsp. salt
1 tsp. cinnamon
½ tsp. nutmeg
8-oz. can pineapple slices, drained
¼ cup chopped pecans

1. Combine mashed sweet potatoes, eggs, milk, butter, vanilla, lemon extract, salt, cinnamon, and nutmeg in slow cooker.
2. Top with pineapple slices and pecans.
3. Cover. Cook on Low 4-5 hours, or until thermometer reaches 160 degrees in middle of potatoes.

Tips:

1. If you need to cook the sweet potatoes, scrub 4-5 large potatoes. Peel them. Cut into chunks. Place in stockpot. Add about 2 inches of water.
2. Cover and cook over medium heat.
3. Check every 10 minutes or so to make sure they don't cook dry. Cook until very soft.
4. Mash with electric mixer or potato masher.
5. Drain off water. Then proceed with Step 1 above.

or

Follow recipe for "Baked" Sweet Potatoes on page 217 of this cookbook. When potatoes are finished cooking, and when they're cool enough to handle, peel. Then proceed with Steps 4 and 5 immediately above.

Sweet Potato-Cranberry Casserole

Mary E. Wheatley
Mashpee, MA

Makes 6-8 servings

Prep. Time: 20-30 minutes
Cooking Time: 3-4 hours
Ideal slow cooker size: 4- to 6-qt.

¼ cup orange juice
1 stick (8 Tbsp.) butter
2-3 Tbsp. brown sugar
1 tsp. ground cinnamon
1 cup dried cranberries
salt
4 lbs. sweet potatoes, *or* **yams, peeled and cut into 1" pieces**

1. Place all ingredients except sweet potatoes in slow cooker. Mix together.
2. Cover. Cook on High while preparing potatoes.
3. Add potato pieces to warm mixture.
4. Cover. Cook on High 3-4 hours.
5. When potatoes are soft, stir until they're mashed and then serve.

Barbecued Black Beans with Sweet Potatoes

Barbara Jean Fabel
Wausau, WI

Makes 4-6 servings

Prep. Time: 10-15 minutes
Cooking Time: 2-4 hours
Ideal slow cooker size: 3-qt.

4 large sweet potatoes, peeled and cut into 8 chunks each
15-oz. can black beans, rinsed and drained
1 medium onion, diced
2 ribs celery, sliced
9 oz. Sweet Baby Ray's Barbecue Sauce

1. Place sweet potatoes in slow cooker.
2. Stir in additional ingredients.
3. Cover. Cook on High 2-3 hours, or on Low 4 hours.

Mashed Potatoes

Mrs. Audrey L. Kneer
Williamsfield, IL

Makes 1 serving, multiplied

Prep. Time: 15 minutes
Cooking Time: 2 hours
Ideal slow cooker size: large enough to hold desired number of servings

1-2 medium-sized potatoes per person
3 Tbsp. milk per potato
½ Tbsp. butter per potato, melted
⅛ tsp. salt per potato

1. Peel potatoes. Place in stockpot. Add at least an inch of water to stockpot. Cover. Cook on stovetop over medium heat until soft.
2. Check after about 20 minutes to make sure potatoes aren't cooking dry. If nearly dry, add another inch of water or so.
3. When potatoes are falling-apart-soft, mash with electric mixer or hand-held potato masher.
4. While mashing potatoes, heat milk to scalding. Then add hot milk, butter, and salt to mashed potatoes, stirring in well.
5. Put in slow cooker a couple of hours before serving. Set cooker on Low. Stir once in a while. These will be the same as fresh mashed potatoes when you're ready to serve the meal.

Tip:
This saves needing to mash potatoes at the last minute.

Garlic Mashed Potatoes

Katrine Rose
Woodbridge, VA

Makes 6 servings

Prep. Time: 10 minutes
Cooking Time: 4-7 hours
Ideal slow cooker size: 4-qt.

2 lbs. baking potatoes, unpeeled and cut into ½" cubes
¼ cup water
3 Tbsp. butter, sliced
1 tsp. salt
¾ tsp. garlic powder
¼ tsp. black pepper
1 cup milk

1. Combine all ingredients, except milk, in slow cooker. Toss to combine.
2. Cover. Cook on Low 7 hours, or on High 4 hours.
3. Add milk to potatoes during last 30 minutes of cooking time.
4. Mash potatoes with potato masher or electric mixer until fairly smooth.

Make Ahead Mixed Potatoes Florentine

Becky Frey
Lebanon, PA

Makes 10-12 servings

Prep. Time: 45-60 minutes
Cooking Time: 8-10 hours
Ideal slow cooker size: 4-qt.

6 medium-sized white potatoes
3 medium-sized sweet potatoes
¼ stick (2 Tbsp.) butter
2 Tbsp. olive oil
1 large onion, chopped
1-2 cloves garlic, pressed
8 oz. low-fat, *or* non-fat, cream cheese, at room temperature
½ cup non-fat sour cream
½ cup non-fat plain yogurt
1 tsp. salt, *or* to taste
1-1½ tsp. dill weed
¼ tsp. black pepper
10-oz. pkg. frozen, chopped spinach, thawed and squeezed dry

1. Peel and quarter both white and sweet potatoes. Place in slow cooker. Barely cover with water.
2. Cover. Cook on Low 6-8 hours, or until potatoes are falling-apart-tender.

Stockings are one tradition we all love. I shop all year for special treats for the youngest to the oldest. It is super fun!
Carol Duree, Salina, KS

3. Meanwhile, in a saucepan sauté onion and garlic in butter and olive oil, on low heat, until soft and golden.

4. In an electric mixer bowl, combine sautéed onion and garlic with cream cheese, sour cream, yogurt, salt, dill weed, and pepper. Whip until well blended. Set aside.

5. Drain off some of the potato cooking water, but reserve. Mash potatoes in some of their cooking water until soft and creamy. Add more cooking water if you'd like a creamier result.

6. Stir onion-cheese mixture into mashed potatoes.

7. Fold spinach into potato mixture.

8. Turn into greased 4-qt. slow cooker. Cook for 2 hours on Low, or until heated through.

9. If you've made the potatoes a day or so in advance of serving them, refrigerate them until the day of your gathering. Then heat potatoes in slow cooker for 3-4 hours on Low, or until heated through.

Variation:

You can use 1 cup plain yogurt and omit the sour cream, or vice versa. The more yogurt, the greater the savory tang.

Refrigerator Mashed Potatoes

Deborah Swartz
Grottoes, VA

Makes 8-10 servings

Prep. Time: 30 minutes
Cooking Time: 2 hours
Ideal slow cooker size: 6-qt.

5 lbs. potatoes
8-oz. pkg. cream cheese, softened
1 cup sour cream
1 tsp. salt
¼ tsp. pepper
¼ cup crisp bacon, crumbled
¼ stick (2 Tbsp.) butter

1. Cook and mash potatoes.*
2. Place mashed potatoes in lightly greased slow cooker.
3. Stir in all remaining ingredients except butter.
4. Dot with butter.
5. Cover. Cook on Low 2 hours.

Variations:

1. These potatoes can be made several days ahead and refrigerated.
2. Cook cold, refrigerated potatoes on Low 5 hours, or until heated through.
3. If you wish, sprinkle 1 cup cheddar cheese over top of potatoes during their last half hour in slow cooker.
4. Substitute chopped ham for bacon.
5. Add 2 Tbsp. chopped fresh chives to Step 2.

*For instructions for cooking and mashing potatoes, see recipe for Mashed Potatoes on page 220 of this Cookbook.

Creamy Mashed Potatoes

Brenda S. Burkholder
Port Republic, VA

Makes 10-12 servings

Prep. Time: 10-15 minutes
Cooking Time: 3-5 hours
Ideal slow cooker size: 6-qt.

2 tsp. salt
¾ stick (6 Tbsp.) butter, melted
2¼ cups milk
6⅞ cups potato flakes
6 cups water
1 cup sour cream
4-5 oz. (approximately half a large pkg.) cream cheese, softened

1. Combine first five ingredients as directed on potato flakes box.
2. Whip cream cheese with electric mixer until creamy. Blend in sour cream.
3. Fold potatoes into cheese and sour cream. Beat well. Place in slow cooker.
4. Cover. Cook on Low 3-5 hours.

Creamy Red Potatoes

Kayla Snyder
North East, PA

Makes 8 servings

Prep. Time: 20-30 minutes
Cooking Time: 3½ hours
Ideal slow cooker size: 3-qt.

3 Tbsp. butter
3 Tbsp. flour
1 cup milk
½ tsp. garlic powder
¾ tsp. salt
1 Tbsp. dried onion flakes
1 tsp. parsley flakes
2 3-oz. pkgs. cream cheese, at room temperature
2 lbs. red potatoes

1. Make a white sauce in a saucepan by melting butter, stirring in flour, and adding milk. Whisk and stir until smooth and thickened.
2. Add seasonings. Beat in cream cheese until smooth.
3. Cut up unpeeled potatoes into 1"-2" cubes.
4. Layer potatoes and sauce in slow cooker.
5. Cover. Cook on High 3½ hours, or until potatoes are as soft as you like them.

Tips:

1. 5 lbs. of potatoes fills up a 3-qt. slow-cooker nicely.
2. Mix up the sauce ahead of time and refrigerate it. Then when you're ready, cut up the potatoes, and put them and the sauce in your slow cooker.

Sunday Dinner Potatoes

Ruth Ann Penner
Hillsboro, KS

Makes 8 servings

Prep. Time: 15 minutes
Cooking Time: 2-5 hours
Ideal slow cooker size: 3-qt.

4 cups cooked, sliced potatoes
5⅔ Tbsp. (⅓ cup) butter
¼ cup flour
2 cups milk
1 tsp. salt
pepper to taste
1 tsp. onion powder

1. Place potatoes in slow cooker.
2. Melt butter in small skillet. Add flour and stir. Slowly add milk, stirring constantly.
3. Add salt, pepper, and onion powder. When smooth and thickened, pour over potatoes.
4. Cover. Cook on High 2-3 hours or on Low 4-5 hours.

Swiss-Irish Hot Sauce— A Great Potato Topping!

Jo Haberkamp
Fairbank, IA

Makes 6-8 servings

Prep. Time: 15 minutes
Cooking Time: 4 hours
Ideal slow cooker size: 3-qt.

2 medium onions, diced
5 garlic cloves, minced
¼ cup oil
14½-oz. can puréed tomatoes
15-oz. can tomato sauce
12-oz. can tomato paste
2 Tbsp. parsley, fresh *or* **dried**
½ tsp. red pepper
½ tsp. black pepper
1 tsp. chili powder
1 tsp. dried basil
2 tsp. Worcestershire sauce
2 tsp. Tabasco sauce
¼ cup red wine

1. Sauté onions and garlic in oil in skillet.
2. Combine all ingredients in slow cooker.
3. Cover. Cook on Low 4 hours.
4. This is a flavorful sauce for eating over baked potatoes or pasta.

Herbed Potatoes

Jo Haberkamp
Fairbank, IA

Makes 6 servings

Prep. Time: 10 minutes
Cooking Time: 2½-3 hours
Ideal slow cooker size: 3-qt.

1½ lbs. small new potatoes
¼ cup water
half a stick (4 Tbsp.) butter, melted
3 Tbsp. chopped fresh parsley
1 Tbsp. lemon juice
1 Tbsp. chopped fresh chives
1 Tbsp. dill weed
¼-½ tsp. salt, according to your taste preference
⅛-¼ tsp. pepper, according to your taste preference

1. Wash potatoes. Peel a strip around the middle of each potato. Place prepared potatoes in slow cooker.
2. Add water.
3. Cover. Cook on High 2½-3 hours. Drain well.
4. In saucepan, heat butter, parsley, lemon juice, chives, dill, salt, and pepper.
5. Pour over potatoes.

*Serving suggestion: Serve with **ham** or any **meat dish** that does not make its own gravy.*

Onion Potatoes

Donna Lantgen
Rapid City, SD

Makes 6 servings

Prep. Time: 5-10 minutes
Cooking Time: 3-6 hours
Ideal slow cooker size: 3-qt.

6 medium potatoes, peeled or unpeeled, diced
⅓ cup olive oil
1 envelope dry onion soup mix

1. Combine potatoes and olive oil in plastic bag. Shake well.
2. Add onion soup mix. Shake well.
3. Pour into slow cooker.
4. Cover. Cook on Low 6 hours or on High 3 hours.

Variations:

Add more zest to the potatoes by stirring in 1 small onion, chopped; 1 bell pepper, chopped; ½ tsp. salt; and ¼ tsp. black pepper, after pouring the potatoes into the slow cooker. Then continue with Step 4.

Potatoes Perfect

Naomi Ressler
Harrisonburg, VA

Makes 4-6 servings

Prep. Time: 15 minutes
Cooking Time: 3-10 hours
Ideal slow cooker size: 3½-qt.

¼ lb. bacon, diced and browned in a skillet until crisp, *divided*
2 medium-sized onions, thinly sliced, *divided*
6-8 medium-sized potatoes, thinly sliced, *divided*
½ lb. cheddar cheese, thinly sliced, *divided*
salt to taste
pepper to taste
¼-½ stick (2-4 Tbsp.) butter

1. Layer half of bacon, onions, potatoes, and cheese in greased slow cooker. Season to taste.
2. Dot with butter. Repeat layers.
3. Cover. Cook on Low 8-10 hours or on High 3-4 hours, or until potatoes are soft.

Pete's Scalloped Potatoes

Dede Peterson
Rapid City, SD

Makes 8-10 servings

Prep. Time: 15 minutes
Cooking Time: 6-7 hours
Ideal slow cooker size: 6-qt.

5 lbs. red potatoes, peeled or unpeeled and sliced, *divided*
2 cups water
1 tsp. cream of tartar
¼ lb. bacon, cut in 1" squares, browned until crisp, and drained, *divided*
dash of salt
½ pt. whipping cream
1 pt. half-and-half

1. In large bowl, toss sliced potatoes in water and cream of tartar. Drain.
2. Layer half of potatoes and half of bacon in large slow cooker. Sprinkle each layer with salt.
3. Repeat layers using all remaining potatoes and bacon.
4. Mix whipping cream and half-and-half in bowl. Pour over potatoes.
5. Cover. Cook on Low 6-7 hours.

Variations:

For added flavor, cut one large onion into thin rings. Sauté in bacon drippings; then layer onion along with potatoes and bacon into slow cooker. Sprinkle each layer of potatoes with salt and pepper. Continue with Step 4.

Lotsa Scalloped Potatoes

Fannie Miller
Hutchinson, KS

Makes 20-25 servings

Prep. Time: 25 minutes
Cooking Time: 2-3 hours
Ideal slow cooker size: 6-qt. *or* ***2 4-qt. cookers***

5 lbs. potatoes, cooked* and sliced
2 lbs. cooked ham, cubed
half a stick (4 Tbsp.) butter
½ cup flour
2 cups cream, *or* **milk**
¼ lb. mild cheese, your favorite, shredded
1½ tsp. salt
¼-½ tsp. pepper

1. Place layers of sliced potatoes and ham in very large, or two smaller, slow cooker(s).
2. Melt butter in saucepan on stove. Stir in flour. Gradually add milk to make a white sauce, stirring constantly until smooth and thickened.
3. Stir cheese, salt, and pepper into white sauce.
4. Continue stirring until cheese is melted. Pour over potatoes and ham.
5. Cover. Cook on Low 2-3 hours.

Tip:

A great way to free up oven space.

*To prepare cooked potatoes for Step 1, peel them if you wish. Place whole potatoes, peeled or unpeeled, in stockpot. Add at least an inch of water to stockpot. Cover. Cook on stovetop over medium heat until soft.

Check frequently to make sure potatoes aren't cooking dry. Add more water if needed.

Allow potatoes to cool enough to handle. Then slice thin, using a knife or mandolin.

Proceed with Step 1 above.

My extended family usually meets at our home for a Christmas season gathering. Now, instead of preparing a lot of food, we provide hot sandwiches, and guests bring either a salad or a dessert. The 40-50 guests enjoy the more relaxed atmosphere, and the pressure to prepare many dishes is taken off the host and guests alike.

Sharon Miller, Holmesville, OH

Company Potatoes

Deborah Swartz
Grottoes, VA
Julia A. Fisher
New Carlisle, OH

Makes 6-8 servings

Prep. Time: 20 minutes
Cooking Time: 4 hours
Ideal slow cooker size: 3½- to 4-qt.

6 medium-sized potatoes, cooked,* cooled, and shredded
2 cups shredded cheddar cheese
⅓ cup finely chopped onions
half a stick (4 Tbsp.) butter, melted
1 tsp. salt
¼ tsp. pepper
1½-2 cups sour cream
butter

1. Combine potatoes, cheese, onions, melted butter, salt, pepper, and sour cream in slow cooker. Dot with butter.
2. Cover. Cook on Low 4 hours.

*To prepare cooked potatoes for Step 1, first peel potatoes. Place whole potatoes in stockpot. Add at least an inch of water to stockpot. Cover. Cook on stovetop over medium heat until soft.

Check frequently to make sure potatoes aren't cooking dry. Add water if needed.

Cool potatoes to room temperature. Then refrigerate 4-8 hours, or until thoroughly chilled. Shred into slow cooker.

Continue with Step 1 above.

Variations:

1. Use garlic salt instead of regular salt.
2. Add ½ tsp. chopped parsley to Step 1.
3. Use 1 cup milk and 1 cup sour cream instead of 1½-2 cups sour cream.

Kim Stoltzfus
New Holland, PA

Cheese Potatoes

Joyce Shackelford, Green Bay, WI

Makes 10 servings

Prep. Time: 10-15 minutes • Cooking Time: 8¼ hours
Ideal slow cooker size: 5-qt.

6 potatoes, peeled and cut into ¼" strips
2 cups sharp cheddar cheese, shredded
10¾-oz. can cream of chicken soup
1 small onion, chopped
half a stick (4 Tbsp.) butter, melted
1 tsp. salt
1 tsp. pepper
1 cup sour cream
2 cups seasoned stuffing cubes
3 Tbsp. butter, melted

1. Toss together potatoes and cheese in slow cooker.
2. In a bowl, combine soup, onion, 4 Tbsp. melted butter, salt, and pepper. Pour over potatoes. Mix together gently.
3. Cover. Cook on Low 8 hours.
4. Stir in sour cream. Cover and heat 10 more minutes.
5. Meanwhile, toss together stuffing cubes and 3 Tbsp. butter in bowl. Sprinkle over potatoes just before serving.

Christmas Potatoes with Cheese

Jean Turner
Williams Lake, B.C.

Makes 6 servings

Prep. Time: 30 minutes
Cooking Time: 3-7 hours
Ideal slow cooker size: 2½-qt.

5 Tbsp. butter, *divided*
2 Tbsp. flour
½ tsp. dry mustard
½ tsp. Worcestershire sauce
1½ tsp. salt
⅛ tsp. pepper
3 cups milk
1 cup shredded Swiss cheese
6 medium potatoes, peeled and thinly sliced (6 cups)
4-oz. jar sliced pimento, chopped and drained
¼ cup finely chopped onion
1½ cups soft bread crumbs

1. Melt 3 Tbsp. butter in saucepan. Blend in flour, mustard, Worcestershire sauce, salt, pepper, and milk. Cook and stir until thickened and bubbly. (I do this in the microwave.)
2. Add cheese. Stir to melt.
3. Place potatoes, pimento, and onion in slow cooker. Stir in cheesy sauce and blend well.
4. Cover. Cook on Low 5½-6½ hours or on High 2½-3½ hours, or until potatoes are as soft as you wish.
5. Melt remaining butter in saucepan. Toss with bread crumbs. Sprinkle over potatoes. Cook 30 minutes more, uncovered.

Creamy Potatoes

Lena Sheafer
Port Matilda, PA
Gloria Julien
Gladstone, MI
Jena Hammond
Traverse City, MI

Makes 8-10 servings

Prep. Time: 20-30 minutes
Cooking Time: 4-5 hours
Ideal slow cooker size: 5-qt.

2 lbs. frozen cubed hash browns, thawed, *or* **parboiled* fresh potato cubes**
2 cups sharp cheddar, *or* **mozzarella, cheese, shredded**
2 cups sour cream
10¾-oz. can cream of celery soup
10¾-oz. can cream of chicken soup
1 large onion, chopped
half a stick (4 Tbsp.) butter, melted
¼ tsp. pepper
1 lb. cooked ham, *or* **crispy bacon pieces,** *or* **other cooked meat, cut up**

1. Place potatoes in slow cooker.
2. Combine cheese, sour cream, soups, onion, butter, and pepper in large mixing bowl. Pour over potatoes and mix well.
3. Cover. Cook on Low 4-5 hours.
4. Thirty minutes before end of the cooking time, stir in meat.

*To parboil potatoes, cut peeled or unpeeled potatoes into cubes. Place in stockpot. Add at least an inch of water to stockpot. Cover.

Cook on stovetop over medium heat until potatoes are no longer crispy, but are not yet soft. Drain.

Proceed with Step 1.

Tips:

1. This is a great way to use up leftovers: extra potatoes in that 5-lb. bag, hashbrowns in the freezer, leftover meat, extra veggies.
2. This works equally well as a main dish or a side dish.

Variation:

You can skip the meat if you wish.

Jena Hammond
Traverse City, MI

Shredded Potatoes with Canadian Bacon

Carol Eberly
Harrisonburg, VA

Makes 8 serving

Prep. Time: 10 minutes
Cooking Time: 5 hours
Ideal slow cooker size: 4-qt.

32-oz. bag frozen hash browns, *divided*
6-8 thin slices Canadian bacon, *or* **fully cooked ham,** *divided*
1 cup shredded sharp cheese, *divided*
2 cups shredded mild cheddar cheese, *divided*
¾ cup chopped onions, *divided*
salt to taste
pepper to taste
10¾-oz. can cream of mushroom soup
10¾-oz. can cream of chicken soup

1. Layer half of potatoes, meat, cheeses, and onions in slow cooker. Season with salt and pepper.
2. Repeat layers. Pour over top of mixture in slow cooker.
4. Cover. Cook on Low 5 hours.

Note:

We used this recipe, minus the meat, for our daughter's wedding reception meal.

We made 12 slow-cookers-full. We put the recipe together the night before, put the mixture in the refrigerator overnight, and got up at 4 a.m. to plug in the cookers. They were ready for lunch.

Get out your serving dishes before your guests arrive. Place a piece of paper in each one, designating what goes in or on it, along with its serving utensil. When your guests ask if they may help you, they can follow your plan.

Linda Sluiter, Schererville, IN

Hot German Potato Salad

Judi Manos
West Islip, NY

Makes 6 servings

Prep. Time: 15 minutes
Cooking Time: 8-10 hours
Ideal slow cooker size: 3-qt.

5 medium-sized potatoes, cut ¼" thick
1 large onion, chopped
⅓ cup water
⅓ cup vinegar
2 Tbsp. flour
2 Tbsp. sugar
1 tsp. salt
½ tsp. celery seed
¼ tsp. pepper
4 slices bacon, cooked crisp and crumbled
chopped fresh parsley

1. Combine potatoes and onions in slow cooker.
2. Combine remaining ingredients, except bacon and parsley, in bowl. Pour over potatoes.
3. Cover. Cook on Low 8-10 hours, or until potatoes are tender.
4. Stir in bacon and parsley.
5. Serve warm or at room temperature.

Serving suggestion: Prepare a full German meal and serve this with grilled ***bratwurst*** *or* ***Polish sausage, dill pickles, pickled beets,*** *and* ***sliced apples.***

Rudolph's Nose Wild Rice

Darla Sathre
Baxter, MN

Makes 8 servings

Prep. Time: 15 minutes
Cooking Time: 3 hours
Ideal slow cooker size: 3-qt.

6 cups cooked wild rice, *or* **3 15-oz. cans wild rice, drained**
3.8-oz. can sliced black olives, drained
4-oz. can sliced button mushrooms, rinsed and drained
1 large onion chopped (about 2 cups)
1 pint (2 cups) grape, *or* **cherry, tomatoes, halved**
8-oz. pkg. cheddar cheese, cubed
¼ cup olive oil
black pepper, to taste

1. Mix all ingredients together gently in slow cooker.
2. Cover. Cook on Low 3 hours.

Tips:

1. The proportions of this recipe can be adjusted to your personal preferences quite easily.
2. When we have just a small amount of leftovers of this recipe, we use it as a pizza topping, and it is delicious!

Holiday Wild Rice

Susan Kasting, Jenks, OK

Makes 4 servings

Prep. Time: 10 minutes • Cooking Time: 2½-3 hours
Ideal slow cooker size: 4-qt.

1½ cups wild rice, uncooked
3 cups chicken stock
3 Tbsp. orange zest
2 Tbsp. orange juice
½ cup raisins (I like golden raisins)
1½ tsp. curry powder
1 Tbsp. butter, softened
½ cup fresh parsley
½ cup chopped pecans
½ cup chopped green onion

1. Mix rice, chicken stock, orange zest, orange juice, raisins, curry powder, and butter in slow cooker.
2. Cover and cook on High 2½-3 hours, or until rice is tender and has absorbed most of the liquid, but is not dry.
3. Stir in parsley, pecans, and green onion just before serving.

Note:

Dear family friends gave us this to use as an oven recipe years ago. We have since adapted it for a slow cooker. While eating it one Christmas Eve, someone commented that the cut tomatoes resembled the reindeer Rudolph's red nose. From then on, we changed the name from Wild Rice Hot Dish to Rudolph's Nose Wild Rice.

Fruited Wild Rice with Pecans

Dottie Schmidt
Kansas City, MO

Makes 4 servings

Prep. Time: 15 minutes
Cooking Time: 2-2½ hours
Ideal slow cooker size: 3-qt.

½ cup chopped onions
¼ stick (2 Tbsp.) butter, cut in chunks
6-oz. pkg. long-grain and wild rice, uncooked
seasoning packet from wild rice pkg.
1½ cups hot water

⅔ cup apple juice
1 large tart apple, chopped
¼ cup raisins
¼ cup coarsely chopped pecans

1. Combine all ingredients except pecans in greased slow cooker.
2. Cover. Cook on High 2-2½ hours, or until rice is fully cooked.
3. Stir in pecans. Serve.

Mjeddrah

Dianna Milhizer
Brighton, MI

Makes 20-24 servings

Prep. Time: 10 minutes
Cooking Time: 10 hours
Ideal slow cooker size: 6-qt.

10 cups water
4 cups dried lentils, rinsed
2 cups uncooked brown rice
¼ cup olive oil
2 tsp. salt

1. Combine all ingredients in large slow cooker
2. Cover. Cook on High 8 hours and then on Low 2 hours.
3. Check after cooking 8 hours on High. Add 2 more cups water, if needed, to allow rice to continue cooking and to prevent dish from drying out.

Serving suggestion: This is traditionally eaten with a ***salad*** *with an* ***oil-and-vinegar dressing*** *over the lentil-rice mixture, similar to a tostada without the tortilla.*

Mushroom Stuffing

Laverne Stoner
Scottdale, PA

Makes 7-8 cups stuffing

Prep. Time: 15 minutes
Cooking Time: 2-3 hours
Ideal slow cooker size: 5-qt.

1 stick (8 Tbsp.) butter
1 cup finely chopped onions
1 cup finely chopped celery
8-oz. can sliced mushrooms, drained
¼ cup chopped parsley
1½-2 tsp. poultry seasoning
½ tsp. salt
⅛ tsp. pepper
12 cups toasted bread cubes*
2 eggs, well beaten
1½ cups chicken broth

1. Sauté onions and celery in butter in skillet until cooked. Stir in mushrooms and parsley.
2. Combine seasonings and sprinkle over bread cubes in large mixing bowl.
3. Gently add remaining ingredients. Spoon lightly into slow cooker.
4. Cover. Cook on High 1 hour, and then reduce to Low and cook 1-2 hours.

*Lay 18-22 slices of bread on baking sheets. Toast in oven for 15 minutes at 300°.

Tip:
This is not as much a time-saver as it is a space-saver. If your oven is full, make your stuffing in your slow cooker.

Variations:
1. Add extra flavor to your stuffing by adding 1 tsp. dried sage, ¾ tsp. dried thyme, and ¼ tsp. dried marjoram to Step 2.
Mary H. Nolt, East Earl, PA
Jean Turner, Williams Lake, BC
Mary Rogers, Waseca, MN
Kristi See, Weskan, KS

2. Add 1 lb. loose sausage, browned and drained, to Step 3.
Dede Peterson
Rapid City, SD

Slow-Cooker Stuffing

Allison Ingels
Maynard, IA

Makes 10-12 servings

Prep. Time: 15 minutes
Cooking Time: 3 hours
Ideal slow cooker size: 5-qt.

12-13 cups dry bread cubes (equal to a 20-oz. loaf of bread)
¼ cup dried parsley
2 eggs, beaten
giblets, cooked and chopped, broth reserved*
1 tsp. salt
¼ tsp. pepper
½ tsp. sage
1½ tsp. poultry seasoning
3½-4½ cups turkey broth (from cooking giblets)
2 chicken bouillon cubes
2 cups finely chopped celery
1 cup finely chopped onion
2 sticks (16 Tbsp.) butter

1. Combine bread cubes and parsley in slow cooker.
2. Stir in eggs, giblets, and seasonings.
3. Dissolve bouillon in heated turkey broth in stockpot. Add to slow cooker.
4. Sauté celery and onion in butter in stockpot. Stir into bread mixture in slow cooker.
5. Cover. Cook on High 1 hour and then on Low 2 hours, stirring occasionally if you're home and able to do so.

*Place giblets in 3½-4½ cups water in stockpot. Cover. Cook over medium heat until giblets are tender.

Remove giblets from broth and allow them to cool enough to handle. Then cut up giblets and proceed with Step 2.

Reserve broth and keep warm in stockpot for Step 3.

Variations:

1. Add 1 lb. loose sausage, browned and drained, to Step 2.

Dorothy VanDeest
Memphis, TN

2. Use 6 cups cubed day-old white bread and 6 cups cubed day-old wheat bread to add flavor and fiber.

Jean M. Butzer
Batavia, NY

Tip:

A convenient way to free up oven space—or keep your kitchen cool.

Slow-Cooker Dressing

Marie Shank
Harrisonburg, VA

Makes 16 servings

Prep. Time: 10 minutes, plus baking time for cornbread
Cooking Time: 2-8 hours
Ideal slow cooker size: 6-qt., or 2 4-qt. cookers

2 boxes Jiffy Cornbread mix
8 slices day-old bread
4 eggs
1 onion, chopped
½ cup chopped celery
2 10¾-oz. cans cream of chicken soup
2 cups chicken broth
1 tsp. salt
½ tsp. pepper
1½ Tbsp. sage, *or* **poultry seasoning**
1-1½ sticks (8-12 Tbsp.) butter

1. Prepare cornbread according to package instructions.
2. Crumble cornbread and bread together in large bowl.
3. Stir in all other ingredients, except butter.
4. Spoon into 6-qt. greased cooker, or into 2 greased 4-qt. cookers. Dot top(s) with butter.
5. Cover. Cook on High 2-4 hours or on Low 3-8 hours.

Variations:

1. Prepare your favorite cornbread recipe in an 8"-square baking pan instead of using cornbread mix.
2. For a more moist Dressing, use 2 14½-oz. cans chicken broth instead of 2 cups chicken broth.
3. You may reduce butter to 2 Tbsp.

Helen Kenagy
Carlsbad, NM

Old-Fashioned Stuffing

Elaine Rineer
Lancaster, PA
Rhonda Freed
Croghan, NY

Makes 6 servings

Prep. Time: 20-30 minutes
Cooking Time: 5 hours
Ideal slow cooker size: 4-qt.

1 stick (8 Tbsp.) butter
1½ cups chopped celery
1 small onion, chopped
12-oz. pkg. bread cubes, *or* **about 15 slices stale bread**
½-¾ tsp. salt
⅛ tsp. pepper
1-2 Tbsp. fresh parsley, chopped
2 eggs
1½ cups milk

1. Melt butter in skillet. Sauté celery and onion in it.
2. Meanwhile, spray interior of slow cooker with non-stick cooking spray. Place bread cubes, salt, pepper, and parsley in cooker.
3. Pour in sautéed vegetables, eggs, and milk. Stir together gently until well mixed.
4. Cover. Cook on High 1 hour. Stir.
5. Cover. Cook on High 4 more hours.

Tip:
This is delicious and an easy way to free up oven space for the rest of your meal.

Corn Stuffing Balls

Mable Shirk
Mt. Crawford, VA

Makes 4-5 servings

Prep. Time: 30 minutes
Cooking Time: 3-4 hours
Ideal slow cooker size: 2- to 4-qt.

½ cup celery with leaves, chopped
1 small onion, chopped
2 cups cream-style corn, canned, *or* **frozen**
¼ cup water
⅛ tsp. pepper
1 tsp. poultry seasoning
8-oz. pkg. herb-seasoned stuffing mix
2 slightly beaten eggs
half a stick (4 Tbsp.) melted butter

1. In mixing bowl, combine celery, onion, corn, water, pepper, poultry seasoning, stuffing mix, and eggs.
2. Shape into 7 or 8 balls. Arrange in slow cooker. Pour butter over top.
3. Cover. Cook on Low 3-4 hours.

Serving suggestion: Serve with ***gravy*** *and alongside* ***broiled meats*** *or* ***roasts****, or use as extra stuffing with* ***turkey****.*

Mashed Potato Filling

Betty K. Drescher
Quakertown, PA

Makes 8-10 servings

Prep. Time: 15-20 minutes
Cooking Time: 4 hours
Ideal slow cooker size: 5-qt.

½ cup diced onions
1 cup diced celery
1 stick (8 Tbsp.) butter
2½ cups milk
4 large eggs, beaten
8 oz. bread cubes
4 cups mashed potatoes
1½ tsp. salt
¼ tsp. pepper

1. Sauté onions and celery in butter in skillet for 5-10 minutes, or until vegetables are tender.
2. Combine onions and celery, milk, and eggs in mixing bowl.
3. Place bread cubes in large mixing bowl. Pour vegetable-milk-egg mixture over bread cubes. Mix lightly.
4. Stir in potatoes and seasonings.
5. Spoon into greased slow cooker.
6. Cover. Cook on Low 4 hours.

Sweet Potato Stuffing

Tina Snyder
Manheim, PA

Makes 8 servings

Prep. Time: 15 minutes
Cooking Time: 4 hours
Ideal slow cooker size: 4-qt.

½ cup chopped celery
½ cup chopped onions
half a stick (4 Tbsp.) butter
6 cups dry bread cubes
1 large sweet potato, cooked,* peeled, and cubed
½ cup chicken broth
¼ cup chopped pecans
½ tsp. poultry seasoning
½ tsp. rubbed sage
½ tsp. salt
¼ tsp. pepper

1. Sauté celery and onions in skillet in butter until tender. Pour into greased slow cooker.
2. Add remaining ingredients. Toss gently.
3. Cover. Cook on Low 4 hours.

*To prepare a cooked sweet potato, wash, dry, and prick it at about 4 different places with a sharp fork. Lay on a paper towel in the microwave. Cook on High 1½ minutes. Turn over. Cook on High another minute. Jag with fork to see if it's tender. If not, continue cooking for 30-second intervals on High, turning over each time, until tender.

Allow to cool. When you're able to handle it, gently peel and cube.

Scalloped Pineapple

June Groff
Denver, PA

Makes 8 servings

Prep. Time: 10 minutes
Cooking Time: 3 hours
Ideal slow cooker size: 2- to 3-qt.

1 stick (8 Tbsp.) butter, softened
½ cup sugar
4 eggs
20-oz. can crushed pineapple, drained
5 slices fresh bread, cubed

1. Cream butter and sugar together in a medium-sized mixing bowl.
2. Add eggs. Mix well.
3. Add drained pineapple. Blend.
4. Fold bread into mixture.
5. Pour into slow cooker.
6. Cover. Cook on High 2 hours and then on Low 1 hour.

*Serving suggestion: This is a good accompaniment to **turkey**, **ham**, and **chicken**, especially at holiday-time. Small individual servings add a bright sweetness to special meals.*

Back in the 1930s, a doctor and his wife lived in Wausau, WI, where the local hospital served a large, mostly rural region. Many children in the area were pretty confined during the holidays. This couple baked and frosted cookies by the hundreds. Walking into their house was like going to Mrs. Claus' kitchen; there were cookies everywhere. They distributed the cookies to the children on Christmas Day.

My aunt lived with them and shared the recipe with our family. This year my 7 grandchildren continue the tradition of baking these cookies into the 5th generation. It's not Christmas until those cookies are decorated.

Carol Findling, Carol Stream, IL

Beverages

Cider Snap

Cathy Boshart
Lebanon, PA

Makes 12-16 servings

Prep. Time: 5-10 minutes
Cooking Time: 2 hours
Ideal slow cooker size: 3½-qt.

2 qts. apple cider, *or* **apple juice**
4 Tbsp. red cinnamon candies
at least 16 apple slices
at least 16 cinnamon sticks

1. Combine cider and cinnamon candies in slow cooker.
2. Cover. Cook on High 2 hours, or until candies dissolve and cider is hot.
3. Ladle into mugs and serve with apple-slice floaters and cinnamon-stick stirrers.

Note:
This is a cold-winter-night luxury. Make it in the morning and keep it on Low throughout the day so its good fragrance can fill the house.

Variation:
Use cran-apple juice instead of apple cider or juice.
Anita Troyer
Fairview, MI

Maple Mulled Cider

Leesa Lesenski
Wheatley, MA

Makes 8-10 servings

Prep. Time: 5-10 minutes
Cooking Time: 2 hours
Ideal slow cooker size: 3½-qt.

½ gallon cider
3-4 cinnamon sticks
2 tsp. whole cloves
2 tsp. whole allspice
1-2 Tbsp. orange juice concentrate, *optional*
1-2 Tbsp. maple syrup, *optional*

1. Combine ingredients in slow cooker.
2. Cover. Heat on Low 2 hours. Serve warm.

Note:
Serve at Halloween, after Christmas caroling, or for sledding parties.

Matthew's Hot Mulled Cider

Shirley Unternahrer, Wayland, IA

Makes 12 servings

Prep. Time: 5 minutes • Cooking Time: 5 hours
Ideal slow cooker size: 3½-qt.

2 qts. apple cider
¼ cup brown sugar
½ tsp. vanilla
1 cinnamon stick
4 cloves

1. Combine ingredients in slow cooker.
2. Cover. Cook on Low 5 hours. Stir.

Note:
Our kids just tried hot mulled cider for the first time this past Christmas. They loved it. It's fun to try new old things.

Orange Cider Punch

Naomi Ressler
Harrisonburg, VA

Makes 9-12 6-oz. servings

Prep. Time: 5-10 minutes
Cooking Time: 2-10 hours
Ideal slow cooker size: 3½-qt.

1 cup sugar
2 cinnamon sticks
1 tsp. whole nutmeg
2 cups apple cider, *or* **apple juice**
6 cups orange juice
fresh orange thinly sliced

1. Combine all ingredients except orange slices in slow cooker.
2. Cover. Cook on Low 4-10 hours or on High 2-3 hours, until heated through.
3. Float thin slices of orange in cooker before serving.

Deep Red Apple Cider

Judi Manos
West Islip, NY

Makes 8-9 servings

Prep. Time: 5-10 minutes
Cooking Time: 3-4 hours
Ideal slow cooker size: 3½-qt.

5 cups apple cider
3 cups dry red wine
¼ cup brown sugar
½ tsp. whole cloves
¼ tsp. whole allspice
1 stick cinnamon

1. Combine all ingredients in slow cooker.
2. Cover. Cook on Low 3-4 hours.
3. Remove cloves, allspice, and cinnamon before serving.

Variation:
You can use 8 cups apple cider and no red wine.

I like to sit down a couple of weeks before the holidays and write an outline of what needs to be done and how many days I need to do the work. I try to plan enough time so I don't run out of time on the last day.

Jane Geigley, Honey Brook, PA

Wassail

Virginia Bender
Dover, DE

Makes 16-18 servings

Prep. Time: 10 minutes
Cooking Time: 2-8 hours
Ideal slow cooker size: 6-qt.

1 gallon cider
6-oz. container frozen orange juice concentrate
6-oz. container frozen lemonade concentrate
½-1 cup brown sugar, according to your taste preference
1 tsp. whole nutmeg
1 Tbsp. whole cloves
1 Tbsp. whole allspice
orange slices
cinnamon sticks

1. Combine cider, orange juice and lemonade concentrates, and brown sugar in slow cooker. Mix well.
2. Place nutmeg, cloves, and allspice in cheesecloth bag or spice ball. Add to juices in slow cooker.
3. Cover. Cook on Low 2-8 hours, until the Wassail is as hot as you like it.
4. Float orange slices and cinnamon sticks on top. Ladle from slow cooker to serve.

Hot Cranberry Cider

Kristi See
Weskan, KS

Makes 10-12 servings

Prep. Time: 10 minutes
Cooking Time: 5-9 hours
Ideal slow cooker size: 4-qt.

½ gallon apple cider, *or* **apple juice**
2 cups cranberry juice
½-¾ cup sugar, according to your taste preference
2 cinnamon sticks
1 tsp. whole allspice
whole orange studded with cloves

1. Put all ingredients except orange studded with cloves in slow cooker.
2. Cover. Cook on High 1 hour, and then on Low 4-8 hours, until thoroughly hot.
3. Float clove-studded orange in cooker. Serve hot.

Serving suggestion: To garnish Cider with an ***orange****, insert 10-12½"-long* ***whole cloves*** *halfway into orange. Place studded orange in flat baking pan with sides. Pour in ¼ cup water. Bake at 325° for 30 minutes. Just before serving, float orange on top of hot Cider.*

Note:

I come from a family of eight children, and every Christmas we all get together. We eat dinner, and then play games while drinking Hot Cranberry Cider.

Pomegranate Punch

Lindsey Spencer
Marrow, OH

Makes 8 servings

Prep. Time: 5-7 minutes
Cooking Time: 1-2 hours
Ideal slow cooker size: 3-qt.

3 cups pomegranate juice
1-1½ cups cranberry juice cocktail, according to your taste preference
½ cup orange juice
3"-long cinnamon stick
1 tsp. grated ginger

1. Put all ingredients in slow cooker.
2. Cover. Cook on Low 1-2 hours, or until heated through.

Christmas Wassail

Dottie Schmidt
Kansas City, MO

Makes 6-8 servings

Prep. Time: 5-10 minutes
Cooking Time: 1 hour
Ideal slow cooker size: 3-qt.

2 cups cranberry juice
3¼ cups hot water
⅓ cup sugar
6-oz. can frozen lemonade concentrate
1 stick cinnamon
5 whole cloves
2 oranges, cut in thin slices

1. Combine all ingredients except oranges in slow cooker. Stir until sugar is dissolved.
2. Cover. Cook on High 1 hour. Strain out spices.
3. Serve hot with an orange slice floating in each cup.

Fruity Hot Punch

Evelyn L. Ward
Greeley, CO

Makes 12 servings

Prep. Time: 10 minutes
Cooking Time: 4 hours
Ideal slow cooker size: 5-qt.

2 16-oz. cans jellied cranberry sauce
4 cups water
1 qt. pineapple juice
¾ cup brown sugar
¼ tsp. salt
¼ tsp. ground nutmeg
¾ tsp. ground cloves
½ tsp. ground allspice
12 cinnamon sticks
butter, *optional*

1. Place cranberry sauce in slow cooker and mash with a potato masher.
2. Add all remaining ingredients to slow cooker except cinnamon sticks and butter. Mix well.
3. Cover. Heat on Low 4 hours.
4. Serve in mugs with cinnamon-stick stirrers. Dot each serving with butter if you wish.

Note:
My daughter is a teacher and has served this at faculty meetings when it's her turn to treat.

Fruity Wassail

Kelly Evenson
Pittsboro, NC

Makes 20 cups

Prep. Time: 10 minutes
Cooking Time: 1-2 hours
Ideal slow cooker size: 5-qt.

6 cups apple cider
1 cinnamon stick
¼ tsp. ground nutmeg
¼ cup honey
3 Tbsp. lemon juice
1 tsp. grated lemon rind
46-oz. can pineapple juice

1. Combine ingredients in slow cooker.
2. Cover. Cook on Low 1-2 hours, or until hot.
3. Serve warm from slow cooker.

Variation:
Use 3 cups cranberry juice, and reduce the amount of pineapple juice by 3 cups, to add more color and to change the flavor of the Wassail.

Spicy Citrus Warmer

Jean Butzer
Batavia, NY
Barbara Walker
Sturgis, SD

Makes 12 servings

Prep. Time: 5-10 minutes
Cooking Time: 2-3 hours
Ideal slow cooker size: 5-qt.

2½ qts. water
1½ cups sugar
1½ cups orange juice (with pulp is great!)
⅔ cup freshly squeezed lemon juice
⅓ cup pineapple juice
6"-long cinnamon stick, *or* **two 3" sticks**
1 tsp. whole cloves

1. Combine water, sugar, and juices in slow cooker. Stir until sugar is dissolved.
2. Add cinnamon stick to cooker. Place cloves in a tea ball. Close tightly and place in slow cooker.
3. Cover. Cook on Low 2-3 hours, or until heated through.

Tester Idea:
Add a half slice of oran or lime on the edge of eac individual cup before serv

Golden Wassail Punch

Susan Segraves
Lansdale, PA

Makes 9 cups

Prep. Time: 10 minutes
Cooking Time: 1-3 hours
Ideal slow cooker size: 3- to 4-qt.

3 cups apricot nectar
3 cups orange juice
3 cups white grape juice
¼ cup lemon juice
2 Tbsp. brown sugar
8"-long stick cinnamon, broken
½ tsp. cardamom, coarsely crushed

1. Combine juices and brown sugar in slow cooker. Stir until sugar is dissolved.
2. Lay stick cinnamon and cardamom on a square of cheesecloth. Tie shut securely. Place in slow cooker and push down into liquid.
3. Cover. Cook on High 1 hour, or on Low 2-3 hours. Remove spice bag before serving.

Hot Buttered Lemonade

Janie Steele
Moore, OK

Makes 5-6 servings

Prep. Time: 5-10 minutes
Cooking Time: 2½ hours
Ideal slow cooker size: 2-qt.

4½ cups water
¾ cup sugar
1½ tsp. grated lemon peel
¾ cup lemon juice
2 Tbsp. butter
6 cinnamon sticks

1. Combine water, sugar, lemon peel, lemon juice, and butter in slow cooker.
2. Cover. Cook on High 2½ hours, or until well heated through.
3. Serve very hot with a cinnamon stick in each mug.

When juicing a lemon, let it come to room temperature. You'll get more juice if you do. Then, using some pressure, roll it under your hand on the counter before juicing it so that it releases its juice more easily. Freeze any extra juice in 1 Tbsp. amounts in an ice cube tray.

Becky Frey, Lebanon, PA

Hot Fruit Tea

Kelly Evenson
Pittsboro, NC

Makes 20 servings

Prep. Time: 20 minutes
Ideal slow cooker size: 5-qt.

5-6 tea bags, fruit flavor of your choice
2 cups boiling water
1¾ cups sugar
2 cinnamon sticks
2½ qts. water
1¼ tsp. vanilla
1¼ tsp. almond extract
juice of 3 lemons
juice of 3 oranges

1. Steep tea bags in 2 cups boiling water for 5 minutes.
2. Bring tea water, sugar, cinnamon sticks, and 2½ qts. water to boil in saucepan.
3. Pour into slow cooker. Stir in remaining ingredients.
4. Turn slow cooker to Low. Keep tea warm on Low while serving.

Serving suggestion: Float thinly cut fresh ***lemon*** *and/or* ***orange*** *slices in tea.*

Johnny Appleseed Tea

Sheila Plock
Boalsburg, PA

Makes 8-9 cups

Prep. Time: 15 minutes
Cooking Time: 1-2 hours
Ideal slow cooker size: 3½-qt.

2 qts. water, *divided*
6 tea bags of your favorite flavor
6 ozs. frozen apple juice, thawed
¼ cup, plus 2 Tbsp., firmly packed brown sugar

1. Bring 1 qt. water to boil in large saucepan. Add tea bags. Remove from heat. Cover and let steep 5 minutes. Pour into slow cooker.
2. Add remaining ingredients and mix well.
3. Cover. Heat on Low until hot. Continue on Low while serving from slow cooker.

Note:
I serve this wonderful hot beverage with cookies at our Open House Tea and Cookies afternoon, which I host at Christmas-time for friends and neighbors.

Ginger Tea

Evelyn Page
Gillette, WY

Makes 8 cups

Prep. Time: 5-15 minutes
Cooking Time: 2 hours
Ideal slow cooker size: 3-qt.

4 cups boiling water
15 single green tea bags
4 cups white grape juice
1-2 Tbsp. honey, according to your taste preference
1 Tbsp. minced fresh gingerroot
candied ginger pieces, *optional*

1. Place boiling water and tea bags in slow cooker. Cover and let stand 10 minutes. Discard tea bags.
2. Stir in juice, honey, and gingerroot.
3. Cover. Cook on Low 2 hours, or until heated through.
4. Strain if you wish before pouring into individual cups.
5. Garnish each cup with candied ginger, if you wish.

Triple Delicious Hot Chocolate

Jennifer Freed
Harrisonburg, VA

Makes 6 servings

Prep. Time: 15 minutes
Cooking Time: 2¼ hours
Ideal slow cooker size: 2- to 3-qt.

⅓ cup sugar
¼ cup unsweetened cocoa powder
¼ tsp. salt
3 cups milk, *divided*
¾ tsp. vanilla
1 cup heavy cream
1 square (1 oz.) bittersweet chocolate
1 square (1 oz.) white chocolate
¾ cup whipped topping
6 tsp. mini-chocolate chips, *or* **shaved bittersweet chocolate**

1. Combine sugar, cocoa powder, salt, and ½ cup milk in medium-sized bowl. Stir until smooth. Pour into slow cooker.
2. Add remaining 2½ cups milk and vanilla to slow cooker. Cover. Cook on Low 2 hours.
3. Stir in cream. Cover. Cook on Low 10 minutes.
4. Stir in bittersweet and white chocolates until melted.
5. Pour hot chocolate into 6 mugs. Top each with 2 Tbsp. whipped topping and 1 tsp. chocolate chips or shavings.

Crockery Cocoa

Betty Hostetler, Allensville, PA

Makes 9-12 servings, depending on size of mugs

Prep. Time: 10 minutes
Cooking Time: 1-4 hours
Ideal slow cooker size: 3½-qt.

½ cup sugar
½ cup unsweetened cocoa powder
2 cups boiling water
3½ cups nonfat dry milk powder
6 cups water
1 tsp. vanilla
mini-marshmallows
1 tsp. ground cinnamon

1. Combine sugar and cocoa powder in slow cooker. Add 2 cups boiling water. Stir well to dissolve.
2. Add dry milk powder, 6 cups water, and vanilla. Stir well to dissolve.
3. Cover. Cook on Low 4 hours or on High 1-1½ hours.
4. Before serving, beat with rotary beater to make frothy. Ladle into mugs. Top with marshmallows and sprinkle with cinnamon.

Variations:

1. Add ⅛ tsp. ground nutmeg, along with ground cinnamon in Step 4.
2. Mocha-style—Stir ¾ tsp. instant coffee crystals into each serving in Step 4.
3. Coffee-Cocoa—Pour half-cups of freshly brewed, high quality coffee. Top with half-cups of Crockery Cocoa.

Hot Chocolate with Stir-Ins

Stacy Schmucker Stoltzfus
Enola, PA

Makes 12 6-oz. servings

Prep. Time: 5 minutes
Cooking Time: 1-2 hours
Ideal slow cooker size: 4-qt.

9½ cups water
1½ cups hot chocolate mix

Stir-ins:
smooth peanut butter
chocolate-mint candies, chopped
candy canes, broken
assorted flavored syrups: hazelnut, almond, raspberry, Irish creme
instant coffee granules
cinnamon
nutmeg

whipped topping
candy sprinkles

1. Pour water into slow cooker. Heat on High 1-2 hours. (Or heat water in tea kettle and pour into slow cooker.) Turn cooker to Low to keep hot for hours.
2. Stir in hot chocolate mix until blended.
3. Arrange stir-ins in small bowls.
4. Instruct guests to place approximately 1 Tbsp. of their choice of stir-ins in their mugs before ladling in hot chocolate. Stir well.
5. Top each filled mug with whipped topping and candy sprinkles.

Vanilla Steamer

Anita Troyer, Fairview, MI

Makes 8 servings

Prep. Time: 5-10 minutes • Cooking Time: 2-3 hours
Ideal slow cooker size: 3-qt.

8 cups milk
⅛ tsp. cinnamon, *or*
2 3"-long cinnamon sticks
3 Tbsp. sugar
2 Tbsp. vanilla
pinch of salt
pinch of nutmeg
whipped topping, *optional*
sprinkling of ground cinnamon, *optional*

1. Put all ingredients except whipped topping and sprinkling of ground cinnamon in slow cooker.
2. Cover. Cook on Low 2-3 hours, taking care to make sure it doesn't boil.
3. Garnish individual servings with whipped topping and a sprinkling of cinnamon if you wish.

Tip:
I usually make a larger recipe than I will need, and then refrigerate the leftovers. We like it either reheated, or as creamer in our coffee. This drink is very soothing and helps everyone relax!

Viennese Coffee

Evelyn Page
Gillette, WY

Makes 4 servings

Prep. Time: 15 minutes
Cooking Time: 3 hours
Ideal slow cooker size: 1½- to 2-qt.

3 cups strong brewed coffee
3 Tbsp. chocolate syrup
1 tsp. sugar
⅓ cup heavy whipping cream
¼ cup crème de cacao, *or*
Irish cream liqueur
whipped cream, *optional*
chocolate curls, *optional*

1. In a slow cooker, combine coffee, chocolate syrup, and sugar.
2. Cover. Cook on Low 2½ hours.
3. Stir in heavy cream and crème de cacao.
4. Cover. Cook 30 minutes more, or until heated through.
5. Ladle into mugs. Garnish if you wish with whipped cream and chocolate curls.

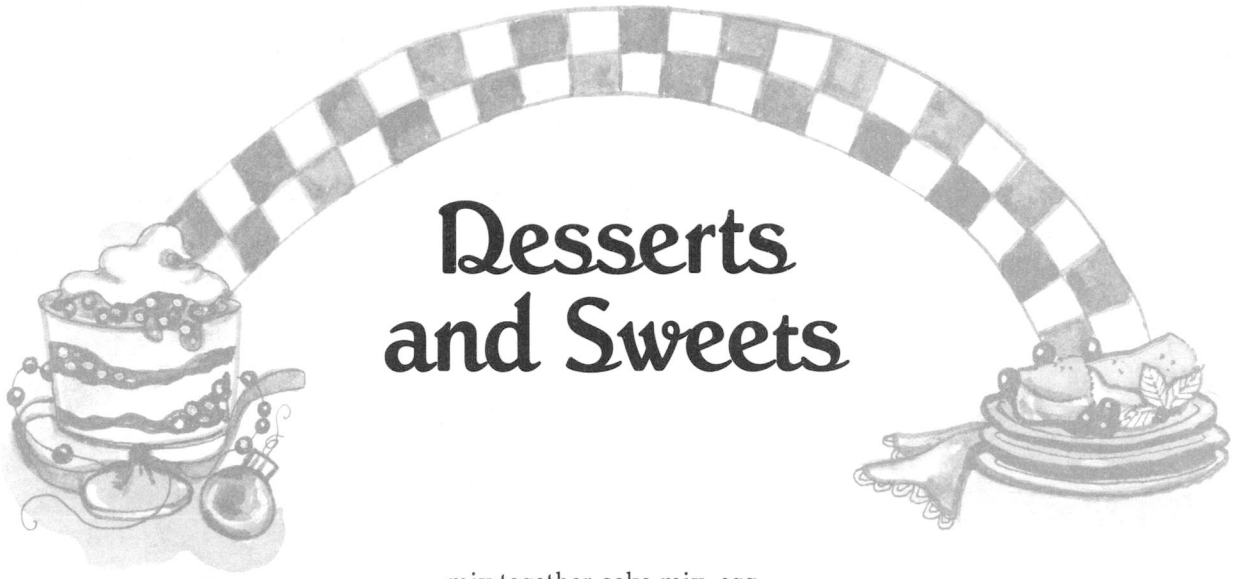

Desserts and Sweets

Holiday Cherry Cobbler

Colleen Heatwole
Burton, MI

Makes 5-6 servings

Prep. Time: 15 minutes
Cooking Time: 2½-3½ hours
Ideal slow cooker size: 4-qt.

16-oz. can cherry filling (light *or* regular)
1 pkg. cake mix for 1 layer white, *or* yellow, cake
1 egg
3 Tbsp. evaporated milk
½ tsp. cinnamon
½ cup walnuts, chopped

1. Spray slow cooker with cooking spray.
2. Spread pie filling in bottom of cooker.
3. Cover. Cook on High 30 minutes.
4. Meanwhile, in a medium-sized mixing bowl mix together cake mix, egg, evaporated milk, cinnamon, and walnuts.
5. Spoon over hot pie filling. Do not stir.
6. Cover. Cook on Low 2-3 hours, or until toothpick inserted in cake layer comes out clean.

Use a special holiday kitchen tool. I use my grandmother's 100-year-old tin cookie cutters to make sugar cookies from her recipe box. The angel and lady cutters are my favorite. They make the best "dunking" shapes.
Susan J. Heil, Strasburg, PA

Gingerbread Pudding Cake

Katrina Eberly
Wernersville, PA

Makes 6-8 servings

Prep. Time: 20 minutes
Cooking Time: 2-2½ hours
Standing Time: 15 minutes
Ideal slow cooker size: 3-qt.

half a stick (4 Tbsp.) butter, softened
¼ cup sugar
1 egg white
1 tsp. vanilla extract
½ cup molasses
1 cup water
1¼ cups flour
¾ tsp. baking soda
½ tsp. ground cinnamon
½ tsp. ground ginger
¼ tsp. salt
¼ tsp. ground allspice
⅛ tsp. ground nutmeg
½ cup chopped pecans
6 Tbsp. brown sugar

Topping:
¾ cup hot water
5⅔ Tbsp. (⅓ cup) butter, melted

1. Spray interior of slow cooker with cooking spray.
2. In a large mixing bowl, cream 4 Tbsp. butter and sugar until light and fluffy. Beat in egg white and vanilla.
3. In a separate bowl, combine molasses and water until blended.
4. In another bowl, combine flour, baking soda, and spices. Add to creamed mixture alternately with molasses mixture, beating well after each addition.
5. Fold in pecans. Spoon into slow cooker. Sprinkle with brown sugar
6. In a small bowl, combine hot water and 5⅔ Tbsp. butter. Pour over batter. Do *not* stir.
7. Cover. Cook on High 2-2½ hours, or until toothpick inserted in center of cake comes out clean.
8. Turn off cooker. Let stand 15 minutes. Serve cake warm.

Note from Tester:
I used blackstrap molasses, and the flavor didn't overpower the cake.

At the end of our Christmas meal we serve chocolate cake. I write "Happy Birthday, Jesus" on it in yellow frosting. I use extra frosting to make a hay bed for a small baby figurine to rest on. We have one candle for each grandchild to blow out after we sing Happy Birthday to Baby Jesus. Usually amid laughter, we relight some accidentally blown-out candles.

Anne Townsend, Albuquerque, NM

Christmas Apple Date Pudding

Colleen Heatwole
Burton, MI

Makes 8 servings

Prep. Time: 30 minutes
Cooking Time: 3-4 hours
Ideal slow cooker size: 2-qt.

4-5 apples, peeled, cored, and diced
½ cup sugar
½ cup chopped dates
½ cup toasted, chopped pecans
1 Tbsp. flour
1 tsp. baking powder
⅛ tsp. salt
½ tsp. cinnamon
2 Tbsp. melted butter
1 beaten egg

1. In a greased slow cooker, mix together apples, sugar, dates, and pecans.
2. In a separate bowl, mix together flour, baking powder, salt, and cinnamon. Stir into apple mixture.
3. Drizzle melted butter over batter and stir.
4. Stir in egg.
5. Cover. Cook on Low 3-4 hours. Serve warm.

Date and Nut Loaf

Jean Butzer
Batavia, NY

Makes 16 servings

Prep. Time: 20 minutes
Cooking Time: 3½-4 hours
Ideal slow cooker size: large enough to hold 2 coffee cans, or your baking insert

1½ cups boiling water
1½ cups chopped dates
1¼ cups sugar
1 egg
2 tsp. baking soda
½ tsp. salt
1 tsp. vanilla
1 Tbsp. melted butter
2½ cups flour
1 cup walnuts, chopped
2 cups hot water

1. In a large mixing bowl, pour 1½ cups boiling water over dates. Let stand 5-10 minutes.
2. Stir in sugar, egg, baking soda, salt, vanilla, and butter.
3. In a separate bowl, combine flour and nuts. Stir into date mixture and combine well.
4. Pour into 2 greased 11½-oz. coffee cans, or one 8-cup baking insert.
5. If using coffee cans, cover with foil and tie securely with kitchen twine. If using baking insert, cover with its lid.
6. Place cans or insert on rack in slow cooker. (If you don't have a rack, use rubber jar rings instead.)
7. Pour 2 cups hot water around cans or insert, up to half their/its height.
8. Cover slow cooker tightly. Cook on High 3½-4 hours. Insert toothpick into loaves of bread to see if it comes out clean. If it does, the bread is finished. If it doesn't, allow to cook 30 more minutes. Check again to see if bread is done. If not, continue cooking in 30-minute intervals.
9. When bread is finished, remove cans or insert from cooker. Let bread stand in coffee cans or baking insert for 10 minutes. Turn out onto cooling rack.
10. When thoroughly cooled, slice. Spread with butter, cream cheese, or peanut butter.

Banana Loaf

Sue Hamilton, Minooka, IL

Makes 6-8 servings

Prep. Time: 5-10 minutes • Cooking Time: 2-2½ hours
Ideal slow cooker size: large enough to hold 2-lb. coffee can upright, or a baking insert

3 very ripe bananas
1 stick (8 Tbsp.) butter, softened
2 eggs
1 tsp. vanilla
1 cup sugar
1 cup flour
1 tsp. baking soda

1. Combine all ingredients in an electric mixing bowl. Beat 2 minutes, or until well blended. Pour into well greased 2-lb. coffee can or baking insert.
2. Place can or insert in slow cooker. Cover can with 6 layers of paper towels between cooker lid and bread. Or cover with baking insert lid.
3. Cover cooker. Bake on High 2-2½ hours, or until toothpick inserted in center comes out clean. Cool 15 minutes before removing from pan.

Slow-Cooker Spoon Peaches

Jeanette Oberholtzer
Manheim, PA

Makes 6 servings

Prep. Time: 10 minutes
Cooking Time: 6-8 hours
Ideal slow cooker size: 1½-qt.

⅓ cup sugar
½ cup brown sugar
¾ cup buttermilk baking mix
2 eggs
2 tsp. vanilla
1 Tbsp. butter, melted
half a 12-oz. can evaporated milk
2 cups mashed peaches, fresh, frozen, *or* **canned (if canned, drain slightly)**
¾ tsp. cinnamon

1. Combine sugar, brown sugar, and baking mix in a good-sized mixing bowl.
2. Add eggs and vanilla. Mix well.
3. Add butter and milk. Mix well.
4. Add peaches and cinnamon. Mix well. Pour into greased slow cooker.
5. Cover. Cook on Low 6-8 hours.

Serving suggestion: Serve warm with ***whipped cream*** *or* ***vanilla ice cream.***

Note:
This is a great warm dessert for a cold winter evening.

Zesty Pears

Barbara Walker, Sturgis, SD

Makes 6 servings

Prep. Time: 15 minutes • Cooking Time: 4-6 hours
Ideal slow cooker size: 2- to 3-qt.

6 fresh pears
½ cup raisins
¼ cup brown sugar
1 tsp. grated lemon peel
¼ cup brandy
½ cup sauterne wine
½ cup macaroon crumbs
sour cream, *optional*

1. Peel and core pears. Cut into thin slices and place in bowl.
2. In a separate small bowl, combine raisins, sugar, and lemon peel. Layer alternately with pear slices in slow cooker.
3. Pour brandy and wine over top.
4. Cover. Cook on Low 4-6 hours.
5. Spoon into serving dishes. Cool. Sprinkle with macaroons. Serve plain or topped with sour cream.

Cranberry Sauce with Red Wine and Oranges

Donna Treloar
Muncie, IN

Makes 3-4 servings

Prep. Time: 5-10 minutes
Cooking Time: 2-2½ hours
Ideal slow cooker size: 2-qt.

12-oz. bag fresh cranberries, rinsed
1½ cups sugar
1 cup dry red wine
1 cinnamon stick
grated zest of one orange, then cut orange in half
4 whole cloves

1. Combine cranberries, sugar, wine, cinnamon, and zest in slow cooker.
2. Place 2 cloves in each orange half. Push down into cranberry mixture.
3. Cover. Cook on High 2-2½ hours, or until cranberries have popped. Turn off cooker.
4. Discard cinnamon stick and orange halves with cloves.
5. Remove lid and let Sauce cool to room temperature.

Serving suggestion: Serve chilled or at room temperature over ***ice cream*** *or* ***pound cake.***

Apple Cranberry Compote

Charlotte Shaffer
East Earl, PA

Makes 8 servings

Prep. Time: 15-20 minutes
Cooking Time: 3-4 hours
Ideal slow cooker size: 3- to 4-qt.

6 apples, peeled and sliced
1 cup fresh cranberries
1 cup sugar
½ tsp. grated orange peel
½ cup water
¼ cup port wine
sour cream

1. Combine apples and cranberries in slow cooker. Sprinkle evenly with sugar. Stir in orange peel, water, and wine.
2. Cover. Cook on Low 3-4 hours.
3. Serve with dollops of sour cream on individual servings.

Warmed Spiced Fruit

Susan Segraves
Lansdale, PA

Makes 6-8 servings

Prep. Time: 20 minutes
Cooking Time: 2 hours
Ideal slow cooker size: 6-qt.

3 Golden Delicious, *or* **Granny Smith, apples, peeled, cored, and sliced**
3 pears, peeled, cored, and sliced
11-oz. can mandarin oranges, drained
1 cup fresh cranberries, rinsed, and coarsely chopped
¼ cup firmly packed brown sugar
2 Tbsp. cornstarch
¼ tsp. ground cinnamon
¼ tsp. ground ginger
⅛ tsp. ground cloves
1 cup apple, white grape, *or* **cranberry juice**

1. Layer fruit in order given in slow cooker.
2. In a medium-sized bowl, stir together brown sugar, cornstarch, and spices. Slowly stir in juice. Pour over fruit.
3. Cover. Cook on High 2 hours. Serve warm or chilled.

Note from Tester:
Cranberries were out of season when I tested the recipe, so I used 1 cup craisins instead. Excellent results!

Fruit Compote

Janet Batdorf
Harrisburg, PA

Makes 5 servings

Prep. Time: 15 minutes
Cooking Time: 6 hours
Ideal slow cooker size: 5-qt.

1 qt. canned peach slices with juice
1 cup dried apricots
½ cup brown sugar
¼ cup water
1 tsp. grated orange peel
⅓ cup orange juice
½ tsp. grated lemon peel
2 Tbsp. lemon juice
16-oz. can pitted dark sweet cherries, drained

1. Combine peaches with their juice, apricots, brown sugar, water, orange peel, orange juice, lemon peel, and lemon juice in slow cooker.
2. Cover. Cook on Low 6 hours.
3. Fifteen minutes before end of cooking time, stir in cherries. Cover. Cook 15 more minutes.

Serving suggestion: Serve over ***ice cream*** *or* ***pound cake****, or alongside a plate of* ***cookies****.*

Festive Fruit Compote

Maryann Markano
Wilmington, DE

Makes 10-12 servings

Prep. Time: 10-15 minutes
Cooking Time: 3-8 hours
Ideal slow cooker size: 4- to 5-qt.

1 lb. dried prunes
1⅓ cups dried apricots
13½-oz. can pineapple chunks, undrained
16-oz. can pitted dark sweet cherries, undrained
¼ cup dry white wine
2 cups water

1. Place all ingredients in slow cooker.
2. Cover. Cook on Low 7-8 hours or on High 3-4 hours.
3. Serve warm.

Note:
You can substitute other dried fruits in place of the prunes and apricots.

Fruit Dessert Topping

Lavina Hochstedler
Grand Blanc, MI

Makes 6 cups

Prep. Time: 20 minutes
Cooking Time: 3½-4¾ hours
Ideal slow cooker size: 3½-qt.

3 tart apples, peeled and sliced
3 pears, peeled and sliced
1 Tbsp. lemon juice
½ cup packed brown sugar
½ cup maple syrup
half a stick (4 Tbsp.) butter, melted
½ cup chopped pecans
¼ cup raisins
2 cinnamon sticks
1 Tbsp. cornstarch
2 Tbsp. cold water

1. Toss apples and pears in lemon juice in slow cooker.
2. In a small bowl, combine brown sugar, maple syrup, and butter. Pour over fruit.
3. Stir in pecans, raisins, and cinnamon sticks.
4. Cover. Cook on Low 3-4 hours.
5. In a small bowl, combine cornstarch and water until smooth. Gradually stir into slow cooker.
6. Cover. Cook on High 30-40 minutes, or until fruit thickens.
7. Discard cinnamon sticks.

*Serving suggestion: Serve over **pound cake** or **ice cream**.*

Note:
We also like this served along with pancakes or an egg casserole. We always use Fruit Topping for our breakfasts at church camp.

Wagon Master Apple-Cherry Sauce

Sharon Timpe
Mequon, WI

Makes 12-15 servings

Prep. Time: 5-10 minutes
Cooking Time: 3-4 hours
Ideal slow cooker size: 3½-qt.

2 21-oz. cans apple pie filling
2-3 cups frozen tart red cherries
1 Tbsp. butter
½ tsp. ground cinnamon
½ tsp. ground nutmeg
⅛ tsp. ground ginger
⅛ tsp. ground cloves

1. Combine all ingredients except whipped cream in slow cooker.
2. Cover. Heat on Low 3-4 hours, or until mixture is hot and bubbly. Stir occasionally.

*Serving suggestion: Serve warm over **vanilla ice cream**, **pudding**, **pound cake**, or **shortcake biscuits**. Top with **whipped cream** or **whipped topping** if you wish.*

Curried Fruit

Jane Meiser
Harrisonburg, VA

Makes 8-10 servings

Prep. Time: 10 minutes
Marinating Time: 2-8 hours
Cooking Time: 8-10 hours
Ideal slow cooker size: 3½- to 4-qt.

1 can peaches, cut into chunks and undrained
1 can apricots, cut into chunks and undrained
1 can pears, cut into chunks and undrained
1 large can pineapple chunks, undrained
1 can black cherries, undrained
½ cup brown sugar
1 tsp. curry powder
3-4 Tbsp. quick-cooking tapioca, depending upon how thick you'd like the finished dish to be
butter, *optional*

1. Combine fruit in slow cooker. Let stand without heating for at least 2 hours, or up to 8 hours, to allow flavors to blend.
2. Drain off juices.
3. Add remaining ingredients. Mix well. Top with butter chunks, if you wish.
4. Cover. Cook on Low 8-10 hours.
5. Serve warm or at room temperature.

Southwest Cranberries

Bernita Boyts
Shawnee Mission, KS

Makes 8 servings

Prep. Time: 5 minutes
Cooking Time: 2-3 hours
Ideal slow cooker size: 1½- to 2-qt.

16-oz. can whole berry cranberry sauce
10½-oz. jar jalapeño jelly
2 Tbsp. chopped fresh cilantro

1. Combine all ingredients in slow cooker.
2. Cover. Cook on Low 2-3 hours.

Serving suggestion: Cool. Serve at room temperature as a side dish or as a ***marinade*** *for poultry or pork.*

Cranberry Applesauce

Susan Segraves
Lansdale, PA

Makes 12 servings

Prep. Time: 20 minutes
Cooking Time: 3-8 hours
Ideal slow cooker size: 4- to 5-qt.

10 cups peeled, cubed apples (about 3 lbs. Granny Smith, *or* **McIntosh)**
2 cups fresh cranberries
½ cup sugar
½ cup maple-flavored pancake syrup
⅓ cup water
½ tsp. cinnamon
¼ tsp. nutmeg

1. Mix all ingredients in slow cooker.
2. Cover. Cook on High 3-4 hours or on Low 6-8 hours.
3. In cooker, mash apples and cranberries with potato masher.
4. Reduce heat to warm. Hold in slow cooker until serving time. Or chill if you prefer until ready to serve.

Serving suggestion: Use this as is for dessert, or as a topping for ***ice cream*** *or* ***pound cake****. Or serve warm as* ***an accompaniment*** *to a turkey dinner.*

For Christmas Eve I prepare plain sugar cookies. I also put out bowls of sprinkles and frosting for the kids to use to decorate the cookies. Michele Ruvola, Vestal, NY

Homemade Applesauce

Renita Denlinger
Denver, PA

Makes 7-8 servings

Prep. Time: 10-20 minutes
Cooking Time: 3½ hours
Ideal slow cooker size: 5- to 6-qt.

10 large apples, halved, cored, and peeled
½ tsp. cinnamon
dash of nutmeg
dash of ground cloves
1 Tbsp. water

1. Spray slow cooker with non-stick spray.
2. Put apples in slow cooker.
3. Sprinkle cinnamon, nutmeg, cloves, and water over apples. Stir.
4. Cover. Cook on Low 3½ hours, or until apples are soft. If you're home and available, stir the apples after they've cooked for 2 hours. It's okay to mash them up a bit as you stir.
5. Serve warm or chilled.

Note:
This makes the whole house smell wonderful.

Cranberry Baked Apples

Judi Manos
West Islip, NY

Makes 4 servings

Prep. Time: 15 minutes
Cooking Time: 4-6 hours
Ideal slow cooker size: 4- to 5-qt.

⅓ cup packed brown sugar
¼ cup dried cranberries
4 large cooking apples
½ cup cran-apple juice cocktail
¼ stick (2 Tbsp.) butter, melted
½ tsp. ground cinnamon
¼ tsp. ground nutmeg
chopped nuts, *optional*

1. In a small bowl, mix brown sugar and cranberries together.
2. Core apples but leave whole. Fill centers with brown sugar and cranberry mixture.
3. Set apples upright in slow cooker. (Don't stack them.)
4. In the same small bowl, combine cran-apple juice and butter. Pour over apples.
5. Sprinkle with cinnamon and nutmeg.
6. Cover. Cook on Low 4-6 hours.
7. To serve, spoon sauce over apples and sprinkle with nuts.

Serving suggestion: A great accompaniment to ***vanilla ice cream****.*

Note:
This was one of our favorite recipes while growing up. When it's cooking, the house smells delicious. I'm suddenly full of memories of days gone by and a much more relaxing time. My mother passed away in October, and I re-found this recipe among her collection of favorites.

Apple Schnitz

Betty Hostetler
Allensville, PA

Makes 6-8 servings

Prep. Time: 5 minutes
Cooking Time: 2½-6 hours
Ideal slow cooker size: 3-qt.

16 oz. dried apples
3 cups water
1 cup sugar
1 tsp. ground cinnamon
1 tsp. salt

1. Combine apples, water, sugar, cinnamon, and salt in slow cooker.
2. Cover. Cook on Low 6 hours, or on High 2½ hours.
3. Serve warm as a side dish with bean soup, or as filling for Half Moon Pies (see below).
4. For pie filling, remove apples from slow cooker. Mash until smooth with potato masher, or put through food mill. Cool.

Pie Crust:
4 cups flour
2 tsp. salt
4 Tbsp. shortening
¼ cold water, *or* **more**

1. Combine flour and salt in large bowl. Cut in shortening until mixture resembles small peas.
2. Add ¼ cup cold water to dough, adding more by tablespoonfuls as needed to make a soft pie dough.
3. Pinch off small pieces of dough, each about the size of a large walnut. Roll into round pieces, each about 8" in diameter.
4. Jag one half of the circle a few times with a sharp fork to create holes for the steam to escape while baking. On the other half, place a heaping tablespoon of Apple Schnitz.
5. Fold one-half of dough up over the half holding the Apple Schnitz, shaping the pie like a half moon. Press edges of dough together. Cut off remaining dough and crimp edges.
6. Bake at 350° for 30 minutes.

Note:
On a cold winter day, Mother would prepare dried beans to make soup. After the beans were soft, she added milk to the soup pot. She heated the mixture to the boiling point, then added rivels. While the beans were cooking, she cooked dried apples until they were soft. She served these Half Moon Pies as a side dish/dessert with the soup.

Caramel Apples

Becky Harder, Monument, CO
Jeanette Oberholtzer, Manheim, PA

Makes 8-10 servings

Prep. Time: 20-30 minutes • Cooking Time: 1-1½ hours
Ideal slow cooker size: 2-qt.

2 14-oz. bags of caramels
¼ cup water
8-10 medium apples
12-15 sticks, in case a few break
granulated sugar in a dish
waxed paper, lightly greased

1. Remove wrapping from caramels. Combine candies and water in slow cooker.
2. Cover. Cook on High 1-1½ hours, stirring every 5 minutes. (This is a good job for a child who's tall enough to take the lid off and stir without steaming him/herself.)
3. Meanwhile, wash and dry apples. Insert a stick into stem end of each apple. Turn cooker to Low.
4. Dip apple into hot caramel, turning to coat entire surface. (This is definitely a task for children, if adults are nearby to help.)
5. Holding apple above cooker, scrape off excess accumulation of caramel from bottom of apple.
6. Then dip bottom of caramel-coated apple in granulated sugar to keep it from sticking. Place apple on greased waxed paper to cool.

Note:
This is a good recipe for Fall/Harvest/Halloween parties. Children won't forget the hands-on experience of dipping their own apples. Room mothers can make the caramel mix ahead of time and bring it into the classroom. This recipe is also a fun intergenerational activity for church groups or family reunions.

In the late 1950s and early 1960s, my sister and I were rewarded with a store-bought caramel apple, only after our Saturday night baths and our Sunday school lessons had been completed. I remember that the waxed paper wrapped around each apple had colorful clowns printed on it, and they sold for less than 50¢ each.

Becky Harder

Apple Caramel Dessert

Jeanette Oberholtzer
Manheim, PA

Makes 7 servings

Prep. Time: 15 minutes
Cooking Time: 6 hours
Ideal slow cooker size: 2-qt.

½ cup apple juice
7 ozs. caramels, unwrapped
1 tsp. vanilla
⅛ tsp. ground cardamom
½ tsp. ground cinnamon
⅓ cup creamy peanut butter
2 medium apples, peeled, cored, and cut in wedges

1. Combine apple juice, caramel candies, vanilla, and spices in slow cooker.
2. Drop peanut butter, 1 Tbsp. at a time, into slow cooker. Stir well after each addition.
3. Gently stir in apple wedges.
4. Cover. Cook on Low 5 hours.
5. Stir well.
6. Cover. Then cook 1 more hour on Low.

Serving suggestion: Serve about ⅓ cup warm mixture over each slice of ***angel food cake****, and then top each with* ***ice cream****.*

Apple Crisp

Michelle Strite
Goshen, IN

Makes 6-8 servings

Prep. Time: 5-10 minutes
Cooking Time: 2-3 hours
Ideal slow cooker size: 2-qt.

2 21-oz. cans apple pie filling, *or*
⅔ cup sugar
1¼ cups water
3 Tbsp. cornstarch
4 cups sliced, peeled apples
½ tsp. ground cinnamon
¼ tsp. ground allspice
¾ cup uncooked quick oatmeal
½ cup brown sugar
½ cup flour
half a stick (4 Tbsp.) butter, at room temperature

1. Place pie filling in slow cooker. If not using prepared filling, combine ⅔ cup sugar, water, cornstarch, apples, cinnamon, and allspice in cooker. Stir until well mixed.
2. In a mixing bowl, combine remaining ingredients until crumbly. Sprinkle over apple filling.
3. Cover. Cook on Low 2-3 hours.

Dried Cranberry Pudding

Evelyn L. Ward
Greeley, CO

Makes 8 servings

Prep. Time: 10-15 minutes
Cooking Time: 3 hours
Ideal slow cooker size: large enough to hold your baking insert

half a stick (4 Tbsp.) butter, softened
½ cup brown sugar
½ cup molasses
1 egg
½ tsp. baking soda
½ cup hot water
1½ cups flour, *divided*
1 tsp. baking powder
½ cup dried cranberries

Butter Sauce:
½ cup sugar
1 Tbsp. flour
½ cup water
pinch salt
1 Tbsp. butter
2 tsp. vanilla

1. To make Pudding, cream together butter, sugar, and molasses in a good-sized mixing bowl.
2. Add egg. Beat well.
3. In a small bowl, dissolve baking soda in hot water. Stir into creamed mixture until well mixed.
4. Beat in 1 cup flour and baking powder.
5. In a small bowl, combine cranberries with ½ cup flour. Stir into batter.

6. Pour into well-greased baking insert or coffee can. Cover tightly with lid or double layer of foil.
7. Place upright on rack in slow cooker.
8. Pour boiling water into cooker, until halfway up sides of insert.
9. Cover cooker. Cook 3 hours on High.
10. Remove insert or can from cooker. Cool 2 minutes on baking rack. Run knife around edge of insert or can, and then turn upside down to unmold onto plate.
11. Serve with hot Butter Sauce.
12. To make Butter Sauce, combine sugar, flour, water, and salt in saucepan until well blended. Cook over medium heat, stirring constantly until thickened. Remove from heat. Stir in butter and vanilla. Serve hot with slices of Pudding.

Tips:

1. A coffee can that stands upright in your slow cooker works as a good pudding mold.
2. You can use a jar ring as a rack under the mold.

Steamed Chocolate Pudding

Evelyn L. Ward
Greeley, CO

Makes 8 servings

Prep. Time: 10 minutes
Cooking Time: 2½ hours
Ideal slow cooker size: large enough to hold your baking insert or a coffee can standing upright

1 stick (8 Tbsp.) butter, softened
¾ cup sugar
¾ cup flour
3 Tbsp. cocoa powder
¼ tsp. salt
3 eggs
½ tsp. vanilla
¼ cup half-and-half

1. Cream together butter and sugar with electric mixer.
2. In a separate bowl, sift together flour, cocoa powder, and salt.
3. Add alternately with eggs to creamed mixture. Beat well.
4. Add vanilla and half-and-half. Beat well.
5. Spoon into greased and floured slow cooker baking insert.* Cover tightly with lid or double layer of foil.
6. Place insert on a rack in slow cooker. Add boiling water to slow cooker, halfway up sides of insert.
7. Cover slow cooker. Cook on High 2½ hours.
8. Remove insert from cooker. Cool 2 minutes. Unmold.

Serving suggestion: Cut into wedges. Serve with ***frozen whipped topping, thawed,*** *or* ***ice cream.***

Tips:

* 1. A coffee can that stands upright inside your slow cooker serves as a good pudding mold.
2. You can use a jar ring for a rack under the can or baking insert.

Slow-Cooker Rice Pudding

Dede Peterson
Rapid City, SD

Makes 5 servings

Prep. Time: 10 minutes
Cooking Time: 3-4 hours
Cooling Time: 2-5 hours
Ideal slow cooker size: 2-qt.

1 pkg. vanilla cook-and-serve pudding mix
1 cup cooked white rice
1 cup raisins
1 tsp. cinnamon
2 tsp. vanilla
3 cups half-and-half, *or* **milk**

1. Combine ingredients in slow cooker.
2. Cover. Cook on Low 3-4 hours.
3. Serve warm, at room temperature, or chilled.

Rice Pudding

Vera Schmucker
Goshen, IN

Makes 4-6 servings

Prep. Time: 10 minutes
Cooking Time: 2-6 hours
Chilling Time: 2-5 hours
Ideal slow cooker size: 1½- to 2-qt.

2½ cups cooked rice
1½ cups evaporated, *or* scalded, milk
⅔ cup sugar
1 Tbsp. butter, melted
½-1 tsp. ground nutmeg

1. Combine all ingredients in lightly greased slow cooker.
2. Cover. Cook on High 2 hours, or on Low 4-6 hours.
3. Stir after first hour.
4. Cool to slightly warm or to room temperature before serving. Or chill until cold if you wish.

Serving suggestion: Serve topped with ***whipped cream*** *and/or* ***maraschino cherries****, if you wish.*

Chocolate Rice Pudding

Michele Ruvola
Selden, NY

Makes 4 servings

Prep. Time: 10 minutes
Cooking Time: 2½-3½ hours
Chilling Time: 2-5 hours
Ideal slow cooker size: 3-qt.

4 cups cooked white rice
¾ cup sugar
¼ cup baking cocoa powder
3 Tbsp. butter, melted
1 tsp. vanilla
2 12-oz. cans evaporated milk

1. Combine first 6 ingredients in greased slow cooker.
2. Cover. Cook on Low 2½-3½ hours, or until liquid is absorbed.

Serving suggestion: Serve warm or chilled. Top individual servings with a dollop of ***whipped cream, sliced toasted almonds****, and/or a* ***maraschino cherry*** *if you wish.*

Deluxe Tapioca Pudding

Michelle Showalter
Bridgewater, VA

Makes 16 servings

Prep. Time: 10 minutes
Cooking Time: 3½ hours
Chilling Time: 4-5 hours, or longer
Ideal slow cooker size: 4-qt.

2 qts. milk
¾ cup dry small pearl tapioca
1½ cups sugar
4 eggs, beaten
2 tsp. vanilla
3-4 cups whipped cream, *or* **frozen whipped topping, thawed**
chocolate candy bar

1. Combine milk, tapioca, and sugar in slow cooker.
2. Cook on High 3 hours.
3. In a medium-sized mixing bowl, add a little hot milk mixture to beaten eggs. Stir.
4. Whisk eggs into milk mixture in slow cooker. Stir in vanilla.
5. Cover. Cook on High 20-30 minutes.
6. Cool to room temperature. Chill in refrigerator.
7. When fully chilled, beat with hand mixer to fluff Pudding.
8. Fold in whipped cream or whipped topping. Garnish with chopped candy bar.

Our neighborhood has a cookie exchange, and we try to surprise each other with interesting containers to take them home in. We bring as many dozen cookies (of the same kind of cookie) as there are people attending, and we go home with that many different ones.

Donna Conto, Saylorsburg, PA

Lemon Pudding

Jean M. Butzer
Batavia, NY

Makes 4 servings

Prep. Time: 10-15 minutes
Cooking Time: 1½-2 hours
Standing/Cooling Time: 30 minutes-3 hours
Ideal slow cooker size: 3-qt.

1 cup sugar
¼ cup flour
¼ tsp. salt
1 cup buttermilk
¼ cup lemon juice
3 eggs, separated

1. Spray slow cooker with cooking spray.
2. Combine sugar, flour, and salt in a good-sized mixing bowl.
3. Make a well in the center and add buttermilk and lemon juice. Stir until smooth. Stir in egg yolks.
4. In a separate bowl, beat egg whites until stiff and able to hold a peak. Fold into batter. Pour into slow cooker.
5. Cover. Cook on High 1½-2 hours, or until top is set and pudding is brown around the edges.
6. Turn off cooker. Let stand at least 30 minutes before serving. Serve warm or cold.

Note:

This recipe is similar to an old-fashioned lemon soufflé that has been a favorite of my family for years. I use a lot of buttermilk when baking for the holiday season. This recipe helps use up any extra I might have.

Eggnog Gingersnap Custard

Sue Hamilton, Minooka, IL

Makes 4-6 servings

Prep. Time: 5 minutes • Cooking Time: 3½-4 hours
Cooling/Chilling Time: 20 minutes-4 hours
Ideal slow cooker size: 3- to 4-qt.

24 small gingersnaps
1 qt. eggnog
4 eggs

1. Spray interior of slow cooker with cooking spray.
2. Lay all cookies on bottom of slow cooker.
3. In a large mixing bowl, beat eggs. Stir in eggnog.
4. Slowly pour into slow cooker. The cookies will rise in a layer to the top.
5. Cover. Cook on Low 3½-4 hours, or until Custard is set.
6. Remove cover. Let cool 20 minutes for a warm Custard, or chill 4 or more hours for a cold Custard.

Slow-Cooker Pumpkin Pie

Colleen Heatwole
Burton, MI

Makes 5-6 servings

Prep. Time: 10 minutes
Cooking Time: 3-4 hours
Cooling Time: 2-4 hours
Ideal slow cooker size: 3-qt.

15-oz. can solid-pack pumpkin
12-oz. can evaporated milk
¾ cup sugar
½ cup low-fat buttermilk baking mix
2 eggs, beaten
¼ stick (2 Tbsp.) butter, melted
1½ tsp. cinnamon
¾ tsp. ground ginger
¼ tsp. ground nutmeg
whipped topping

1. Spray slow cooker with cooking spray.
2. Mix all ingredients together in slow cooker, except whipped topping.
3. Cover. Cook on Low 3-4 hours, or until a toothpick inserted in center comes out clean.
4. Allow to cool to warm, or chill, before serving with whipped topping.

Variation:

You can substitute 2½ Tbsp. pumpkin pie spice in place of cinnamon, ginger, and nutmeg.

White Chocolate Bread Pudding

Linda E. Wilcox
Blythewood, SC

Makes 5-6 servings

Prep Time: 30 minutes
Cooking Time: 1¾ hours
Cooling Time: 30 minutes, and then 1-2 hours
Ideal slow-cooker size: 3- to 4-qt.

½ cup dried cranberries, *or* **dried cherries**
3 Tbsp. apple cider, *or* **brandy**
3-oz. white chocolate bar
¼ stick (2 Tbsp.) butter
6 cups stale French bread, cubed, ***divided***
4 eggs
½ cup sugar
1 cup half-and-half
1 tsp. vanilla

1. Combine dried fruit with cider or brandy in a microwave-safe bowl.
2. Microwave on High for 30 seconds. Set aside to cool (about 30 minutes).
3. Coarsely chop the chocolate. Set aside.
4. Drain the dried fruit. Set aside.
5. Spray interior of slow cooker with cooking spray.
6. Cover bottom of slow cooker with half the bread cubes.
7. Sprinkle half the chocolate and half the fruit over bread cubes.
8. Layer in remaining bread cubes. Top with a layer of remaining fruit and a layer of remaining chocolate.
9. In a bowl beat eggs with whisk. Add sugar, half-and-half, and vanilla to eggs. Mix together thoroughly.
10. Pour over bread mixture and press to make sure egg mixture covers all bread.
11. Cover and cook on High 1¾ hours.
12. Cool until warm or at room temperature.

Note:
My grandchildren love this dessert.

Apple-Nut Bread Pudding

Ruth Ann Hoover
New Holland, PA

Makes 6-8 servings

Prep. Time: 15 minutes
Cooking Time: 3-4 hours
Cooling Time: 3-4 hours
Ideal slow cooker size: 4-qt.

8 slices raisin bread, cubed
2-3 medium-sized tart apples, peeled and sliced
1 cup chopped pecans, toasted
1 cup sugar
1 tsp. ground cinnamon
½ tsp. ground nutmeg
3 eggs, lightly beaten
2 cups half-and-half
¼ cup apple juice
half a stick (4 Tbsp.) butter, melted

1. Place bread cubes, apples, and pecans in greased slow cooker and mix together gently.
2. Combine sugar, cinnamon, and nutmeg in a good-sized mixing bowl.
3. Add remaining ingredients. Mix well.
4. Pour over bread mixture. Stir gently to mix thoroughly.
5. Cover. Cook on Low 3-4 hours, or until knife inserted in center comes out clean.
6. Serve warm (but not hot) or at room temperature.

Serving suggestion: ***Ice cream*** *is a great accompaniment.*

Simple Bread Pudding

Melanie L. Thrower
McPherson, KS

Makes 6-8 servings

Prep. Time: 5-10 minutes
Cooking Time: 2-2½ hours
Chilling Time: 2-5 hours
Ideal slow cooker size: 1½- to 2-qt.

6-8 slices of bread, cubed
2 cups milk
2 eggs
¼ cup sugar
1 tsp. ground cinnamon
1 tsp. vanilla

Sauce:
6-oz. can concentrated grape juice
1 Tbsp. cornstarch

1. Place cubed bread in slow cooker.
2. In a good-sized bowl, whisk together milk, eggs, sugar, cinnamon, and vanilla. Pour over bread. Press bread down into liquid to dampen.
3. Cover. Cook on High 2-2½ hours, or until mixture is set.
4. Allow Pudding to cool to warm or to room temperature before serving. Or chill until cold.
5. Combine cornstarch and concentrated juice in saucepan. Heat until boiling, stirring constantly, until sauce is thickened. Serve drizzled over bread pudding.

Tip:
This is a fine dessert with a cold salad main dish.

Home-Style Bread Pudding

Lizzie Weaver
Ephrata, PA

Makes 4-6 servings

Prep. Time: 10 minutes
Cooking Time: 2-3 hours
Chilling Time: 1-4 hours
Ideal slow cooker size: large enough to hold your baking insert

2 eggs, beaten
2¼ cups milk
½ tsp. cinnamon
¼ tsp. salt
½ cup brown sugar
1 tsp. vanilla
2 cups 1" bread cubes
½ cup raisins *or* **dates**

1. Combine all ingredients in good-sized mixing bowl. Pour into slow cooker baking insert.
2. Cover baking insert. Place on metal rack (or rubber jar rings) in bottom of slow cooker.
3. Pour ½ cup hot water into cooker around sides of insert.
4. Cover slow cooker. Cook on High 2-3 hours.

Serving suggestion: Serve Pudding warm or cold, topped with ***cherry pie filling*** *and/or* ***whipped topping*** *if you wish.*

Pineapple Upside Down Cake

Vera M. Kuhns
Harrisonburg, VA

Makes 10 servings

Prep. Time: 20 minutes
Cooking Time: 4-5 hours
Cooling Time: 10 minutes
Ideal slow cooker size: 4-qt.

1 stick (8 Tbsp.) butter, melted
1 cup brown sugar
1 medium-sized can pineapple slices, drained, juice reserved
6-8 maraschino cherries
1 box yellow cake mix

1. Combine butter and brown sugar in well-greased slow cooker. Spread over cooker bottom.
2. Lay pineapple slices over top. Place a cherry in the center of each slice.
3. In a good-sized mixing bowl, prepare cake according to package directions, using pineapple juice for part of liquid.
4. Spoon cake batter into cooker over top fruit.
5. Cover cooker with 2 tea towels and then with its own lid. Cook on High 1 hour, and then on Low 3-4 hours.
6. Insert toothpick in center of cake. If it comes out clean, cake is finished. If it doesn't, continue to cook in 15-minute increments, checking after each one, until pick comes out clean.
7. Allow cake to cool for 10 minutes. Then run knife around edge and invert cake onto large platter.

Make your favorite Christmas cookies and have a bag ready to send home with each guest.
Leona M Slabaugh, Apple Creek, OH

Low-Fat Apple Cake

Sue Hamilton
Minooka, IL

Makes 8 servings

Prep. Time: 15 minutes
Cooking Time: 2½-3 hours
Cooling Time: 1 hour
Ideal slow cooker size: 3-qt.

1 cup flour
1 cup sugar
2 tsp. baking powder
1 tsp. ground cinnamon
¼ tsp. salt
4 medium-sized cooking apples, chopped
2 eggs, beaten
2 tsp. vanilla

1. Combine flour, sugar, baking powder, cinnamon, and salt in lightly greased slow cooker.
2. Add apples, stirring gently to coat.
3. In a small bowl, combine eggs and vanilla. Add to apple mixture. Stir until just moistened.
4. Cover. Bake on High 2½-3 hours. Insert toothpick in center of Cake. If tester comes out clean, Cake is finished. If it doesn't, continue cooking for 15-minute intervals, checking after each one with pick until it comes out clean.

Serving suggestion: Serve warm. Top with ***whipped topping*** *or* ***ice cream*** *and a sprinkle of* ***cinnamon****.*

Variation:
Stir ½ cup broken English or black walnuts, or ½ cup raisins, into Step 2.

Note:
The slow cooker is great for "baking" desserts. Your guests will be pleasantly surprised to see a cake coming from your slow cooker.

Creamy Orange Cheesecake

Jeanette Oberholtzer
Manheim, PA

Makes 10 servings

Prep. Time: 15 minutes
Cooking Time: 2½-3 hours
Standing Time: 1-2 hours
Chilling Time: 2-4 hours
Ideal slow cooker size: large enough to hold your baking insert

Crust:
¾ cup graham cracker crumbs
2 Tbsp. sugar
3 Tbsp. melted butter

Filling:
2 8-oz. pkgs. cream cheese, at room temperature
⅔ cup sugar
2 eggs
1 egg yolk
¼ cup frozen orange juice concentrate
1 tsp. orange zest
1 Tbsp. flour
½ tsp. vanilla

1. Combine crust ingredients in a small bowl. Pat into 7"or 9" springform pan, whichever size fits into your slow cooker.
2. In a large mixing bowl, cream together cream cheese and sugar. Add eggs and yolk. Beat 3 minutes.
3. Add juice, zest, flour, and vanilla. Beat 2 more minutes.
4. Pour batter into crust. Place on rack (or jar rings) in slow cooker.
5. Cover. Cook on High 2½-3 hours. Turn off and let stand 1-2 hours, or until cool enough to remove from cooker.
6. Cool completely before removing sides of pan. Chill before serving.

Serving suggestion: Serve with thawed ***frozen whipped topping*** *and* ***fresh or mandarin orange slices****.*

Invest in a microplane wand. They are wonderful for zesting citrus. Freeze amounts of lemon or orange zest to use in any given recipe. Orange zest is great in blueberry muffins or sweet potato casserole. Anything that calls for lemon juice will be even better if you also add some lemon zest.

Becky Frey, Lebanon, PA

Orange Slice Cake

Steven Lantz
Denver, CO

Makes 10-12 servings

Prep. Time: 20 minutes
Cooking Time: 2-3 hours
Cooling Time: 3-4 hours
Ideal slow cooker size: 3-qt.

1 cup chopped dates
½ lb. candied orange slices, cut into thirds
½ cup chopped walnuts
1 cup flaked, unsweetened coconut
1 Tbsp. grated orange rind, *optional*
1¾ cups flour, *divided*
1 stick (8 Tbsp.) butter, at room temperature
1 cup sugar
2 eggs
½ tsp. baking soda
¼ cup buttermilk

1. In a good-sized mixing bowl, combine dates, orange slices, nuts, coconut, and orange rind if you wish.
2. Pour ¼ cup flour over mixture and stir together.
3. In a separate big bowl, cream butter and sugar together. Add eggs and beat well.
4. In a small bowl, dissolve baking soda in buttermilk.
5. Add remaining 1½ cups flour and buttermilk, in which soda has been dissolved, to creamed mixture.
6. Stir in fruit and nut mixture.
7. Pour into greased slow cooker.
8. Cover. Cook on High 2-3 hours, or until toothpick inserted in center comes out clean.
9. Allow cake to cool completely before removing from slow cooker.

Tip:
This cake is perfect with coffee in the morning or later in the day as dessert.

Note from Tester:
I chopped the dates and nuts in my food processor. I spooned them into a mixing bowl where I combined them with the other ingredients in Steps 1 and 2.

Then I continued using my food processor for Steps 3 and 5. No need to wash it in between.

I believe in saving time whenever I can.

Carrot Cake

Colleen Heatwole
Burton, MI

Makes 6-8 servings

Prep. Time: 20 minutes
Cooking Time: 3-4 hours
Ideal slow cooker size: large enough to hold your baking insert

½ cup vegetable oil
2 eggs
1 Tbsp. hot water
½ cup grated raw carrots
¾ cup flour
¾ cup sugar
½ tsp. baking powder
⅛ tsp. salt
¼ tsp. ground allspice
½ tsp. ground cinnamon
⅛ tsp. ground cloves
½ cup chopped nuts
½ cup raisins, *or* **chopped dates**
2 Tbsp. flour

1. In large bowl, beat oil, eggs, and water for 1 minute.
2. Add carrots. Mix well.
3. In a separate bowl, stir together flour, sugar, baking powder, salt, allspice, cinnamon, and cloves. Add to creamed mixture.
4. Toss nuts and raisins in bowl with 2 Tbsp. flour. Add to creamed mixture. Mix well.
5. Pour into greased and floured 3-lb. shortening can or slow-cooker baking insert. Place can or baking insert in slow cooker.
6. Cover insert with its lid, or cover can with 8 paper towels, folded down over edge of slow cooker to absorb moisture. Cover paper towels with cooker lid. Cook on High 3-4 hours, or until toothpick inserted in center of cake comes out clean.
7. Remove can or insert from cooker and allow to cool on rack for 10 minutes. Run knife around edge of cake. Invert onto serving plate.

Easy Easy Cake

Janice Muller
Derwood, MD

Makes 8-10 servings

Prep. Time: 10 minutes
Cooking Time: 2-3 hours
Ideal slow cooker size: 3½-qt.

20-oz. can crushed pineapple, undrained
21-oz. can blueberry, *or* **cherry, pie filling**
18½-oz. pkg. yellow cake mix
cinnamon
1 stick (8 Tbsp.) butter
1 cup chopped nuts
vanilla ice cream

1. Grease bottom and sides of interior of slow cooker.
2. Spread a layer of pineapple in bottom.
3. Top with a layer of blueberry pie filling.
4. Top that with a layer of dry cake mix. Be careful not to mix the layers!
5. Sprinkle with cinnamon.
6. Top with thin layers of butter chunks and nuts.
7. Cover cooker. Cook on High 2-3 hours, or until toothpick inserted in center comes out clean.
8. Serve warm with vanilla ice cream.

Variation:

Substitute a pkg. of spice cake mix and apple pie filling.

Fudgy Peanut Butter Cake

Betty Moore
Plano, IL

Makes 4 servings

Prep. Time: 15 minutes
Cooking Time: 1½ hours
Ideal slow cooker size: 2- to 3-qt.

¾ cup sugar, *divided*
½ cup flour
¾ tsp. baking powder
⅓ cup milk
¼ cup peanut butter
1 Tbsp. oil
½ tsp. vanilla
2 Tbsp. dry cocoa powder
1 cup boiling water

1. Butter or spray interior of slow cooker.
2. Mix ¼ cup sugar, flour, and baking powder together in a small bowl.
3. In another larger bowl, mix milk, peanut butter, oil, and vanilla together. Beat well.
4. Stir dry ingredients into milk-peanut butter mixture just until combined. Spread in buttered slow cooker.
5. In bowl, combine cocoa powder and remaining ½ cup sugar. Add water, stirring until well mixed. Pour slowly into slow cooker. Do *not* stir.
6. Cover. Cook on High 1½ hours, or until toothpick inserted in center of cake comes out clean.

Serving suggestion: Serve warm with ***vanilla ice cream.***

Note:

I take this to potlucks and it is always a hit.

Notes from Tester:

1. I was pretty sure my kids would love this, so I doubled the recipe. I cooked that larger recipe for 2 hours. The kids came back for second and third helpings!
2. This is a pretty sturdy cake. I kept one of my test cakes for over an hour before serving it, and it was just as good, if not better, than the one we ate right away.

Lemon Poppy Seed Upside-Down Cake

Jeanette Oberholtzer
Manheim, PA

Makes 8-10 servings

Prep. Time: 10-15 minutes
Cooking Time: 2-2½ hours
Cooling Time: 2 hours
Ideal slow cooker size: 2-qt.

1 pkg. lemon poppy seed bread mix
1 egg
8 oz. light sour cream
½ cup water

Sauce:

1 Tbsp. butter
¾ cup water
½ cup sugar
¼ cup lemon juice

1. Combine first four ingredients until well moistened in

Crusty Baked Potatoes

Anna Stoltzfus,
Honey Brook, PA

Makes 6 servings

Prep. Time: 20 minutes
Baking Time: 60 minutes

1 cup cracker crumbs
½ tsp. salt
1 tsp. dried oregano
1 tsp. seasoning salt
1 tsp. parsley flakes
4 Tbsp. butter, melted
4 medium-sized potatoes, sliced

1. In a shallow bowl, add seasonings to cracker crumbs.
2. Place melted butter in another shallow bowl.
3. Dip potato slices in butter. Then dredge in cracker crumbs.
4. When coated, place slices in a greased baking dish.
5. Bake, uncovered, at 375° for 60 minutes.

Variation:
Add ½ tsp. baking powder to every 2 cups of potatoes to mash. Sprinkle it into the potatoes before adding milk. This helps to keep them white and not stiffen up.

SALADS

Festive Tossed Salad

Cheryl A. Lapp
Parkesburg, PA
Yvonne Kauffman Boettger
Harrisonburg, VA
Sally Holzem
Schofield, WI

Makes 8-10 servings

Prep Time: 30 minutes

½ cup sugar
⅓ cup cider *or* red wine vinegar
2 Tbsp. lemon juice
2 Tbsp. finely chopped onions
½ tsp. salt
⅔ cup olive oil
2 tsp. poppy seeds
10 cups torn romaine lettuce
1 cup shredded Swiss cheese
1 medium-sized apple, cored and cubed
1 medium-sized pear, cored and cubed
¼ cup dried cranberries
½ cup chopped cashews

1. In a blender, combine first 5 ingredients until well blended.
2. With a blender running, gradually add oil. Add poppy seeds and blend.
3. In salad bowl, combine lettuce, cheese, apple, pear, and cranberries.
4. Just before serving, drizzle salad with desired amount of dressing. (You'll have more dressing than you need, so save what's left for a future salad.) Add cashews and toss to coat.

Variation:
Add 1 tsp. Dijon mustard to the dressing in Step 1.
Jennifer Eberly
Harrisonburg, VA

Tip:
If you're delayed in tossing a salad, you can keep the greens fresh under a drape of paper towels, wrung out of ice water.

Dried Cherry Salad

Stacy Schmucker Stoltzfus
Enola, PA

Makes 12 servings

Prep Time: 20 minutes
Cooking Time: 10 minutes

half a head of romaine lettuce, chopped
half a head of red leaf lettuce, chopped
half a large red onion, sliced
1 cup dried cherries
1 cup feta cheese
⅓ cup sugar
1 cup pecan halves

Raspberry Dressing:
4 Tbsp. raspberry vinegar
½ tsp. Tabasco sauce
½ tsp. salt
4 Tbsp. sugar
pepper to taste
1 Tbsp. chopped parsley
½ cup vegetable oil

1. Place lettuces in a large salad bowl. Sprinkle with onion slices, dried cherries, and feta cheese.
2. In skillet, over medium heat, combine ⅓ cup sugar and pecans. Stir constantly until sugar melts and pecans are coated. Immediately pour pecans onto waxed paper to cool.
3. Sprinkle cooled nuts over salad.
4. To make dressing, combine vinegar, Tabasco sauce, salt, 4 Tbsp. sugar, pepper, and parsley in a small mixing bowl. While whisking, slowly pour in oil until emulsified. Just before serving, pour over salad.

Spinach Salad with Walnut Dressing

Dolores Metzler
Lewistown, PA

Makes 8 servings

Prep Time: 15 minutes
Standing Time: 30 minutes

Dressing:
¼ cup vegetable oil
1 Tbsp. honey
¼ tsp. salt
2 Tbsp. lemon juice
2 tsp. Dijon mustard
dash of pepper
⅔ cup walnuts, chopped
2 Tbsp. sliced green onions

Salad:
4-6 cups spinach andlor other greens
1 cup diced Swiss cheese
1 cup diced fresh fruit (apples, peaches, and pears are all good, dipped in lemon juice to keep from discolring)

1. Mix oil, honey, salt, lemon juice, mustard, pepper, walnuts, and onions in a jar with a tight-fitting lid.
2. Cover and shake until well mixed. Then let stand for 30 minutes to enhance flavor.
3. Mix spinach, Swiss cheese, and diced fruit in a large mixing bowl.
4. Just before serving, add dressing to salad and toss together.

Trees & Seeds Salad

Nanci Keatley
Salem, OR

Makes 8-10 servings

Prep Time: 10-20 minutes
Chilling Time: 30 minutes

4 cups cauliflower florets
3 cups cut-up broccoli
1 cup diced red onions
2 pts. cherry tomatoes, halved
½-I lb. bacon, cooked and diced, according to your preference
3 Tbsp. sesame seeds
¼ cup sunflower seeds
¼ cup slivered almonds

Dressing:
1 cup mayonnaise
½ cup sugar or sugar substitute
3 Tbsp. cider vinegar
½ tsp. salt
½ tsp. pepper

1. In a large serving bowl, combine cauliflower, broccoli, onions, tomatoes, bacon, seeds, and nuts.
2. In a separate bowl, mix together mayonnaise, sugar, vinegar, salt, and pepper. Pour over vegetables.
3. Refrigerate at least 30 minutes to blend flavors.

Tip:
This is great to make ahead. Mix all ingredients together except the dressing. Chill, then add the dressing half an hour before serving. Refrigerate until serving time.

Variations:

1. Change the "green" base of this salad to: 3 cups shredded cabbage or coleslaw mix;
2 cups broken cauliflower;
2 cups chopped broccoli.

— **Teresa Martin**
Gordonville, PA

2. Add ⅓ cup grated Parmesan cheese to the Dressing in Step 2.

— **Phyllis Smith**
Goshen, IN

3. Add 8 sliced radishes to Step 1.

— **Sara Wilson**
Blairstown, MO

Cranberry Coleslaw

Carolyn Baer
Conrath, WI

Makes 6-7 servings

Prep Time: 15 minutes
Chilling Time: 45 minutes

½ cup mayonnaise
2 Tbsp. honey
2 Tbsp. vinegar
¼ cup fresh cranberries, chopped, *or* snipped dried cranberries
5 cups shredded cabbage (1 small head)

1. Combine mayonnaise, honey, and vinegar. Stir in cranberries.
2. Place shredded cabbage in a large bowl.
3. Pour dressing over cabbage. Toss to coat.
4. Cover and chill for 45 minutes.

This salad is very pretty for holiday parties, but it is delicious anytime.

Sweet Potato Salad

Jean Johnson
Dallas, OR

Makes 6 servings

Prep Time: 10 minutes
Cooking Time: 20 minutes
Chilling Time: 3 hours

4 medium-sized sweet potatoes
½ cup mayonnaise
½ cup plain yogurt
1-1½ tsp. curry powder salt to taste
2 medium-sized Granny Smith apples, chopped
2 medium-sized oranges, peeled and chopped, *or* 2 11-oz. cans mandarin oranges, drained
½ cup raisins
½ cup chopped dates
20-oz. can pineapple chunks, drained
1 cup sliced celery

1. Place whole, unpeeled sweet potatoes in a saucepan. Add 2 inches of water. Cover and cook over medium-high heat until tender in the middle, but not mushy.
2. Meanwhile, combine mayonnaise, yogurt, curry powder, and salt in a large bowl. Mix well.
3. When the cooked sweet potatoes are cool enough to handle, peel them. Then cut into chunks about the size of the pineapple chunks. Add to mayonnaise mixture.
4. Add remaining ingredients. Toss well.
5. Refrigerate at least 3 hours before serving.

Linguine Salad with Peanut Sauce

Gretchen H. Maust
Keezletown, VA

Makes 6 servings

Prep Time: 15 minutes
Cooking Time: 15 minutes

8-oz. box dry linguine
1½-1 cup chopped scallions
1 diced cucumber
¼ cup peanut butter
⅓ cup cider *or* rice vinegar
¼ cup soy sauce
¼ cup warm water
⅓ cup sesame oil
2 cloves minced garlic
½ tsp. 5-spice powder
hot sauce to taste
dark green lettuce leaves
toasted sesame seeds and tomato wedges for garnish

1. Cook linguine as directed on box, but undercook slightly. Drain. Rinse with cool water.
2. In a large bowl, combine linguini, scallions, and cucumber.
3. In a separate bowl, whisk together peanut butter, vinegar, soy sauce, water, oil, garlic, 5-spice powder, and hot sauce.
4. Arrange lettuce on platter. Spoon linguine mixture into the middle. Drizzle dressing over top. Garnish with sesame seeds and tomato wedges.

Variations:

1. For a heartier dish, add cubed cooked chicken or turkey.
2. Serve hot, replacing the cucumbers with cooked zucchini.

Tip:

I like to triple the peanut sauce and keep it in the refrigerator to use as a salad dressing or dipping sauce for grilled chicken.

Black Bean Fiesta Salad

Lorraine Pflederer
Goshen, IN

Makes 6 servings

Prep Time: 30 minutes
Chilling Time: 2-8 hours, or overnight

15-oz. can black beans, rinsed and drained
1 cup frozen corn, thawed
1 green pepper, diced
1 sweet red pepper, diced
1 cup diced red onions
2 celery ribs, chopped
¾ cup cubed Monterey Jack cheese
3 Tbsp. lemon juice
3 Tbsp. red wine, *or* cider, vinegar
2 Tbsp. olive oil
2 garlic cloves, minced
1 Tbsp. Italian seasoning
1 tsp. pepper
½ tsp. ground cumin

1. In a large bowl, combine beans, corn, peppers, onions, celery, and cheese.
2. In a jar with a tight-fitting lid, combine the remaining ingredients. Shake well.
3. Pour over vegetable mixture and toss gently.
4. Cover and chill for 2 hours or overnight.

Marinated Mushrooms

Lisa Harnish
Christiana, PA

Makes 12 servings

Prep Time: 10 minutes
Cooking Time: 20 minutes

2 lbs. (50-60) medium-sized fresh mushrooms
2 cloves garlic
1 cup red wine vinegar
1 cup water
½ cup olive oil
½ cup vegetable oil
1 bay leaf
1 tsp. salt
½ tsp. dried thyme leaves
12 whole black peppercorns
fresh parsley

1. Clean mushrooms and set aside.
2. Flatten garlic or use garlic press.
3. In Dutch oven, combine all ingredients except mushrooms and parsley.
4. Bring to a boil. Reduce heat and simmer 5 minutes.
5. Add mushrooms and simmer uncovered 10 minutes.
6. Remove from heat and let stand until cooled slightly.
7. Transfer mushrooms and marinade to a storage container. Cover and refrigerate until ready to serve.
8. To serve, remove mushrooms from marinade and place in serving dish. Garnish with fresh parsley.

Bright Beet Salad

Dorothy Lingerfelt
Stonyford, CA

Makes 6 servings

Prep Time: 10 minutes
Cooking Time: 5 minutes
Chilling Time: 4 hours

16-oz. can diced beets, drained, juice reserved
3-oz. pkg. lemon gelatin
⅔ cup orange juice
1 tsp. grated onion
2-3 tsp. grated horseradish, depending upon how much zip you like
1 tsp. vinegar
1 tsp. salt
⅔ cup chopped celery

1. Drain beets, reserving juice.
2. Pour beet juice into a 1-cup measure. Fill to the top with water. Pour into a small saucepan. Bring to a boil.
3. Dissolve gelatin in boiling beet juice. Stir in orange juice, onion, horseradish, vinegar, and salt. Mix well.
4. Chill beet-gelatin mixture until slightly thickened.
5. Stir in beets and celery. Pour into mold.
6. Chill until firm. Unmold on a serving plate.

Tip:
Have one or two "company specials" you can make when friends show up unexpectedly.

Frozen Waldorf Salad

Bonita Ensenberger
Albuquerque, NM

Makes 6-9 servings

Prep Time: 20 minutes
Freezing Time: 8 hours, or overnight

8 ozs. cream cheese, softened
½ cup mayonnaise
2 cups frozen whipped topping, slightly thawed
1 cup apples, unpeeled and chopped
½ cup celery, sliced
1 cup seedless grapes, halved
¾ cup crushed pineapple, drained
¾ cup English walnuts, toasted and chopped

1. In a large mixing bowl, whip together cream cheese and mayonnaise, either by hand or with a mixer or food processor. Fold in whipped topping.
2. Fold in apples, celery, grapes, and pineapple.
3. Pour into a greased 8 x 8 baking dish. Cover and freeze for 8 hours or overnight.
4. Remove from freezer 10-15 minute before serving. Cut into squares. Top each serving with toasted walnuts.

Cranberry Salad

Mary Lynn Miller
Reinholds, PA

Makes 6-8 servings

Prep Time: 30-40 minutes
Chilling Time: 6-8 hours, or overnight

4 cups fresh cranberries, rinsed and drained
4 oranges (2 peeled, 2 unpeeled)
4 apples, peeled and cut into quarters
2 cups sugar

1. Grind cranberries, oranges, and apples. Mix well.
2. Pour sugar over fruit and mix well.
3. Refrigerate for 6-8 hours before serving.

Saucy Fruit Salad

Tracey Hanson Schramel
Windom, MN

Makes 6-8 servings

Prep Time: 10-15 minutes
Chilling Time: 1-2 hours

2 11-oz. cans mandarin oranges, drained
2 20-oz. cans pineapple chunks, drained
4 bananas, sliced
2 red apples, sliced, *optional*

Fruit sauce:
3.4-oz. box instant vanilla pudding
1 cup milk
⅓ cup orange juice concentrate
6-oz. carton banana, *or* French vanilla, yogurt

1. Mix all fruit in a large bowl and set aside.
2. In a small mixing bowl, combine dry pudding with milk, orange juice, and yogurt. Beat with wire whisk until smooth.
3. Pour sauce over fruit and fold together. Chill for 1-2 hours.

Honey Apple Salad

Esther Becker
Gordonville, PA

Makes 6 servings

Prep Time: 15-20 minutes

3½ cups diced red apples, unpeeled
2 Tbsp. lemon juice
2 cups green grapes, halved
1 cup thinly sliced celery
½ cup raisins or craisins
2 Tbsp. sour cream
½ cup mayonnaise
½ tsp. salt
¼ cup honey
½ cup chopped walnuts *or* pecans

1. In a large bowl, toss apples with lemon juice. Add grapes, celery, and raisins.
2. In a small bowl, combine sour cream, mayonnaise, salt, and honey. Mix well. Pour over apple mixture and stir to coat.
3. Stir in nuts just before serving.

Raspberry Vinaigrette

Colleen Heatwole
Burton, MI

Makes 1-1½ cups dressing

Prep Time: 5-10 minutes

1 cup raspberries, fresh *or* frozen and thawed
¼ cup raspberry vinegar
2 Tbsp. olive oil
1 Tbsp. honey
¼ tsp. dry mustard

1. Blend all ingredients in food processor or blender.
2. Refrigerate.

Zesty French Dressing

Erma Rutt
Newmanstown, PA

Makes about 2 cups dressing

Prep Time: 5-10 minutes

1 small onion, chopped
⅔ cup vegetable oil
½ cup white sugar
⅓ cup vinegar
2 Tbsp. ketchup
1½ tsp. Worcestershire sauce
1 tsp. salt
1 tsp. prepared mustard
1 tsp. paprika
½ tsp. garlic powder
½ tsp. celery seed

1. Combine all ingredients in blender.
2. Blend until smooth.
3. Store in refrigerator.

Favorite Balsamic Dressing

Ann Bender
Fort Defiance, VA

Makes about ½ cup dressing

Prep Time: 5 minutes

¼ cup olive oil
2 Tbsp. balsamic vinegar
1 tsp. prepared mustard
1 clove garlic
2 Tbsp. sugar
⅛ tsp. salt
⅛ tsp. pepper

1. Combine olive oil, vinegar, mustard, garlic, sugar, salt, and pepper in blender.
2. Blend until smooth.
3. Store in refrigerator.

Ranch Dressing

Pat Unternahrer
Wayland, IA

Makes ¾ cup dressing

Prep Time: 5 minutes

⅔ cup cottage cheese
2 Tbsp. milk
1 Tbsp. tarragon vinegar
1 garlic clove, minced
1 Tbsp. sliced green onions

1. Blend cottage cheese, milk, vinegar, and garlic in blender or food processor.
2. Add green onions and blend just to combine.
3. Store in refrigerator.

DESSERTS

Cranberry Pudding

Barbara Jean Fabel
Wausau, WI

Makes 9 servings

Prep Time: 10 minutes
Baking Time: 30 minutes

Pudding:

2 cups flour
1 cup sugar
¼ tsp. salt
4 tsp. baking powder
1 cup milk, or more
3 Tbsp. butter, melted
2 cups raw cranberries, cut in half

Sauce:

2 cups half-and-half
⅔ cup sugar
2 Tbsp. cornstarch
⅛ tsp. salt
2-4 Tbsp. butter

1. To make pudding, mix ingredients together in order named.
2. Bake in a greased 9 x 9 baking pan at 400° for 30 minutes.
3. While the pudding is baking, make the sauce by scalding the half-and-half.
4. In a small bowl, combine the sugar, cornstarch, and salt. When thoroughly mixed add to the hot half-and-half in the saucepan.
5. Bring to a boil, stirring constantly until mixture thickens. Stir in butter.
6. Serve hot over hot pudding.

This has been family's Christmas dessert for 3 generations!

Frozen Heath Bar Mocha Mousse

Ida Stoltzfus
Free Union, VA

Makes 15-18 servings

Prep Time: 20-30 minutes
Chilling Time: 30-60 minutes
Freezing Time: 6 hours, or overnight
Thawing Time: 1 hour

1½ cups crushed Oreo cookies
¼ cup butter, melted
2¾ cups cold milk
2 3.9-oz. pkgs. instant chocolate pudding
3 tsp. instant coffee powder
2 Tbsp. hot water
1 ice cube
8 ozs. frozen whipped topping, thawed
1 cup, plus 2 Tbsp., crushed Heath Bars, *divided*

1. Mix crushed Oreos and butter. Press into a 9 x 13 pan. Put into freezer until pudding is made.
2. In a mixing bowl, stir together pudding and milk. Chill until of soft-set consistency.
3. Mix coffee powder with hot water in a mug until dissolved. Add ice cube until mixture cools. Remove any remaining cube.
4. Fold cooled coffee and whipped topping into soft-set pudding until blended.
5. Add 1 cup crushed Heath Bars.
6. Spoon into cookie crust in pan, being careful not to disturb the crust crumbs.
7. Garnish with 2 tablespoons crushed Heath Bars.
8. Freeze for 6 hours, or overnight.
9. Thaw in refrigerator for 1 hour prior to serving.

Pumpkin Cream

Esther J. Mast
Lancaster, PA

Makes 8-10 servings

Prep Time: 5 minutes
Cooking Time: 15-20 minutes
Chillinn Time: 1-2 hours

2 cups pumpkin, canned or freshly sieved
2 cups milk
4 Tbsp. cornstarch
1 cup sugar
1 tsp. salt
1 tsp. cinnamon
½ tsp. nutmeg
2 eggs, beaten
1 tsp. cold water
8-oz. container whipped topping

1. Combine pumpkin and milk in a microwavable dish. Microwave on high for 10-15 minutes, or until liquid reaches boiling point.
2. In a mixing bowl, mix together cornstarch, sugar, salt, cinnamon, and nutmeg. Beat in the eggs and water.
3. Stir into the pumpkinl milk mixture and microwave on high an additional 5 minutes, or until thickened.
4. Chill in refrigerator.
5. Reserve some of the whipped topping as a garnish and mix the remainder into the cooled, thickened pumpkin.

This is a creamy alternative to pumpkin pie, with much less work.

Pumpkin Ginger Squares

Margaret Culbert
Lebanon, PA
Gina Hargitt
Quinter, KS

Makes 16-20 servings

Prep Time: 20 minutes
Baking Time: 50-55 minutes
Chilling Time: 2 hours

1 cup flour
½ cup dry quick oats
½ cup brown sugar
1 stick (½ cup) butter, softened
2 cups pumpkin
12-oz. can evaporated milk
2 eggs
¾ cup sugar
¾ tsp. salt
1 tsp. cinnamon
½ tsp ginger
½ cup chopped pecans or walnuts
½ cup brown sugar
2 Tbsp. butter, melted

1. In a large mixing bowl, mix together flour, quick oats, and ½ cup brown sugar. When well blended, cut in ½ cup butter with a pastry cutter until mixture is crumbly.
2. Press into the bottom of a lightly greased 9 x 13 baking pan. Bake at 350° for 15 minutes.
3. In the same mixing bowl, combine pumpkin, evaporated milk, eggs, sugar, salt, cinnamon, and ginger. Mix well.
4. Spoon pumpkin mixture over baked crust, being careful not to disturb the crumbs. Return to oven and bake another 20 minutes at 350°.
5. Meanwhile, combine pecans or walnuts, ½ cup brown sugar and 2 Tbsp. melted butter. Sprinkle over baked pumpkin.
6. Return to oven and bake 15-20 minutes more at 350°.
7. Allow to cool completely before cutting into squares to serve.

Tip:
When a recipe calls for eggs, break them into a separate bowl or cup. You can remove any loose shells before adding the eggs to the recipe you're preparing.

Lemon Almond Torte

Kathy Hertzler
Lancaster, PA

Makes 10 servings

Prep Time: 15-20 minutes
Baking Time: 50 minutes
cooling Time: 15 minutes

2 sticks (1 cup) butter, softened
1 cup sugar
1½ cups finely ground almonds, *divided*
4 large eggs
1 tsp. vanilla
1 tsp. lemon extract
1 tsp. almond extract
1 Tbsp. grated lemon rind
1 cup flour
1 tsp. baking powder
¼ tsp. salt
¼ cup fresh lemon juice

Glaze:
¼ cup fresh lemon juice
1½-2 cups confectioners sugar
10 whole almonds, *optional*

1. In a large electric mixing bowl, cream together butter, sugar, and 1 cup finely ground almonds until fluffy.
2. Add eggs, one at a time, beating well after each addition.
3. Add 3 extracts and lemon rind. Beat again to incorporate.
4. In a separate mixing bowl, stir together flour, baking powder, and salt. Add to creamed mixture alternately with lemon juice.
5. Spoon batter into a greased and floured 8" springform pan.
6. Bake at 350° for 50 minutes. Cool for 15 minutes. Release springform pan.
7. While cake is still warm, and with the pan sides removed, whisk together lemon juice and confectioners sugar to make the glaze.
8. Spread glaze generously over top and sides of cake. Sprinkle remaining ground almonds over glaze while it is still wet. Garnish with whole almonds if you wish.

Colossal Caramel Apple Trifle

Jane Hindal
Grandin, MI

Makes 35-40 servings

Prep Time: 35 minutes
Baking Time: 30 minutes
Cooling Time: 50-60 minutes

1 pkg. yellow cake mix
6 cups cold milk
3 3.4-02. pkgs. instant vanilla pudding
1 tsp. cinnamon
12.25-02. container of caramel ice cream topping
1½ cups chopped pecans, *divided*
2 21-oz. cans apple pie filling
2 16-oz. cartons frozen whipped topping, thawed

1. Make cake according to package directions. Bake in two greased 9" round cake pans.
2. Cool 10 minutes in pans before removing to wire racks to cool completely.
3. In a large bowl, whisk milk, dry pudding mix, and cinnamon for 2 minutes. Let stand 2 minutes or until soft-set.
4. Cut (if necessary) one cake layer to fit evenly in a clear 8-qt. punch bowl. Poke holes in cake with a long wooden skewer. Gradually pour ⅓ of the caramel topping over the cake.
5. Sprinkle with ½ cup pecans and spread with half the pudding mixture.
6. Spoon one can pie filling over pudding.
7. Spread one carton whipped topping over pie filling.
8. Top with remaining cake and repeat layers
9. Drizzle with remaining caramel topping and sprinkle with remaining pecans.

Tips for building this Colossus:

1. If your punch bowl is larger in the middle than at the bottom and top, use the cut-off pieces of cake from the first layer to fill in around the edges of the cake on the second layer.
2. Again, if your bowl is larger in the middle than at the bottom and top, you'll need a scant third of the caramel topping on the first layer, and more than a third on the second layer.
3. When spreading the top layer of whipped topping, use the back of a large spoon to even it out. Then touch the spoon here-and-there to the top- ping and lift to form peaks.

Tip:

Buy an oven thermometer so you can check your oven's true heat and temperature.

Apple Bake

Barbara Sparks
Glen Burnie, MD

Makes 6-8 servings

Prep Time: 10-15 minutes
Baking Time: 20-30 minutes

⅔ cup sugar
¾ cup flour
pinch of salt
1½ tsp. baking powder
1½ tsp. cinnamon, *or* to taste
2 eggs
¾ tsp. vanilla
¾ cup chopped nuts
1½ cups Gala apples, chopped, *or* other baking apple, peeled *or* unpeeled
a little water to thin

1. Lightly grease an 8" or 9" pie plate.
2. Thoroughly mix all ingredients and spread in pie plate.
3. Bake at 350° for 20-30 minutes, until top is browned. (The mix will puff up to fit the pie plate.)

Variation:

Cut the cake into wedges and spoon the following warm sauce over top:

1 cup sugar
1 stick (½ cup) butter, cut in pieces
½ cup heavy cream
1 tsp. vanilla

Place all ingredients in a saucepan. Stir. Bring to a boil over medium-high heat. Cook 3 minutes, stirring frequently.

—Christine Heuser
Farmingdale, NJ

Gooey Apple Dumplings

Kathy Deal
Noblesville, IN

Makes 8 servings

Prep Time: 15-25 minutes
Cooking/Baking Time: 50-70 minutes

2 8" pie crusts, unbaked
3-4 firm baking apples (Granny Smith are good)
8 tsp. brown sugar
8 tsp. butter
8 dashes of cinnamon

Syrup:
1 cup sugar
2 cups water
3 Tbsp. butter
¼ tsp. cinnamon

1. In a medium-sized saucepan, mix the syrup ingredients together. Boil 3 minutes, watching carefully that the mixture doesn't boil over.
2. Meanwhile, cut the pie crusts into quarters.
3. Divide sliced, pared apples over the crust quarters. Top each with 1 teaspoon brown sugar, 1 teaspoon butter, and a dash of cinnamon.
4. Wrap up each dumpling. Seal the seam with a dab of water.
5. Place in a greased 9 x 13 baking pan. Pour syrup over top.
6. Bake at 350° for 40-60 minutes, or until nicely browned.

Butter Rum Bananas

Shari Jensen
Fountain, CO

Makes 4 servings

Prep Time: 5 minutes
Cooking Time: 10 minutes

2 Tbsp. butter
½ cup sugar
2 Tbsp. water
2 Tbsp. light rum
½ Tbsp. lemon juice grated rind of half a lemon
½ tsp. vanilla *or* rum flavoring
4 small bananas, peeled and halved
whipping cream *or* ice cream

1. Melt butter in a large skillet. Add sugar and water. Stir well. Cook until reduced to heavy syrup, stirring occasionally so the mixture doesn't stick to the bottom of the pan.
2. Add rum, lemon juice, rind, and your choice of flavoring. Cook 2 minutes, or until golden in color.
3. Remove from stove and add banana pieces. Plunge them into the syrup, covering them as well as possible.
4. Serve warm, not hot, topped with a dollop of whipped cream or alongside scoops of ice cream.

Blueberry Tart

Susan Kasting
Jenks, OK

Makes 6-8 servings

Prep Time: 20 minutes
Cooking and Baking Time: 25 minutes
Chilling Time: 1-2 hours

1 pkg. frozen puff pastry, thawed
1 egg
3 Tbsb. water, *divided*
½ cup, plus 2 Tbsp., sugar, divided
3½ cups blueberries, fresh *or* frozen
2 Tbsp. instant tapioca
2 tsp. finely grated lemon peel
1 Tbsp. lemon juice

1. Roll dough into a 12" square. Fit into 10" tart or pie pan. Cut off excess dough.
2. Roll out scraps and cut into small shapes with cookie cutters.
3. In a small bowl, beat together egg and 1 Tbsp. water. With a pastry brush, brush sides of tart and small cut-outs with egg wash. Sprinkle tart shell and cutouts with 2 Tbsp. sugar.
4. Lay cut-outs in a cake pan. Place in oven, along with the tart shell. Bake at 400° for 12-15 minutes, until golden brown.
5. While the pastry is baking combine in a saucepan, the blueberries, ½ cup sugar, 2 Tbsp. water, tapioca, lemon peel, and lemon juice. Bring to a boil until berries burst.
6. Lower temperature and simmer until tapioca dissolves (about 10 minutes) and mixture has thickened. Stir occasionally.
7. Pour berry mixture into shell. Lay pastry cut-outs over top.
8. Chill for 1-2 hours before serving.

Chocolate Raspberry Torte

Pam McAllister
Wooster, OH

Makes 10-12 servings

Prep Time: 35 minutes
Baking Time: 25-30 minutes
Cooling Time: 1 hour

18.25-02. pkg. chocolate cake mix
3-oz. pkg. cream cheese, softened
¾ cup cold milk
3.4-oz. pkg. instant vanilla pudding
8-oz. container frozen whipped topping, thawed
2 cups fresh raspberries confectioners sugar fresh mint and additional raspberries, *optional*

1. Prepare the cake according to package directions, using 3 greased and floured 9" round cake pans.
2. Bake at 350° for 25-30 minutes, or until toothpick inserted in center comes out clean.
3. Cool for 10 minutes in pan. Remove from pans to wire racks to cool completely.
4. While the cake is baking, beat the cream cheese in a mixing bowl until fluffy.
5. In a separate bowl, combine milk and pudding. Add to cream cheese mixture and mix well.
6. Fold whipped topping and raspberries into creamy mixture.
7. Place one cake layer on a serving plate. Spread with half the creamy fruit filling. Repeat layers, ending with a cake layer.
8. Just before serving, dust with confectioners sugar. Garnish with mint leaves and raspberries if you wish. Store in the refrigerator until the moment you're ready to serve.

Tip:
You can substitute sliced fresh strawberries for raspberries.

Tip:
Use light brown sugar for a caramel flavor. Use dark brown sugar when you prefer a molasses flavor and color.

Chocolate Chip Date Cake

Shari Jensen
Fountain, CO
Rebecca Meyerkorth
Wamego, KS

Makes 9 servings

Prep Time: 20 minutes
Baking Time: 30-35 minutes

1 cup chopped dates
1½ cups boiling water
1¾ tsp. baking soda, *divided*
½ cup butter, at room temperature
1 cup sugar
1½ cups flour
2 eggs
1 tsp. vanilla

Topping:
½ cup sugar
½ cup chopped walnuts
6-oz. pkg. chocolate chips

1. Combine dates, boiling water, and 1 tsp. baking soda in a small bowl. Let cool.
2. In a large mixing bowl, cream together butter and sugar.
3. In a separate bowl, combine flour and ¾ tsp. baking soda. Stir into creamed mixture.
4. Add eggs and vanilla. Stir well.
5. Stir in cooled dates.
6. Pour into a lightly greased 9" square baking dish.
7. Make topping by combining sugar, walnuts, and chocolate chips. Sprinkle over cake batter.
8. Bake at 375° for 30-35 minutes. (Warning: The cake will likely sink in the middle. Despite that, it's ready to serve when a toothpick inserted in the center comes out clean.) Serve warm or cold.

Tip:
Try baking with glass paas and metal pans to see which You prefer. You may have to lower the oven temperature by 25-50 degrees when cooking in glass pans to prevent burning.

Variation:
Bake the cake according to Step 8 after com- pleting Step 6 above. In other words, eliminate the topping. Instead, make the following sauce, cube the finished cake, and layer the cake and sauce together in a sewing bowl.

Sauce:
3-4 Tbsp. flour
½ cup cold water
1 cup brown sugar
1½ cups hot water
1 Tbsp. butter
1 tsp. vanilla
pinch of salt
whipped cream

1. Combine flour and cold water in a jar with a tight-fitting lid. Shake until well mixed and without lumps. Set aside.
2. Combine the brown sugar, hot water, butter, vanilla, and salt in a saucepan. Bring to a gently boil.
3. Shake flour-water mixture again. Then pour slowly into boiling syrup mixture in saucepan. Stir constantly until mixture thickens and becomes smooth.
4. Cool sauce to room temperature.
5. To serve, break the cake into small pieces. In a serving bowl, place a layer of cake cubes. Top with sauce. Continue layering until all cake and all sauce are used. Top with whipped cream.

Chocolate-Almond Biscotti

Beth Maurer
Columbus Grove, OH

Makes 48 biscotti slices

Prep Time: 30-40 minutes
Baking Time: 40-47 minutes per sheet
Cooling Time: 2 hours

1½ cups sliced almonds, toasted, *divided*
2 sticks (1 cup) butter, softened
2 cups sugar
⅔ cup unsweetened cocoa powder
1 tsp. baking powder
1 tsp. baking soda
½ tsp. salt
3 eggs
1 tsp. almond extract
3½ cups flour
4 blocks white almond bark, melted

1. Preheat the oven to 350°. Lightly grease a cookie sheet and set it aside.
2. Place ¾ cup almonds in a food processor and pulse until ground.
3. In a large electric mixer bowl, beat butter with mixer. Add sugar and beat until well mixed.
4. Add cocoa powder, baking powder, baking soda, and salt to mixer bowl. Beat until combined.
5. Beat in eggs and almond extract.
6. Add flour by cupfuls, mixing well after each addition. Batter will be quite stiff, and you may need to add the last cup of flour by hand.
7. Remove from mixer, and by hand stir in remaining ¾ cup sliced almonds.
8. Divide dough in half. On waxed paper, and with floured hands, shape dough into two 14"-long rolls
9. Place rolls on greased and floured cookie sheet, at least 5" apart. Flatten slightly.
10. Bake 25-30 minutes, or until wooden pick inserted near center comes out clean.
11. Cool on cookie sheet for 1 hour. On a cutting board, cut each roll diagonally into ½" thick slices, about 24 slices from each roll.
12. Place slices cut-side down on the same cookie sheets you used for the first baking. Bake at 350° for 8 minutes.
13. Turn cookies over and bake 7-9 more minutes, or until cookies are dry and beginning to get crisp.
14. Remove from cookie sheets to wire racks. Cool completely.
15. With a spoon, drizzle melted almond bark over tops of biscotti.
16. Store in an airtight container.

These are great in the morning with coffee or in the evening as dessert. They are perfect for dipping in your favorite hot beverage.

I made these for my mother as part of her Christmas gift. They disappeared very quickly, and she keeps asking me to make more!

Tip:

I have several "half-sheet" commercial baking pans. They are a little heavier than regular cookie sheets and I never have trouble with burned cookies. They are wonderful. Mine came from a bigbox store, but they are likely available at restaurant supply stores, as well.

Peanut Butter Chocolate Chip Cookies

Wendy B. Martzall
New Holland, PA

Makes 100 small cookies

Prep Time: 10 minutes
Baking Time: 8-10 minutes per sheet

1 cup peanut butter
¾ cup butter, at room temperature
¾ cup sugar
¾ cup packed brown sugar
1 tsp. vanilla
2 large eggs
2 cups flour
1 tsp. baking soda
2 cups semi-sweet chocolate chips

1. Preheat oven to 375°.
2. Beat together peanut butter, butter, sugars, and vanilla with an electric mixer.
3. Beat in eggs. Gradually beat in flour and baking soda.
4. Stir in chocolate chips by hand.
5. Drop by rounded teaspoons, 2 inches apart, on ungreased cookie sheets.
6. Bake 8-10 minutes, or until lightly browned.
7. Cool on cookie sheets for 1 minute before removing. Cool completely on wire racks.

Variations:

1. Use the same dough, but get a different result! After

Step 3, refrigerate the dough for half an hour or so, so that it's easy to handle.

Using a 7-oz. pkg. of miniature peanut butter cups, wrap a ball of cookie dough around each little peanut butter cup. Place the wrapped balls in the fridge for 1 hour.

When ready to bake, place balls 2 inches apart on ungreased cookie sheets. Bake at 350° for 12-14 minutes, or until the bottom edges of the balls are golden.

After the baked balls have cooled, drizzle them with melted chocolate chips.

— Stacy Schmucker Stoltzfus,
Enola, PA

2. After Step 3, chill the dough for half an hour in the fridge. Then roll into small walnut-sized balls and place each ball in a cup in a mini-muffin tin.

Bake at 375° for 8-9 minutes. Remove from oven. Gently press 1 miniature peanut butter cup into each cookie.

Cool in pan 10 minutes. Remove from pan and finish cooling on a wire rack.

—Carol Sherwood
Batavia, NY

Soft, Chewy Molasses Cookies

Martha Ann Auker
Landisburg, PA

Makes 3 dozen cookies

Prep Time: 10 minutes
Baking Time: 8-10 minutes per cookie sheet

1 stick (½ cup) butter, at room temperature
1 cup brown sugar
1 egg
2 cups flour
2 tsp. baking soda
2 tsp. ginger
2 tsp. cinnamon
4 Tbsp. black strap molasses sugar

1. In an electric mixing bowl, cream together butter and sugar. Add egg. Mix well.
2. In a separate bowl, mix together flour, baking soda, ginger, and cinnamon. Add to creamed mixture, alternately with the molasses, until well blended.
3. Shape batter into 1" balls. Roll each in sugar. Place 2" apart on a greased cookie sheet.
4. Bake at 350° for 8-10 minutes.
5. Let stand on cookie sheet about 2 minutes before removing to wire rack to cool.

Variation:

Add ½ tsp. ground cloves to Step 2, if you wish.

—Marjora Mier
Archbold, OH

Butter Crescents

Janet Hardy
Arp, TX

Makes 3 dozen cookies

Prep Time: 10 minutes
Baking Time: 10-14 minutes per sheet

2 sticks (1 cup) butter, softened (no substitutes)
5 Tbsp. sifted confectioners sugar
1 tsp. vanilla
1 Tbsp. water
2 cups flour
1 cup chopped pecans
sifted confectioners sugar for dusting

1. Blend butter and sugar together in a mixing bowl with an electric mixer.
2. Mix in vanilla, water, flour, and pecans.
3. Shape into crescents and place on an ungreased baking sheet.
4. Bake at 350° just until slightly browned, about 10-14 minutes.
5. Remove from oven and allow to cool for 3 minutes. Then roll immediately in sifted confectioners sugar.
6. Place on wire racks and allow to coolfully. Watch them disappear!

Raspberry Almond Shortbread Thumbprints

sherlyn Hess
Millersville, PA

Makes 3-3½ dozen cookies

Prep Time: 35 minutes
Baking Time: 8-10 minutes per sheet

⅔ cup sugar
2 sticks (1 cup) butter, softened
½ tsp. almond extract
2 cups flour
½ cup raspberry jelly

Glaze:

1 cup confectioners sugar
1½ tsp. almond extract
2-3 tsp. water

1. In an electric mixer bowl, combine sugar, butter, and ½ tsp. almond extract until creamy.
2. Add flour. Mix well.
3. Shape into 1" balls. Place 2" apart on ungreased cookie sheets.
4. With your thumb, make an indentation in the center of each cookie. Fill each indentation with ¼ tsp. jam.
5. Bake at 350° for 8-10 minutes. Do not brown.
6. Remove from cookie sheets onto wire racks. Cool 10 minutes.
7. Combine confectioners sugar, 1½ tsp. almond extract, and water. Drizzle over cookies. Cool completely.

Tip:

I cool these cookies on racks. Then when I drizzle them with the glaze, the excess falls through the rack and the cookies have a nicer look than when the glaze puddles around them.

Tip:

I usually make cookie dough and put it in the refrigerator instead of immediately baking it. Then I bake the cookies the next day. The dough is usually easier to work with when it's cold, and if I'm short on time, I've spread the job over two days.

Butterscotch Bars

Dottie Geraci
Burtonsville, MD

Makes 25 bars

Prep Time: 20 minutes
Baking Time: 40 minutes

6 Tbsp. butter, at room temperature
1½ cups brown sugar, *divided*
1¼ cups all-purpose flour, *divided*
2 eggs
1½ tsp. vanilla extract
1 tsp. baking powder
½ tsp. salt
½ cup chopped walnuts
1 cup butterscotch morsels

1. In a small mixing bowl, cream butter and ½ cup brown sugar together until light and fluffy. Blend in 1 cup flour and mix until crumbly.
2. Pat mixture into an ungreased 7 x 11 x 1½ baking pan. Bake at 350° for 10 minutes. Remove from oven.
3. In the mixing bowl, beat eggs until thick and lemon-colored. Add 1 cup brown sugar and vanilla. Continue beating.
4. In a separate bowl, combine ¼ cup flour, baking powder, and salt. Add to egg mixture. Stir in nuts.
5. Spread over baked crust. Sprinkle with butterscotch morsels.
6. Bake 30 minutes more. Cool and cut into 2 x 1% bars.

Cheesecake Bars

Leona Yoder
Hartville, OH

Makes 12 bars

Prep Time: 10-15 minutes
Baking Time: 40 minutes

1 cup flour
⅓ cup brown sugar
⅓ cup butter, melted
8-oz. pkg. cream cheese, at room temperature
¼ cup sugar
1 large egg
1 Tbsp. lemon juice
2 Tbsp. milk
1 tsp. vanilla

1. Mix flour, brown sugar, and butter together in an electric mixing bowl. Reserve 1 cup mixture. Press remainder into a greased 8 x 8 bak- ing pan.
2. Bake at 350° for 15 minutes.
3. Meanwhile, in the mixing bowl, beat together the remaining ingredients. Spread on baked crust.
4. Top with reserved crumbs and bake for 25 minutes, or until set.

Black Bottom Cake or Cupcakes

Joleen Albrecht
Gladstone, MI

Makes 15 servings of cake, or about 18 cupcakes

Prep Time: 20 minutes
Baking Time: 20-25 minutes

8 ozs. cream cheese, at room temperature
1 egg
1⅓ cups sugar, *divided*
⅜ tsp. salt, *divided*
12 ozs. semi-sweet chocolate chips
1½ cups flour
¼ cup unsweetened cocoa powder
1 cup sugar
¼ tsp. salt
½ tsp. baking soda
1 cup cold water
⅓ cup vegetable oil
1 Tbsp. vinegar
1 Tbsp. vanilla

1. Mix cream cheese, egg, ⅓ cup sugar, and ⅛ tsp. salt together with an electric mixer.
2. Stir in the chocolate chips by hand. Set aside.
3. Combine and mix the remaining ingredients in a separate bowl.
4. Pour cake batter into a greased 9 x 13 baking pan.
5. Spoon cream cheese mixture on top. Swirl with a fork.
6. Bake at 350° for 25 minutes, or until a toothpick inserted in the center comes out clean.

To make cupcakes, line cupcake pans with cupcake papers.

Spoon batter into the cups, making each about half-full. Put about 1 tablespoon cream cheese mixture on top of each. Bake at 350° for 20-25 minutes, or until toothpick inserted in centers comes out clean.

Tip:

Do not open the oven door when baking an angel food cake. Use an electric knife in order to cut an angel food cake with a clean cut.

Cajun Pineapple Cake

Jan Sams
Lancaster, PA
Kay Magruder
Seminole, OK

Makes 12-16 servings

Prep Time: 20 minutes
Baking Time: 50 minutes

3 cups flour
½ tsp. salt
1½ cups sugar
1½ tsp. baking soda
2 eggs
15-oz. can crushed pineapple, undrained
¼ cup orange juice

Frosting:

¾ cup sugar
¼ cup evaporated milk
1 stick (½ cup) butter
1 cup chopped pecans
1 cup shredded coconut

1. Make the cake by combining the flour, salt, sugar, and baking soda in a large mixing bowl.
2. In a separate bowl, mix together eggs, pineapple, and orange juice.
3. Add wet ingredients to dry ingredients. Mix well.
4. Pour into a greased 9 x 13 baking pan.
5. Bake at 325° for 50 minutes, or until a toothpick inserted in the center comes out clean.
6. While the cake is baking, place the sugar, milk, and butter for the frosting in a saucepan. Bring to a boil. Continue simmering until the butter is melted. Cool.
7. Stir in pecans and coconut. Mix well.
8. Spread topping on hot cake. Place under broiler for a few minutes until lightly browned. But watch carefully so the topping doesn't burn!

Topping Variation:

1 stick (½ cup) butter, softened
8-oz. pkg. cream cheese, softened
1½ cups confectioners sugar
1 tsp. vanilla
chopped walnuts

1. Cream together butter and cream cheese.
2. Stir in sugar and vanilla, stirring until well mixed and creamy.
3. Spread on lukewarm cake.
4. Garnish with walnuts.

—Erma Hoover
Lititz, PA

—Linda Overholt
Abbeville, SC

Coconut Cake

Michele Ruvola
Selden, NY

Makes 12 servings

Prep Time: 15-20 minutes
Baking Time: 30-35 minutes
Cooling Time: 1 hour

2 cups flour
1 tsp. baking powder
2 sticks (1 cup) butter, softened
1⅓ cups white sugar
3 eggs
1 tsp. vanilla
1 cup milk 1-1 ½ cups shredded coconut, according to your preference
confectioners sugar

1. In a medium-sized mixing bowl, combine flour and baking powder. Set aside.
2. Beat the butter with an electric mixer until creamy. Gradually add sugar. Blend until fluffy.
3. Add eggs, one at a time, beating well between each. Add vanilla.
4. Add flour mixture alter-nately with milk. Beat well after each addition.
5. Fold in coconut.
6. Spoon into a lightly greased 9" springform pan. Bake at 350° for 30-35 minutes, or until golden brown.
7. Sprinkle cooled cake with confectioners sugar before serving.

Harvest Cranberry Apple Pie

Janelle Reitz
Lancaster, PA

Makes 6-8 servings

Prep Time: 20 minutes
Baking Time: 55-60 minutes

1 cup sugar
2 Tbsp. cornstarch
½ tsp. allspice
2 tsp. cinnamon
4 large tart baking apples, pared, cored, and sliced
1 cup fresh, whole cranberries*
½ cup chopped walnuts
dough for a double-crust 9" pie
2 Tbsp. butter, cut into pieces
1 egg white, beaten

1. In a large mixing bowl, combine sugar, cornstarch, allspice, and cinnamon.
2. Add apples, cranberries, and nuts. (*Frozen cranberries also work in this pie. Allow them to thaw before stirring them into the mix.) Toss to coat.
3. Divide dough. Roll out one half. Fit into a 9" pie pan.
4. Fill with fruit mixture and dot with butter.
5. Roll out second half. Place pie crust on top. Seal, trim, and flute edges. Brush top with egg whites.
6. Bake at 400° for 55-60 minutes, or until crust is golden brown and filling is bubbly. (You may need to loosely cover the edges of the crust with foil to prevent it from burning during the last 30 minutes of the baking time.)

Greatest Apple Pie

Lynette Nisly
Lancaster, PA

Makes 8 servings

Prep Time: 30 minutes
Baking Time: 45-55 minutes

Filling:
1 cup sugar
2 Tbsp. flour
1 tsp. cinnamon
dash of nutmeg
dash of salt
6 cups peeled and sliced apples (Rome is my favorite)
unbaked 9" pie shell

Crumb Topping:
¼ cup brown sugar
¼ cup sugar
¾ cup flour
scant ⅓ cup solid shortening

1. To prepare filling, combine sugar, flour, cinnamon, nutmeg, and salt in a large bowl.
2. Add sliced apples and mix well. Put apple mixture in unbaked pie crust.
3. To prepare topping, combine sugars and flour in a medium-sized bowl.
4. Cut in shortening with a pastry blender or fork until crumbly. Sprinkle over apples.
5. Bake at 400° for 45-55 minutes.

When my husband and I were dating, I made this pie for him and he loved it. After that, he decided to think more seriously about our future together. He has convinced our children that I make the best apple pie, which they are not shy about stating whenever apple pie is sewed.

White Chocolate Pie

Jeanne Allen
Rye, CO

Makes 6 servings

Prep Time: 15-30 minutes
Chilling Time: 6 hours

8 ozs. white chocolate
20 large marshmallows
½ cup milk
½ pt. whipping cream
½ tsp. vanilla
½ cup toasted almonds, cut in half *or* coarsely chopped
9" baked pie crust

1. Over hot water in double boiler, melt chocolate and marshmallows over medium heat.
2. Stir in milk. Cool completely.
3. Whip cream in a chilled bowl until stiff.
4. Fold in vanilla.
5. Fold cooled chocolate mixture into flavored whipped cream.
6. Fold in almonds. Pour into pie shell.
7. Chill several hours before serving.

White Chocolate Crunch

Becky Harder
Monument, CO

Makes 20½-cup servings

Prep Time: 10 minutes
Cooking Time: 5-10 minutes

1 whole block of white chocolate
6 cups Chex cereal
2 cups M&Ms
2 cups small pretzels

1. Chop the white chocolate block into pieces. Place in a microwave-safe bowl. Microwave at 50% power for 2-3 minutes. Stir. Heat again at 50% power for 15 seconds. Stir. Continue heating for 15-second periods, following each by stirring, until the pieces around the edges are melted and the center of the bowl feels hot. Let stand for a minute and then stir. If solid pieces remain, continue the heating for 15-second periods, followed by stirring.
2. When the chocolate is fully melted, stir in cereal, M&Ms, and pretzels.
3. Spread out on waxed paper and let harden.
4. Break into chunks/pieces to serve.

Salted Peanut Squares

John D. Allen
Rye, CO

Makes 20-24 servings

Prep Time: 5 minutes
Cooking Time: 5 minutes
Chilling Time: 1 hour

16-oz. jar salted peanuts
3 Tbsp. butter
10-oz. pkg. peanut butter chips
2 cups miniature marshmallows
14-oz. can sweetened condensed milk

1. Cover the bottom of a greased 9 x 13 baking pan with half the salted peanuts.
2. In a saucepan, melt butter and peanut butter chips.
3. Stir in marshmallows and milk. Heat until melted.
4. Pour over peanuts.
5. Top with remaining peanuts.
6. Chill. Cut into squares.

Equivalent Measurements

dash = little less than ⅛ tsp.

3 teaspoons = 1 Tablespoon

2 Tablespoons = 1 oz.

4 Tablespoons = ¼ cup

5 Tablespoons plus 1 tsp. = ⅓ cup

8 Tablespoons = ½ cup

12 Tablespoons = ¾ cup

16 Tablespoons = 1 cup

1 cup = 8 oz. liquid

2 cups = 1 pint

4 cups = 1 quart

4 quarts = 1 gallon

1 stick butter = ¼ lb.

1 stick butter = ½ cup

1 stick butter = 8 Tbsp.

Beans, 1 lb. dried = 2-2½ cups (depending upon the size of the beans)

Bell peppers, 1 large = 1 cup chopped

Cheese, hard (for example, cheddar, Swiss, Monterey Jack, mozzarella), 1 lb. grated = 4 cups

Cheese, cottage, 1 lb. = 2 cups

Chocolate chips, 6-oz. pkg. = 1 scant cup

Crackers (butter, saltines, snack), 20 single crackers = 1 cup crumbs

Herbs, 1 Tbsp. fresh = 1 tsp. dried

Lemon, 1 medium-sized = 2-3 Tbsp. juice

Lemon, 1 medium-sized = 2-3 tsp. grated rind

Mustard, 1 Tbsp. prepared = 1 tsp. dry or ground mustard

Oatmeal, 1 lb. dry = about 5 cups dry

Onion, 1 medium-sized = ½ cup chopped

Macaronis, penne, and other small or tubular shapes, 1 lb. dry = 4 cups uncooked

Noodles, 1 lb. dry = 6 cups uncooked

Spaghetti, linguine, fettucine, 1 lb. dry = 4 cups uncooked

Potatoes, white, 1 lb. = 3 medium-sized potatoes = 2 cups mashed

Potatoes, sweet, 1 lb. = 3 medium-sized potatoes = 2 cups mashed

Rice, 1 lb. dry = 2 cups uncooked

Sugar, confectioners, 1 lb. = 3½ cups sifted

Whipping cream, 1 cup unwhipped = 2 cups whipped

Whipped topping, 8-oz. container = 3 cups

Yeast, dry, 1 envelope (¼ oz.) = 1 Tbsp.

Assumptions about Ingredients

flour = unbleached *or* white, and all-purpose

oatmeal or oats = dry, quick *or* rolled (old-fashioned), unless specified

pepper = black, finely ground

rice = regular, long-grain (not minute or instant unless specified)

salt = table salt

shortening = solid, not liquid

sugar = granulated sugar (not brown and not confectioners)

Three Hints

1 If you'd like to cook more at home–without being in a frenzy–go off by yourself with your cookbook some evening and make a week of menus. Then make a grocery list from that. Shop from your grocery list.

2 Thaw frozen food in a bowl in the fridge (not on the counter-top). If you forget to stick the food in the fridge, put it in a microwave-safe bowl and defrost it in the microwave just before you're ready to use it.

3 Let roasted meat, as well as pasta dishes with cheese, rest for 10-20 minutes before slicing or dishing. That will allow the juices to re-distribute themselves throughout the cooked food. You'll have juicier meat, and a better presentation of your pasta dish.

Substitute Ingredients
for when you're in a pinch

For one cup **buttermilk**—use 1 cup plain yogurt; or pour 1⅓ Tbsp. lemon juice or vinegar into a 1-cup measure. Fill the cup with milk. Stir and let stand for 5 minutes. Stir again before using.

For 1 oz. **unsweetened baking chocolate**—stir together 3 Tbsp. unsweetened cocoa powder and 1 Tbsp. butter, softened.

For 1 Tbsp. **cornstarch**—use 2 Tbsp. all-purpose flour; or 4 tsp. minute tapioca.

For 1 **garlic clove**—use ¼ tsp. garlic salt (reduce salt in recipe by ⅛ tsp.); or ⅛ tsp. garlic powder.

For 1 Tbsp. **fresh herbs**—use 1 tsp. dried herbs.

For ½ lb. **fresh mushrooms**—use 1 6-oz. can mushrooms, drained.

For 1 Tbsp. **prepared mustard**—use 1 tsp. dry or ground mustard.

For 1 **medium-sized fresh onion**—use 2 Tbsp. minced dried onion; or 2 tsp. onion salt (reduce salt in recipe by 1 tsp.); or 1 tsp. onion powder. Note: These substitutions will work for meat balls and meat loaf, but not for sautéing.

For 1 cup **sour milk**—use 1 cup plain yogurt; or pour 1 Tbsp. lemon juice or vinegar into a 1-cup measure. Fill with milk. Stir and then let stand for 5 minutes. Stir again before using.

For 2 Tbsp. **tapioca**—use 3 Tbsp. all-purpose flour.

For 1 cup canned **tomatoes**—use 1⅓ cups diced fresh tomatoes, cooked gently for 10 minutes.

For 1 Tbsp. **tomato paste**—use 1 Tbsp. ketchup.

For 1 Tbsp. **vinegar**—use 1 Tbsp. lemon juice.

For 1 cup **heavy cream**—add ⅓ cup melted butter to ¾ cup milk. ***Note:*** *This will work for baking and cooking, but not for whipping.*

For 1 cup **whipping cream**—chill thoroughly ⅔ cup evaporated milk, plus the bowl and beaters, then whip; or use 2 cups bought whipped topping.

For ½ cup **wine**—pour 2 Tbsp. wine vinegar into a ½-cup measure. Fill with broth (chicken, beef, or vegetable). Stir and then let stand for 5 minutes. Stir again before using.

Kitchen Tools and Equipment You Really Ought to Have

1 Make sure you have a little electric vegetable chopper, the size that will handle 1 cup of ingredients at a time.

2 Don't try to cook without a good paring knife that's sharp (and holds its edge) and fits in your hand.

3 Almost as important—a good chef's knife (we always called it a "butcher" knife) with a wide, sharp blade that's about 8 inches long, good for making strong cuts through meats.

4 You really ought to have a good serrated knife with a long blade, perfect for slicing bread.

5 Invest in at least one broad, flexible, heat-resistant spatula. And also a narrow one.

6 You ought to have a minimum of 2 wooden spoons, each with a 10-12 inch-long handle. They're perfect for stirring without scratching.

7 Get a washable cutting board. You'll still need it, even though you have an electric vegetable chopper (#1 above).

8 A medium-sized whisk takes care of persistent lumps in batters, gravies, and sauces when there aren't supposed to be any.

9 Get yourself a salad spinner.

Index

1-2-3-4 Casserole, 115
1-2-3 Barbecued Country Ribs, 128
8-Hour Tangy Beef, 78

A

After-Work Stew, 94
Almonds
  Cheese and Crab Dip, 18
  Chicken Rice Special, 177
  Company Casserole, 177
  Spicy Party Mix, 19
  Tuna Noodle Casserole, 202
Angel Chicken Pasta, 168
Apple and Brown Sugar Corned Beef, 88
Apple and Onion Beef Pot Roast, 78
Apple Caramel Dessert, 250
Apple Chicken Stew, 67
Apple Cider *See Cider*
Apple Cranberry Compote, 245
Apple Crisp, 250
Apple-Nut Bread Pudding, 254
Apple Oatmeal, 22
Apple Pie Filling
  Wagon Master Apple-Cherry Sauce, 246
Apple Schnitz, 248
Apple Walnut Squash, 214
Apples 'n' Yams, 218
Apples, Sauerkraut, and Chops, 136
Apples
  Apple and Onion Beef Pot Roast, 78
  Apple Caramel Dessert, 250
  Apple Chicken Stew, 67
  Apple Cranberry Compote, 245
  Apple Crisp, 250
  Apple-Nut Bread Pudding, 254
  Apple Oatmeal, 22
  Apple Walnut Squash, 214
  Apples 'n' Yams, 218
  Apples, Sauerkraut, and Chops, 136
  Autumn Harvest Pork Loin, 129
  Brats and Spuds, 141
  Breakfast Apple Cobbler, 25
  Butternut Squash and Apple Soup, 43
  Caramel Apples, 249
  Caramel Peanut Butter Dip, 19
  Chocolate Fondue, 259
  Christmas Apple Date Pudding, 242
  Chunky Sweet Spiced Apple Butter, 20
  Country-Style Ribs and Sauerkraut, 128
  Cranberry Applesauce, 247
  Cranberry Baked Apples, 248
  Fruit and Grains Breakfast Cereal, 23
  Fruit Dessert Topping, 246
  Fruited Wild Rice with Pecans, 228
  Golden Autumn Stew, 145
  Homemade Applesauce, 248
  Hot Applesauce Breakfast, 25
  Low-Fat Apple Cake, 256
  No Fuss Sauerkraut, 131
  Orange Yams, 217
  Sauerkraut & Pork Ribs, 129
  Sausage and Sweet Potatoes, 142
  Slow-Cooker Kidney Beans, 197
  Sweet Potatoes and Apples, 218
  Turkey Thighs, Acorn Squash, and Apples, 186
  Tzimmes, 214
  Warmed Spiced Fruit, 245
  Wine Tender Roast, 75
Apples, Dried
  Apple Schnitz, 248
  Schnitz und Knepp, 149
Applesauce Meatballs, 106
Applesauce
  Applesauce Meatballs, 106
  Chicken with Applesauce, 167
  Edna's Baked Beans, 198
  Harvest Kielbasa, 143
  Pork Roast with Applesauce "Pulled Pork", 138
  Sweet Potatoes with Applesauce, 218
Apricots
  Curried Fruit, 247
  Saucy Apricot Chicken, 167
Apricots, Dried
  Festive Fruit Compote, 246
  Fruit and Grains Breakfast Cereal, 23
  Fruit Compote, 245
  Fruited Turkey and Yams, 187
  Oxford Canal Chops Deluxe, 135
  Pork Loin with Spiced Fruit Sauce, 130
  Russian Red Lentil Soup, 31
  Tzimmes, 214
Arlene's BBQ Meatballs, 103
Arroz con Queso, 204
Artichokes
  Creamy Artichoke Dip, 9
Asian Meatballs, 106
Asian Pork Soup, 62
Asparagus
  Delicious Chicken with Curried Cream Sauce, 161
Au Gratin Green Beans, 206
Auntie Ginny's Baked Beans, 195
Aunt Thelma's Homemade Soup, 46
Autumn Harvest Pork Loin, 129

B

Back-on-Track Soup, 30
Bacon Cheese Dip, 13
Baked Acorn Squash, 213
Baked Beans and Chops, 134
Baked Chicken and Rice, 178
"Baked" Sweet Potatoes, 217
Bananas
  Banana Loaf, 243
  Chocolate Fondue, 259
Barbara Jean's Junior Beef, 96
Barbara Jean's Whole Pork Tenderloin, 129
Barbecue Sauce and Hamburgers, 108
Barbecue
  1-2-3 Barbecued Country Ribs, 128
  Arlene's BBQ Meatballs, 103
  Barbecue Sauce and Hamburgers, 108
  Barbecued Beans, 191
  Barbecued Black Beans with Sweet Potatoes, 219
  Barbecued Chicken, 164
  Barbecued Chicken Sandwiches, 181
  Barbecued Chicken with Peppers, Onions, and Celery, 164
  Barbecued Hamburgers, 114
  Barbecued Pork and Beef Sandwiches, 155
  Barbecued Pork Chops, 132
  Barbecued Ribs, 127
  Barbecued Turkey Cutlets, 187
  Barbecued Turkey Legs, 186
  Beef Barbecue Sandwiches, 97
  Beef-Venison Barbecue, 200
  Dianna's Barbecue, 110
  Easy Meatballs for a Group, 104
  Easy Roast Beef Barbecue, 98
  Ham Barbecue, 156
  No-More-Bottled Barbecue Sauce, 109
  Pork Barbecue, 155
  Pork Roast with Applesauce "Pulled Pork", 138
  Potluck Beef Barbecue Sandwiches, 96
  Pulled Pork BBQ, 138
  Tender Barbecued Chicken, 166
  There's-No-Easier Roast Beef, 78
  Turkey Barbecue, 187
  Zesty Pulled Pork, 138
Barbecued Beans, 191
Barbecued Black Beans with Sweet Potatoes, 219
Barbecued Chicken, 164
Barbecued Chicken Sandwiches, 181
Barbecued Chicken with Peppers, Onions, and Celery, 164
Barbecued Chuck Steak, 87
Barbecued Hamburgers, 114
Barbecued Pork and Beef Sandwiches, 155
Barbecued Pork Chops, 132
Barbecued Ribs, 127
Barbecued Turkey Legs, 186
Barley
  Beef Barley Soup, 50
  Grandma's Barley Soup, 35
  Hungarian Barley Stew, 95
  Meatball-Barley Casserole, 108
  Your-Choice-of-Vegetables Soup, 48
Basil
  Caponata, 216
Bavarian Beef, 80
Bean Sprouts
  Asian Pork Soup, 62
  Chicken Cashew Dish, 174
Beans, Baked
  Baked Beans and Chops, 134
  Calico Beans, 193
  Galloping Beans, 194
  Lotsa-Beans Pot, 194
  Zesty Calico Beans, 198
Beans, Black
  Barbecued Black Beans with Sweet Potatoes, 219
  Black Bean and Ham Soup, 32
  Black Bean and Tomato Soup, 32
  Black Bean Chili con Carne, 59
  Black Beans with Ham, 151
  Chicken Azteca, 175
  Creole Black Beans, 195
  Partytime Beans, 197
  Pumpkin Black-Bean Turkey Chili, 69
  Red Pepper Chicken, 176
  Southwestern Bean Soup with Cornmeal Dumplings, 29

Taco Soup with Corn, 52
Three-Bean Burrito Bake, 125
Three-Bean Chili, 56
Vegetarian Baked Beans, 198
Wintertime Vegetable Chili, 47
Beans, Black-Eyed Peas
Black-Eyed Pea Chili, 62
Black-Eyed Peas and Ham, 212
Lotsa-Beans Pot, 194
Partytime Beans, 197
Beans, Butter
Calico Beans, 193
Dawn's Special Beans, 196
Easy Hamburger Vegetable Soup, 49
Election Lunch, 144
Galloping Beans, 194
Hamburger Beans, 192
One-Pot Dinner, 193
Beans, Cannellini
Italian Chicken Chili, 66
Pasta Bean Pot, 192
Beans, Chili
Chili Casserole, 146
Extra Easy Chili, 57
Grandma's Chili, 58
Haystacks, 123
Hot Chili Dip, 11
Our Favorite Chili, 54
Beans, Garbanzo
Election Lunch, 144
Garbanzo Souper, 31
Minestra Di Ceci, 204
Three-Bean Chili, 56
Wash-Day Stew, 96
White Chili, 66
Beans, Great Northern
Calico Beans, 193
Great Northern Bean Soup, 29
Ground Beef Soup, 51
Keilbasa Stew, 143
Partytime Beans, 197
Polish Sausage Bean Soup, 35
Slow-Cooker Bean Soup, 28
Southwestern Bean Soup with Cornmeal Dumplings, 29
White Chili, 66
Zesty Calico Beans, 198
Beans, Green *See Green Beans*
Beans, Kidney
Back-on-Track Soup, 30
Calico Beans, 193
Chili con Carne Supreme, 53
Chili Soup, 54
Country Auction Chili Soup, 55
Dawn's Special Beans, 196
Easy Hamburger Vegetable Soup, 49
Election Lunch, 144
Galloping Beans, 194
Grandma's Chili, 58
Hamburger Beans, 192
Hearty Chili, 56
Hearty Potato Chili, 58
Hot and Good Chili, 55
Italian Chicken Chili, 66
Lotsa-Beans Pot, 194
Mexican Goulash, 124
Mexican Rice and Bean Soup, 37
Naturally Colorful Vegetable Soup, 44
Norma's Vegetarian Chili, 47
One-Pot Dinner, 193
Our Favorite Chili, 54
Partytime Beans, 197
Pasta Bean Pot, 192
Pizza Beans, 196
Rice and Beans—and Sausage, 144
Sausage Pasta Stew, 145
Slow-Cooked Chili, 54
Slow-Cooker Chili, 53
Slow-Cooker Kidney Beans, 197
Slowly Cooked Chili, 55
Southwestern Bean Soup with Cornmeal Dumplings, 29
Taco Soup with Corn, 52
The Chili Connection, 57
Three-Bean Burrito Bake, 125
Three-Bean Chili, 56
Trio Bean Casserole, 193
Turkey Chili, 71
Zesty Calico Beans, 198
Zesty Minestrone, 28
Beans, Lima
Aunt Thelma's Homemade Soup, 46
Election Lunch, 144
Grandma's Barley Soup, 35
Ham and Lima Beans, 151
Hungarian Barley Stew, 95
Hungarian Beef Stew, 95
Lotsa-Beans Pot, 194
Partytime Beans, 197
Pioneer Beans, 196
Ribs and Limas, 84
Beans, Marrow
White Marrow Bean Soup, 36
Beans, Mexican-Style
Arroz con Queso, 204
Beans, Navy
Hearty Bean and Vegetable Soup, 27
Navy Bean and Bacon Chowder, 34
Navy Bean Soup, 34
Party Bean Soup, 33
Red and Green Bean Soup, 33
White Chicken Chili, 65
Beans, Pinto
Back-on-Track Soup, 30
Cassoulet Chowder, 35
Galloping Beans, 194
Hearty Chili, 56
Lotsa-Beans Pot, 194
Minestrone, 28
Pizza Beans, 196
Slow-Cooker Bean Soup, 28
Slow-Cooker Chili, 53
Southwestern Bean Soup with Cornmeal Dumplings, 29
Taco Soup with Hominy, 52
Three-Bean Burrito Bake, 125
Turkey Chili, 71
White Chili, 66
Beans, Pork and
Auntie Ginny's Baked Beans, 195
Barbecued Beans, 191
Cowboy Beans, 192
Deb's Baked Beans, 194
Edna's Baked Beans, 198
"Famous" Baked Beans, 191
Hamburger Beans, 192
One-Pot Dinner, 193
Trio Bean Casserole, 193
Beans, Ranch-Style
Taco Soup with Corn, 52
Beans, Red
Dawn's Special Beans, 196
Red Beans and Pasta, 197
Beans, Refried
Cheesy Hot Bean Dip, 11
M&T's Chili, 59
Taco Appetizer, 13
Tiajuana Tacos, 126
Beans, White
Dawn's Special Beans, 196
Rice & Bean Soup, 37
Sauerkraut-Sausage Bean Soup, 64
Three-Bean Chili, 56
Vegetarian Baked Beans, 198
Wash-Day Stew, 96
White Marrow Bean Soup, 36
Beef and Macaroni, 120
Beef and Pepper Rice, 122
Beef and Sausage Spaghetti Sauce, 112
Beef Barbecue Sandwiches, 97
Beef Barley Soup, 50
Beef Dumpling Soup, 49
Beef Mushroom Casserole, 90
Beef Pot Roast, 81
Beef Ribs with Sauerkraut, 83
Beef Roast in Beer, 79
Beef Stew with Wine, 92
Beef Tortellini Soup, 60
Beef-Venison Barbecue, 200
Beef
After-Work Stew, 94
Easy Beef Stew, 94
Fruited Beef Tagine, 89
Home-Style Beef Cubes, 88
Hungarian Barley Stew, 95
Hungarian Beef Stew, 95
Middle Eastern Sandwiches (for a crowd), 99
Salsa Beef, 89
Wash-Day Stew, 96
Beef, Brisket
Apple and Brown Sugar Corned Beef, 88
Cranberry Brisket, 76
Smoked Beef Brisket, 77
Spicy Beef Roast, 75
Beef, Chipped Dried
Hot Beef Dip, 12
Beef, Chuck
Barbecued Chuck Steak, 87
Bavarian Beef, 80
Beef Pot Roast, 81
Herby Beef Sandwiches, 98
Hot Beef Sandwiches, 98
Melt-in-Your-Mouth Mexican Meat Dish, 77
Potluck Beef Barbecue Sandwiches, 96
Pot-Roast Complete, 82
Ranch Hand Beef, 97
Salsa Chuck Roast, 77
Sunday Roast Beef, 80
Wine Tender Roast, 75
Beef, Corned
Apple and Brown Sugar Corned Beef, 88
Corned Beef, 88
Slow Cooker Reuben Dip, 15
Beef, Dried
Gourmet Chicken Breasts, 173
Mexican Rice and Bean Soup, 37
Beef, Flank
Fruited Flank Steak, 86
Slow Cooker Beef with Mushrooms, 87
Stuffed Flank Steak, 86
Three-Pepper Steak, 85
Beef, Ground
1-2-3-4 Casserole, 115
Applesauce Meatballs, 106
Arlene's BBQ Meatballs, 103
Asian Meatballs, 106
Barbecued Beans, 191
Barbecued Hamburgers, 114
Beef and Macaroni, 120
Beef and Pepper Rice, 122
Beef and Sausage Spaghetti Sauce, 112
Beef Barley Soup, 50
Beef Tortellini Soup, 60
Beef-Venison Barbecue, 200
Black Bean Chili con Carne, 59
Brunswick Stew, 180
Calico Beans, 193

Casserole Verde, 126
Cedric's Casserole, 119
Cheese and Pasta in a Pot, 120
Cheese Meat Loaf, 101
Cheese Pizza Fondue, 14
Cheeseburger Casserole, 118
Chili con Carne Supreme, 53
Chili Soup, 54
Chili Spaghetti, 110
Christmas Meat Loaf, 100
Cocktail Meatballs, 104
Country Auction Chili Soup, 55
Cowboy Beans, 192
Cranberry Meatballs, 16
Creamy Taco Dip, 12
Dawn's Spaghetti and Meat Sauce, 110
Dianna's Barbecue, 110
Easy Hamburger Vegetable Soup, 49
Easy Veggie-Beef Soup, 50
Extra Easy Chili, 57
"Famous" Baked Beans, 191
Festive Meatballs, 102
Gourmet Meat Loaf, 101
Grandma's Chili, 58
Ground Beef Soup, 51
Ground Beef Stew, 117
Ground Beef Stroganoff, 99
Ham Balls, 154
Ham Loaf or Balls, 154
Hamburger Beans, 192
Hamburger Casserole, 116
Hamburger/Green Bean Dish, 118
Hamburger Potato Casserole, 116
Hamburger-Potato Slow Cooker Dinner, 115
Hamburger Rice Casserole, 121
Hamburger Sausage Soup, 63
Hamburger Soup, 51
Hamburger Vegetable Soup, 51
Haystacks, 123
Hearty Chili, 56
Hearty Potato Chili, 58
Hearty Rice Casserole, 121
Hot and Good Chili, 55
Hot Hamburger Dip, 11
Italian Meatball Subs, 103
M&T's Chili, 59
Magic Meat Loaf, 100
Meal-in-One, 119
Meat Loaf, 100
Meat Loaf Burgers, 114
Meatball-Barley Casserole, 108
Meatballs with Bounce, 107
Mexican Goulash, 124
Now That's Lasagna, 113
One-Pot Dinner, 193
Our Favorite Chili, 54
Pizzaburgers, 109
Plenty More in the Kitchen, 120
Prompt, 118
Quick and Easy Spaghetti, 111
Ruth's Ground Beef Vegetable Soup, 49
Sloppy Beef Sandwiches, 108
Slow-Cooked Chili, 54
Slow Cooker Almost Lasagna, 114
Slow Cooker Lasagna, 112
Slowly Cooked Chili, 55
Snappy Meatballs, 105
Snowmobile Soup, 52
So Easy Chili, 56
Spaghetti Sauce for a Crowd, 111
Spaghetti Sauce with a Kick, 112
Spanish Stuffed Peppers, 123
Spicy Chili, 58
Spicy Sausage Soup, 64
Stuffed Baked Topping, 117
Stuffed Green Peppers, 122
Swedish Meat Balls, 102
Sweet and Sour Meatballs, 106
Sweet 'n' Tangy Meatballs, 104
Taco Appetizer, 13
Taco Casserole, 125
Taco Soup with Corn, 52
Taco Soup with Hominy, 52
The Chili Connection, 57
Three-Bean Chili, 56
TNT Dip, 12
Tortilla Bake, 124
Wholesome Hamburger Dinner, 116
Yum-Yums, 109
Zesty Calico Beans, 198

Beef, Hamburgers
Barbecue Sauce and Hamburgers, 108

Beef, Ribs
Beef Ribs with Sauerkraut, 83
Ribs and Limas, 84
Slow-Cooked Short Ribs, 83
Spicy Short Ribs, 82

Beef, Roast
8-Hour Tangy Beef, 78
Apple and Onion Beef Pot Roast, 78
Barbara Jean's Junior Beef, 96
Bavarian Beef, 80
Beef Barbecue Sandwiches, 97
Beef Pot Roast, 81
Beef Roast in Beer, 79
Cranberry Brisket, 76
Easy Roast Beef Barbecue, 98
Herby Beef Sandwiches, 98
Hot Beef Sandwiches, 98
Italian Beef au Jus, 79
Machaca Beef, 76
Melt-in-Your-Mouth Mexican Meat Dish, 77
Plum Roast, 76
Potluck Beef Barbecue Sandwiches, 96
Pot-Roast Complete, 82
Ranch Hand Beef, 97
Salsa Chuck Roast, 77
Saucy Italian Roast, 79
Sauerbraten, 81
Simply Super Supper, 80
Smoked Beef Brisket, 77
Spicy Beef Roast, 75
Sunday Roast Beef, 80
There's-No-Easier Roast Beef, 78
Wine Tender Roast, 75

Beef, Round
Beef Barbecue Sandwiches, 97
Beef Burgundy, 91
Easy Stroganoff, 90
Garlic Beef Stroganoff, 90
Pigs in Blankets, 87
Salsa Chuck Roast, 77
Sauerbraten, 81
Savory Pepper Steak, 85
Slow Cooker Beef with Mushrooms, 87
Spicy Beef Roast, 75
Swiss Steak, 84

Beef, Rump
Beef Barbecue Sandwiches, 97
Saucy Italian Roast, 79

Beef, Sirloin
Beef Burgundy, 91
Beef Mushroom Casserole, 90
Dawn's Mushroom Beef Stew, 92

Beef, Steak
Barbecued Chuck Steak, 87
Fruited Flank Steak, 86
Pigs in Blankets, 87
Savory Pepper Steak, 85
Slow Cooker Beef with Mushrooms, 87
Stuffed Flank Steak, 86
Swiss Steak, 84
Tender Texas-Style Steaks, 84
Three-Pepper Steak, 85
Tiajuana Tacos, 126

Beef, Stewing
Barbecued Pork and Beef Sandwiches, 155
Beef Dumpling Soup, 49
Beef Stew with Shiitake Mushrooms, 93
Beef Stew with Wine, 92
Best Ever Beef Stew, 93
Easy Stroganoff, 90
Easy Veggie-Beef Soup, 50
Everyone's Hungry Soup, 63
Homemade Vegetable Soup, 48
Italian Beef Stew, 91
New Mexico Stew, 95
Slow-Cooker Chili, 53
Stay-in-Bed Stew, 48
Tempting Beef Stew, 92
Tomato-y Beef Stew, 94
Your-Choice-of-Vegetables Soup, 48
Best Ever Beef Stew, 93
Black Bean and Ham Soup, 32
Black Bean and Tomato Soup, 32
Black Bean Chili con Carne, 59
Black Beans with Ham, 151
Black-Eyed Pea Chili, 62
Black-Eyed Peas and Ham, 212
Black-Eyed Peas *See Beans, Black-Eyed Peas*
Blessing Soup, 30

Blueberry Pie Filling
Easy Easy Cake, 258

Boston Brown Bread, 26
Brats and Spuds, 141
Bratwurst in Sauce, 141

Bread
Apple-Nut Bread Pudding, 254
Boston Brown Bread, 26
Home-Style Bread Pudding, 255
Simple Bread Pudding, 254
White Chocolate Bread Pudding, 254

Breakfast Apple Cobbler, 25
Breakfast Prunes, 25
Breakfast Skillet, 22
Broccoli and Cauliflower Soup, 38
Broccoli and Rice Casserole, 210
Broccoli Casserole, 152
Broccoli, Potato, and Cheese Soup, 38

Broccoli
Broccoli and Cauliflower Soup, 38
Broccoli and Rice Casserole, 210
Broccoli Casserole, 152
Broccoli, Potato, and Cheese Soup, 38
Cheesy Broccoli Casserole, 210
Cheesy Broccoli Soup, 39
Cheesy Ham and Broccoli, 152
Chicken Broccoli Rice Casserole, 177
Creamy Chicken and Vegetables, 171
Ham and Broccoli, 152
Ham and Broccoli Chowder, 39
Quick Broccoli Fix, 211
Szechwan-Style Chicken and Broccoli, 172
Turkey Frame Soup, 70
Your-Choice-of-Vegetables Soup, 48

Brookville Hotel Creamed Corn, 206
Brunswick Stew, 180
Buffalo Chicken Dip, 16
Butternut Squash and Apple Soup, 43

C

Cabbage
- Apple and Brown Sugar Corned Beef, 88
- Cedric's Casserole, 119
- Corned Beef, 88
- Diet Soup Unlimited, 46
- Hamburger Soup, 51
- Ham 'n' Cabbage Stew, 151
- Hearty Bean and Vegetable Soup, 27
- Kielbasa and Cabbage, 143
- Minestrone, 28
- New England Boiled Dinner, 149
- Sweet-Sour Red Cabbage, 212

Cake
- Banana Loaf, 243
- Carrot Cake, 257
- Chocolate Fondue, 259
- Creamy Orange Cheesecake, 256
- Date and Nut Loaf, 243
- Easy Easy Cake, 258
- Fudgy Peanut Butter Cake, 258
- Gingerbread Pudding Cake, 242
- Holiday Cherry Cobbler, 241
- Lemon Poppy Seed Upside-Down Cake, 258
- Low-Fat Apple Cake, 256
- Orange Slice Cake, 257

Calico Beans, 193
Candied Sweet Potatoes, 216
Caponata, 216
Caramel Peanut Butter Dip, 19
Carrot Cake, 257

Carrots
- 1-2-3-4 Casserole, 115
- After-Work Stew, 94
- Apple and Brown Sugar Corned Beef, 88
- Apple Chicken Stew, 67
- Asian Pork Soup, 62
- Basil Chicken, 160
- Bavarian Beef, 80
- Beef Barley Soup, 50
- Beef Stew with Shiitake Mushrooms, 93
- Beef Stew with Wine, 92
- Best Ever Beef Stew, 93
- Carrot Cake, 257
- Carrot Ginger Soup, 39
- Cassoulet Chowder, 35
- Chicken and Dumplings, 180
- Chicken Stew with Peppers and Pineapples, 165
- Christmas Carrots, 211
- Corned Beef, 88
- Creamy Chicken and Noodles, 172
- Curried Carrot Soup, 40
- Delicious Sausage Soup, 64
- Easy Beef Stew, 94
- Easy Veggie-Beef Soup, 50
- Everyone's Hungry Soup, 63
- Garbanzo Souper, 31
- Glazed Carrots, 212
- Golden Autumn Stew, 145
- Grandma's Barley Soup, 35
- Green Beans and Ham Soup, 37
- Ground Beef Stew, 117
- Ham 'n' Cabbage Stew, 151
- Hamburger Casserole, 116
- Hamburger Potato Casserole, 116
- Hamburger Sausage Soup, 63
- Hamburger Soup, 51
- Hearty Bean and Vegetable Soup, 27
- Homemade Vegetable Soup, 48
- Lamb Stew, 199
- Lentil Soup, 32
- Many-Bean Soup, 30
- Minestrone, 28
- Moo Shu Pork, 137
- Naturally Colorful Vegetable Soup, 44
- New England Boiled Dinner, 149
- New Mexico Stew, 95
- One-Pot Easy Chicken, 158
- Orange-Glazed Carrots, 211
- Ribs and Limas, 84
- Rice & Bean Soup, 37
- Ruth's Ground Beef Vegetable Soup, 49
- Sauerkraut & Pork Ribs, 129
- Sausage Tortellini Soup, 60
- Simply Super Supper, 80
- Slow-Cooker Bean Soup, 28
- Stay-in-Bed Stew, 48
- Sunday Roast Beef, 80
- Tempting Beef Stew, 92
- The Soup, 46
- Tomato-y Beef Stew, 94
- Turkey Meatball Soup, 71
- Turkey Mushroom Soup, 71
- Tzimmes, 214
- Vegetable Pork Soup, 61
- Your-Choice-of-Vegetables Soup, 48

Cashews
- Chicken Cashew Dish, 174
- Norma's Vegetarian Chili, 47
- Spicy Party Mix, 19

Casserole Verde, 126

Casserole
- 1-2-3-4 Casserole, 115
- Beef Mushroom Casserole, 90
- Broccoli and Rice Casserole, 210
- Broccoli Casserole, 152
- Casserole Verde, 126
- Cedric's Casserole, 119
- Cheese Souffle Casserole, 203
- Cheesy Broccoli Casserole, 210
- Chicken Broccoli Rice Casserole, 177
- Chili Casserole, 146
- Company Casserole, 177
- Cornbread Casserole, 209
- Creamy Green Bean Casserole, 205
- Green Bean Casserole, 206
- Ham and Corn Slow-Cooker Casserole, 152
- Hamburger Casserole, 116
- Hamburger Potato Casserole, 116
- Hamburger Rice Casserole, 121
- Hearty Rice Casserole, 121
- Meatball-Barley Casserole, 108
- Pork Chop Slow Cooker Casserole, 135
- Spicy Corn Casserole, 209
- Tuna Noodle Casserole, 202
- Western Omelet Casserole, 21

Cassoulet Chowder, 35

Cauliflower
- Broccoli and Cauliflower Soup, 38
- Creamy Chicken and Vegetables, 171
- Turkey Frame Soup, 70
- Your-Choice-of-Vegetables Soup, 48

Cedric's Casserole, 119

Celery
- Hearty Bean and Vegetable Soup, 27

Cereal
- Cornmeal Mush, 24
- Fruit and Grains Breakfast Cereal, 23
- Hot Wheatberry Cereal, 24
- Snack Mix, 18

Chard
- Red and Green Bean Soup, 33

Cheese and Pasta in a Pot, 120
Cheese Meat Loaf, 101
Cheese Pizza Fondue, 14
Cheese Souffle Casserole, 203

Cheese, American
- Cheese Meat Loaf, 101

Cheese, Bleu
- Buffalo Chicken Dip, 16

Cheese, Cheddar
- Bacon Cheese Dip, 13
- Barbara Jean's Junior Beef, 96
- Breakfast Skillet, 22
- Broccoli and Cauliflower Soup, 38
- Broccoli and Rice Casserole, 210
- Cheese Meat Loaf, 101
- Cheese Pizza Fondue, 14
- Cheese Potatoes, 225
- Cheese Souffle Casserole, 203
- Cheesy Hominy, 209
- Cheesy Hot Bean Dip, 11
- Chili Casserole, 146
- Company Potatoes, 225
- Creamy Chicken and Vegetables, 171
- Creamy Potatoes, 226
- Creamy Taco Dip, 12
- Delicious Chicken with Curried Cream Sauce, 161
- Easy Cheese Soup, 45
- Green Bean Casserole, 206
- Ham and Corn Slow-Cooker Casserole, 152
- Hamburger Potato Casserole, 116
- Hamburger-Potato Slow Cooker Dinner, 115
- Hot Beef Dip, 12
- Hot Cheddar Mushroom Spread, 10
- Macaroni and Cheese, 202
- Nacho Dip, 10
- Party Bean Soup, 33
- Pizzaburgers, 109
- Plenty More in the Kitchen, 120
- Potatoes Perfect, 223
- Quick Broccoli Fix, 211
- Rudolph's Nose Wild Rice, 228
- Sausage-Potato Slow Cooker Dinner, 142
- Savory Cheese Soup, 45
- Slow and Easy Macaroni and Cheese, 203
- Smoked Salmon Corn Chowder, 72
- Snowmobile Soup, 52
- Spicy Corn Casserole, 209
- Stuffed Baked Topping, 117
- Taco Casserole, 125
- Tamale Chicken, 175
- Tuna Noodle Casserole, 202
- Western Omelet Casserole, 21

Cheese, Colby
- Creamy Green Bean Casserole, 205

Cheese, Cream
- Bacon Cheese Dip, 13
- Cheese and Crab Dip, 18
- Cheesy Hot Bean Dip, 11
- Cheesy Spinach and Bacon Dip, 14
- Creamy Artichoke Dip, 9
- Creamy Orange Cheesecake, 256
- Creamy Pizza Dip, 14
- Creamy Taco Dip, 12
- Hot Beef Dip, 12
- Hot Crab Dip, 17
- Savory Cheese Soup, 45
- Slow Cooker Reuben Dip, 15
- Super Creamed Corn, 207

Cheese, Feta
- Red Pepper-Cheese Dip, 9

Cheese, Gouda
Chicken Pasta, 178
Cheese, Monterey Jack
Arroz con Queso, 204
Cheesy Hot Bean Dip, 11
Company Seafood Pasta, 201
Easy Ravioli, 113
Meal-in-One, 119
Taco Appetizer, 13
Cheese, Mozzarella
Cheese and Pasta in a Pot, 120
Cheese Pizza Fondue, 14
Chicken Alfredo, 171
Creamy Artichoke Dip, 9
Creamy Pizza Dip, 14
Easy Ravioli, 113
Meatless Pizza Fondue, 15
Now That's Lasagna, 113
Onion Soup, 42
Pizza Rigatoni, 146
Sausage, Tomato, Spinach Soup, 60
Slow Cooker Almost Lasagna, 114
Slow Cooker Lasagna, 112
Slow-Cooker Pizza, 146
Turkey Lasagna, 189
Cheese, Parmesan
Chicken Alfredo, 171
Creamy Artichoke Dip, 9
Meatballs and Spaghetti Sauce, 105
Meatless Pizza Fondue, 15
Onion Soup, 42
Slow Cooker Almost Lasagna, 114
Turkey Meatball Soup, 71
Zesty Minestrone, 28
Cheese, Provolone
Cheese and Pasta in a Pot, 120
Zucchini and Turkey Dish, 185
Cheese, Romano
Meatballs and Spaghetti Sauce, 105
Cheese, Swiss
Barbara Jean's Junior Beef, 96
Christmas Potatoes with Cheese, 226
Creamy Artichoke Dip, 9
Ham and Broccoli Chowder, 39
Our Favorite Chicken and Stuffing, 178
Red French Onion Soup, 41
Slow Cooker Reuben Dip, 15
Tuna Noodle Casserole, 202
Cheese, Velveeta
Au Gratin Green Beans, 206
Broccoli and Rice Casserole, 210
Broccoli, Potato, and Cheese Soup, 38
Cheesy Broccoli Soup, 39
Cheesy Sausage Dip, 13
Cheesy Spinach and Bacon Dip, 14
Chicken Broccoli Rice Casserole, 177
Hamburger Rice Casserole, 121
Hot Hamburger Dip, 11
Mexican-Style Grits, 24
Santa Fe Chicken Soup, 68
TNT Dip, 12
Underground Ham and Cheese, 153
Cheeseburger Casserole, 118
Cheesy Broccoli Casserole, 210
Cheesy Broccoli Soup, 39
Cheesy Ham and Broccoli, 152
Cheesy Hominy, 209
Cheesy Sausage Dip, 13
Cheesy Spinach and Bacon Dip, 14
Cherries
Curried Fruit, 247
Easy and Elegant Ham, 147
Festive Fruit Compote, 246
Fruit Compote, 245
Wagon Master Apple-Cherry Sauce, 246
Cherries, Dried
White Chocolate Bread Pudding, 254
Cherry Pie Filling
Easy Easy Cake, 258
Holiday Cherry Cobbler, 241
Chicken ala Orange, 168
Chicken Alfredo, 171
Chicken and Dumplings, 180
Chicken and Sausage Cacciatore, 160
Chicken and Seafood Gumbo, 176
Chicken and Stuffing Dinner, 179
Chicken Azteca, 175
Chicken Broccoli Rice Casserole, 177
Chicken Cacciatore, 159
Chicken Cashew Dish, 174
Chicken Corn Soup, 41
Chicken Dressing, 179
Chicken Gumbo, 172
Chicken in a Hurry, 166
Chicken Noodle Soup, 68
Chicken Pasta, 178
Chicken Rice Special, 177
Chicken Sausage Fennel Soup, 67
Chicken Stew with Peppers and Pineapples, 165
Chicken Wings Colorado, 182
Chicken with Applesauce, 167
Chicken
Cassoulet Chowder, 35
Chicken Dressing, 179
Chicken Noodle Soup, 68
Scalloped Chicken, 180
White Chili, 66
Chicken, Breast
Angel Chicken Pasta, 168
Apple Chicken Stew, 67
Baked Chicken and Rice, 178
Barbecued Chicken, 164
Barbecued Chicken with Peppers, Onions, and Celery, 164
Brunswick Stew, 180
Buffalo Chicken Dip, 16
Chicken ala Orange, 168
Chicken Alfredo, 171
Chicken and Dumplings, 180
Chicken and Sausage Cacciatore, 160
Chicken and Stuffing Dinner, 179
Chicken Azteca, 175
Chicken Cashew Dish, 174
Chicken Gumbo, 172
Chicken Pasta, 178
Chicken Rice Special, 177
Chicken Sausage Fennel Soup, 67
Chicken Stew with Peppers and Pineapples, 165
Chicken with Applesauce, 167
Company Casserole, 177
Creamy Chicken and Vegetables, 171
Creamy Chicken Breasts, 169
Creamy Nutmeg Chicken, 173
Delicious Chicken with Curried Cream Sauce, 161
Elegant Chicken with Gravy, 170
Garlic Lime Chicken, 163
Gourmet Chicken Breasts, 173
Hawaiian Chicken, 164
Herbed Chicken, 163
Indonesian Peanut Chicken, 174
Italian Chicken Chili, 66
Jambalaya, 65
Maui Chicken, 166
Miriam's Chicken, 169
Mushroom Chicken in Sour Cream Sauce, 174
Our Favorite Chicken and Stuffing, 178
Pineapple-Glazed Chicken with Sweet Potatoes, 165
Red Pepper Chicken, 176
Santa Fe Chicken Soup, 68
Saucy Apricot Chicken, 167
Savory Chicken, Meal #1, 170
Savory Chicken, Meal #2, 171
Scrumptious Chicken, 168
Slow Cooker Creamy Chicken Italian, 173
Sweet Chili Chicken Bites, 17
Szechwan-Style Chicken and Broccoli, 172
Tamale Chicken, 175
Tex-Mex Chicken and Rice, 176
White Chicken Chili, 65
Chicken, Drumsticks
See Chicken, Pieces
Chicken, Ground
Asian Pork Soup, 62
Chicken, Legs
See Chicken, Pieces
Chicken, Liver
Liver Paté, 18
Chicken, Pieces
Baked Chicken and Rice, 178
Barbecued Chicken Sandwiches, 181
Basil Chicken, 160
Chicken and Seafood Gumbo, 176
Chicken Broccoli Rice Casserole, 177
Chicken Cacciatore, 159
Chicken Cacciatore with Spaghetti, 159
Chicken Corn Soup, 41
Chicken in a Hurry, 166
Con Pollo, 160
Creamy Chicken and Noodles, 172
Curried Chicken, 162
Dad's Spicy Chicken Curry, 161
Delicious Chicken with Curried Cream Sauce, 161
Hot Chicken Sandwiches, 181
Janie's Chicken a La King, 170
Lemon Chicken, 162
Old-Fashioned Stewed Chicken, 158
One-Pot Easy Chicken, 158
Savory Chicken, Meal #1, 170
Savory Chicken, Meal #2, 171
Spicy Sweet Chicken, 167
Sunday Chicken, 169
Tender Barbecued Chicken, 166
Teriyaki Chicken, 163
Chicken, Quarters
See Chicken, Pieces
Chicken, Thighs *See Chicken, Pieces*
Chicken, Whole
Hot Chicken Sandwiches, 181
Pixie's Chicken Stew, 68
Sunday Roast Chicken, 157
Tender Barbecued Chicken, 166
Chicken, Wings
Chicken Wings Colorado, 182
Levi's Sesame Chicken Wings, 182
Sweet and Sour Chicken Wings, 17
Chili Casserole, 146
Chili con Carne Supreme, 53

Chili Soup, 54
Chili Spaghetti, 110
Chili
Black Bean Chili con Carne, 59
Black-Eyed Pea Chili, 62
Chili Casserole, 146
Chili con Carne Supreme, 53
Chili Soup, 54
Chili Spaghetti, 110
Chilly Chili, 72
Country Auction Chili Soup, 55
Extra Easy Chili, 57
Flautas with Pork Filling, 131
Grandma's Chili, 58
Haystacks, 123
Hearty Chili, 56
Hearty Potato Chili, 58
Hot and Good Chili, 55
Hot Chili Dip, 11
Italian Chicken Chili, 66
M&T's Chili, 59
Norma's Vegetarian Chili, 47
Our Favorite Chili, 54
Pork Chile, 61
Pumpkin Black-Bean Turkey Chili, 69
Slow-Cooked Chili, 54
Slow-Cooker Chili, 53
Slowly Cooked Chili, 55
So Easy Chili, 56
Spicy Chili, 58
The Chili Connection, 57
Three-Bean Chili, 56
Turkey Chili, 71
Turkey Green Chili Chowder, 70
White Chicken Chili, 65
White Chili, 66
Wintertime Vegetable Chili, 47
Chilies, Green
Arroz con Queso, 204
Casserole Verde, 126
Flautas with Pork Filling, 131
Green Chile Corn Chowder, 40
Hot Crab Dip, 17
Keilbasa Stew, 143
Machaca Beef, 76
Melt-in-Your-Mouth Mexican Meat Dish, 77
Mexican-Style Grits, 24
Nacho Dip, 10
New Mexico Stew, 95
Pork Chile, 61
Slow-Cooker Chili, 53
Southwest Posole, 210
Southwestern Bean Soup with Cornmeal Dumplings, 29
Taco Appetizer, 13
Tamale Chicken, 175
Tex-Mex Chicken and Rice, 176
Three-Bean Burrito Bake, 125
Turkey Green Chili Chowder, 70
White Chicken Chili, 65
Wintertime Vegetable Chili, 47
Chilly Chili, 72
Chocolate Covered Pretzels, 260
Chocolate Fondue, 259
Chocolate Rice Pudding, 252
Chocolate
Chocolate Covered Pretzels, 260
Chocolate Fondue, 259
Graham Cracker Cookies, 259
Hot Fudge Sauce, 260
Triple Delicious Hot Chocolate, 239
White Chocolate Bread Pudding, 254
Chowder
Cassoulet Chowder, 35
Clam Chowder, 74
Corn and Shrimp Chowder, 73
Corn Chowder, 40
Green Chile Corn Chowder, 40
Ham and Potato Chowder, 42
Navy Bean and Bacon Chowder, 34
Smoked Salmon Corn Chowder, 72
Wonderful Clam Chowder, 74
Christmas Apple Date Pudding, 242
Christmas Carrots, 211
Christmas Meat Loaf, 100
Christmas Potatoes with Cheese, 226
Christmas Smells, 4
Christmas Sugared Walnuts, 19
Christmas Wassail, 236
Chunky Sweet Spiced Apple Butter, 20
Cider Snap, 233
Cider
Cider Snap, 233
Deep Red Apple Cider, 234
Fruity Wassail, 236
Hot Cranberry Cider, 235
Maple Mulled Cider, 233
Matthew's Hot Mulled Cider, 234
Orange Cider Punch, 234
Wassail, 235
Cinnamon
Christmas Smells, 4
Cider Snap, 233
Fruity Hot Punch, 236
Golden Wassail Punch, 237
Maple Mulled Cider, 233
Matthew's Hot Mulled Cider, 234
Clam Chowder, 74
Cobbler
Breakfast Apple Cobbler, 25
Holiday Cherry Cobbler, 241
Cocktail Meatballs, 104
Cocoa *See Hot Chocolate*
Coconut
Christmas Carrots, 211
Orange Slice Cake, 257
Coffee
Viennese Coffee, 240
Cole Slaw
Hamburger Vegetable Soup, 51
Moo Shu Pork, 137
Rob's Sweet and Sour Joe, 139
Company Casserole, 177
Company Potatoes, 225
Company Seafood Pasta, 201
Compote
Apple Cranberry Compote, 245
Festive Fruit Compote, 246
Fruit Compote, 245
Con Pollo, 160
Confetti Scalloped Corn, 208
Corn and Macaroni, 207
Corn Chowder, 40
Corn Stuffing Balls, 231
Corn
Aunt Thelma's Homemade Soup, 46
Baked Corn, 207
Brookville Hotel Creamed Corn, 206
Brunswick Stew, 180
Chicken Azteca, 175
Chicken Corn Soup, 41
Chicken Noodle Soup, 68
Confetti Scalloped Corn, 208
Corn and Macaroni, 207
Corn and Shrimp Chowder, 73
Corn Chowder, 40
Cornbread Casserole, 209
Easy Beef Stew, 94
Easy Veggie-Beef Soup, 50
Everyone's Hungry Soup, 63
Hamburger Vegetable Soup, 51
Hearty Bean and Vegetable Soup, 27
Mexican Corn, 208
Mexican Goulash, 124
Naturally Colorful Vegetable Soup, 44
Pixie's Chicken Stew, 68
Plenty More in the Kitchen, 120
Santa Fe Chicken Soup, 68
Sausage Tortellini Soup, 60
Shepherd's Pie, 154
Smoked Salmon Corn Chowder, 72
Southwestern Bean Soup with Cornmeal Dumplings, 29
Spicy Corn Casserole, 209
Super Creamed Corn, 207
Taco Soup with Corn, 52
White Chili, 66
Your-Choice-of-Vegetables Soup, 48
Corn, Creamed
Brunswick Stew, 180
Corn and Macaroni, 207
Corn Stuffing Balls, 231
Ham and Corn Slow-Cooker Casserole, 152
Smoked Salmon Corn Chowder, 72
Turkey Green Chili Chowder, 70
Corn, Dried
Dried Corn, 208
Cornbread Casserole, 209
Cornbread
Confetti Scalloped Corn, 208
Cornbread Casserole, 209
Slow-Cooker Dressing, 230
Stuffed Flank Steak, 86
Corned Beef, 88
Cornmeal Mush, 24
Country Auction Chili Soup, 55
Country-Style Ribs and Sauerkraut, 128
Couscous
Easy Wheatberries, 204
Cowboy Beans, 192
Crabmeat
Cheese and Crab Dip, 18
Hot Crab Dip, 17
Cranberries
Apple Cranberry Compote, 245
Cranberry Applesauce, 247
Cranberry Baked Apples, 248
Cranberry Sauce with Red Wine and Oranges, 244
Warmed Spiced Fruit, 245
Cranberries, Dried
Christmas Meat Loaf, 100
Dried Cranberry Pudding, 250
Easy Wheatberries, 204
Fruit and Grains Breakfast Cereal, 23
Oatmeal Morning, 23
Slow Cooker Turkey and Dressing, 185
Stuffed Acorn Squash, 214
Sweet Potato-Cranberry Casserole, 219
White Chocolate Bread Pudding, 254
Cranberry Applesauce, 247
Cranberry Baked Apples, 248
Cranberry Brisket, 76
Cranberry Franks, 156
Cranberry Meatballs, 16
Cranberry Pork, 130
Cranberry Sauce with Red Wine and Oranges, 244
Cranberry Sauce
Christmas Meat Loaf, 100

Cranberry Brisket, 76
Cranberry Franks, 156
Cranberry Meatballs, 16
Cranberry Pork, 130
Fruity Hot Punch, 236
Southwest Cranberries, 247
Spicy Sweet Chicken, 167
Tricia's Cranberry Turkey Meatballs, 190
Turkey Slow Cooker, 184
Cream of Pumpkin Soup, 44
Creamy Artichoke Dip, 9
Creamy Chicken and Noodles, 172
Creamy Chicken and Vegetables, 171
Creamy Chicken Breasts, 169
Creamy Green Bean Casserole, 205
Creamy Ham Topping (for baked potatoes), 150
Creamy Mashed Potatoes, 221
Creamy Nutmeg Chicken, 173
Creamy Orange Cheesecake, 256
Creamy Pizza Dip, 14
Creamy Potato Soup, 42
Creamy Potatoes, 226
Creamy Red Potatoes, 222
Creamy Taco Dip, 12
Creamy Tomato Soup, 43
Creole Black Beans, 195
Crisp
Apple Crisp, 250
Crockery Cocoa, 239
Curried Carrot Soup, 40
Curried Chicken, 162
Curried Fruit, 247
Curried Shrimp, 202
Curry
Curried Carrot Soup, 40
Curried Chicken, 162
Curried Fruit, 247
Curried Shrimp, 202
Dad's Spicy Chicken Curry, 161
Delicious Chicken with Curried Cream Sauce, 161
Pork Chops and Stuffing with Curry, 137
Custard
Eggnog Gingersnap Custard, 253

D

Dad's Spicy Chicken Curry, 161
Date and Nut Loaf, 243
Dates
Auntie Ginny's Baked Beans, 195
Carrot Cake, 257
Christmas Apple Date Pudding, 242
Date and Nut Loaf, 243
Fruit and Grains Breakfast Cereal, 23
Home-Style Bread Pudding, 255
Orange Slice Cake, 257
Dawn's Mushroom Beef Stew, 92
Dawn's Sausage and Peppers, 140
Dawn's Spaghetti and Meat Sauce, 110
Dawn's Special Beans, 196
Deb's Baked Beans, 194
Deep Red Apple Cider, 234
Delicious Chicken with Curried Cream Sauce, 161
Delicious Sausage Soup, 64
Deluxe Tapioca Pudding, 252
Dianna's Barbecue, 110
Diet Soup Unlimited, 46
Dips
Bacon Cheese Dip, 13
Buffalo Chicken Dip, 16
Caramel Peanut Butter Dip, 19
Cheese and Crab Dip, 18
Cheese Pizza Fondue, 14
Cheesy Hot Bean Dip, 11
Cheesy Sausage Dip, 13
Cheesy Spinach and Bacon Dip, 14
Creamy Artichoke Dip, 9
Creamy Taco Dip, 12
Hot Beef Dip, 12
Hot Cheddar Mushroom Spread, 10
Hot Chili Dip, 11
Hot Crab Dip, 17
Hot Hamburger Dip, 11
Meatless Pizza Fondue, 15
Nacho Dip, 10
Red Pepper-Cheese Dip, 9
Slow Cooker Reuben Dip, 15
Taco Appetizer, 13
TNT Dip, 12
Dressing *See Stuffing*
Dried Corn, 208
Dried Cranberry Pudding, 250
Dulce de Leche (Sweet Milk), 26
Dumplings
Beef Dumpling Soup, 49
Chicken and Dumplings, 180
Schnitz und Knepp, 149
Southwestern Bean Soup with Cornmeal Dumplings, 29

E

Easy and Elegant Ham, 147
Easy Beef Stew, 94
Easy Cheese Soup, 45
Easy Easy Cake, 258
Easy Flavor-Filled Green Beans, 205
Easy Hamburger Vegetable Soup, 49
Easy Meatballs, 102
Easy Meatballs for a Group, 104
Easy Olive Bake, 215
Easy Ravioli, 113
Easy Roast Beef Barbecue, 98
Easy Stroganoff, 90
Easy Stuffed Shells, 203
Easy Veggie-Beef Soup, 50
Easy Wheatberries, 204
Edna's Baked Beans, 198
Eggplant
Caponata, 216
Eggs 'n' Spinach, 21
Eggs
Apple-Nut Bread Pudding, 254
Breakfast Skillet, 22
Cheesy Broccoli Casserole, 210
Deluxe Tapioca Pudding, 252
Eggnog Gingersnap Custard, 253
Eggs 'n' Spinach, 21
Lemon Pudding, 253
Mashed Potato Filling, 231
Matzoh Ball Soup, 69
Pineapple Sweet Potatoes, 219
Scalloped Pineapple, 232
Spicy Corn Casserole, 209
Verenike (or Creamy Lasagna), 153
Western Omelet Casserole, 21
White Chocolate Bread Pudding, 254
Election Lunch, 144
Escarole
Turkey Meatball Soup, 71
Everyone's Hungry Soup, 63
Extra Easy Chili, 57

F

"Famous" Baked Beans, 191
Fennel
Chicken Sausage Fennel Soup, 67
Festive Fruit Compote, 246
Festive Meatballs, 102
Flautas with Pork Filling, 131
Fondue
Cheese Pizza Fondue, 14
Meatless Pizza Fondue, 15
Fruit and Grains Breakfast Cereal, 23
Fruit Compote, 245
Fruit Dessert Topping, 246
Fruited Beef Tagine, 89
Fruited Flank Steak, 86
Fruited Turkey and Yams, 187
Fruited Wild Rice with Pecans, 228
Fruity Hot Punch, 236
Fruity Wassail, 236
Fudgy Peanut Butter Cake, 258

G

Galloping Beans, 194
Garbanzo Souper, 31
Garlic Beef Stroganoff, 90
Garlic Lime Chicken, 163
Garlic Mashed Potatoes, 220
Ginger Tea, 238
Ginger
Carrot Ginger Soup, 39
Ginger Tea, 238
Gingerbread Pudding Cake, 242
Gingersnaps
Eggnog Gingersnap Custard, 253
Glazed Carrots, 212
Glazed Ham in a Bag, 148
Golden Wassail Punch, 237
Gourmet Chicken Breasts, 173
Gourmet Meat Loaf, 101
Graham Cracker Cookies, 259
Grandma's Barley Soup, 35
Grandma's Chili, 58
Granola
Breakfast Apple Cobbler, 25
Gravy
Creamy Ham Topping (for baked potatoes), 150
Great Northern Bean Soup, 29
Green Bean Casserole, 206
Green Beans and Ham Soup, 37
Green Beans and Sausage Soup, 38
Green Beans
Au Gratin Green Beans, 206
Beef Tortellini Soup, 60
Chicken and Stuffing Dinner, 179
Chicken Noodle Soup, 68
Creamy Green Bean Casserole, 205
Diet Soup Unlimited, 46
Easy Beef Stew, 94
Easy Flavor-Filled Green Beans, 205
Easy Stuffed Shells, 203
Easy Veggie-Beef Soup, 50
Everyone's Hungry Soup, 63
Green Bean Casserole, 206
Green Beans and Ham Soup, 37
Green Beans and Sausage Soup, 38
Ham, Bean, and Potato Dish, 149
Hamburger/Green Bean Dish, 118
Hamburger Vegetable Soup, 51
Homemade Vegetable Soup, 48
Mexican Goulash, 124
Pork Chop Slow Cooker Casserole, 135
Pork Loin with Spiced Fruit Sauce, 130
Spicy Sausage Soup, 64

Tempting Beef Stew, 92
Trio Bean Casserole, 193
Wholesome Hamburger Dinner, 116
Your-Choice-of-Vegetables Soup, 48
Green Chile Corn Chowder, 40
Green Peppers
See Peppers, Bell Sweet
Grits
Mexican-Style Grits, 24
Ground Beef Soup, 51
Ground Beef Stew, 117
Ground Beef Stroganoff, 99
Gumbo
Chicken and Seafood Gumbo, 176
Chicken Gumbo, 172

H

Ham and Broccoli, 152
Ham and Broccoli Chowder, 39
Ham and Corn Slow-Cooker Casserole, 152
Ham and Hash Browns, 150
Ham and Lima Beans, 151
Ham and Potato Chowder, 42
Ham Balls, 154
Ham Barbecue, 156
Ham, Bean, and Potato Dish, 149
Ham in Foil, 147
Ham Loaf or Balls, 154
Ham 'n' Cabbage Stew, 151
Ham with Pineapple Sauce, 148
Hamburger Beans, 192
Hamburger Casserole, 116
Hamburger/Green Bean Dish, 118
Hamburger Potato Casserole, 116
Hamburger-Potato Slow Cooker Dinner, 115
Hamburger Rice Casserole, 121
Hamburger Sausage Soup, 63
Hamburger Soup, 51
Hamburger Vegetable Soup, 51
Hamburgers
Barbecued Hamburgers, 114
Meat Loaf Burgers, 114
Harvest Kielbasa, 143
Hawaiian Chicken, 164
Haystacks, 123
Hearty Bean and Vegetable Soup, 27
Hearty Chili, 56
Hearty Potato Chili, 58
Hearty Rice Casserole, 121
Herb-Roasted Turkey Breast, 183
Herbed Chicken, 163
Herbed Potatoes, 223
Herby Beef Sandwiches, 98
Holiday Cherry Cobbler, 241
Holiday Meatballs, 107
Homemade Applesauce, 248
Homemade Vegetable Soup, 48
Home-Style Beef Cubes, 88
Home-Style Bread Pudding, 255
Hominy
Cheesy Hominy, 209
Taco Soup with Hominy, 52
Honey-Dijon Holiday Ham, 147
Hot and Good Chili, 55
Hot Applesauce Breakfast, 25
Hot Beef Dip, 12
Hot Beef Sandwiches, 98
Hot Buttered Lemonade, 237
Hot Cheddar Mushroom Spread, 10
Hot Chicken Sandwiches, 181
Hot Chili Dip, 11
Hot Chocolate with Stir-Ins, 239
Hot Chocolate
Crockery Cocoa, 239
Hot Chocolate with Stir-Ins, 239
Triple Delicious Hot Chocolate, 239
Hot Crab Dip, 17
Hot Cranberry Cider, 235
Hot Fruit Tea, 238
Hot German Potato Salad, 227
Hot Hamburger Dip, 11
Hot Wheatberry Cereal, 24
Hungarian Barley Stew, 95
Hungarian Beef Stew, 95

I

Indonesian Peanut Chicken, 174
Italian Beef au Jus, 79
Italian Beef Stew, 91
Italian Meatball Subs, 103
Italian Sausage, 140

J

Jalapeños
See Peppers, Jalapeños
Jambalaya, 65
Janie's Chicken a La King, 170
Johnny Appleseed Tea, 238

K

Kale
Delicious Sausage Soup, 64
Red and Green Bean Soup, 33
Kielbasa and Cabbage, 143
Kielbasa Stew, 143

L

Lamb Chops, 199
Lamb Stew, 199
Lamb
Lamb Chops, 199
Lamb Stew, 199
Wash-Day Stew, 96
Lasagna
Now That's Lasagna, 113
Slow Cooker Almost Lasagna, 114
Slow Cooker Lasagna, 112
Turkey Lasagna, 189
Verenike (or Creamy Lasagna), 153
Lemon Chicken, 162
Lemon Poppy Seed Upside-Down Cake, 258
Lemon Pudding, 253
Lemonade
Hot Buttered Lemonade, 237
Lemons
Christmas Smells, 4
Hot Fruit Tea, 238
Lentil Soup, 32
Lentil Soup with Ham Bone, 62
Lentils
Lentil Soup, 32
Lentil Soup with Ham Bone, 62
Mjeddrah, 229
Russian Red Lentil Soup, 31
Levi's Sesame Chicken Wings, 182
Liver Paté, 18
Lotsa-Beans Pot, 194
Lotsa Scalloped Potatoes, 224
Low-Fat Apple Cake, 256

M

Macaroni and Cheese, 202
Macaroons
Zesty Pears, 244
Magic Meat Loaf, 100
Make Ahead Mixed Potatoes Florentine, 220
Many-Bean Soup, 30
Maple Mulled Cider, 233
Maple Syrup
Cranberry Applesauce, 247
Fruit Dessert Topping, 246
Maple Mulled Cider, 233
Sweet Potatoes and Apples, 218
Sweet Potatoes That Can Wait, 217
Mashed Potatoes, 220
Mashed Potato Filling, 231
Matzoh Ball Soup, 69
Matzoh
Matzoh Ball Soup, 69
Meal-in-One, 119
Meat Loaf, 100
Meat Loaf Burgers, 114
Meat Loaf
Cheese Meat Loaf, 101
Christmas Meat Loaf, 100
Gourmet Meat Loaf, 101
Ham Loaf or Balls, 154
Magic Meat Loaf, 100
Meat Loaf, 100
Meat Loaf Burgers, 114
Meatball-Barley Casserole, 108
Meatballs and Peppers, 105
Meatballs and Spaghetti Sauce, 105
Meatballs with Bounce, 107
Meatballs
Applesauce Meatballs, 106
Arlene's BBQ Meatballs, 103
Asian Meatballs, 106
Cocktail Meatballs, 104
Cranberry Meatballs, 16
Easy Meatballs, 102
Easy Meatballs for a Group, 104
Festive Meatballs, 102
Ham Balls, 154
Ham Loaf or Balls, 154
Holiday Meatballs, 107
Italian Meatball Subs, 103
Meatball-Barley Casserole, 108
Meatballs and Peppers, 105
Meatballs and Spaghetti Sauce, 105
Meatballs with Bounce, 107
Savory Turkey Meatballs in Italian Sauce, 189
Snappy Meatballs, 105
Swedish Meat Balls, 102
Sweet and Sour Meatballs, 106
Tricia's Cranberry Turkey Meatballs, 190
Turkey Meatball Soup, 71
Turkey Meatballs and Gravy, 190
Meatless Pizza Fondue, 15
Melt-in-Your-Mouth Mexican Meat Dish, 77
Mexican Corn, 208
Mexican Goulash, 124
Mexican Rice and Bean Soup, 37
Mexican-Style Grits, 24
Middle Eastern Sandwiches (for a crowd), 99
Milk, Sweetened Condensed
Dulce Leche (Sweet Milk), 26
Minestra Di Ceci, 204
Minestrone, 28
Minestrone
Minestrone, 28
Zesty Minestrone, 28
Mint
Russian Red Lentil Soup, 31
Miriam's Chicken, 169
Mjeddrah, 229
Molasses
Boston Brown Bread, 26
Moo Shu Pork, 137
M&T's Chili, 59
Mushroom Chicken in Sour Cream Sauce, 174
Mushroom Stuffing, 229
Mushrooms
Asian Pork Soup, 62
Barbara Jean's Junior Beef, 96

Barbara Jean's Whole Pork Tenderloin, 129
Beef Burgundy, 91
Beef Mushroom Casserole, 90
Beef Stew with Shiitake Mushrooms, 93
Best Ever Beef Stew, 93
Breakfast Skillet, 22
Chicken and Sausage Cacciatore, 160
Chicken Cacciatore, 159
Creamy Ham Topping (for baked potatoes), 150
Dawn's Mushroom Beef Stew, 92
Dawn's Spaghetti and Meat Sauce, 110
Easy Meatballs, 102
Garlic Beef Stroganoff, 90
Hearty Potato Chili, 58
Home-Style Beef Cubes, 88
Hot Cheddar Mushroom Spread, 10
Italian Chicken Chili, 66
Mushroom Chicken in Sour Cream Sauce, 174
Mushroom Stuffing, 229
Oxford Canal Chops Deluxe, 135
Pot-Roast Complete, 82
Quick and Easy Spaghetti, 111
Quick Broccoli Fix, 211
Rudolph's Nose Wild Rice, 228
Saucy Italian Roast, 79
Slow Cooker Beef with Mushrooms, 87
Spicy Chili, 58
Stuffed Mushrooms, 215
Your-Choice-of-Vegetables Soup, 48

N

Nacho Dip, 10
Naturally Colorful Vegetable Soup, 44
Navy Bean and Bacon Chowder, 34
Navy Bean Soup, 34
New England Boiled Dinner, 149
New Mexico Stew, 95
No Fuss Sauerkraut, 131
No-More-Bottled Barbecue Sauce, 109
Now That's Lasagna, 113

O

Oatmeal Morning, 23
Oats
Apple Oatmeal, 22
Meat Loaf, 100
Oatmeal Morning, 23
Slow-Cooker Oatmeal, 22
Okra
Chicken and Seafood Gumbo, 176
Chicken Gumbo, 172
Everyone's Hungry Soup, 63
Old-Fashioned Stewed Chicken, 158
Old-Fashioned Stuffing, 231
Olives
Casserole Verde, 126
Creamy Pizza Dip, 14
Easy Olive Bake, 215
Hot Chili Dip, 11
Mexican Goulash, 124
Rudolph's Nose Wild Rice, 228
Sloppy Beef Sandwiches, 108
Three-Bean Burrito Bake, 125
One-Pot Dinner, 193
One-Pot Easy Chicken, 158
Onion Potatoes, 223
Onion Soup, 42
Onions
Apple and Onion Beef Pot Roast, 78
Aunt Thelma's Homemade Soup, 46
Baked Beans and Chops, 134
Bavarian Beef, 80
Best Ever Beef Stew, 93
Brunswick Stew, 180
Butternut Squash and Apple Soup, 43
Dawn's Sausage and Peppers, 140
Fruited Beef Tagine, 89
Harvest Kielbasa, 143
Hearty Bean and Vegetable Soup, 27
Hot Hamburger Dip, 11
Italian Sausage, 140
Lamb Stew, 199
Middle Eastern Sandwiches (for a crowd), 99
Nacho Dip, 10
Onion Soup, 42
Ratatouille, 10
Red French Onion Soup, 41
Simply Super Supper, 80
Taco Appetizer, 13
Wash-Day Stew, 96
Yum-Yums, 109
Onions, Green
Asian Pork Soup, 62
Black Bean and Ham Soup, 32
Chicken Cashew Dish, 174
Company Casserole, 177
Holiday Wild Rice, 228
Home-Style Beef Cubes, 88
Hot Crab Dip, 17
Pioneer Beans, 196
Orange Candied Sweet Potatoes, 216
Orange Cider Punch, 234
Orange-Glazed Carrots, 211
Orange Slice Cake, 257
Orange Yams, 217
Oranges
Chocolate Fondue, 259
Christmas Smells, 4
Christmas Wassail, 236
Cranberry Sauce with Red Wine and Oranges, 244
Ham with Sweet Potatoes and Oranges, 150
Hawaiian Chicken, 164
Hot Cranberry Cider, 235
Hot Fruit Tea, 238
Pork Chops in Orange Sauce, 134
Warmed Spiced Fruit, 245
Oranges, Candied
Orange Slice Cake, 257
Our Favorite Chicken and Stuffing, 178
Our Favorite Chili, 54
Oyster and Potato Filling Yuletide, 201
Oyster Stew, 74

P

Parsley
Chicken and Seafood Gumbo, 176
Fruited Turkey and Yams, 187
Holiday Wild Rice, 228
Italian Chicken Chili, 66
Spaghetti Sauce for a Crowd, 111
Stuffed Flank Steak, 86
Party Bean Soup, 33
Partytime Beans, 197
Pasta, Acini di Pepe
Minestrone, 28
Pasta Bean Pot, 192
Pasta, Chow Mein Noodles
Cheesy Ham and Broccoli, 152
Pasta, Kluski Noodles
Chicken Noodle Soup, 68
Pasta, Lasagna
Now That's Lasagna, 113
Slow Cooker Lasagna, 112
Turkey Lasagna, 189
Verenike (or Creamy Lasagna), 153
Pasta, Macaroni
Beef and Macaroni, 120
Cheese and Pasta in a Pot, 120
Chicken Pasta, 178
Corn and Macaroni, 207
Hamburger Sausage Soup, 63
Macaroni and Cheese, 202
Pasta Bean Pot, 192
Plenty More in the Kitchen, 120
Slow and Easy Macaroni and Cheese, 203
Zesty Minestrone, 28
Pasta, Noodles
Chicken Alfredo, 171
Chicken Corn Soup, 41
Easy Stroganoff, 90
Slow-Cooker Pizza, 146
Tuna Noodle Casserole, 202
Turkey Frame Soup, 70
Pasta, Orzo
Easy Wheatberries, 204
Your-Choice-of-Vegetables Soup, 48
Pasta, Penne
Minestra Di Ceci, 204
Pasta, Ravioli
Easy Ravioli, 113
Pasta, Rigatoni
Pizza Rigatoni, 146
Pasta, Rotini
Slow Cooker Almost Lasagna, 114
Pasta Sauce
Angel Chicken Pasta, 168
Beef and Sausage Spaghetti Sauce, 112
Chicken and Sausage Cacciatore, 160
Chicken Cacciatore, 159
Chicken Cacciatore with Spaghetti, 159
Chili Spaghetti, 110
Dawn's Spaghetti and Meat Sauce, 110
Meatballs and Spaghetti Sauce, 105
Quick and Easy Spaghetti, 111
Spaghetti Sauce for a Crowd, 111
Spaghetti Sauce with a Kick, 112
Pasta, Shells
Cheese and Pasta in a Pot, 120
Easy Stuffed Shells, 203
Your-Choice-of-Vegetables Soup, 48
Pasta, Soba Noodles
Indonesian Peanut Chicken, 174
Pasta, Spiral
Red Beans and Pasta, 197
Sausage Pasta Stew, 145
Pasta, Tortellini
Beef Tortellini Soup, 60
Sausage Tortellini Soup, 60
Pasta, Ziti
Slow Cooker Almost Lasagna, 114
Paté
Liver Paté, 18
Peaches
Curried Chicken, 162
Curried Fruit, 247

Fruit Compote, 245
Slow-Cooker Spoon Peaches, 244
Peanut Butter
Apple Caramel Dessert, 250
Caramel Peanut Butter Dip, 19
Fudgy Peanut Butter Cake, 258
Hot Chocolate with Stir-Ins, 239
Indonesian Peanut Chicken, 174
Peanut Butter Pumpkin Soup, 44
Peanuts
Caramel Peanut Butter Dip, 19
Indonesian Peanut Chicken, 174
Pear Butter, 20
Pears
Curried Fruit, 247
Fruit Dessert Topping, 246
Pear Butter, 20
Warmed Spiced Fruit, 245
Zesty Pears, 244
Peas
Aunt Thelma's Homemade Soup, 46
Brunswick Stew, 180
Chicken Noodle Soup, 68
Creamy Chicken and Noodles, 172
Easy Beef Stew, 94
Everyone's Hungry Soup, 63
Hamburger Casserole, 116
Hamburger Potato Casserole, 116
Italian Beef Stew, 91
Janie's Chicken a La King, 170
Naturally Colorful Vegetable Soup, 44
Ribs and Limas, 84
Sausage Pasta Stew, 145
Scalloped Chicken, 180
Stay-in-Bed Stew, 48
Tempting Beef Stew, 92
Tuna Noodle Casserole, 202
Your-Choice-of-Vegetables Soup, 48
Peas, Split
Split Pea Soup, 36
Pecans
Apple-Nut Bread Pudding, 254
Baked Acorn Squash, 213
Candied Sweet Potatoes, 216
Christmas Apple Date Pudding, 242
Fruit Dessert Topping, 246
Fruited Wild Rice with Pecans, 228
Gingerbread Pudding Cake, 242
Holiday Wild Rice, 228
Pineapple Sweet Potatoes, 219
Spicy Party Mix, 19
Sweet Potato Stuffing, 232
Peppers, Bell Sweet
Asian Meatballs, 106
Barbecued Chicken with Peppers, Onions, and Celery, 164
Barbecued Pork and Beef Sandwiches, 155
Beef and Pepper Rice, 122
Chicken Cacciatore, 159
Chicken Stew with Peppers and Pineapples, 165
Chilly Chili, 72
Creole Black Beans, 195
Dawn's Sausage and Peppers, 140
Garbanzo Souper, 31
Great Northern Bean Soup, 29
Hearty Chili, 56
Hearty Potato Chili, 58
Hearty Rice Casserole, 121
Hot and Good Chili, 55
Hot Beef Dip, 12
Italian Sausage, 140
Jambalaya, 65
Meal-in-One, 119
Meatballs and Peppers, 105
Norma's Vegetarian Chili, 47
Pork Chops Pierre, 133
Pumpkin Black-Bean Turkey Chili, 69
Red Beans and Pasta, 197
Red Pepper-Cheese Dip, 9
Savory Pepper Steak, 85
Slow-Cooker Bean Soup, 28
Slow-Cooker Kidney Beans, 197
Spanish Stuffed Peppers, 123
Spicy Corn Casserole, 209
Stuffed Baked Topping, 117
Stuffed Green Peppers, 122
Sunday Roast Chicken, 157
Szechwan-Style Chicken and Broccoli, 172
Three-Pepper Steak, 85
Peppers, Jalapeños
Creamy Artichoke Dip, 9
Mexican Goulash, 124
White Chicken Chili, 65
Peppers, Roasted Red
Red Pepper Chicken, 176
Pete's Scalloped Potatoes, 224
Pickles, Dill
Barbara Jean's Junior Beef, 96
Bavarian Beef, 80
Pigs in Blankets, 87
Pimentos
Chicken Rice Special, 177
Christmas Potatoes with Cheese, 226
Green Chile Corn Chowder, 40
Ham and Hash Browns, 150
Mexican Corn, 208
Stuffed Baked Topping, 117
Pineapple-Glazed Chicken with Sweet Potatoes, 165
Pineapple Sweet Potatoes, 219
Pineapple Upside Down Cake, 255
Pineapple
Chicken Stew with Peppers and Pineapples, 165
Chocolate Fondue, 259
Christmas Carrots, 211
Curried Fruit, 247
Easy and Elegant Ham, 147
Easy Easy Cake, 258
Festive Fruit Compote, 246
Ham with Pineapple Sauce, 148
Hawaiian Chicken, 164
Maui Chicken, 166
Pineapple Sweet Potatoes, 219
Pineapple Upside Down Cake, 255
Scalloped Pineapple, 232
Sweet and Sour Meatballs, 106
Sweet and Sour Ribs, 127
Pioneer Beans, 196
Pitas
Middle Eastern Sandwiches (for a crowd), 99
Wash-Day Stew, 96
Pixie's Chicken Stew, 68
Pizza Beans, 196
Pizza Rigatoni, 146
Pizza
Cheese Pizza Fondue, 14
Meatless Pizza Fondue, 15
Pizzaburgers, 109
Pizza Rigatoni, 146
Slow-Cooker Pizza, 146
Pizzaburgers, 109
Plenty More in the Kitchen, 120
Plum Roast, 76
Plums
Plum Roast, 76
Polish Sausage Bean Soup, 35
Pomegranate Punch, 235
Pork Barbecue, 155
Pork Chile, 61
Pork Chops, 132
Pork Chops and Gravy, 132
Pork Chops and Potatoes, 133
Pork Chops and Stuffing with Curry, 137
Pork Chops in Orange Sauce, 134
Pork Chop Slow Cooker Casserole, 135
Pork Chops on Rice, 134
Pork Chops Pierre, 133
Pork Chops with Stuffing, 136
Pork Loin with Spiced Fruit Sauce, 130
Pork Roast with Applesauce "Pulled Pork", 138
Pork
Barbecued Pork and Beef Sandwiches, 155
Pork, Bacon
Auntie Ginny's Baked Beans, 195
Bacon Cheese Dip, 13
Beef Burgundy, 91
Breakfast Skillet, 22
Calico Beans, 193
Cheesy Spinach and Bacon Dip, 14
Clam Chowder, 74
Corn and Shrimp Chowder, 73
Creamy Potatoes, 226
Deb's Baked Beans, 194
Eggs 'n' Spinach, 21
Everyone's Hungry Soup, 63
Galloping Beans, 194
Gourmet Chicken Breasts, 173
Hot German Potato Salad, 227
Keilbasa Stew, 143
Lotsa-Beans Pot, 194
Navy Bean and Bacon Chowder, 34
One-Pot Dinner, 193
Pete's Scalloped Potatoes, 224
Pigs in Blankets, 87
Potatoes Perfect, 223
Refrigerator Mashed Potatoes, 221
Squash Medley, 213
Sweet-Sour Red Cabbage, 212
Trio Bean Casserole, 193
Underground Ham and Cheese, 153
Zesty Calico Beans, 198
Pork, Bratwurst
Brats and Spuds, 141
Bratwurst in Sauce, 141
Pork, Butt
Pulled Pork BBQ, 138
Pork, Canadian Bacon
Shredded Potatoes with Canadian Bacon, 227
Pork, Chops
Apples, Sauerkraut, and Chops, 136
Baked Beans and Chops, 134
Barbecued Pork Chops, 132
Flautas with Pork Filling, 131
Moo Shu Pork, 137
Oxford Canal Chops Deluxe, 135
Pork Chop Slow Cooker Casserole, 135
Pork Chops, 132
Pork Chops and Gravy, 132
Pork Chops and Potatoes, 133
Pork Chops and Stuffing with Curry, 137

Pork Chops in Orange Sauce, 134
Pork Chops on Rice, 134
Pork Chops Pierre, 133
Pork Chops with Stuffing, 136
Teriyaki Pineapple Pork Chops, 136
Pork, Deviled Ham
Festive Meatballs, 102
Pork, Ground
Applesauce Meatballs, 106
Asian Pork Soup, 62
Ham Balls, 154
Ham Loaf or Balls, 154
Rob's Sweet and Sour Joe, 139
Shepherd's Pie, 154
Swedish Meat Balls, 102
Pork, Ground Ham
Ham Balls, 154
Ham Loaf or Balls, 154
Pork, Ham
Black Bean and Ham Soup, 32
Black Beans with Ham, 151
Blessing Soup, 30
Broccoli Casserole, 152
Cassoulet Chowder, 35
Cheesy Ham and Broccoli, 152
Corn Chowder, 40
Creamy Ham Topping (for baked potatoes), 150
Creamy Potatoes, 226
Easy and Elegant Ham, 147
Glazed Ham in a Bag, 148
Green Beans and Ham Soup, 37
Green Chile Corn Chowder, 40
Ham and Broccoli, 152
Ham and Broccoli Chowder, 39
Ham and Corn Slow-Cooker Casserole, 152
Ham and Hash Browns, 150
Ham and Lima Beans, 151
Ham and Potato Chowder, 42
Ham Barbecue, 156
Ham, Bean, and Potato Dish, 149
Ham in Foil, 147
Ham 'n' Cabbage Stew, 151
Ham with Pineapple Sauce, 148
Ham with Sweet Potatoes and Oranges, 150
Honey-Dijon Holiday Ham, 147
Lotsa Scalloped Potatoes, 224
Navy Bean Soup, 34
New England Boiled Dinner, 149
Party Bean Soup, 33
Raspberry-Glazed Ham, 148
Schnitz und Knepp, 149
Trio Bean Casserole, 193
Underground Ham and Cheese, 153
Verenike (or Creamy Lasagna), 153
Western Omelet Casserole, 21
White Marrow Bean Soup, 36
Pork, Ham Bone
Black Bean and Ham Soup, 32
Green Beans and Ham Soup, 37
Lentil Soup with Ham Bone, 62
Polish Sausage Bean Soup, 35
Pork, Ham Hock
Black Bean and Ham Soup, 32
Black-Eyed Peas and Ham, 212
Grandma's Barley Soup, 35
Party Bean Soup, 33
Polish Sausage Bean Soup, 35
Red and Green Bean Soup, 33
Split Pea Soup, 36
Pork, Hot Dogs
Edna's Baked Beans, 198
Pork, Italian Sausage
Rice & Bean Soup, 37
Taco Appetizer, 13
Pork, Kielbasa
Harvest Kielbasa, 143
Keilbasa Stew, 143
Kielbasa and Cabbage, 143
Lentil Soup with Ham Bone, 62
Rice and Beans—and Sausage, 144
Pork, Loin
Autumn Harvest Pork Loin, 129
Cranberry Pork, 130
Moo Shu Pork, 137
Pork Barbecue, 155
Pork Chops and Potatoes, 133
Pork Loin with Spiced Fruit Sauce, 130
Teriyaki Pineapple Pork Chops, 136
Pork, Pepperoni
Creamy Pizza Dip, 14
Now That's Lasagna, 113
Pizza Rigatoni, 146
Slow-Cooker Pizza, 146
Pork, Ribs
1-2-3 Barbecued Country Ribs, 128
Baked Beans and Chops, 134
Barbecued Ribs, 127
Country-Style Ribs and Sauerkraut, 128
Pork Chile, 61
Sauerkraut & Pork Ribs, 129
Sweet and Sour Ribs, 127
Tender 'n' Tangy Ribs, 128
Pork, Roast
Flautas with Pork Filling, 131
No Fuss Sauerkraut, 131
Pork Loin with Spiced Fruit Sauce, 130
Pork Roast with Applesauce "Pulled Pork", 138
Zesty Pulled Pork, 138
Pork, Sausage
Beef and Sausage Spaghetti Sauce, 112
Black-Eyed Pea Chili, 62
Cassoulet Chowder, 35
Cheesy Sausage Dip, 13
Chicken and Sausage Cacciatore, 160
Chicken Rice Special, 177
Chili Casserole, 146
Creole Black Beans, 195
Dawn's Sausage and Peppers, 140
Delicious Sausage Soup, 64
Eggs 'n' Spinach, 21
Election Lunch, 144
Golden Autumn Stew, 145
Gourmet Meat Loaf, 101
Green Beans and Sausage Soup, 38
Hamburger Sausage Soup, 63
Hearty Rice Casserole, 121
Italian Chicken Chili, 66
Italian Meatball Subs, 103
Italian Sausage, 140
Jambalaya, 65
Lentil Soup with Ham Bone, 62
M&T's Chili, 59
New Mexico Stew, 95
Now That's Lasagna, 113
Pioneer Beans, 196
Pizza Beans, 196
Pizza Rigatoni, 146
Polish Sausage Bean Soup, 35
Sauerkraut-Sausage Bean Soup, 64
Sausage and Scalloped Potatoes, 141
Sausage and Sweet Potatoes, 142
Sausage Pasta Stew, 145
Sausage-Potato Slow Cooker Dinner, 142
Sausage, Tomato, Spinach Soup, 60
Sausage Tortellini Soup, 60
Savory Sausage Sandwiches, 139
Slow Cooker Almost Lasagna, 114
Slow-Cooker Pizza, 146
Spaghetti Sauce with a Kick, 112
Spicy Chili, 58
Spicy Sausage Soup, 64
Super-Simple Sausage and Sauerkraut, 140
Pork, Shoulder
Zesty Pulled Pork, 138
Pork, Sirloin
Zesty Pulled Pork, 138
Pork, Smoked Ham
Party Bean Soup, 33
Pork, Smokies
Cranberry Franks, 156
Super-Bowl Little Smokies, 156
Pork, Stewing
Everyone's Hungry Soup, 63
Pork, Tenderloin
Barbara Jean's Whole Pork Tenderloin, 129
Vegetable Pork Soup, 61
Posole
Southwest Posole, 210
Potato, Flakes
Creamy Mashed Potatoes, 221
Potatoes Perfect, 223
Potatoes
1-2-3-4 Casserole, 115
After-Work Stew, 94
Apple and Brown Sugar Corned Beef, 88
Apple Chicken Stew, 67
Aunt Thelma's Homemade Soup, 46
Back-on-Track Soup, 30
Beef Stew with Shiitake Mushrooms, 93
Beef Stew with Wine, 92
Best Ever Beef Stew, 93
Brats and Spuds, 141
Broccoli, Potato, and Cheese Soup, 38
Cheese Potatoes, 225
Chicken and Stuffing Dinner, 179
Christmas Potatoes with Cheese, 226
Company Potatoes, 225
Corn and Shrimp Chowder, 73
Corned Beef, 88
Creamy Potato Soup, 42
Creamy Red Potatoes, 222
Dad's Spicy Chicken Curry, 161
Dawn's Mushroom Beef Stew, 92
Delicious Sausage Soup, 64
Everyone's Hungry Soup, 63
Garlic Mashed Potatoes, 220
Golden Autumn Stew, 145
Grandma's Barley Soup, 35
Green Beans and Ham Soup, 37
Green Beans and Sausage Soup, 38
Green Chile Corn Chowder, 40
Ground Beef Soup, 51
Ground Beef Stew, 117
Ham and Corn Slow-Cooker Casserole, 152
Ham and Potato Chowder, 42
Ham, Bean, and Potato Dish, 149
Hamburger Casserole, 116
Hamburger Potato Casserole, 116
Hamburger-Potato Slow Cooker Dinner, 115

Hearty Bean and Vegetable Soup, 27
Herbed Potatoes, 223
Homemade Vegetable Soup, 48
Hot German Potato Salad, 227
Hungarian Beef Stew, 95
Kielbasa and Cabbage, 143
Lamb Stew, 199
Lentil Soup, 32
Lotsa Scalloped Potatoes, 224
Magic Meat Loaf, 100
Make Ahead Mixed Potatoes Florentine, 220
Mashed Potatoes, 220
New England Boiled Dinner, 149
New Mexico Stew, 95
One-Pot Easy Chicken, 158
Onion Potatoes, 223
Pete's Scalloped Potatoes, 224
Pork Chops and Potatoes, 133
Pork Chop Slow Cooker Casserole, 135
Potatoes Perfect, 223
Prompt, 118
Refrigerator Mashed Potatoes, 221
Ruth's Ground Beef Vegetable Soup, 49
Sausage and Scalloped Potatoes, 141
Sausage-Potato Slow Cooker Dinner, 142
Shepherd's Pie, 154
Simply Super Supper, 80
Slow-Cooked Turkey Dinner, 186
Slow-Cooker Bean Soup, 28
Smoked Salmon Corn Chowder, 72
Snowmobile Soup, 52
Split Pea Soup, 36
Stay-in-Bed Stew, 48
Sunday Dinner Potatoes, 222
Sunday Roast Beef, 80
Tomato-y Beef Stew, 94
Turkey Green Chili Chowder, 70
Turkey Mushroom Soup, 71
Vegetable Pork Soup, 61
White Marrow Bean Soup, 36
Wonderful Clam Chowder, 74

Potatoes, Au Gratin
Breakfast Skillet, 22

Potatoes, Hash Brown
Corn Chowder, 40
Creamy Potatoes, 226
Ham and Hash Browns, 150
Meal-in-One, 119
Shredded Potatoes with Canadian Bacon, 227
Western Omelet Casserole, 21

Potatoes, Mashed
Cheeseburger Casserole, 118
Hamburger/Green Bean Dish, 118
Mashed Potato Filling, 231
Oyster and Potato Filling Yuletide, 201
Underground Ham and Cheese, 153

Potluck Beef Barbecue Sandwiches, 96

Pretzels
Chocolate Covered Pretzels, 260
Snack Mix, 18
Spicy Party Mix, 19

Prompt, 118

Prunes
Breakfast Prunes, 25
Curried Chicken, 162
Festive Fruit Compote, 246
Fruited Beef Tagine, 89
Pork Loin with Spiced Fruit Sauce, 130

Pudding
Apple-Nut Bread Pudding, 254
Chocolate Rice Pudding, 252
Christmas Apple Date Pudding, 242
Deluxe Tapioca Pudding, 252
Dried Cranberry Pudding, 250
Gingerbread Pudding Cake, 242
Home-Style Bread Pudding, 255
Lemon Pudding, 253
Rice Pudding, 252
Simple Bread Pudding, 254
Slow-Cooker Rice Pudding, 251
Steamed Chocolate Pudding, 251
White Chocolate Bread Pudding, 254

Pulled Pork BBQ, 138

Pumpkin Black-Bean Turkey Chili, 69

Pumpkin Butter, 20

Pumpkin
Cream of Pumpkin Soup, 44
Peanut Butter Pumpkin Soup, 44
Pumpkin Black-Bean Turkey Chili, 69
Pumpkin Butter, 20
Slow-Cooker Pumpkin Pie, 253

Punch
Fruity Hot Punch, 236
Golden Wassail Punch, 237
Pomegranate Punch, 235
Spicy Citrus Warmer, 237

Q

Quick and Easy Spaghetti, 111

R

Raisins
Boston Brown Bread, 26
Carrot Cake, 257
Fruit and Grains Breakfast Cereal, 23
Fruit Dessert Topping, 246
Fruited Wild Rice with Pecans, 228
Holiday Wild Rice, 228
Home-Style Bread Pudding, 255
Norma's Vegetarian Chili, 47
Pork Loin with Spiced Fruit Sauce, 130
Slow-Cooker Oatmeal, 22
Slow-Cooker Rice Pudding, 251
Zesty Pears, 244

Ranch Hand Beef, 97

Raspberry-Glazed Ham, 148

Ratatouille, 10

Red and Green Bean Soup, 33

Red French Onion Soup, 41

Red Pepper-Cheese Dip, 9

Red Pepper Chicken, 176

Refrigerator Mashed Potatoes, 221

Ribs and Limas, 84

Rice & Bean Soup, 37

Rice and Beans—and Sausage, 144

Rice Pudding, 252

Rice
Arroz con Queso, 204
Baked Chicken and Rice, 178
Beef and Pepper Rice, 122
Broccoli and Rice Casserole, 210
Broccoli Casserole, 152
Cheesy Ham and Broccoli, 152
Chicken Broccoli Rice Casserole, 177
Chicken Rice Special, 177
Chili Casserole, 146
Chocolate Rice Pudding, 252
Company Casserole, 177
Easy Hamburger Vegetable Soup, 49
Easy Olive Bake, 215
Fruited Wild Rice with Pecans, 228
Ham and Broccoli, 152
Hamburger Rice Casserole, 121
Hearty Rice Casserole, 121
Holiday Wild Rice, 228
Indonesian Peanut Chicken, 174
Jambalaya, 65
Mexican Rice and Bean Soup, 37
Mjeddrah, 229
Pork Chops on Rice, 134
Prompt, 118
Rice & Bean Soup, 37
Rice Pudding, 252
Rudolph's Nose Wild Rice, 228
Ruth's Ground Beef Vegetable Soup, 49
Slow-Cooker Rice Pudding, 251
Spanish Stuffed Peppers, 123
Spicy Corn Casserole, 209
Spicy Sausage Soup, 64
Stuffed Green Peppers, 122
Tex-Mex Chicken and Rice, 176
Turkey Mushroom Soup, 71
Your-Choice-of-Vegetables Soup, 48

Rob's Sweet and Sour Joe, 139

Rudolph's Nose Wild Rice, 228

Russian Red Lentil Soup, 31

Rutabaga
Golden Autumn Stew, 145
Turkey Frame Soup, 70

Ruth's Ground Beef Vegetable Soup, 49

S

Salsa Beef, 89

Salsa Chuck Roast, 77

Salsa
Caponata, 216
Cheesy Hot Bean Dip, 11
Chicken Azteca, 175
Creamy Taco Dip, 12
Flautas with Pork Filling, 131
Hot Chili Dip, 11
Salsa Beef, 89
Salsa Chuck Roast, 77
Sloppy Beef Sandwiches, 108
TNT Dip, 12

Sandwiches
Barbara Jean's Junior Beef, 96
Barbecued Chicken Sandwiches, 181
Barbecued Hamburgers, 114
Barbecued Pork and Beef Sandwiches, 155
Beef Barbecue Sandwiches, 97
Dianna's Barbecue, 110
Easy Roast Beef Barbecue, 98
Herby Beef Sandwiches, 98
Hot Beef Sandwiches, 98
Hot Chicken Sandwiches, 181
Italian Meatball Subs, 103
Meat Loaf Burgers, 114
Pizzaburgers, 109
Pork Barbecue, 155
Pork Roast with Applesauce "Pulled Pork", 138
Potluck Beef Barbecue Sandwiches, 96
Pulled Pork BBQ, 138
Ranch Hand Beef, 97
Rob's Sweet and Sour Joe, 139
Savory Sausage Sandwiches, 139
Sloppy Beef Sandwiches, 108
Turkey Sloppy Joes, 188
Yum-Yums, 109
Zesty Pulled Pork, 138

Santa Fe Chicken Soup, 68

Saucy Apricot Chicken, 167
Saucy Italian Roast, 79
Sauerbraten, 81
Sauerkraut & Pork Ribs, 129
Sauerkraut-Sausage Bean Soup, 64
Sauerkraut
  Apples, Sauerkraut, and Chops, 136
  Beef Ribs with Sauerkraut, 83
  Brats and Spuds, 141
  Country-Style Ribs and Sauerkraut, 128
  No Fuss Sauerkraut, 131
  Sauerkraut & Pork Ribs, 129
  Sauerkraut-Sausage Bean Soup, 64
  Slow Cooker Reuben Dip, 15
  Super-Simple Sausage and Sauerkraut, 140
Sausage and Scalloped Potatoes, 141
Sausage and Sweet Potatoes, 142
Sausage Pasta Stew, 145
Sausage-Potato Slow Cooker Dinner, 142
Sausage Tortellini Soup, 60
Savory Cheese Soup, 45
Savory Chicken, Meal #1, 170
Savory Chicken, Meal #2, 171
Savory Pepper Steak, 85
Savory Sausage Sandwiches, 139
Savory Turkey Meatballs in Italian Sauce, 189
Scalloped Chicken, 180
Scalloped Pineapple, 232
Schnitz und Knepp, 149
Scrumptious Chicken, 168
Seafood, Clams
  Clam Chowder, 74
  Wonderful Clam Chowder, 74
Seafood, Crabmeat
  Company Seafood Pasta, 201
Seafood, Oysters
  Oyster and Potato Filling Yuletide, 201
  Oyster Stew, 74
Seafood, Scallops
  Company Seafood Pasta, 201
Seafood, Shrimp
  Cheese and Crab Dip, 18
  Chicken and Seafood Gumbo, 176
  Company Casserole, 177
  Company Seafood Pasta, 201
  Corn and Shrimp Chowder, 73
  Curried Shrimp, 202
  Jambalaya, 65
Seafood, Smoked Salmon
  Smoked Salmon Corn Chowder, 72
Seafood, Tuna
  Tuna Noodle Casserole, 202
Shallots
  Home-Style Beef Cubes, 88
Shepherd's Pie, 154
Shredded Potatoes with Canadian Bacon, 227
Simple Bread Pudding, 254
Simply Super Supper, 80
Sloppy Beef Sandwiches, 108
Slow and Easy Macaroni and Cheese, 203
Slow-Cooked Chili, 54
Slow-Cooked Short Ribs, 83
Slow-Cooked Turkey Dinner, 186
Slow Cooker Almost Lasagna, 114
Slow-Cooker Bean Soup, 28
Slow Cooker Beef with Mushrooms, 87
Slow-Cooker Chili, 53
Slow Cooker Creamy Chicken Italian, 173
Slow-Cooker Dressing, 230
Slow-Cooker Kidney Beans, 197
Slow Cooker Lasagna, 112
Slow-Cooker Oatmeal, 22
Slow-Cooker Pizza, 146
Slow-Cooker Pumpkin Pie, 253
Slow Cooker Reuben Dip, 15
Slow-Cooker Rice Pudding, 251
Slow-Cooker Spoon Peaches, 244
Slow-Cooker Stuffing, 230
Slow Cooker Turkey and Dressing, 185
Slowly Cooked Chili, 55
Smoked Beef Brisket, 77
Smoked Salmon Corn Chowder, 72
Snack Mix, 18
Snappy Meatballs, 105
Snowmobile Soup, 52
So Easy Chili, 56
Southwest Cranberries, 247
Southwest Posole, 210
Southwestern Bean Soup with Cornmeal Dumplings, 29
Spaghetti Sauce for a Crowd, 111
Spaghetti Sauce with a Kick, 112
Spanish Stuffed Peppers, 123
Spicy Beef Roast, 75
Spicy Chili, 58
Spicy Citrus Warmer, 237
Spicy Corn Casserole, 209
Spicy Party Mix, 19
Spicy Sausage Soup, 64
Spicy Short Ribs, 82
Spicy Sweet Chicken, 167
Spinach
  Back-on-Track Soup, 30
  Cheesy Spinach and Bacon Dip, 14
  Dad's Spicy Chicken Curry, 161
  Eggs 'n' Spinach, 21
  Make Ahead Mixed Potatoes Florentine, 220
  Pot-Roast Complete, 82
  Red and Green Bean Soup, 33
  Sausage, Tomato, Spinach Soup, 60
Split Pea Soup, 36
Spreads
  Chunky Sweet Spiced Apple Butter, 20
  Pear Butter, 20
  Pumpkin Butter, 20
Squash Medley, 213
Squash, Acorn
  Apple Walnut Squash, 214
  Baked Acorn Squash, 213
  Stuffed Acorn Squash, 214
  Turkey Thighs, Acorn Squash, and Apples, 186
Squash, Butternut
  Autumn Harvest Pork Loin, 129
  Butternut Squash and Apple Soup, 43
  Golden Autumn Stew, 145
  Tzimmes, 214
  Wintertime Vegetable Chili, 47
Squash, Summer
  Sausage Pasta Stew, 145
  Squash Medley, 213
Squash, Yellow
  Sausage Pasta Stew, 145
  The Soup, 46
Stay-in-Bed Stew, 48
Steamed Chocolate Pudding, 251
Stewed Tomatoes, 215
Strawberries
  Chocolate Fondue, 259
String Beans *See Green Beans*
Stroganoff
  Easy Stroganoff, 90
  Garlic Beef Stroganoff, 90
  Ground Beef Stroganoff, 99
Stuffed Acorn Squash, 214
Stuffed Baked Topping, 117
Stuffed Flank Steak, 86
Stuffed Green Peppers, 122
Stuffed Mushrooms, 215
Stuffed Turkey Breast, 184
Stuffing
  Chicken and Stuffing Dinner, 179
  Chicken Dressing, 179
  Corn Stuffing Balls, 231
  Mashed Potato Filling, 231
  Mushroom Stuffing, 229
  Old-Fashioned Stuffing, 231
  Our Favorite Chicken and Stuffing, 178
  Oyster and Potato Filling Yuletide, 201
  Pork Chops and Stuffing with Curry, 137
  Pork Chops with Stuffing, 136
  Slow-Cooker Dressing, 230
  Slow-Cooker Stuffing, 230
  Slow Cooker Turkey and Dressing, 185
  Stuffed Turkey Breast, 184
  Sweet Potato Stuffing, 232
Sunday Chicken, 169
Sunday Dinner Potatoes, 222
Sunday Roast Beef, 80
Sunday Roast Chicken, 157
Super-Bowl Little Smokies, 156
Super Creamed Corn, 207
Super-Simple Sausage and Sauerkraut, 140
Swedish Meat Balls, 102
Sweet and Sour Meatballs, 106
Sweet and Sour Ribs, 127
Sweet Chili Chicken Bites, 17
Sweet 'n' Tangy Meatballs, 104
Sweet Peppers
  See Peppers, Bell Sweet
Sweet Potato-Cranberry Casserole, 219
Sweet Potato Stuffing, 232
Sweet Potatoes and Apples, 218
Sweet Potatoes That Can Wait, 217
Sweet Potatoes with Applesauce, 218
Sweet Potatoes
  Apples 'n' Yams, 218
  "Baked" Sweet Potatoes, 217
  Barbecued Black Beans with Sweet Potatoes, 219
  Candied Sweet Potatoes, 216
  Fruited Turkey and Yams, 187
  Golden Autumn Stew, 145
  Ham with Sweet Potatoes and Oranges, 150
  Make Ahead Mixed Potatoes Florentine, 220
  Orange Candied Sweet Potatoes, 216
  Orange Yams, 217
  Peanut Butter Pumpkin Soup, 44
  Pineapple-Glazed Chicken with Sweet Potatoes, 165
  Pineapple Sweet Potatoes, 219
  Sausage and Sweet Potatoes, 142
  Sweet Potato-Cranberry Casserole, 219
  Sweet Potato Stuffing, 232
  Sweet Potatoes and Apples, 218
  Sweet Potatoes That Can Wait, 217
  Sweet Potatoes with Applesauce, 218
  Tzimmes, 214
Sweet-Sour Red Cabbage, 212
Swiss-Irish Hot Sauce—A Great Potato Topping!, 222
Swiss Steak, 84

T

Taco Appetizer, 13
Taco Casserole, 125
Taco Soup with Corn, 52
Taco Soup with Hominy, 52
Tacos
  Casserole Verde, 126
  Creamy Taco Dip, 12
  Mexican Goulash, 124
  Taco Appetizer, 13
  Taco Casserole, 125
  Three-Bean Burrito Bake, 125
  Tiajuana Tacos, 126
  Tortilla Bake, 124
  Turkey Fajitas, 188
Tamale Chicken, 175
Tea
  Ginger Tea, 238
  Hot Fruit Tea, 238
  Johnny Appleseed Tea, 238
Tempting Beef Stew, 92
Tender Barbecued Chicken, 166
Tender Texas-Style Steaks, 84
Teriyaki Chicken, 163
Teriyaki Pineapple Pork Chops, 136
Tex-Mex Chicken and Rice, 176
The Chili Connection, 57
The Soup, 46
There's-No-Easier Roast Beef, 78
Three-Bean Burrito Bake, 125
Three-Bean Chili, 56
Three-Pepper Steak, 85
Tiajuana Tacos, 126
TNT Dip, 12
Tomato-y Beef Stew, 94
Tomatoes
  Arroz con Queso, 204
  Aunt Thelma's Homemade Soup, 46
  Beef Barley Soup, 50
  Beef Stew with Wine, 92
  Black Bean and Tomato Soup, 32
  Black Beans with Ham, 151
  Black-Eyed Pea Chili, 62
  Blessing Soup, 30
  Brunswick Stew, 180
  Cheesy Sausage Dip, 13
  Cheesy Spinach and Bacon Dip, 14
  Chicken Cacciatore, 159
  Chicken Gumbo, 172
  Chili con Carne Supreme, 53
  Creamy Pizza Dip, 14
  Creamy Tomato Soup, 43
  Easy Hamburger Vegetable Soup, 49
  Easy Olive Bake, 215
  Easy Veggie-Beef Soup, 50
  Everyone's Hungry Soup, 63
  Extra Easy Chili, 57
  Grandma's Chili, 58
  Great Northern Bean Soup, 29
  Hot and Good Chili, 55
  Hot Hamburger Dip, 11
  Italian Chicken Chili, 66
  Kielbasa and Cabbage, 143
  Lentil Soup, 32
  Many-Bean Soup, 30
  Meatballs and Peppers, 105
  Mexican Goulash, 124
  M&T's Chili, 59
  Nacho Dip, 10
  Naturally Colorful Vegetable Soup, 44
  Norma's Vegetarian Chili, 47
  Our Favorite Chili, 54
  Pasta Bean Pot, 192
  Pizza Beans, 196
  Polish Sausage Bean Soup, 35
  Pork Chile, 61
  Prompt, 118
  Quick and Easy Spaghetti, 111
  Ratatouille, 10
  Red Pepper Chicken, 176
  Rudolph's Nose Wild Rice, 228
  Russian Red Lentil Soup, 31
  Santa Fe Chicken Soup, 68
  Sausage, Tomato, Spinach Soup, 60
  Savory Turkey Meatballs in Italian Sauce, 189
  Slow-Cooker Kidney Beans, 197
  Southwest Posole, 210
  Southwestern Bean Soup with Cornmeal Dumplings, 29
  Spaghetti Sauce with a Kick, 112
  Spanish Stuffed Peppers, 123
  Squash Medley, 213
  Stewed Tomatoes, 215
  Swiss-Irish Hot Sauce—A Great Potato Topping!, 222
  Taco Casserole, 125
  Taco Soup with Corn, 52
  Taco Soup with Hominy, 52
  Tempting Beef Stew, 92
  Tex-Mex Chicken and Rice, 176
  The Chili Connection, 57
  The Soup, 46
  Three-Bean Burrito Bake, 125
  Three-Bean Chili, 56
  Tomato-y Beef Stew, 94
  Tortilla Bake, 124
  Turkey Chili, 71
  Turkey Fajitas, 188
  Vegetable Pork Soup, 61
  Wintertime Vegetable Chili, 47
  Zesty Minestrone, 28
  Zucchini and Turkey Dish, 185
Tortilla Bake, 124
Tortillas
  Moo Shu Pork, 137
  Taco Casserole, 125
  Three-Bean Burrito Bake, 125
  Tortilla Bake, 124
Tricia's Cranberry Turkey Meatballs, 190
Trio Bean Casserole, 193
Triple Delicious Hot Chocolate, 239
Tuna Noodle Casserole, 202
Turkey Barbecue, 187
Turkey Breast with Orange Sauce, 184
Turkey Cacciatore, 188
Turkey Chili, 71
Turkey Fajitas, 188
Turkey Frame Soup, 70
Turkey Green Chili Chowder, 70
Turkey Lasagna, 189
Turkey Meatball Soup, 71
Turkey Meatballs and Gravy, 190
Turkey Mushroom Soup, 71
Turkey Sloppy Joes, 188
Turkey Slow Cooker, 184
Turkey Thighs, Acorn Squash, and Apples, 186
Turkey
  Jambalaya, 65
  Pumpkin Black-Bean Turkey Chili, 69
  Turkey Cacciatore, 188
  Turkey Frame Soup, 70
  Turkey Green Chili Chowder, 70
  Turkey Mushroom Soup, 71
  Turkey Sloppy Joes, 188
  Zucchini and Turkey Dish, 185
Turkey, Breast
  Herb-Roasted Turkey Breast, 183
  Slow Cooker Turkey and Dressing, 185
  Stuffed Turkey Breast, 184
  Turkey Breast with Orange Sauce, 184
  Turkey Slow Cooker, 184
Turkey, Cutlets
  Barbecued Turkey Cutlets, 187
Turkey, Drumsticks
  Barbecued Turkey Legs, 186
Turkey, Ground
  Asian Pork Soup, 62
  Chilly Chili, 72
  Extra Easy Chili, 57
  Savory Turkey Meatballs in Italian Sauce, 189
  Slowly Cooked Chili, 55
  Spaghetti Sauce for a Crowd, 111
  Tricia's Cranberry Turkey Meatballs, 190
  Turkey Chili, 71
  Turkey Lasagna, 189
  Turkey Meatball Soup, 71
  Turkey Meatballs and Gravy, 190
Turkey, Sausage
  Chicken Rice Special, 177
  Chicken Sausage Fennel Soup, 67
  Rice and Beans—and Sausage, 144
  Sausage, Tomato, Spinach Soup, 60
Turkey, Tenderloin
  Turkey Fajitas, 188
Turkey, Thighs
  Fruited Turkey and Yams, 187
  Slow-Cooked Turkey Dinner, 186
  Turkey Barbecue, 187
  Turkey Thighs, Acorn Squash, and Apples, 186
Tzimmes, 214

U

Underground Ham and Cheese, 153

V

Vegetable Pork Soup, 61
Vegetarian Baked Beans, 198
Venison in Sauce, 200
Venison Roast, 200
Venison
  Middle Eastern Sandwiches (for a crowd), 99
  Venison in Sauce, 200
  Venison Roast, 200
Verenike (or Creamy Lasagna), 153
Viennese Coffee, 240

W

Wagon Master Apple-Cherry Sauce, 246
Walnuts
  Apple Oatmeal, 22
  Apple Walnut Squash, 214
  Boston Brown Bread, 26
  Carrot Cake, 257
  Christmas Sugared Walnuts, 19
  Date and Nut Loaf, 243
  Easy Easy Cake, 258
  Graham Cracker Cookies, 259
  Holiday Cherry Cobbler, 241
  Oatmeal Morning, 23
  Orange Slice Cake, 257
  Spicy Party Mix, 19
Warmed Spiced Fruit, 245
Wash-Day Stew, 96
Wassail, 235
Wassail
  Christmas Wassail, 236
  Golden Wassail Punch, 237
  Wassail, 235
Water Chestnuts
  Asian Meatballs, 106

Green Bean Casserole, 206
Ham and Broccoli, 152
Western Omelet Casserole, 21
Wheatberries
Easy Wheatberries, 204
Hot Wheatberry Cereal, 24
White Chicken Chili, 65
White Chili, 66
White Chocolate Bread Pudding, 254
White Marrow Bean Soup, 36
Wholesome Hamburger Dinner, 116
Wine Tender Roast, 75
Wintertime Vegetable Chili, 47
Wonderful Clam Chowder, 74

Y

Yams
Apples 'n' Yams, 218
Fruited Turkey and Yams, 187
Orange Yams, 217
Sweet Potato-Cranberry Casserole, 219
Sweet Potatoes with Applesauce, 218
Your-Choice-of-Vegetables Soup, 48
Yum-Yums, 109

Z

Zesty Calico Beans, 198
Zesty Minestrone, 28
Zesty Pulled Pork, 138
Zucchini and Turkey Dish, 185
Zucchini
Beef Tortellini Soup, 60
Chicken Pasta, 178
Italian Chicken Chili, 66
Minestrone, 28
Ratatouille, 10
Sausage Tortellini Soup, 60
Squash Medley, 213
The Soup, 46
Zucchini and Turkey Dish, 185

About the Author

Phyllis Good is a *New York Times* bestselling author whose books have sold nearly 14 million copies.

Good is the author of the nationally acclaimed *Fix-It and Forget-It* slow-cooker cookbooks, several of which have appeared on *The New York Times* bestseller list, as well as the bestseller lists of *USA Today*, *Publishers Weekly*, and *Book Sense*.

In addition to this book, the series includes:

- ***Fix-It and Forget-It Cookbook (Revised and Updated)***
  700 Great Slow-Cooker Recipes
- ***Fix-It and Forget-It Cooking Light for Slow Cookers***
  600 Healthy, Low-Fat Recipes for Your Slow Cooker
- ***Fix-It and Forget-It 5-Ingredient Favorites***
  Comforting Slow-Cooker Recipes
- ***Fix-It and Forget-It Slow Cooker Diabetic Cookbook***
  550 Slow Cooker Favorites—to Include Everyone
  (with the American Diabetes Association)
- ***Fix-It and Forget-It Slow Cooker Magic***
  550 Amazing Everyday Recipes
- ***Fix-It and Forget-It Kids' Cookbook***
  50 Favorite Recipes to Make in a Slow Cooker
- ***Fix-it and Forget-It Slow Cooker Champion Recipes***
  450 of Our Very Best Recipes
- ***Fix-it and Forget-It Baking with Your Slow Cooker***
  150 Slow Cooker Recipes for Breads, Pizza, Cakes, Tarts, Crisps, Bars, Pies, Cupcakes, and More!

Good is also the author of the *Fix-It and Enjoy-It* series, a "cousin" series to the phenomenally successful *Fix-It and Forget-It* cookbooks. There are currently four books in that series:

- ***Fix-It and Enjoy-It Cookbook***
  All-Purpose, Welcome-Home Recipes
- ***Fix-It and Enjoy-It 5-Ingredient Recipes***
  Quick and Easy—for Stove-Top and Oven!
- ***Fix-It and Enjoy-It Diabetic Cookbook***
  Stove-Top and Oven Recipes—for Everyone!
  (with the American Diabetes Association)
- ***Fix-It and Enjoy-It Healthy Cookbook***
  400 Great Stove-Top and Oven Recipes
  (with nutritional expertise from Mayo Clinic)

Among Good's other cookbooks are:

- ***The Best of Amish Cooking***
- ***"Fresh From Central Market" Cookbook***

Phyllis Good received her B.A. and M.A. in English from New York University. She and her husband Merle live in Lancaster, Pennsylvania. They are the parents of two young-adult daughters.

For a complete listing of books by Phyllis, visit www.Fix-ItandForget-It.com or www.GoodBooks.com.